MW01672624

Introduction to UNIX

Kate Wrightson and Joe Merlino

McGraw-Hill Irwin

Boston Burr Ridge, IL Dubuque, IA Madison, WI New York San Francisco St. Louis
Bangkok Bogotá Caracas Kuala Lumpur Lisbon London Madrid Mexico City
Milan Montreal New Delhi Santiago Seoul Singapore Sydney Taipei Toronto

McGraw-Hill Higher Education

A Division of The ***McGraw-Hill*** *Companies*

INTRODUCTION TO UNIX

Published by McGraw-Hill/Irwin, a business unit of The McGraw-Hill Companies, Inc., 1221 Avenue of the Americas, New York, NY, 10020.

This book is printed on acid-free paper.

1 2 3 4 5 6 7 8 9 0 DOC/DOC 0 9 8 7 6 5 4 3 2

ISBN 0-07-283620-2

Publisher: *George Werthman*
Sponsoring editor: *Dan Silverburg*
Developmental editor: *Diana Del Castillo*
Marketing manager: *Greta Kleinert*
Media producer: *Greg Bates*
Project manager: *Scott Scheidt*
Lead production supervisor: *Heather D. Burbridge*
Designer: *Adam Rooke*
Senior supplement producer: *Rose M. Range*
Senior digital content specialist: *Brian Nacik*
Cover design: *Ryan Brown*
Cover image: *© Corbis*
Typeface: *10/12 New Baskerville*
Compositor: *Black Dot Group*
Printer: *R. R. Donnelley*

Library of Congress Cataloging-in-Publication Data

Wrightson, Katherine.
Introduction to UNIX/Kate Wrightson and Joe Merlino.
p. cm.
ISBN 0-07-283620-2 (alk. paper)
1. UNIX (Computer file) 2. Operating systems (Computers) I. Merlino, Joseph. II. Title.
QA76.76.O63 W73 2003
0054'32–dc21

www.mhhe.com 2002030944

InformationTechnology

Information Technology at McGraw-Hill/Irwin

At McGraw-Hill Higher education, we publish instructional materials for the higher education market. In order to expand the tools of higher learning, we publish everything you may need: texts, lab manuals, study guides, testing materials, software, and multimedia products—the Total Solution.

We realize that technology has created and will continue to create new mediums for professors and students to use in managing resources and communicating information to one another. McGraw-Hill/Irwin continues to provide the most flexible and complete teaching and learning tools available as well as offer solutions to the changing world of teaching and learning. McGraw-Hill/Irwin is dedicated to providing the tools for today's instructors and students which will enable them to successfully navigate the world of Information Technology.

- Seminar Series and Focus Groups—McGraw-Hill/Irwin's seminar series and focus groups are offered across the country every year. At the seminar series we provide you with the latest technology products and encourage collaboration among teaching professionals. We conduct many focus groups year round where we can hear from you what we need to publish.
- ITAP—Information Technology Advisory Panel. This is a "super focus group," where we gather many of the country's top IT educators for three days to tell us how to publish the best IT texts possible. ITAP's are very instrumental in driving our publishing plans.
- McGraw-Hill/Osborne—This leading trade division company of family of McGraw-Hill Companies is known for its best-selling Internet titles, Harley Hahn's Internet & Web yellow pages, and the Internet Complete Reference. If we don't have it in our CIT/MIS, you can find it at Osborne. For more information, visit Osborne at **www.osborne.com**.
- Digital Solutions—Whether you want to teach a class online or just post your "bricks-n-mortar" class syllabus, McGraw-Hill/Irwin is committed to publishing digital solutions. Taking your course online doesn't have to be a solitary adventure, nor does it have to be a difficult one. We offer several solutions that will allow you to enjoy all the benefits of having your course material online.
- Packaging Options—For more information about our discount options, contact your McGraw-Hill/Irwin Sales representative at 1-800-338-3987 or visit our website at **www.mhhe.com/it**.

Brief Table of Contents

Extended Table of Contents

Preface

To the Student

This text is a basic introduction to the complex world of the Unix operating system. Here, you will find information about several aspects of working with Unix, from simple personal tasks to shell programming and system administration. Unix is a powerful and ever-evolving system, which is now available in variants designed for every hardware platform and with configurations to suit any preferences or needs. It powers much of the world's academic and business information technology, and is increasingly popular for home networks and machines.

You may find Unix intimidating, especially if you have not worked with text-based operating systems before. Although it might be unfamiliar territory, explore the systems available to you and practice the various commands you see in this book or find elsewhere. You will come to see that, although the user interface can initially be uncomfortable, working with Unix is much like working on any other operating system, especially if you are working on a Unix installation which offers a graphical user interface, some of which are virtually indistinguishable from Windows or MacOS.

If you have a spare computer available to you, we strongly encourage you to consider downloading and installing a Unix variant for your own practice and exploration. The most popular Unix variants for personal computers are Linux and FreeBSD. There are more than a hundred Linux variants available on the Internet, but the Red Hat and Debian distributions tend to be the friendliest for new users. FreeBSD has only one distribution, but it is also good for newcomers. While you are learning, it would be best to keep your Unix machine separate from your regular home computer, should you have one. You can run Linux on a 486, as long as you work primarily in text mode. Using the graphical interfaces can slow the system significantly if there is not enough RAM or a fast enough chip. Unix is best learned hands on.

Whether this is the only Unix course you take or whether you are interested in pursuing a career related to Unix administration or development, this course will expose you to the various elements that make up the day of most professional Unix people. The Unix employment outlook is still vibrant, especially in academic and large corporate arenas. Even those who plan to work with Microsoft or Apple products will benefit from Unix knowledge, since heterogeneous networks are increasingly the norm rather than the deviation.

To the Teacher

This text is designed to provide an overview of several critical areas of the Unix operating system. With this text, you can expose your students to a range of activities related to Unix, from simple filesystem navigation to scripting with sed and awk, as well as the various functions which system administrators perform regularly. No matter what the focus of your particular course—from a survey of operating systems to a class designed for IT majors—you should find information here which will support your classroom activities.

The text is divided into several sections so that it can be used in a variety of courses with different syllabi and emphasis. Most instructors will use the first two sections in their courses, especially if their students have little experience with multi-user operating systems.

- Chapters 1-6 provide an overview of Unix history, how the operating system works, how commands are given and processed, the file system, and jobs and processes. This section also introduces the shell environment. The bash shell is the default shell used in this book.
- Chapters 7-9 introduce your students to common Unix applications: various text editors, with an emphasis on vi, and some popular Internet applications which your students can put to use immediately if you are working in a networked environment. For those instructors who use electronic mail to communicate with their students, several e-mail clients are covered in this section.
- Chapters 10 and 11 introduce networking. From the most basic concepts of Unix networking to a case study in which students can build a small local network and connect it to the Internet, the ideas presented here are useful for students no matter what their major or eventual career goal.
- Chapters 12-15 concentrate on bash shell programming. Some instructors may not cover this material in their courses, while others find that shell programming is an excellent introduction to programming in general, especially if students are required to take more complex programming courses in their course of study. The basic concepts of shell scripting are introduced here, with increasingly complex scripts and examples.
- Chapters 16-19 are focused on system administration. Since sysadmin jobs are one of the most common destinations for Unix-skilled students, the jobs that routinely make up an administrator's day are an important focus. These chapters introduce user and disk management, working with software, the X Window System, and running networked services: printing, Internet services, and remote access. Attention is also paid to security management and to working with disabled users.
- The appendices contain a brief command compendium, a glossary, a set of configuration files which you can use for examples or illustration, and a set of URLs for further study or exploration.

The text is general enough that it can be used with almost every Unix variant, and all the variants which are likely to be found in an academic setting. Of course, hands-on work is the best way to gain comfort with Unix, and we encourage students (and instructors) to consider installing Linux or FreeBSD on a spare machine. This allows students to explore root-restricted programs and functions, as well as demystifying the operating system through familiarity. Red Hat or Debian Linux and FreeBSD are the most user-friendly choices. If your academic set-up offers both graphical interfaces and text mode, note that we have concentrated on text mode, or terminal window access, throughout the book, since it is hard to predict how many systems still run as text-only.

Acknowledgments

Our thanks to the McGraw-Hill team who put this book together and shepherded it through the process. Particular thanks go to Dan Silverburg, who acquired the project, and Diana del Castillo, who managed it. The entire team, from proofreading to production, was a pleasure to work with. The academic reviewers who previewed each chapter offered useful suggestions that made this a better text.

As always, our thanks to David Fugate at Waterside Productions. Russ Allbery and Matt Gerber offered constructive suggestions and comments while we put together the table of contents and wrote the bulk of the book.

CHAPTER 1

What Is Unix?

IN THIS CHAPTER

1. Unix history and background
2. The rise of the operating system
3. C and Unix
4. The growth of Unix
5. Unix today
6. Unix as cultural phenomenon
7. The Free Software movement
8. Linux and FreeBSD
9. The Open Source movement
10. Flavors of Unix
11. BSD vs. SysV
12. The Unix philosophy

In order to work with Unix, it is not necessary to know anything about its history. However, knowing something about the background of the operating system can be helpful in understanding how the system works, and why certain Unix functions work in the way that they do. Those who are interested enough in Unix to continue studying the system or to install it on a personal computer will benefit from an introduction to the current factions in the Unix community, whether or not they choose to become involved in the political side of the operating system. This chapter provides a general overview of Unix history in order to set the context for the remainder of the text.

Unix History and Background

The world of computers is vastly different today than it was fifty years ago. Were it possible for you to visit a computing laboratory in the mid-1950s, or for a scientist from that lab to visit you in your classroom today, it might seem like you were not speaking the same language or performing the same tasks. The biggest difference is in the size of the computers; where the original computers took up entire rooms, you can do your homework on a desktop or laptop machine, or even on a computer small enough to fit in your hand. As the size of a computer has dropped, the amount of memory in the machine, and the speed of its processor, have grown dramatically.

Apart from the physical differences between these early machines and the machines used today, there are significant differences in the way they work. In fact, the original computers did not have operating systems. To those who came of age in the modern era of computing (roughly defined as anything after 1980), this is nearly unimaginable. The concept of an operating system, however, did not appear until well after computers were established as useful machines and not merely an unusual fad.

If there was no operating system, then how did the machines work? In the earliest days, the computer operator had to set up the machine to perform a particular task. That is, if the computer was needed to sort a batch of data, the operator would manually configure the computer's electric circuits for that

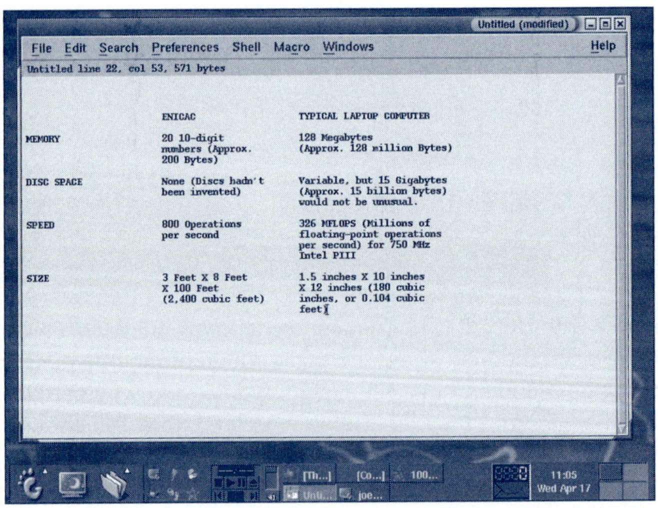

FIGURE 1.1 **Early computers, such as ENIAC, had far less computing power than the average laptop available today.**

task. The circuits needed to be changed for each different job. Obviously, this took time and effort, but it was justified by the fact that changing the circuits was less work than it would require to do the computing task by hand. Most computers were configured to perform one job and were rarely reconfigured. This was the most efficient use of computing power, but didn't allow for much flexibility.

Compare that world to computing today. Now, we use small computers to perform a vast array of tasks, and can change from job to job without opening the machine, adding new hardware, or cutting off the power. The giant machines of the past are in museums or being sold on eBay. While we did not come from room-size computers to palmtops overnight, the change has been rapid. Those fifty years have been exciting scientifically and historically and have affected the world's population more deeply than almost any other 50-year period of technological change.

The Rise of the Operating System

One of the driving forces behind the advance of computer technology is the desire to conserve effort. Computers were designed as timesaving devices, meant to free up human minds and hands for other, less tedious, work. It is easy to characterize this desire as "laziness," but not in the sense that sitting down to watch eight hours of television is lazy. Rather, the desire grows from a dislike of inefficient or repetitive work and a need to eliminate unnecessary effort. If you have to open your computer and change the wiring every time you want to do a different task, you will spend a lot of time with your head inside the machine rather than using that time to get work done. Consequently, computer scientists are always looking for ways to get the computer to do its own work, conserving their own efforts.

While it's fun to debate which idea is the greatest labor-saving innovation, most lists will include the development of the operating system. An *operating system* is a program whose function is to enable other programs to use the computer's hardware. The advantage of this system is clear: instead of creating programs that require direct use of specific hardware, programmers can write programs that make use of the operating system. This saves time and effort, since the operating system is a known entity. It also removes the need for a human operator to reconfigure the machine for each step in the process.

Consider the popular financial program Quicken. You can buy Quicken for Windows and install it on any kind of computer, as long as that computer is running the Windows operating system. It doesn't matter what the specific hardware configuration is; as long as Windows runs properly, Quicken will too. In contrast, without an operating system, a program like Quicken would have to be rewritten for each individual computer because the hardware configuration changes from machine to machine.

Note: The reality of applications and operating systems is, of course, far more complicated than this example.

The first operating systems were written especially for each machine. This was still an era of large computers, so it was not as onerous a task as it might seem. Each computer's hardware was different, so the commands that made that particular set of hardware work were encoded into the machine's specific operating system. With this new convenience, programmers could write programs for their computer far more quickly—as long as they understood the operating system.

Note that, in the years leading up to the early 1980s, there was no such thing as *commodity software.* That is, you couldn't go to the store and buy a packaged program; most software was written in-house by company programmers who would be the computer's primary users. These programs were still written for specific machines' operating systems rather than the generic operating systems in use on most personal computers today.

C and Unix

In 1969, two researchers at Bell Labs became dissatisfied with the operating system running on their DEC PDP-7 computer. So, Ken Thompson and Dennis Ritchie wrote a new operating system. This new program was the first incarnation of Unix. Shortly after they wrote their operating system, Bell Labs bought a new computer, the DEC PDP-11/20. Thompson and Ritchie wanted to keep using their operating system, so they decided to *port,* or transfer, the software to the new machine. As described earlier in this chapter, porting the operating system meant that it had to be completely rewritten to take the new computer's hardware configuration into account. Ritchie and Thompson felt that there had to be an easier way to port software; the result was the C programming language.

The concept behind C is that it should be possible, in theory, to write a program in language which can be converted into any given machine's native command language, regardless of what that native language might be. The problem with machine languages is that they are not very comprehensible to humans. To port a program by hand, the programmer must keep track of every bit of data and how a given machine handles that data type. Thompson and Ritchie wanted to write a program once and then convert it to the native language of any computer they wanted to use to run the program.

Their solution uses a helper program called a *compiler.* The compiler is a program that is specific to a particular computer; a computer running Windows will use a different compiler than a computer running Linux, and the Linux compiler is different from the FreeBSD compiler. Individual versions of compilers for the same operating system will differ as well, if the hardware configuration of the individual machines is different. To port a program from one operating system to another, the programmer uses a program written in C as input for the compiler. The compiler then produces a machine language version of that program, which can be run on the compiler's home machine. With this technique, when a new computer arrived in the laboratory, all Thompson and Ritchie had to do was to write a new compiler and recompile all the old programs for the new machine.

In practice, of course, compiling and porting are not as simple as that. Even with the appropriate compiler, most programs have to be modified or tweaked before they run efficiently on a new computer. Still, this is far easier than rewriting the entire program from scratch. In fact, Thompson and Ritchie found the concept so useful that, in 1974, they rewrote their Unix operating system in the C language. Even today, C remains popular among programmers, especially those who work primarily with Unix. Unix is still written in C, and C compilers exist for almost every piece of computing hardware available.

The Growth of Unix

At about the same time as Ritchie and Thompson were working on Unix and C, their employer, Bell Labs, became embroiled in a legal argument that would have a great effect on computing. The federal government ruled that Bell Labs' parent company, AT&T, was a monopoly in the telecommunications market, and demanded that AT&T take steps to break their stranglehold and permit competition. One of these steps involved Unix, as AT&T began to give the operating system to academic institutions free of charge. Universities, of course, loved this gift, and Unix became very popular in the academic world. As graduates left college, they took their fondness for Unix with them, and the operating system began to establish itself in the corporate world as well.

In 1978, however, AT&T announced that it would start charging for Unix. The universities, which had formerly acquired the software for free, were understandably irritated. In reaction to AT&T's announcement, the University of California at Berkeley announced that it would create its own version of Unix. This version, known as Berkeley Software Development Unix (BSD Unix), was distributed not only free of charge but free of any license restrictions—unlike AT&T's Unix.

At this point, the Unix genie was out of the bottle and destined to stay that way. With the permissiveness of the BSD Unix license, along with all the copies of free AT&T Unix still in existence, anybody who wanted Unix could get it. Even better, anyone who wanted Unix could write his or her own version, from college students to major computing companies. The result was the wholesale fragmentation of Unix into a family of "Unix-like" systems. Each of these systems shares a Unix feel and many common commands and operations, but each variant also has significant differences. People tend to choose one variant and develop a loyalty to that Unix flavor; some of these loyalties can border on the obsessive.

On one hand, this fragmentation has been good for Unix. Competition in the marketplace has led to steady development and improvement of the operating system, and over the years, the various *Unices* (plural of Unix) have become robust and stable computing platforms. The fact that free versions are readily available means that Unix has never been put aside for a cheaper alternative, and that it has become a valid alternative for college students on a budget. On the other hand, fragmentation has made Unix vulnerable in the corporate and consumer worlds. It has been particularly vulnerable to the aggressive marketing techniques of Microsoft, which has criticized the Unix market as confused and non-standard. (While these criticisms are not without justification, Microsoft has greatly exaggerated their degree and importance. In fact, Microsoft sold its own version of Unix for some years until it was determined to be unprofitable.)

Unix Today

The fragmentation of Unix into hundreds of variants, along with the rise of the personal computer and its operating systems like Microsoft's Windows and Apple's MacOS, has led to a decrease in Unix's popularity in the corporate world. Since colleges and universities must train their students for the world that awaits them after graduation, Unix has also lost ground in the academic world. Most college students of the past ten years—especially those students who are not studying technical disciplines—have never knowingly used a Unix machine. The loss of familiarity with Unix is a shame. It is a powerful and flexible operating system that is far more reliable than most of the personal-computer-based operating systems.

However, Unix is not obsolete, and is returning to visibility in both the corporate and academic arenas. A big part of this return is due to the Internet, which still runs primarily on Unix machines because they can handle the intense workload. Unix is alive and vibrant, and has become as much a cultural phenomenon as a technical convenience.

Unix as Cultural Phenomenon

Today's Unix world is not exclusively concerned with the technological function of the operating system. Rather, Unix has become the focus for several political and cultural movements. These spheres of influence use Unix as an example of decentralization, rather than the centralized and monolithic development of the personal computer operating systems. In this section of the chapter, we cover the three major movements focused on Unix: the Free Software movement, the Linux and FreeBSD communities, and the Open Source movement. Although you may never be involved in the Unix community at a level deep enough that you must "take sides," it is a good idea to learn what the major arguments are so that you can recognize them in conversation or in further reading.

The Free Software Movement

The Free Software movement is attributable to the work of one man: Richard Stallman. Stallman was a programmer at the Massachusetts Institute of Technology's artificial intelligence laboratory. In 1971, he and his lab team were working on a DEC PDP-10 computer for which they had written an effective operating system. At that time, the culture of programming was open. People routinely shared software, and there was no concept that software could be "owned" by any one person or company.

MIT purchased a new PDP-10 that year and asked Stallman to change everything over to DEC's operating system rather than install the lab's own operating system on the new computer. Stallman set to work but soon learned that DEC required him to sign a non-disclosure agreement before he could begin to work with their code. This upset Stallman mightily, since he felt that DEC was trying to keep him from helping his fellow programmers by sharing his insights and innovations. Although non-disclosure agreements are now common, in part because software is such a lucrative field, in 1971 Stallman saw the request as a shift in the moral ground underlying computer programming.

In response to this situation, Stallman began work on a new project: an operating system that would be freely available and open to all. He called it GNU, an acronym for "GNU's Not Unix." Stallman wanted to create an operating system that worked exactly like Unix but contained no proprietary software. In order to ensure that GNU could never become proprietary, he drafted a license that allowed users to use the operating system under certain constraints:

- the software can be used for any purpose
- the user has the right to copy and redistribute the software
- the user has the right to modify the software and distribute the changes
- the user must grant these same rights to all subsequent users

In other words, if you want to modify a piece of GNU-licensed software and then distribute your work, you must permit others to distribute it as well. This license is known as the GNU General Public License, or GPL, and there is a vast amount of software available under these terms.

With the GPL in place, Stallman released the first piece of the operating system: GNU Emacs, a text editor. He felt that a good text editor was necessary in order to work on the rest of the system, and GNU Emacs offered a number of features not found in other text editors of the time. This program is still in use today, and is covered in Chapter 8: Other Text Editors. After GNU Emacs was released, Stallman began to work on other software packages. Many of these programs have become popular utilities among programmers and system administrators, and you will learn about several of them in this book. The popularity of GNU programs stemmed from three major features: they were free of charge, they could be compiled on just about all Unix systems, and—if they didn't work for a particular situation—they could be modified because the source code was freely available.

As GNU software began to take off, Stallman found that he wasn't the only one working on the project. Many programmers began to use their free time to work on GNU software. These volunteers sent their work to Stallman, who would evaluate the code and often wrap it into the "official" GNU releases. Other programmers started to release their own projects under the GNU license; some of these projects were incorporated into Stallman's releases, and some were independent. No matter how the code was released, though, Stallman's original vision was being borne out. Programmers were openly sharing code and modifications without restraint.

The GNU project became so successful that, in 1985, the Free Software Foundation was established. The FSF gives the GNU project an organizational structure and the ability to employ people to work on GNU projects and to accept charitable donations. Learn more about the various projects under the Free Software Foundation umbrella by visiting their Web site: http://www.fsf.org.

Linux and FreeBSD

As successful as the GNU project has been, it has not yet reached its goal of a stand-alone, fully functional, operating system. This is because Stallman has not yet finished creating the *kernel*, the part of the operating system that interacts directly with the computer's hardware. Stallman's design for the GNU kernel is based on advanced computational theory that has proved difficult to implement.

Fortunately, others have stepped in to fill this gap. In 1991, a Finnish university student named Linus Torvalds began to work on his own kernel, a project that would eventually plug the major hole in the GNU software system. Torvalds was unhappy with his IBM 386 and the MS-DOS operating system, which was state of the art at that time. He enjoyed working on his university's Unix computer and wanted to have something similar on his personal machine, but soon learned that, if he wanted something like that, he'd have to write it himself.

By October of 1991, Torvalds was far enough along in his project that he could see a lot of potential. However, he knew he couldn't do all the work himself. Luckily, the Internet was popular enough on college campuses at this point (though hardly visible in the non-academic world) that he could tap a wide range of fellow computing enthusiasts for help. He posted a message to a USENET newsgroup, informing people that his project was available for download and asking for suggestions. In the next few months, enough progress had been made on Torvalds' kernel that it could be called "fairly usable." The group continued to work, and the first official release of a stable Linux kernel came in 1994.

By combining the Linux kernel with the array of utilities available from the GNU project, computer users now had access to a complete operating system that would run on personal computers, and it was all free. As time went by, other programmers began to build bundles of software that contained GNU software, the Linux kernel, and special programs that would install everything properly. These bundles, called *distributions*, are the way that GNU and Linux software is packaged today.

Note: Although most people call this operating system "Linux," Stallman has correctly noted that it should be called "GNU/Linux" since it includes components of both systems. While this is certainly true, "Linux" is now the common name for the package and it is the name used in this book.

Today, there are a number of competing Linux distributions: over 100 at the last count. Each distribution has a different focus. Some are sold for profit, some are available at no charge, some are designed for Macintosh computers, some for handhelds, and others for almost any circumstance you can imagine. Three of the most popular distributions are Red Hat, Debian, and Slackware. Red Hat is designed for ease of use and installation, Debian is focused on free software purity, and Slackware aims to be as true to old-style Unix as possible.

Of course, Linux variants are not the only PC-based Unices available. There are several distributions available that are based on the Berkeley Software Distribution Unix described earlier in this chapter. The most commonly used BSD variant is FreeBSD, which is free of charge and offers the source code to those who want to develop it further. Unlike Linux, however, FreeBSD is not covered by the GNU GPL, so some source code may not be available. While FreeBSD can be freely used, modified, and redistributed, nobody is under obligation to make the source code for modifications available. This means that FreeBSD can be used as part of a proprietary package; in fact, the latest version of the Macintosh operating system, MacOS X, is built on a FreeBSD base.

The other major difference between Linux and FreeBSD is that FreeBSD is developed by a small, closed group of programmers. While they do take some contributions from the FreeBSD community, it is very different from the free-wheeling and open Linux development community. There are advantages to both approaches. In addition, FreeBSD is often preferred by those who want to have a "real Unix" on their machines, since FreeBSD and the other PC BSD variants use original BSD Unix code.

The Open Source Movement

Whether correct or not, many people see an ideological and political conviction in the goals of the Free Software Foundation and, by extension, in the Linux community (because Linux is so closely integrated with GNU software). Richard Stallman's writings rely heavily on his concepts of morality, freedom, assistance, and other philosophical ideas. This has led many casual observers to conclude, with arguable justification, that the thrust of the FSF's efforts are anti-capitalist. Whatever Stallman's personal feelings may be, the GNU license and software documents contain no provisions that prevent commercial use.

However, some advocates of Free Software think that a political or philosophical approach is not the best way to get one's product adopted in the business community, especially if the product is perceived as anti-corporate. Eric Raymond, in particular, has argued that the key to acceptance of Free Software is in getting it into corporate installations and that, in order for this to happen, the case for Free Software must be made in language that is both understandable and appealing to business leaders.

Raymond is a programmer and author who came to prominence as the result of a sociological experiment. He hypothesized that not only was Free Software a good thing from a social point of view, but that the very fact that the software was free created a developmental environment that would build better software in less time. To test this theory, he wrote a program called "fetchmail." This program retrieves electronic mail from a remote server and delivers it to local users' mail programs. At the time Raymond wrote fetchmail, there was no equivalent in any Unix variant. Raymond released fetchmail under the GNU GPL, and was quickly gratified to see that people were working on his program and improving it.

Raymond then wrote an article called "The Cathedral and the Bazaar," which compared the world of commercial software, developed in a closed system or "cathedral," to the world of free software, developed openly in the "bazaar" of public participation. This article has become one of the most influential pieces written about software development and is responsible for at least one company's decision to release its program code rather than keep it private: Netscape.

Note: You can read "The Cathedral and the Bazaar," along with Raymond's other writings, at http://www.tuxedo.org/esr/.

One of the key points in the essay is a subtle shift in semantics. Raymond does not use the term Free Software to describe openly developed code. Rather, he introduces the term Open Source Software. In keeping with Raymond's desire to make this software business-friendly, the change in terms removes the perceived anti-business bias that had hindered Free Software from being widely adopted. Raymond has been criticized for this choice but has noted that he is trying to help the movement and not to steal its thunder: "'Open Source' is a marketing program for 'Free Software'," he has said.

To a great extent, this marketing program has been successful, and Free/Open Source Software has found some acceptance in corporate circles. IBM, for example, has embraced Linux and is now selling servers with Linux pre-installed. Other companies have moved to Linux for significant parts of their technological infrastructure. Like Stallman, Raymond has founded an organization to promote his views. Learn more about the Open Source initiative at http://www.opensource.org.

Flavors of Unix

The fragmentation of Unix into a number of competing variants has led to a divergence in how these varying systems function. To the average end user, this is not a cause for concern since the user interface is reasonably consistent from system to system. To the programmer or system administrator, however, the differences can be of extreme importance. Luckily for the programmers, though, all current Unix variants are POSIX-compliant. This means that all the variants adhere to a particular standard so that they execute critical functions in the same way.

Note: POSIX, or the Portable Operating System Interface, is a set of standard interfaces that allows programs to run on a variety of Unix variants. As long as the operating system uses POSIX-compliant mechanisms, it can run software regardless of the actual variant in use. The POSIX standard is administered by the Institute of Electrical and Electronics Engineers, or IEEE.

As you learn more about Unix, you will see that the internal workings of a Unix system depend on a number of crucial files and configurations. Unfortunately, these are the elements that work differently under different variants, so you must be able to see the differences and know how to work with them. The major cause of these variances is the "family tree" of the particular variant with which you are working.

BSD versus SysV

These family-tree issues stem from the differences between the original AT&T Unix and the Berkeley Software Distribution Unix variant. As described earlier in this chapter, the BSD variant was written in response to AT&T's decision to charge for its Unix. All Unix variants that descend from AT&T/Bell Labs Unix are called *SysV Unices*, after the fifth release of AT&T Unix (the most popular version), while Unix variants that descend from Berkeley Unix are called *BSD Unices.*

SysV and BSD Unices differ significantly in the way that they handle the configuration of various tasks that must be executed when the system is started up. BSD systems use a simple start-up program, while SysV uses a more complicated method that provides far more flexibility. There are several other aspects of the SysV/BSD incompatibility that are beyond the scope of this book, since they deal with the low-level elements of the computer's operation. For our purposes, the differences at boot will be described in most detail. Table 1.1 shows some of the more popular Unices, sorted into BSD and SysV columns.

Since that original fork in the Unix family tree, there has been some cross-development. Sun Microsystem's Solaris Unix, for example, combines elements of both SysV and BSD Unix. Linux also offers elements of both styles. There is no consensus that one style is better than the other. Both systems have adherents and detractors, and it ends up being a matter of personal choice. However, it's good to know how both kinds of Unix work in the event that you are confronted with an unfamiliar flavor of Unix.

The Unix Philosophy

Regardless of the type of Unix being developed, those who work on Unix variants have subscribed to a set of principles that reflect the original theories behind Ritchie and Thompson's work in the late 1960s. Over the years, programmers have taken care to maintain these design concepts and to incorporate them whenever new features are added. These points are so critical to the concept of Unix that they have taken on the character of a design philosophy:

Keep it small: the typical Unix system is composed of many small programs. Small programs are easy to understand, maintain, and improve. While each component may not be particularly powerful on its own, small modules can be combined into complex objects. Clever programmers can often find new uses for existing modules.

TABLE 1.1: Some Unix Variants Sorted by BSD or SysV Heritage

BSD	SysV
OpenBSD	AIX
FreeBSD	HP/UX
BSD/OS	Linux
NetBSD	SCO Unix

Keep it consistent: the modules that make up a Unix system tend to interact with each other in consistent ways. For example, every element of a Unix system is represented as a file. Every text file, every program, every piece of hardware, and every other system element can be dealt with as a file. This consistency makes it easy to deal with all the elements of the operating system.

Keep it configurable: almost all Unix programs can be made to behave in nearly as many ways as you can think of. Users can control the look and feel of their interface; administrators can configure system-wide behaviors; programmers can adapt or modify system functions. It is a rare Unix program that doesn't have multiple configuration options.

Keep it non-captive: Unix programs seek to avoid the "captive user interface." This means that programmers do not assume that the end user is always a human. Consider a Web browser; it does not work independently, but expects you to enter commands. In the Unix world, programs make use of other programs to generate input or process output. Whenever possible, Unix programs include a non-interactive mode that makes automation possible without human input.

Keep it automatable: the idea of non-captive interfaces is related to the idea of automation. Unix administrators prefer to automate tasks whenever possible, and Unix provides the means to do so. Unix commands can be encoded in a script or program that will run the commands automatically, and even provides a task schedule to make use of downtime.

With these principles in action, Unix programmers have developed a robust system that can be used in a vast array of situations: end users, automation, factory management, scientific testing, and many other realms.

Summary

Although Unix is less than fifty years old, its history is surprisingly complex. The earliest computers were programmed by manually moving electrical connections within the machine. The first operating systems were written for individual computers, and were simply the software equivalent of moving the internal wires. In the mid-1960s, two programmers at AT&T's Bell Labs created a method to move software from one computer to another; this method resulted in both the Unix operating system and the concept of a compiler.

When the federal courts determined AT&T was a monopoly, the company had to give away Unix as part of its penalty. The company later began to charge for the operating system, leading to a splinter in Unix development. Over the next twenty years, a number of Unix variants were created, and the Unix community began to separate into philosophical and technical subcommunities. Unix variants themselves generally fall into either the SysV or BSD category, depending on the code that was used to build the basic system. Regardless of the faction or beliefs that produced each variant, however, all Unices adhere to several general principles, including size and consistency.

Review Questions

1. How were the earliest computers programmed? What operating system did they use?
2. Why do computer users and programmers want to eliminate repetition and duplicative effort?
3. Define an operating system and explain how an operating system works with the hardware and the human user.
4. Provide several examples of commodity software.
5. Why was the development of C an advance in computing?
6. Why was free distribution of Unix a valid penalty when AT&T was declared a monopoly?
7. What are the basic beliefs of the Free Software Foundation?
8. Why did Linus Torvalds develop Linux? Was his work motivated by technical or philosophical impulses?
9. What are the basic beliefs of the Open Source initiative?
10. Why are there so many different Linux and FreeBSD distributions?
11. Define the POSIX standard.
12. Describe the "Unix philosophy."

Exercises

1. As computers have become smaller over the past 50 years, their computing power has grown. Research the computing power of any early space mission and compare it to the power contained in your own computer, palmtop, or cellular telephone.
2. Create a detailed "family tree" of Unix variants, starting with Thompson and Ritchie's original Bell Labs version. (Option: concentrate only on the SysV or BSD branches.) This exercise requires external research on the Web or in your school's library.
3. Research current opposition to Unix, particularly from those who sell commodity operating systems. Are these arguments valid? How can invalid arguments be refuted?
4. Compare the positions of the Free Software Foundation and the Open Source initiative. Do you think one side argues its position more effectively than the other? Which position do you agree with, if any? Why?
5. Read Eric Raymond's article "The Cathedral and the Bazaar." What are his major points? Is the cathedral/bazaar model an effective way to describe software development? Do you agree or disagree with him? Why?
6. Find and compare several different software licenses. Show how they differ and provide a scenario for each license, explaining how a user might violate or adhere to the license's provisions.

CHAPTER 2

Basic Unix Concepts

IN THIS CHAPTER

1. What is an operating system?
2. Structure of a Unix operating system
3. The kernel
4. The shell
5. The file system
6. Users
7. Accounts
8. The superuser
9. Logging into your account
10. Logging out of your account

This chapter provides the framework you will need to understand the rest of the material in the text. No matter which flavor of Unix you use while studying the operating system, it will have these basic components. The many Unix variants may use different ways to accomplish the same task, but each of these methods uses the same components to achieve the same goal.

Much like the human body, a Unix system is composed of various parts that work together and mutually support each other. For example, in the human body, the digestive system requires oxygen from the respiratory system, delivered by blood in the circulatory system, in order to digest food. Likewise, the respiratory system requires the energy from digested food in order to keep the lungs and diaphragm moving. In the same way, a Unix system has different cycles and components that interact in order to perform the tasks you request.

Understanding how these parts work together to form a complete operating system is a critical foundation for further work with Unix. If you discover a problem on your Unix system, it is very helpful if you know the general area of the system where the problem is located, and know enough about how that component works in order to begin solving the problem. When things are going well on your machine, you can use the same knowledge to make small changes that bring the machine to an optimum level of performance.

What Is an Operating System?

As defined in Chapter 1, an *operating system* is the software whose function is to enable other programs to use the computer's hardware. This means that the operating system must perform many small functions in order to execute the task desired by the computer's user. For example, assume that you want to see a list of files in your home directory on the Unix computer. At the command prompt, you would type the command **ls**. The **ls** command launches the **ls** program. The program must be identified, found on the computer's hard disk, stored in memory, loaded into the memory and run. Once the program has started, the computer must locate the desired directory on the hard disk, identify all the subdirectories and files in the desired directory, convert the file identities into human-readable characters, and display the output on the screen. Each of these steps are performed in the processor's native language, which typically can only manipulate 32 or 64 *bits*, or discrete binary units, of information at a time.

The user experience is quite different. While all of these microtasks are being executed, the user simply waits for the output. The user has done nothing but execute the command, or perhaps has only clicked the mouse button, in order to get the displayed output. The difference between the user's experience and the actual microtasks that manipulate electrical signals within the machine is the domain of the operating system, which exists to manage the various resources on the computer and allocate them as necessary.

The operating system is responsible for controlling the processor, the hard disk(s), and the memory installed in the computer. It is also responsible for any peripheral devices that may be attached, such as printers, external disk drives, modems, network cards, video or sound cards, and anything else that can be added to a computer either temporarily or permanently. These devices and components use binary code, unintelligible to most humans, to understand their instructions and execute their operations. Without a functional operating system or the ability to communicate in pure binary code, there is no way to make the computer work.

Structure of a Unix Operating System

All Unix variants have the same general structure. Unix is a modular operating system; you can install as many modules as you like to perform a wide array of functions, or you can install as few modules as are needed to keep the machine running. Moreover, these modules can be changed whenever necessary. The modular nature of Unix makes it extremely flexible, since you need only run the software necessary for your current requirements. The operating system has three general components: the kernel, the shell, and the file system.

The Kernel

The kernel is the core of any Unix system. In fact, the only difference between any two given Unix machines might be the kernel. The kernel runs constantly while the computer is powered on, and provides the core operating system functions. It is the supervisory element of the operating system, and is the link between user directions and hardware activity.

Despite the central responsibility and critical nature of the kernel, it is not a program that a user can call up or modify. The kernel will never show up on a list of programs currently running on the machine, even though it is a constantly running program itself. The kernel is always out of sight so that it can work without interference or damage.

The kernel can be thought of as the "traffic cop" of the operating system. Its primary job is to manage the flow of electrical signals through the computer's hardware. These electrical signals force the hardware to react in specific ways and either to perform a function or to generate output. This output is then translated by the kernel into a particular format that is then interpreted by a given program or by the user. Since the computer is an electrical machine, the kernel is the manager of all electrical impulses sent between the various cards and devices within the external case.

Most users will never have direct experience with the kernel; in fact, the system is designed so that there will be little or no reason for the average user to work directly with kernel operation. Unless you are writing a program that requires a particular operating system service, you will probably never issue an operating system command directly to your kernel. This is due to the *user interface,* a piece of software that makes dealing with the operating system and kernel easier for humans. The user interface offers a set of functions and commands that are designed for the user; once the user issues a command, the user interface interprets that command for the operating system itself.

Why this indirect method of interaction between user and computer? The kernel was never designed for direct user manipulation. Rather, the kernel's services are available through commands that are designed to be embedded into programs: programs that will eventually be run by humans or by other programs. These kernel commands are called *system calls* because the programmer is calling upon the system's services when she uses one of these commands in her program. The set of all acceptable system calls is referred to as the *Application Programming Interface*, or API.

Every operating system has its own API, as do many large-scale programs. Before a programmer begins work on a program designed for a particular operating system or a module for a particular software program, he must familiarize himself with the API for that programming environment. Calls that work under one system or program may not work with another, or may have unintended effects.

The Shell

Although the kernel is remote by design, the user interfaces described above make it possible to use the computer. Without the user interface, the computer would simply be a mildly unattractive box sitting on the desk or floor, but it would be neither accessible nor popular. On Unix systems, these user interfaces are called *shells*.

The term "shell" is generally used to describe a text-based user interface, such as those traditionally found on Unix systems. In the last five years, however, graphical user interfaces, or GUIs, have become increasingly popular on Unix systems. GUIs are the interfaces that offer multiple windows, mouse interaction, and attractive visual decoration. Microsoft Windows and MacOS have used graphical user interfaces from the beginning, but GUIs are a latecomer to the Unix community. A GUI could be considered a shell in a technical sense, but the term is not used commonly. Many people run text-based shell sessions within a window on a graphical desktop in order to exploit particular features of the text-based interaction.

As the name suggests, the shell acts as the operating system's outer layer. Just like the shell of a clam or a nut, a user sees the shell instead of the vulnerable contents. There are several types of shells, and an even bigger number of individual shells within each type. Like Unix variants, each shell is slightly different, but they all function in the same general manner. No matter what the specific quirks of any shell may be, the shell provides an interactive environment for the user to work with the operating system and to issue commands that ultimately direct the kernel.

Most text-based shells are operated with keystroke commands. As Figure 2.1 shows, the shell usually provides a *command prompt* and a cursor. Enter your commands by typing them on the keyboard and press the Return or Enter key, and the shell will begin to process the request, passing on the required system calls to the kernel.

FIGURE 2.1 The standard shell interface is text-based.

Most shells, however, are more complex and permit more complicated interaction than the simple translation described above. For example, the **bash** shell includes a number of native features: a text editor, so you can edit your commands if you make an error; a command history function, so you can look up commands issued previously; a program interpreter, so you can build programs from shell commands; and a number of small utilities that make working in the shell easier. A selection of Unix shells is described in Chapter 6: Using the Shell.

Although kernel functions and system calls are well-standardized in the current Unix world, shells also have the advantage of providing a consistent interface from machine to machine, regardless of what Unix variant, hardware, or other software is actually installed. The user will see the same interface on different machines, as long as the shell is configured in the same way. This minimizes the differences between variants, and can be a useful trick for the system administrator when faced with changing Unices or software across a network.

The File System

It is easy to overlook the file system when thinking about the various components of an operating system. It is somewhat non-intuitive to think of the files stored on your computer as being part of the operating system, since they seem much more like data or programs that you have intentionally stored there. Nevertheless, the file system is an especially important part of the Unix operating system.

One of the overarching design features of Unix is that the operating system handles everything as a file. All the programs installed on the machine, all the data created by users or other programs, and all the hardware devices attached to the computer are represented as files. For example, when you create a text file and save it to the hard disk, the kernel sees the hard disk as a file and opens that file in order to write your text data in the correct subdirectory. Likewise, when you run a program, the kernel opens the program file in order to read the executable data contained within it. Files that contain other files are called *directories* to distinguish them from files that contain executable or parsable data.

In addition to these executable and device files, Unix makes use of extensive text files to store information about how the system is configured. These configuration files control a vast number of aspects of the system's behavior. Configuration files can be used to control the programs that are initiated when the machine starts up, what the user sees when he logs in, how network connections are managed, and many other things.

In fact, files may not even be files at all! Unix uses a number of special file types which, though handled as a file by the operating system, have other functions. *Links*, for example, are dummy filenames that point to other files. *Pipes* serve as conduits for communication between programs. Some Unix variants also have "pseudo filesystems," which are used to track running processes. Linux, for example, uses the /proc directory to track these items.

These examples illustrate the fact that files in Unix systems are more than storage devices. The file system itself is integral to the operation of the computer, and determines how smoothly a given process will run. Files are the way Unix represents its various components to itself; they are, in a certain way, Unix's self-image.

Users

People who are used to working with personal operating systems like Microsoft Windows or Apple MacOS may never have given any thought to the role that users play in an operating system's design. Although Windows, for example, does make provisions for multiple user profiles, these profiles are primarily used to alter the graphical user interface rather than to provide hard authentication for security and privacy reasons. Some versions of Windows, such as Windows 95, Windows 98, and Windows ME, have little or no internal security. On machines running these Windows versions, programs and documents stored on the hard disk are available to all users, regardless of the user profile in operation.

Unix, in contrast, was designed from the beginning as a multi-user operating system. This means that Unix not only has separate accounts and restrictions for each user, but that multiple users can use the operating system at the same time. Even personal computers running Unix variants designed for PCs, like FreeBSD or Linux, can host a number of simultaneous users, limited only by the number of network connections available to the machine. This multi-user approach comes from Unix's heritage as an operating system for large mainframe machines that handled many users, both remote and working on the actual host.

Accounts

Before a prospective user can begin to work on a Unix machine, she must have an account created by someone with administrative powers on the machine; users cannot create their own accounts. An *account* contains five distinct components:

- a user name
- a password
- a user ID
- one or more group IDs
- a home directory

The user name identifies all aspects of this account, including e-mail and Web space addresses, as well as any permissions that may be set by the administrator. User and group IDs are identifying numbers; the user ID is often a more effective way to identify a user than the user name, and the group ID is used to create sub-groups of users who have accounts on that machine. Groups may have access to different programs, different security permissions, or particular file-sharing abilities.

All of these components create a defined identity for the person who will use this account. She can log in, has a specified directory that contains her personal data, and can access programs and files on the main machine as long as she has been granted permission to do so. All users on this system will have accounts with the same basic components. In fact, some user accounts will not be intended for humans, but are part of the operating system's regular work.

Having a distinct identity and a personal workspace allows the user to create private files. The level of privacy associated with a particular file is determined by the level of *permission* granted to the file. Unix uses permission attributes to define who has access to a given file, and for what purpose. Permissions determine who can read the file, alter the file, or execute the file if it is an executable program. Permissions are covered in more detail in Chapter 4: The File System.

Distinct identities also allow users to customize their working environments. User accounts have personal versions of the configuration files described earlier in this chapter. These configuration files control the behavior of certain programs, such as the shell. An individual user can change things about these programs to suit his tastes, but his changes will not affect any other users on the machine. For those users who prefer not to make any changes, the system-wide default configuration will still apply, but changes to personal configuration files always override the system default.

The Superuser

Every Unix system has a special account called the *superuser* or *root account.* This account has the user name "root," and is the account that is used to manage everything about the system. The superuser account is all-powerful. It can read, write, or execute any file on the system, including users' private files. It can run any program installed on the machine, including those installed in user accounts. It can create and delete user accounts, alter account settings, and install or delete any type of software. In short, the root account can do anything that is possible on a Unix system.

The superuser account was created for the unique requirements of system administration. The person who manages a Unix system must be able to access every file on the machine immediately, and cannot be hampered by file permissions. The superuser is also ultimately responsible for all files on the machine; should a user place illegal or invasive files in her account, such as a virus or account-cracking program, the superuser must remove it or possibly be liable in legal action.

If you install a Unix variant on your own personal computer, you will own the superuser account. The account is created when the operating system is installed, and the person installing the operating system selects the root password. The root password is the single most important and sensitive piece of information about any Unix system. If someone figures out the root password, she has complete access to your machine and, by extension, to any network connections or hardware devices attached to it. She can even change the root password, effectively locking you out of your own system.

Never use the superuser account for regular work, such as reading and sending e-mail, posting to USENET newsgroups, or doing daily tasks. If you are logged in as the superuser, your actions have superpowers; it is all too easy to delete an important file inadvertently, or to damage your system. It is also tempting to see what your users are doing in their accounts, even if you don't have a legitimate reason to snoop. Always create a normal user account, or two, for your regular and personal use.

For those who do not run their own Unix machines, such as students with accounts on a school Unix system, it is unlikely that root access will ever be available. In these cases, the root account will be held by the system administrator or whoever has ultimate control over the system. In many academic and corporate settings, a small group of people share responsibility for the superuser account so that someone with complete system access is always on duty. However, whenever passwords are shared, overall system security is compromised. The larger the network, the better the tradeoff between security and efficiency when there is more than one person with access to superuser powers.

Note: For many of the exercises in this book, you will not need superuser powers. Should you require them for a particular exercise, your instructor will either make provisions for you, or you must have your own Unix variant running on a personal computer where you have access to root.

Logging Into Your Account

From this point forward, we assume that you have either had a user account created for you or have installed a Unix variant and created an account yourself. Now that you have an account, you can log in. In order to log in, you need to know your user name and the password that was provided when the account was created. For most people, these items will be chosen by the administrator who created your account, though some administrators allow you to select your own user name as long as it adheres to existing user name policies. In any case, you should already have this information.

When you sit down to log in, you will see a system prompt like the one shown in Figure 2.2.

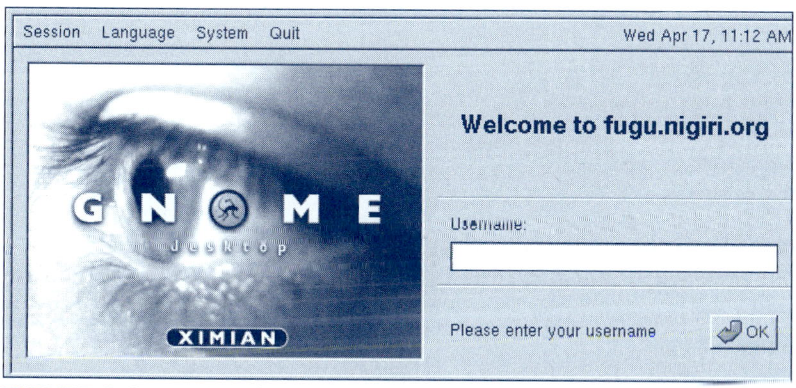

FIGURE 2.2 To log in, enter your username at the login prompt.

Prompts differ from system to system, depending on the Unix installed or local configuration. No matter what it looks like on your system, you should see a space for your user name and, sometimes, a space for the password. On some systems, the password prompt appears after the user name has been entered and verified as a valid account on the machine.

Enter your user name at the prompt. Be sure to spell it exactly as given, including any capitalization, numbers, hyphens, or underscores. The user name **Fran_12** is not the same as **fran_12**, **Fran-12**, or **fran-twelve**. In almost all cases, Unix is *case-sensitive*, so you must be careful to type commands and file names accurately. If you already have a password prompt available, press Tab. If you do not have a password prompt on the screen, press the Enter or Return key to bring it up.

Enter the password given to you. Again, enter it exactly as given. This may be harder because passwords are never shown in clear text as you type them. You will probably see a series of asterisks on the screen instead of your password, though some systems don't show anything at all. Press Enter or Return again.

If you make errors, you will see a message informing you of a failed login attempt. On some systems, three failed attempts lock the account and you must get the system administrator to unlock it for you, so it's advantageous to take care and type correctly. In some cases, you may have been given an incorrect user name or password; ask your instructor or administrator for help if repeated tries still fail.

Once you have successfully logged in, you will see a system prompt. The appearance of this system prompt will differ, depending on the shell environment that is installed on your system and its configuration. However, prompts follow a general pattern. They usually end with a non-alphanumeric character like % or $, and contain mapping information about your current location within the system.

For example, you might see a prompt like this:

```
[Fran_12@darkstar Fran_12$]
```

This prompt contains several points of information. The first component, Fran_12@darkstar, identifies the logged-in user as Fran_12 and the machine logged into as "darkstar." All Unix machines have names, assigned during the operating system installation process. The second component of the prompt, Fran_12, shows the current directory. In this case, Fran_12 is logged into her home directory, also named Fran_12. The complete path name for this directory is /home/Fran_12, but it is shortened to keep the prompt compact.

If you are using a system with a graphical user interface, you might not see a prompt when you log in. It is more likely that you'll see a desktop similar to what you'd find on a Windows or MacOS machine. In this case, you will need to open a *terminal window* in order to complete most of the exercises in this text. A terminal window is a program window that contains a system prompt, and that works like a standard text-based Unix screen. Depending on the GUI installed on your system, the terminal emulator may be called "xterm," "Terminal Emulator," or "Terminal." Your instructor will help you find the appropriate program. You can also try right-clicking your mouse on the desktop, which should bring up a menu. A terminal emulator is usually listed there. Figure 2.3 shows a terminal window open on a graphical desktop.

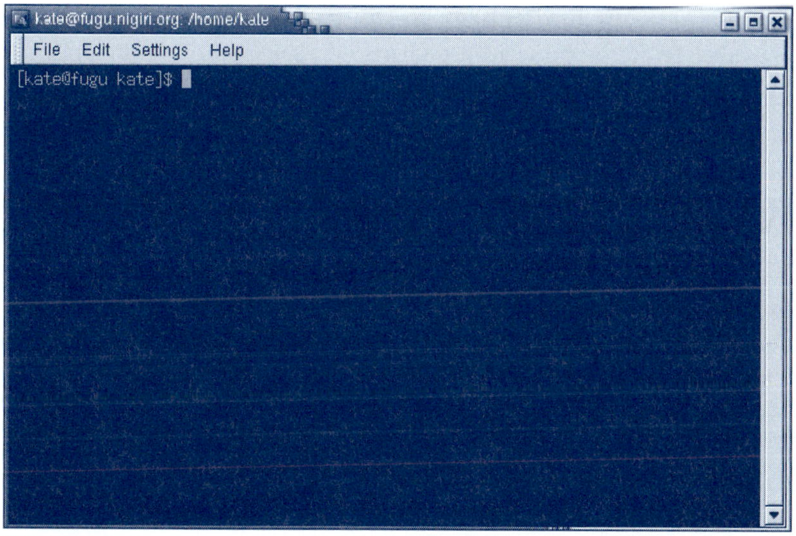

FIGURE 2.3 Use a terminal window to work with the shell in a graphical user environment.

Once you are logged into your account, you can issue some basic commands. Type

```
ls
```

at the command prompt to see a list of files and subdirectories contained in your account. Depending on what was created automatically when your account was set up, you may see several files or none at all. Try some of the commands contained in Appendix A: Common Unix Commands and see what happens.

Note: The cd command will always return you to your home directory. If you are moving through the computer's filesystem and want to return home, simply type cd at the prompt to return to your personal directory.

Logging Out of Your Account

Although knowing how to log into your account is critical, it is also important to know how to log out. Unlike personal operating systems, Unix accounts must be logged out when you are done working. This is done to maintain security over the entire system; because of Unix's multi-user nature, one user's insecure behavior can affect everyone with an account on that machine. It is especially important to log out if you use machines in a lab or public setting, such as a library or Internet café. Leaving your account logged on means that some random person could masquerade as you and cause a great deal of trouble.

If you are working in a text-based shell, you only need to type **logout** at the prompt and press the Enter key. Some shells also permit the commands **exit**, **bye**, or **quit**. Those working in a GUI should select the logout option from their main menu, or click the Logout icon if one is available.

Summary

Unix is a modular operating system that is composed of three main items and a number of optional modules. The three basic components of a Unix system are the kernel, the shell, and the file system. The kernel is a piece of software that actually transmits instructions to the computer's processor. The shell is a user interface that allows commands to be transmitted to the kernel, but which may also have its own native commands. The file system is the method used to organize files, devices, and programs installed on the system. Additional software modules may be installed to add extra functions to the operating system.

Individual users on a Unix system each have user accounts, which must be created by the superuser. User accounts include the user name and password, a home directory, and a set of identification numbers that allow easy management of a large user base. Users can configure their personal accounts by installing new software or changing the way in which default software behaves or appears. The superuser account can perform any action and read any file on the machine, and is used by the system administrator(s); ordinary users never have access to this account and its powers.

Review Questions

1. Define an operating system and give several examples.
2. What is a device? How does a Unix machine represent devices?
3. Why are modules used in Unix? What benefits do modules have, and when are they less useful?
4. How does the kernel work?
5. Define a user interface and provide several examples, at least two of which run under Unix.
6. Why do programmers use Application Programming Interfaces, or APIs?
7. Define a shell environment. What features can a shell incorporate, and why are shells used?
8. Why does Unix represent every component as a file? What are the benefits of this method?
9. What are the basic components of a user account?
10. Define the superuser account. Why does Unix have such a system management method?
11. Who holds root on your machine?
12. List and identify the components of your system prompt.

1. Log into your user account. Issue five commands taken from Appendix A, and write down the output you received. Try using different flags for a particular command and see how that changes the output.
2. Find a computer: perhaps your own, or a computer in your school's computer laboratory. Identify and list all devices attached to the machine, describing their function.
3. Research various modules that can be installed on a Unix system. Which of these modules would be useful to you, and why? Find a list of the modules that are installed by default on a personal computer Unix variant. Why are these modules important enough to be installed automatically?
4. Find an API for a program or operating system. What instructions does it contain? If the API has good documentation, use it to learn what critical functions programmers must understand before programming for that software.
5. What shell is used as the default shell in your user account? What are its features? If multiple shells are installed on your system, log into each shell. What are the differences? What are the features of each shell? If you cannot determine the features from experimentation, consult the shell's documentation.
6. If you have an account on a school or office network, obtain copies of the system's user policies. What are the main components of these policies? Which entries are designed to protect user rights, and which are designed to protect data or the network as a whole?

CHAPTER 3

Understanding Unix Commands

IN THIS CHAPTER

1. Understanding Unix commands
2. The shell prompt
3. What the prompt tells you
4. Anatomy of a command
5. The command word
6. Arguments and options
7. Input and output redirection
8. Redirecting output
9. Redirecting input
10. Pipes
11. Command substitution

Although most modern Unix variants are capable of running a graphical user interface—and many do—Unix is most powerful when run with text-based commands. As operating systems have become more user-friendly over the years, they have traded power and flexibility for that ease of use. Many users of graphical interfaces do not realize that there are commands that their operating system will understand, but which are not part of the windowed menu system; since most people only use a percentage of the commands available in the menus, a large portion of the system's total available power is left dormant.

A typical Unix command can do more than one thing. Most Unix commands have a number of options which modify the original command's behavior, essentially creating a new command. Furthermore, by using some of the built-in features of the shell environment, a user can combine multiple commands to create miniature scripts or programs. This practice can help to automate routine administrative tasks, saving time and keystrokes.

The drawback of text-based commands is that it is not always obvious which commands are part of the Unix operating system and which are part of the shell environment installed on your machine. In practice, it is not important to differentiate between operating system commands and shell commands, but it does become critical when you begin to write shell scripts or to program for Unix. As long as you understand the options and syntax relevant to the command you are using, though, it doesn't matter whether the command is going to the shell or directly to the operating system as long as it performs the task you want to do.

Appendix B, Common Unix Commands, contains a short dictionary of the most useful Unix commands, their syntax, and some common options. You can also get a more detailed description of any given command by issuing the command

```
man command
```

where *command* is the name of the command you want to learn about, at the prompt. Assuming that your system administrator has installed the Unix online manual, you will get full documentation for the command. These manual pages are written by programmers, rather than documentation specialists, and may be difficult to understand. Some are far better than others, but the manual page is always a good place to start when you have questions about a particular command.

The examples and commands in this chapter, and throughout most of the text, are drawn from the Bourne Again Shell, commonly called "bash." If bash is not the shell installed on your system, ask your instructor or system administrator to install it or to provide you with equivalent commands for the shell you are using. If you have permission to install personal programs in your account or you are running your own machine, you can download bash from the GNU Web site at http://www.gnu.org. However, if you cannot get bash, you probably have the regular Bourne shell available to you, called "sh". Most of the examples in this book should work equally well under either sh or bash.

Note: Check to see if you have the bash shell by typing **bash** at the command prompt. If nothing happens, you are already using bash; if the prompt changes, you have invoked the bash shell and can continue. You will see an error message if bash is not installed on the system.

The Shell Prompt

Discussion of Unix commands begins with the shell prompt, since that is where commands are issued. In the previous chapter, you learned that prompts may differ in appearance depending on the shell installed and how it is configured. Even prompts in bash may look different on different systems, since system administrators often do not share opinions about how to configure software. Once you become familiar with configuration files, though, you can set your prompt so that it is most useful to you.

What the Prompt Tells You

Among many other options, the bash prompt can display the time, date, current directory, name of the user, name of the machine, and device name of the terminal. It can also provide identifiers for commands or various processes currently being managed by the shell. The appearance of the prompt will change, depending on the elements configured by the user or by default.

In almost all cases, though, the last character of the bash prompt will be the dollar sign, $. More precisely, the dollar sign is usually the last character of the prompt if you are logged into a regular user account. To keep the superuser account noticeably distinct from user accounts, the final character for the superuser's bash prompt is usually the hashmark, or # character. Although it is possible to change the final character of the prompt, most people choose not to do so because it is useful to keep the two kinds of accounts separate as a reminder.

Anatomy of a Command

The majority of Unix commands follow a general format. There are exceptions where either syntax or options take an unusual format, but such commands are relatively infrequent and are easy to memorize. The common syntax for Unix commands is

```
command option(s) argument(s)
```

Both components of the command are important for proper execution; while you can issue the command alone, not all programs run without options, and many more do not provide useful information without the appropriate arguments.

The Command Word

The *command word* is the name of an installed shell command or the name of a program installed on the machine. The command word may be an abbreviation, such as "sh" for the Bourne shell, or may be the complete name, as in "date" to see the current system date and time. Because there is no systematic way to name commands, it may be difficult to find the appropriate command when you have not used it before. A good command compendium is a useful investment for those who plan on doing a lot of work with Unix; for those who are casual users, a dictionary like the one in Appendix B may be sufficient for most needs.

Arguments and Options

When issuing a command, the command word is always first. Anything typed after the command word is interpreted as an *argument* or an *option*, an additional piece of information that modifies the basic function or performance of the requested program. The additional information may also be used to specify the target for the program's actions, like a text file or a database.

Almost all commands require an argument, though the argument may be implicit. In other words, if you issue the command without providing an argument, the program often infers that you want to run the program with the default argument. A good example of this is the "ls" command, which prints a listing of the contents of any directory you specify. If you do not provide a directory as the explicit target, ls assumes you want a list of the contents in your current directory. Arguments often specify the directory or file upon which the invoked command will operate, which is why arguments are sometimes called *targets.* Issuing the command **ls /home** generates a list of the /home directory's contents, regardless of your current directory.

Options, as the name implies, are not required for the command to function properly. Options increase the number of functions that a command can execute. You can recognize an option because it is always preceded by a dash, as in –l or –verbose. Different commands have different options, often different even for the same function. Learn what options are available for whatever command you are working on by viewing the command's manual page, which usually lists all available options and arguments.

Options and targets can be combined. This is the source of the real power behind Unix, because you can create a command with specific function and target so that you get only the information or action that you really want. Issuing the ls command as **ls –l /home** would result in yet another type of output. Unix commands have no limit on the number of arguments that can be used in a single command, but too many arguments or contradictory arguments may cause trouble when the operating system or shell attempts to carry out your wishes. Several sequential and concise commands will usually produce better results than one confusing and very long command.

Input and Output Redirection

These combined commands can become quite complex, and it may become difficult to trace back to the original intent. It is easier to understand a complex command if you remember the basic function of all commands: Unix commands direct or redirect input and output. *Input* is any data or instruction that is normally fed into a command and is the information that the program uses to perform its task. *Output* is the result of the command's action and may be printed to the screen, piped into a text file, or used as the input for yet another command.

In most situations, input is taken from the keyboard. That is, a user sitting at the keyboard types information that the command will use. Command arguments are one type of input, as are answers to questions posed as part of another program. Input from the keyboard is called the *standard input* because that is where the vast majority of input originates, even if it is stored as a file that itself becomes input at a later time.

Likewise, the *standard output* is usually the monitor. Programs with short output will print the output to the screen so that you can see it. Some programs don't generate output at all; the prompt simply disappears for a moment and then returns. Error messages also count as output, since they print to the screen when a program cannot complete its task.

Note: The keyboard/monitor combination is the most common set of standard input and output, but it is not the only way programs take or generate information. If you are expecting a particular type of input or output and you do not get it, consult that program's manual page or documentation to see if you are looking in the wrong place.

The standard input or output devices may not be convenient for you, or you may want to use a different input source for a particular task. Because Unix treats every component of the operating system as a file, this is simple to fix. Devices like the keyboard and terminal screen are represented as files, as are other devices. If you want input to come from a text file instead of the keyboard, change the input. If you want output to go directly to the printer instead of the screen, change the output. You can often reconfigure the program to take input or produce output from your desired location or device as a permanent change by editing the program's configuration files.

Redirecting Output

Most redirection involves output. Many programs, which use the standard output of the monitor, return more information than can be displayed in a single screen. In other cases, administrators may need to run programs which report on current system status or function, but do not have the time to deal with the output at the same time the command is issued. In both these examples, it makes better sense to redirect the output to a text file so that it can be used more comfortably or studied at a later time.

It is a simple matter to redirect output into a file. Using the directory listing example from the previous section, suppose that you want to get the listing of files in a particular directory which you know to hold over a hundred files, such as a graphics directory on a Web site. Because the output will be large, it will probably scroll off the monitor before you get a chance to see the full listing. Sending the output to a text file is a logical choice.

The command **ls –l /home**, as explained earlier, provides a list of the /home directory's contents in a specified format. In order to send the output to a text file, you must add another component to that command. In this case, the additional component is a *redirection operator*, a character which indicates to the operating system that a redirection instruction will follow. The redirection operator is the right angle bracket character, or >. The redirection operator must be accompanied by the name of the file where you want the output to go. This file can either be one which already exists or one which does not; if the file does not exist, it will be created as part of the process. If the file does exist, its contents will be replaced with new output.

After you have determined the appropriate location for the new output, issue the command as

```
ls -l /home > filename
```

Note that, when you issue the command with a redirection argument, nothing prints to the screen. A new prompt appears when the process is complete. Issue a plain **ls** command; you will see the file you specified in the file listing. It contains the output of the directory listing. Issue the command

```
cat filename
```

to see the output. Once you have used the file for whatever work you need, you can either save it or delete it. You can also use it for other redirection purposes.

For example, you could issue the command

```
ls -l /usr > filename
```

Just as with the previous command, the directory listing for /usr will appear in the named file. However, the listing from the previous command is gone. The redirection operator > causes new output to overwrite any existing data in the named file. Do not reuse any file that you need for archival or current purposes.

If you want to save the original data and still use the same file for new output, use a different redirection operator which causes new output to be appended to the end of whatever data currently exists in the file. The redirection operator >> is used when output needs to be added to old data rather than replace it. The command would then be issued as

```
ls -l /usr >> filename
```

Note: If the named file does not exist or is empty, the doubled redirection operator will perform exactly like the single operator. When you are unsure whether an existing file is empty or whether you are reusing the name of an existing file, use the doubled operator to be safe.

Redirecting Input

A less common situation, but equally helpful in lengthy or complicated datasets, involves the redirection of input for a given command or program. Input redirection is often used to organize lists of names, numbers, or other data which might benefit from a particular Unix program. It is useful whenever you want to use an existing file as the source for another program; that file may be one into which output was directed at an earlier point.

Assume that you have a list of user names and want to alphabetize them:

```
Gordon
Beth
Ricky
```

```
Amanda
Carl
Jack
Homer
Eugene
Rita
Bonnie
Amy
Sabine
Claude
Jennifer
```

The easiest way to finish the task is to use the **sort** command. If you were to do this by hand each time you wanted to sort the list, you would have to enter the data anew each time. Re-keying data often leads to typing errors or inadvertent omissions, so this is not the best solution. If the names are already in a text file, though, you can use that file as the new input each time for **sort**.

Issue the command

```
sort < namefile
```

where *namefile* is the file which contains the unsorted list. The contents of "namefile" are used as input, and the resulting alphabetized output is printed to the screen. Note that the redirection operator for input is the left angle bracket, <, rather than the right angle bracket used for redirecting output.

Use both input and output redirection operators to issue a complex command. Instead of having the sorted output print to the screen, you could send it to a new file. Issue the command as

```
sort < namefile > sortednames
```

to have the alphabetized list sent to the new file *sortednames*. The original namefile remains unchanged until you delete or amend it.

Pipes

A slightly different concept, but one related to input and output redirection, is the *pipe*. A Unix pipe is a method to use the output of one command as the direct input to another command, without the intermediate step of saving the first command's output to a file. Pipes can be used for simple jobs or as part of a complex array of commands, arguments, and redirection. They are a critical component of shell scripts and other programs designed for the Unix system.

Suppose that, as in the previous examples, you wanted to generate directory listings for every directory on your machine. Some directories contain a vast number of files, and a complete listing would certainly scroll far off your screen before it was finished. You could certainly redirect the output of each

ls command to a text file, appending subsequent directory listings to the existing data. However, doing so increases the time and keystrokes you spend on the task, since you must invoke a separate program like **less** or **more** to view the program, or must open the file within a text editor.

The pipe, represented by the vertical bar character |, is a third solution. Pipes take the output from a specified program and transfer it directly to a second program as input. Using the pipe avoids the intermediate step required when redirecting output to a text file, since the second program is invoked with the same command as the first. To view the lengthy directory listings generated by **ls** with **more**, issue the command

```
ls -l /usr | more
```

The output will scroll across the screen as usual, but will pause when the screen is filled. Press the spacebar to advance to the next screen. At the bottom of the screen, a percentage number will appear, indicating the amount of output already viewed.

Pipes can be combined with input and output redirection. Output can also be piped to a text file instead of using the redirection operator >. Pipes and redirection operators overlap in their function, and many users choose one over the other through habit. The sorting example above, which used the command

```
sort < namefile > namefile-sorted
```

could also be produced with the command

```
cat namefile | sort > namefile-sorted
```

Multiple pipes are also common:

```
cat namefile | sort | lp
```

This command would send the sorted data to the printer.

Command Substitution

Like the pipe, command substitution involves using the output of one command as the input for another. Where pipes are used to create a chain of processes, though, command substitution uses the output of one command as an argument for another command. That is, the output of the first command modifies the behavior of the second command rather than merely replacing the command's standard input.

Command substitution is especially useful in tasks which are large and require a number of processes, or which require work which is beyond the patience or skill of most human users. One such task might be to determine how many words exist in a user's home directory. Doing this by hand would be overwhelming and repetitive enough that error is likely to give an incorrect result.

You could use the **wc**, or word count, command on each file, but if there are a number of files it may take a long time. Instead, issue the command

```
wc $(ls)
```

This command takes each file name reported in the **ls** directory listing and passes it as an argument to the **wc** command. In other words, if the directory listing generates the output

```
file1
file2
file3
. . .
```

and so on, then the **wc $(ls)** command is the same thing as issuing the command

```
wc file1 file2 file3 . . .
```

but has much less room for error or omission.

The main difference between pipes and command redirection is that command redirection involves the *subshell.* A subshell is an additional shell which is started automatically to handle a specified process, and which closes itself when the process is finished. When the shell receives a command which includes the **$()** construct, it starts the subshell and uses it to process whatever command is contained within the parentheses.

In contrast, the pipe performs all specified commands within the original shell. Command redirection can be used to force execution in the original shell, should that be preferable, by substituting curly braces for parentheses. Thus, the command

```
wc $(ls)
```

uses the subshell, but

```
wc ${ls}
```

executes in the shell where the command was issued (in bash 2.04 and earlier).

Beyond the matter of subshells, there is a conceptual difference in the way that command substitution and pipes work. Consider the commands

```
wc $(ls)
```

and

```
ls | wc
```

In the first command, the resulting output will be the word count of each file contained in the directory listing. In the second command, the resulting output will contain the word count of the directory listing itself, because the default behavior of **ls** merely lists file names but does not open the files. To choose the proper method of redirection, you must understand what the command will generate as output. Often, two commands that seem identical will produce differing output because they perform different tasks.

Tech Tip

There is another way to construct a command which uses redirection. Instead of using the **$()** construct, use backticks instead. Thus, the command

```
wc $(ls)
```

can be written as

```
wc `ls`
```

Be sure to use the backtick character instead of the apostrophe. Issuing the command as

```
wc 'ls'
```

will probably generate an error message, since the shell will try to count the words in a file named "ls," which probably does not exist.

Summary

Unix commands are multifunctional. Most commands offer a range of options, or arguments, which change the basic behavior of the specified program. These arguments may change output or may change the way in which the program actually executes. Some text commands are actually functions of the shell environment, but in practical use it is not always necessary to know whether the command is an operating system command or a shell command. Commands are issued at the shell prompt, a text string which can be configured to show a range of information.

Text commands can also be issued in combinations or with additional elements which change the default input or output of the command. These command sequences can become quite complex, requiring a number of sequential operations. The simplest combinations usually direct a command's output to a file or a printer rather than the monitor, or cause the command to take information from a specified file as input. Commands can also be sequenced with the pipe method, or nested with command redirection. In the latter case, the shell interface often invokes a subshell to control particular operations.

Review Questions

1. What are the advantages of text-based commands?
2. What information can be configured to appear in the system prompt?
3. Describe the basic syntax of a Unix command.
4. List several command words and the programs they invoke.
5. How does an argument work? List several examples.
6. What are the standard input and output devices?
7. Why is it useful to redirect input or output?
8. Explain the difference between the commands **ls -l > newfile** and **ls -l >> newfile**. When is the first command most appropriate, and when is it better to use the second?
9. Explain the difference between a pipe and command substitution. When is it better to use each method?
10. Define the subshell. When is it invoked?

Exercises

1. Pull up the manual pages for several commands. (You can use Appendix A for ideas if you do not know many Unix commands at this point.) What are the common features of each manual page? How could the pages be improved?
2. Use the manual page to determine the various arguments for a command of your choice. Issue the command with each of the arguments and record the output. What happens when you combine arguments?
3. Run the **ls** command for several directories on your system, redirecting the output to a text file. Append the output to the existing data so that you have a complete listing.
4. Create a list of at least 25 words or numbers. Sort the list and send the output to a printer.
5. Using the command compendium in Appendix A, select two or three basic commands. Construct command sequences using command redirection. What is the output of each of your sequences? Why did the commands create that output, and was it the output you expected? Refine your sequences if you did not get the expected result and explain your changes.

CHAPTER 4

The File System

IN THIS CHAPTER

1. File system types
2. Files and directories
3. Types of files
4. The chmod command
5. Finding yourself on the machine
6. Moving around the file system
7. Creating and destroying files and directories
8. System directories

Of the three components of the Unix operating system, the file system is the one of which users and administrators are most aware. While the shell is used to issue commands which cause the kernel to perform certain actions, it is the file system which provides the programs and data for the commands to use. The file system's structure creates the landscape of the operating system, through which users can navigate with simple commands.

This chapter introduces the basic Unix file system, as well as basic navigational and file management commands. The concept of file permissions is introduced, permitting you to configure your personal files so that they can either be shared or protected from others. You will also learn the functions of various directories common to most Unix variants.

File System Types

The first part of the Unix file system is the way in which the disk itself is organized. The method of organization is defined by the type of file system being used. Because all the data on a hard disk cannot be stored simultaneously in a computer's memory, it must be stored on the disk in a way which makes it quick and easy to obtain the required data when it is called for. There are several different ways to organize the files, programs, and other data used to operate the machine, and different Unix variants rely on different file system types.

All file system types have a *boot block*, which is the sector of the disk which is loaded first when the system is powered on. Because the boot block is loaded before the operating system, it is type-independent and there is only one boot block per disk even if the disk is divided into multiple partitions. The boot block contains information needed to start the operating system, as well as other initialization information.

Note: To the average user, the file system type is not noticeable. However, when you change permissions or start to work with more advanced administrative tools, knowing the file system type will help you to understand how your commands affect the disk and its data.

EXT2

The most common file system type under Linux is the EXT2 file system. Each partition on the disk contains a section called the *superblock*, which contains information about the file system itself. The superblock boots after the boot block. Its data includes information about the size of the filesystem, the number of free blocks on the disk and information about those blocks, the size of the inode list and information about free inodes, and other data important when using disk space to execute or store data.

An *inode* contains a description of the blocks which are occupied by a particular file, when the file was most recently modified, and what the file's type is. As you will see in the subsequent sections, Unix files can be of a number of file types. The inode stores a description that indicates what kind of file is kept at a particular disk location. Each file has its own inode and, in turn, each inode has a unique identifying number. These inodes are all stored together in *inode tables*, which the operating system uses to track empty and occupied inodes. Inodes also track file permissions and file ownership, but they do not store the file's actual name.

UFS

BSD, Solaris, and several other Unix variants use a file system type called UFS, or the Unix File System. UFS resembles EXT2 in that it also uses superblocks and inodes to manage data organization and storage, but it is not as advanced.

Unfortunately, over the years, many Unix vendors and developers have independently added elements to their particular variant's version of UFS. There are a number of file system types now called "UFS" which are incompatible, even though all are derived from the same basic structure.

FAT

Although no Unix uses the FAT file system as its dominant method of organizing data, some variants recognize it in order for compatibility between DOS/Windows files and the Unix operating system. The FAT file system was one of Microsoft's first contributions to the computing world. Unlike UFS or EXT2, the FAT file system does not use inodes. Instead, it stores each file as a string of blocks. If there are not enough blocks in a sequence, FAT places a pointer to the remaining blocks in the last block of the sequence. Compare this to the inode method, which uses a table to identify all blocks that belong to a given file and thus uses disk space more efficiently, as well as conserving system resources. Because of the way in which FAT writes data, the physical disk mechanism must constantly move between the disk space table and the actual location of the multiple blocks and block strings in which the file is stored. System resources are wasted as the operating system searches out each set of blocks which belongs to the requested file, following pointers at the end of each block string rather than pulling the entire set of blocks allocated to this file from an inode table. This method of storing data can lead to fragmented block strings, which can eventually cause slower system response or corrupted data. For this reason, those who use Windows must defragment their disk on a regular basis.

Files and Directories

The core of the Unix file system is the file. Files are organized into directories, which may be contained in other directories. In fact, the entire file system is nested within one root directory. Unix is not the only operating system to use this hierarchical concept; Windows and MacOS have brought the nested directory concept to the average computer user, with the visual construct of the file folder.

What Is a File?

Because files are so central to the Unix concept, it is critical to define *file* as specifically as possible. Unfortunately, it is difficult to create a precise definition that still covers the range of uses which "file" covers. Consider the air surrounding us. It is everywhere around us, it can be felt, and it is vital to life, but it cannot be seen. Likewise, files are so ubiquitous in the Unix operating system that it is hard to define them without saying, essentially, that we know them when we see them. Unfortunately, that glib answer does not lead to a particularly subtle, fruitful, or effective understanding of what files actually do.

A file is a named and ordered collection of bytes which has a unique name and which can be managed or manipulated as a single entity. In Chapter 3, you saw an example of output redirection which created a new file called "sortednames". "sortednames" is the name of the file: literally, the *filename*. The file can also be identified by its specific location on the computer's hard disk or by a numerical entry called an *inode* in the operating system's internal index. View any file's inode by issuing the **ls** command with the -i argument, as in **ls -i**. No matter which identifier you use to denote this particular file, the system will find it.

Types of Files

Files serve many purposes on a Unix machine. For each purpose, there is a file type. These types range from simple text files to placeholders used to manage hardware devices. The only thing some of these types have in common is that they are all identified in the same manner when the operating system needs to call them for a particular task or command.

Text Files

Text files, as the name implies, are files filled with text. Text files contain characters that are readable by humans: ordinary prose, source code for programs, configuration instructions for installed software, electronic mail messages, formatted prose which will display in a particular manner when opened by a specified program, scripts used for administrative jobs, and so on. The only common feature of these files is that, if you open the file, you will be able to read the contents—even if you can't understand what it means.

Binary Files

Binary files contain information that is intended for use by the computer or operating system. Binary files are most often programs which have already been compiled and are ready to run, but they may also be something like a digital music file in .wav or MP3 format, an image, or data intended for use by another program. If you open a binary file in a text editor, you will see an unintelligible mass of gibberish. It is technically readable, but not by humans.

Note: We make the distinction between text and binary files by whether or not the file can be read by human eyes. In the operating system's opinion, there is little difference. It can parse human-readable text as easily as it can parse binary text. In a purely technical sense, text and binary files are the same; however, to the ordinary user, there is a difference. Binary files are meant to be run as a program or viewed through an intermediary program that will interpret the binary language. Text files can be read without interpretation and cannot be executed.

Directories

Directories are also files, though files with a special function. A directory is a file which contains other files. In most graphical operating systems, directories are represented with a small graphic of a file folder, which is exactly how they work. A directory file is not readable by humans, nor is it executable. It is merely a container. Directory files are covered in detail later in this chapter.

Links

Links are files that refer to other files. In some cases, especially when writing shell scripts, it is necessary to refer to a single data construct in more than one way. When using links, one file can have more than one name, so that it can be used in different ways in different situations. This is not a common habit for average users, but it is frequently used by programmers and system administrators.

There are two types of links: *hard links* and *symbolic links.* A hard link is literally a second name for a given file. It is actually another directory entry which corresponds to the same inode as the original file, so that any reference to the link will call up the appropriate inode, and thus the desired file. A symbolic link is actually a second file which contains the name of a given file. If the file is moved or renamed, the symbolic link will fail. Since hard links point to the same inode as the actual file, however, they do not fail.

In most cases, hard links and symbolic links work in the same way. One symbolic link common on many systems is the file /bin/sh, which is a symbolic link to /bin/bash. Any programs which invoke the Bourne shell will trigger this symbolic link, and the program will run in the bash shell instead. Links are created with the **ln** command. The default behavior of **ln** is to create a hard link, as in the syntax

```
ln [options] <linked-to file> <name of link>
```

In order to create a symbolic link, use the option –s.

Device Files

Device files are special constructs that represent the various pieces of hardware connected to the computer. In the same way that a human can read or write a text file, the computer's processor can read from or write to a device. This enables the machine to move data between various hardware devices.

For example, when the operating system instructs the computer to open a file, it first must open the device file representing the hard disk and then copy the contents of the specified file into memory. If the file is modified while it is open, the computer will once again open the device file and copy the modified form of the file back into the correct location. Should the user want to copy a file from a CD-ROM drive to a floppy disk, the operating system will handle files representing both of those devices in executing the command.

For those who run their own Unix machines or who are administrators on large Unix networks, it is not uncommon to spend a goodly amount of time each day working with device files. Printers, sound and video cards, input devices, monitors, modems, and network cards are all handled through device files. The device file construct makes it easier to automate certain tasks with shell scripts, and means that any new piece of hardware can be administered like the existing devices without having to install complicated or unusual new management software.

Named Pipes

In Chapter 3, we introduced the concept of pipes. The pipes described there were issued at the command prompt, and were intended for a single use. On a Unix system, it is possible to create pipelines that do not disappear after the command has been issued. These pipelines are permanent, at least until they are deleted, and can be reused or incorporated into different scripts and commands. They are designed to work as conduits between programs, to pass data as input or output. Named pipes are also called *FIFOs*, an acronym drawn from the maxim "first in, first out."

Directories

As defined above, a directory is a type of file which is designed to contain other files. Directories can contain any kind of file, including other directories, which are then called *subdirectories*. Directories containing subdirectories are called *parent directories*. These names are relative; a given directory may be both a parent directory and a subdirectory, as are most directories on a Unix machine.

Although commonly described with one-word names, the most proper way to refer to a file is to use its full *path name*. The path name contains the file name, the directory which contains it, and any directory which contains the file's home directory. Ultimately, all files on a Unix computer are contained within a single directory called the *root directory*: do not confuse the root directory with the root, or superuser, account.

The root directory is designated by the slash character, /. All files which reside in this directory are named ***/filename***, while subdirectories contained in the root directory use the same syntax with a trailing slash, as in ***/directory/***. The trailing slash is optional in most situations, but is useful in cases where it is important to differentiate between a file and a directory with the same name. A file residing in a subdirectory of / would have the path ***/directory/filename***. It is not unusual for a given file to be located inside a multi-layered nest of directories. For example, on a Linux machine, the configuration file for the mail server program sendmail has the path name /etc/rc.d/init.d/sendmail.

A path that shows the entire set of directories containing a particular file, going all the way back to the root directory, is known as the full path name. It is also possible—and quite common—to use partial, or *relative*, path names. Relative path names are used to refer to files or directories contained within the current directory. If two people are discussing the sendmail configuration file, and both know that the file is contained in the /etc directory, then it is sufficient to use rc.d/init.d/sendmail as the path for that file. However, when using partial path names, it is important that both parties to the conversation (or program) know what the partial path name is relative to.

File Permissions

All files, no matter what type, have a set of attributes called *permissions*. Permissions control who has access to a file and for what purpose. There are three kinds of permissions: read, write, and execute. Each of these permissions uses three classifications to identify the user(s) who are granted that permission: owner, owner's group, and all users. There are nine possible combinations of permissions.

View a file's permission configuration by issuing the **ls** command with the -l flag, as shown in Chapter 2. The output will look something like this:

```
[dave@barracuda WorkFiles]$ ls -l
total 100
-rw-rw-r—   1  dave   dave   28034 Feb 23 13:28 phone.txt
-rw-rw-r—   1  dave   dave   16364 Apr 12 22:15 draft1.txt
-rw-rw-r—   1  dave   dave   13748 Dec 01 08:43 salary.txt
-rw-rw-r—   1  dave   dave    6932 Jan 18 17:56 boise.jpg
```

The group of characters at the beginning of each line indicates the permission status for the file named in that entry. The first character is a dash, indicating that the file is a normal file. If it were a directory, the dash would be replaced by a "d."

The next nine characters are divided into three groups of three characters each. The first group refers to permissions set for the file's owner; the second group refers to members of the owner's user groups; the third group refers to any global users who have access to the file. In the first group of three, the characters are **rw-**. This means that user Dave has both read and write access to the files, but does not have execute permission. This is reasonable since none of these files are executables.

In the second group of three, the characters are also **rw-**. These permissions affect anyone who is part of the same user group as Dave. User groups are assigned by the system administrator, and are used to sort the users on a given machine into similar groups. Members of the same work project might share a group, or a group might be used to identify users who have certain security privileges and administrative abilities. When a file is created, it is automatically assigned a group identification number. To have a user group which has access to that file, the administrator needs to create a new user group with the file's group ID, and add users into that group. Otherwise, the only member of the group will be the file's owner: in this case, the user Dave.

The final group of three characters defines the permissions which apply to all users of the system; in this example, the permissions are **r--**. Users who are neither Dave nor members of his group are restricted to read privileges only. This is the permission set used for static Web page files, since anyone with access to the machine – even through a Web server – is considered a user for permission purposes. Should Dave want to keep his files safe from others, he could change the permissions so that no world permissions were granted, or even so that no group permissions were granted.

Note: No matter what permissions are set on a given file, the superuser can always perform any action on any file stored on the system. Privacy is a relative concept on a Unix machine.

The chmod Command

To change file permissions, use the **chmod** command. **chmod** is an abbreviation for "change mode." The **chmod** command takes arguments which indicate the type of user being granted permission, the type of permission being granted, whether permission is being granted or revoked, and the filename in question. Table 4.1 shows the various arguments to **chmod** and their function.

Assume that you have a file named proposal.txt which contains your ideas for a group project. This file lives in your home directory, and you want to make it available to everyone in your class. Issue the command

```
chmod a+rwx proposal.txt
```

Note that this command not only permits others to read the file, but to make changes to it (even to delete it) or to execute it if it were an executable file. It also extends these permissions to everyone with an account on that machine, not just your classmates. This is an unsafe set of permissions. In general, assign permissions which are as restrictive as possible while still permitting use of the file in the necessary manner.

A safer choice would be to extend read and write permissions to members of your user group. People with a direct interest in the file would then be able to read and edit the file, but random bypassers would not be able to access it at all. For this solution, issue the command

```
chmod ug+rw proposal.txt
```

To be safe, you could issue a second command that explicitly revokes execute permission for all groups:

TABLE 4.1: The chmod Command and Its Arguments

Arguments to chmod	Function
u	Grants specified permission to file's owner
g	Grants specified permission to the user's groups
a	Grants specified permission to all users
+	Adds a new permission
-	Removes an existing permission
r	Grants read permission
w	Grants write permission
x	Grants execute permission

```
chmod uga-x proposal.txt
```

The chmod command can also be issued with numeric arguments rather than letters. While some find the numbers harder to remember, others find them quite useful. This is a good example of Unix offering several ways to accomplish the same task. The chmod manual page offers the opportunity both to learn more about the numerical arguments and to gain experience in reading manual pages:

```
CHMOD(1)                                             CHMOD(1)
NAME

chmod - change the access permissions of files

SYNOPSIS
  chmod  [-Rcfv]  [= recursive]  [= changes]  [= silent]
  [= quiet] [= verbose] [= help] [= version] mode file...

DESCRIPTION
  This documentation is no longer being maintained and may
  be inaccurate or incomplete.  The Texinfo documentation
  is now the authoritative source.

  This manual page documents the GNU version of chmod.

  chmod changes the permissions of each given file
  according to mode, which can be either a symbolic
  representation of changes to  make, or an octal number
  representing the bit pattern for the new permissions.

  The format of a symbolic mode is `[ugoa...][[+-=][rwxXs-
```

tugo...]...][,...]. Multiple symbolic operations can be given, separated by commas.

A combination of the letters 'ugoa' controls which users' access to the file will be changed: the user who owns it (u), other users in the file's group (g), other users not in the file's group (o), or all users (a). If none of these are given, the effect is as if 'a' were given, but bits that are set in the umask are not affected.

The operator '+' causes the permissions selected to be added to the existing permissions of each file; '-' causes them to be removed; and '=' causes them to be the only permissions that the file has.

The letters 'rwxXstugo' select the new permissions for the affected users: read (r), write (w), execute (or access for directories) (x), execute only if the file is a directory or already has execute permission for some user (X), set user or group ID on execution (s), save program text on swap device (t), the permissions that the user who owns the file currently has for it (u), the permissions that other users in the file's group have for it (g), and the permissions that other users not in the file's group have for it (o).

A numeric mode is from one to four octal digits (0-7), derived by adding up the bits with values 4, 2, and 1. Any omitted digits are assumed to be leading zeros. The first digit selects the set user ID (4) and set group ID (2) and save text image (1) attributes. The second digit selects permissions for the user who owns the file: read (4), write (2), and execute (1); the third selects permissions for other users in the file's group, with the same values; and the fourth for other users not in the file's group, with the same values.

chmod never changes the permissions of symbolic links; the chmod system call cannot change their permissions. This is not a problem since the permissions of symbolic links are never used. However, for each symbolic link listed on the command line, chmod changes the permissions of the pointed-to file. In contrast, chmod ignores symbolic links encountered during recursive directory traversals.

```
OPTIONS
  -c, --changes
    Verbosely describe  only  files  whose  permissions
    actually change.

  -f, --silent, --quiet
    Do not print error messages about files whose per-
    missions cannot be changed.

  -v, --verbose
    Verbosely describe changed permissions.

  -R, --recursive
    Recursively change permissions of  directories  and
    their contents.

  --help
    Print  a  usage message on standard output and exit
    successfully.

  --version
    Print version information on standard  output  then
    exit successfully.
```

Finding Yourself on the Machine

For users whose main computing experience is with personal operating systems like Windows or MacOS, the Unix emphasis on location can be difficult to understand. With Unix, though, it is important to know where each file is located, as well as to know where you yourself are located within the system. A user normally works within the confines of a small subset of directories, but it is possible to work on files located almost anywhere else on the machine as long as you know where those files reside.

Your Home Directory

When a new user account is created on a Unix machine, a personal directory for that new user is also created. The location of these personal directories differs from Unix variant to variant, and may also differ according to the preferences of the system administrator or the function of that machine as a standalone or part of a larger network. On a large system with many users, the home directories may be divided among several parent directories to make organization and management easier. On smaller or single systems, all user directories will probably be kept in a single parent directory.

On a small network or standalone machine, the various home directories will probably be kept in a parent directory called /home. The home directory is a subdirectory of the root directory, and is thus a top branch on the organizational chart of the machine's files. A given user's home directory is usually designated by the user name; that is, user "daria" has the home directory /home/daria.

When a user logs into the account, she logs into her home directory and that remains her location unless she explicitly moves to another location. That is, if she creates a new file, that file will automatically receive the path name /home/*username*/*filename*. If you use any partial or relative path names to move to another file, those names will be interpreted as relative to your home directory.

Note:

You can always return to your home directory by issuing the command

```
cd
```

no matter where you are on the machine.

The pwd Command

Although it is often safe to assume that you are in your home directory, the **pwd** command can be used to find your exact location. This command can also be used to learn the complete path name of your current location if you need it to identify a file or return to that location at a later time. **pwd** is an acronym for "print working directory." Issuing this command generates output which contains the complete path to the current directory, as in

```
/usr/local/bin/
```

pwd does not take arguments.

Moving Around the File System

There are many other places on the machine beyond the home user directory. Some of these locations are administrative directories which may not be accessible to the average user, while other directories may contain files and programs which are available for use by anyone who wants to install them in their home directories. Moving between directories requires certain command syntax which, once mastered, offers a large amount of flexibility with a minimal number of keystrokes.

Navigating the File System

On any Unix machine, files and directories are organized in a tree-like hierarchy. At the top of the tree chart is the root directory, or /. All other directories are subdirectories of root. Although the exact organization of the file system can vary from individual machine to machine, or from variant to variant, a typical organizational structure looks like the one shown in Figure 4.1.

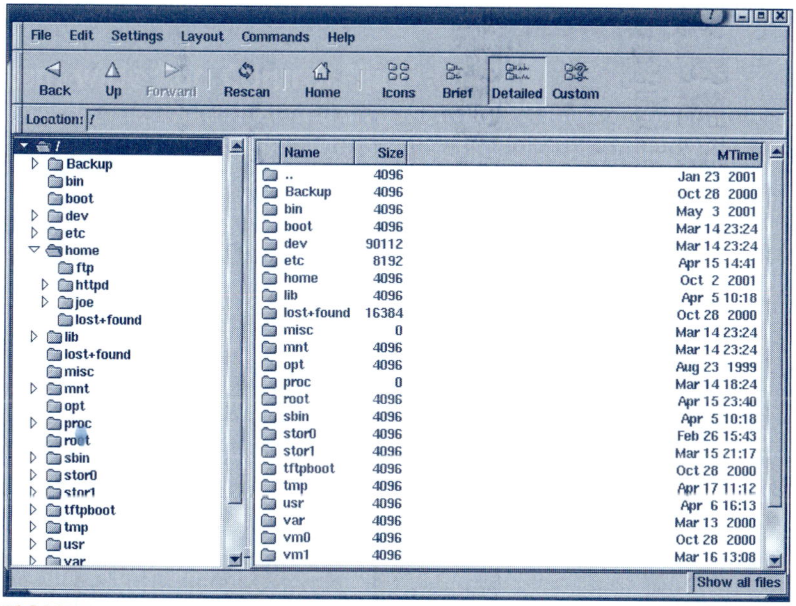

FIGURE 4.1 The file system of a Unix machine, shown in a graphical file manager.

The group of subdirectories immediately below the root directory are often called the *top level directories*. They form the basic organization of the file system. Each directory in this level has a particular purpose and is used to segregate certain types of files. For example, the /bin directory usually contains executable binary files. These directories are described in detail later in this chapter.

Changing Directories

To change from one directory to another, use the **cd** command, an abbreviation for "change directory." **cd** uses the name of the desired directory as an argument; to move to the /bin directory, for example, issue the command

```
cd /bin
```

You can always return to your home directory by issuing the **cd** command without argument.

When giving arguments to **cd**, be aware of the difference between absolute and relative path names. If user Tim is in his home directory and wishes to move to /usr, he must issue the command

```
cd /usr
```

to get there. If he issues the command as

```
cd usr
```

an error message will appear, stating "No such file or directory". If Tim happens to have a subdirectory called usr in his home directory, the **cd usr** command will move him to that subdirectory.

However, if Tim issues the command as **cd usr** when he is in the root directory, he will be taken to the /usr directory. The beginning slash is necessary to move to a directory which is above or outside your current directory; if the slash is omitted, only subdirectories of the current directory are considered as options.

Note: You can only move into a directory if you have execute permission for that directory. If you try to move to a directory without permission, you will see an error message saying "Permission denied". Contact your system administrator if you feel that this is an error; be aware that directories which contain files critical to the system's operating are usually configured so that users do not have access to them.

Learning the Contents of a Directory

It is neither useful nor particularly interesting to move through the file system without a purpose. Once in a new location, it is reasonable to look around and learn the function of the files and subdirectories stored in that directory. The **ls** command, familiar from earlier chapters and exercises, is useful in this situation. Some of **ls's** arguments may be particularly useful as you familiarize yourself with the functions of different directories. Table 4.2 shows the arguments to **ls.**

Note that **ls** expects the name of a directory as an argument. If a directory name is not supplied, **ls** assumes that it should work with the current

TABLE 4.2: The ls Command and Its Arguments

Arguments to ls	Function
-l	Output uses long format, which includes information about file size and other characteristics
-a	Lists all files in the directory, including hidden files (those whose name begins with a dot)
-i	Lists files showing their disk index, or inode, numbers
-R	Recursive mode, which lists all subdirectories in the directory and all files in those subdirectories
-t	Lists files sorted by the timestamp of last modification to each file

directory. **ls** can be used to generate directory listings for any directory on the system for which read permissions are set appropriately, regardless of the user's current location.

Creating and Destroying Files and Directories

After learning to navigate through the file system, the next step is to learn commands used to create new files and directories and destroy ones no longer needed. It is extremely important, especially when deleting files, to know whether or not you are logged in as the superuser. This is likely only if you are running your own Unix variant on a personal computer (or if you are employed as a system administrator), but if you have access to superuser powers, be careful about deleting files that may be critical for system function or that do not belong to you. The superuser is able to delete any file on the system, and removing the wrong files may completely cripple the system and make it unusable.

Creating a Directory

It is simple to create a new directory. Use the **mkdir**, or "make directory," command. **mkdir** takes the name of the new directory as an argument, either as an absolute or relative path name. For example, if user Sandra is in her home directory and issues the command

```
mkdir mynewdir
```

she will create a directory with the absolute path /home/sandra/mynewdir. If she issues the command as

```
mkdir /mynewdir
```

she will create a directory called /mynewdir, which will be a subdirectory of the main root directory. Note that Sandra can do this only if she has write permission on the root directory; however, if she is in a subdirectory in her own home directory, she can use the beginning slash to create a new main subdirectory of her home directory.

Just as it is possible to create a new directory when desired, it is also possible to delete a directory when necessary. Remove a directory with the **rmdir**, or "remove directory," command. Like **mkdir**, **rmdir** takes the name of the desired directory as an argument. Also like **mkdir**, the argument can be either a relative or an absolute pathname.

There are a few restrictions on **rmdir**, in order to keep directories from being deleted inadvertently or maliciously. You cannot delete a directory in which you are currently located, or a directory above your current directory. That is, you cannot be in your home directory and delete either your home directory or the /home directory in which it is stored.

In addition, you cannot remove a directory which has files or subdirectories stored in it. While this second restriction is annoying, it is meant to protect useful files from being deleted unintentionally. You can get past this restriction by issuing the command

```
rm -rf directory
```

where *directory* is the name of the directory you want to remove. **rm** is the command usually used to delete individual files. This is much easier than deleting each file by hand, but it is also **much more destructive**. The emphasis is necessary because, under Unix, a deleted file disappears. Unlike Windows, deleted files do not move to a trash can or other temporary location. The -r and -f options cause **rm** to "force" remove every file "recursively." That is, every file in every subdirectory will be deleted, then the subdirectories themselves, then the main directory. **Be careful with the rm –rf command**, especially if you have superuser powers. Never issue it in the root directory or you will delete every file on the system.

For normal use, it is wise to check through directories before deleting them, even if you eventually use the **rm -rf** option to clear the directory quickly. Many directories have hidden files, which do not appear in a regular ls listing. Hidden files are usually configuration files or other system files; their file names begin with a dot, as in **.rnconf**. Issue the command as **ls -la** and be sure to remove hidden files as well as visible ones before issuing the **rmdir** command.

Creating a File

Creating a new file is less straightforward than creating a new directory. The user must pick one of several commands in order to create the new file; in many cases, the file is generated automatically as the result of some program which needs to save to a new location, such as a text editor. The creation of new files is usually associated with the creation of the data contained in the file.

Chapter 3 explained how files could be created as part of output redirection. For example, the command

```
ls / > newlist
```

creates a file, named newlist, which contains the directory listing for the root directory. A variation on this might be the command

```
echo "This is my new file" > mynewfile
```

This command creates a new file which contains the text string "This is my new file". The **echo** command simply causes whatever text string is supplied as an argument to be printed to the standard output; in this case, the standard output is redirected to a file rather than printed to the screen.

Another way to create a file is to use the **touch** command. **touch** is normally used to update the *time stamp* on a given file. The time stamp is an attribute of the file which denotes the last time the file was modified. However, if the file given as an argument to **touch** does not actually exist, touch will create the file automatically as it executes. Thus, the command

```
touch mynewfile
```

will create a file called mynewfile in the current directory. The file will have no content, unlike the file generated with the **echo** command.

Removing a File

Files are deleted with the **rm**, or "remove," command. The command

```
rm mynewfile
```

will delete the file mynewfile from the system. On most Unix systems, **rm** is configured so that the user must confirm that the file is indeed meant to be deleted. This is a safety mechanism designed to prevent the deletion of the wrong file in case of a typing error. If the **rm** command on your system is not configured to prompt for confirmation, establish the habit of issuing the command with the -i flag, which enables the prompt. Thus, the command

```
rm -i mynewfile
```

will prompt for confirmation. It is an extra step, but one which is well worth the annoyance as it may prevent the deletion of an important or irreplaceable file.

System Directories

These navigation and file management commands are the fundamentals needed to work on a Unix system. Once they are mastered, the user can move on to learn more about the general file system or start to work with specific programs and commands. The basis of the file system is the top level directories introduced earlier. These directories contain all the files of the operating system, specific configurations, user information, software for different functions, active processes, and a vast array of other possible work.

Making Sense of What You See

Different Unix variants have different file systems. Although most variants divide files into the same general categories, the top level directories on your system may have slightly different names from those described here. Regardless of the names on your system, there are some aspects of Unix directory organization that are common practice across the board. The directories described in this chapter are common enough that it is unlikely you'll have a file system which differs significantly. Your instructor will be able to provide information about the directory structure on your class or school network, and how it differs from the structure presented here.

The /bin Directory

The /bin directory usually contains all the executable binary files required for the operating system's software. In the early days of Unix, /bin often held all the software installed on the system. Today, /bin is the repository for the most basic system-level software. Programs like shells and other basic commands are usually stored here.

The /dev Directory

The /dev directory contains device files. All hardware components of the machine, and anything else which is represented by a device file, are represented in this directory. It is generally not necessary to move into this directory unless you want to see what device files are currently available.

The /etc Directory

The /etc directory is the home of most system-wide configuration files. Any program that requires or uses a configuration file usually stores that file in /etc. This includes the operating system itself, as well as more user-oriented programs. Note that, if you create a personal configuration file for a program installed system-wide, your configurations will be stored in your home directory rather than in /etc. Should you want to create a personal configuration file, a good place to start is by copying the system-wide configuration file in the /etc directory if permissions are set to allow it.

The /home Directory

As described earlier in this chapter, the /home directory is usually used to store users' personal directories. Depending on Unix variant, however, the directory which performs this function may differ significantly. Determine the correct location of personal directories on your machine with the pwd command, which will show you the accurate path for your system.

The /lib Directory

The /lib directory is home to various *library files.* Library files are small pieces of software which enable other programs to run. They provide a shared infrastructure for programming, which allows programmers to call the functions of a given library or set of libraries without having to reinvent the wheel and rewrite all those functions directly into the new program.

The /sbin Directory

The /sbin directory is the common home of a certain subset of executable binary files. These programs are usually intended for administrative purposes. For example, the programs used to configure network connections are usually stored in /sbin.

The /tmp Directory

The /tmp directory is a catch-all location for temporary files. If you do not have enough room in your home directory for a large file, for example, you may be able to store it in /tmp. Do not rely on this possibility, though, as system administrators often clean out /tmp regularly to improve system performance. Learn any policies about using /tmp before you move files into that directory. Some programs also create temporary files as they work, and those files are kept in /tmp until they are deleted by their parent program or by the system administrator.

The /usr Directory

Of all directories on a Unix system, the /usr directory probably varies more in its use than any other. In general, this directory is used to house files which pertain to activities of system users. /usr often contains several subdirectories: /usr/local often contains user-level application software; /usr/local/bin contains binary executables for user-level application software; /usr/local/etc contains configuration files for user-level application software. In addition, some systems place the /home directory as a subdirectory of /usr.

The /var Directory

The /var directory is a repository for files which will vary in size. System logs are the most common example of such files, as they grow or shrink depending on the data being tracked and the rate at which they are configured to delete old data. Other files which vary in size might be incoming files on a file server, USENET news feeds, or network administrative data. The /var directory is often configured with a hard limit on the amount of space it is allowed to occupy. With this restriction, files in /var cannot grow so large that they overwhelm the system and cause an operating system crash.

Summary

The Unix file system is the landscape of a given machine. Users and administrators navigate through the file system as if it were a physical place, using maps and markers to identify particular locations. A file can take many forms, ranging from human-readable text data to symbolic constructs intended for programming. Files are organized into directories, which may contain other subdirectories and which themselves are probably nested in parent directories. Every file has a unique identifier called the path name, which states the entire set of directories which contain the file. Access to individual files is controlled by

the file's permissions, a code which determines who can perform what operation on the file. Permissions are changed with the chmod command.

Simple commands are used to move through the file system, and users can move to any directory for which they have permission. Making new directories and files, and removing unused ones, is also a simple task, though removing directories often requires extra steps in order to protect important files which help the system to function. Depending on the function of the new file or directory, it may be stored in a user's home directory or in one of the top level directories used to organize all the files on the operating system. While the exact name and function of these directories may be different from Unix variant to variant, it is likely that they will fall within certain general areas and naming schemes.

Review Questions

1. What is the difference between a file and a directory? Define both terms.
2. Define an inode and explain its function.
3. List several types of files. What is the purpose of each type?
4. When is it appropriate to use a hard link, and when is a symbolic link the better choice?
5. What is the difference between the pipe denoted by the character | and the concept of a named pipe?
6. Define file permissions and explain why they are necessary.
7. What are the nine possible permissions combinations?
8. How are group and individual identification numbers used in the permissions context?
9. How does the chmod command work? Construct several chmod commands which grant or revoke different permissions to different groups.
10. List some commands used to navigate through the file system.
11. How can path names be used to execute commands on files in directories other than your current location?
12. Explain the restrictions on the rmdir command and the reasons for these restrictions.
13. Describe different methods of creating a new file. When is each method appropriate?
14. Name some of the general top level directories and their functions. What top level directory houses your personal account?

Exercises

1. Build a map of the file system on your computer, starting with the root directory. Provide path names for each file.
2. Use the **ls** command to generate a listing of all files in your home directory. Identify the permissions set on each file. Why do these files have these permissions? Should some files have more restrictive or permissive settings? Why?
3. Using a text file generated in an earlier exercise, or one you create specifically for this purpose, change its permissions and test your changes.
4. Consider the World Wide Web. How are permissions used in the Web context? What are the possible security problems involving permissions and Web access? Identify files on your system which are available on the Web; what are their permissions?
5. Identify the top level directories on your system. What is the function of each of these directories, and what kind of files do they contain? Move to a few of these directories and identify the file permissions on their contents. Why do these files have these permissions?

CHAPTER 5

Jobs and Processes

IN THIS CHAPTER

1. Keeping Track of running processes
2. Foreground and background processes
3. Managing processes
4. Managing output
5. Moving jobs between foreground and background
6. The screen program

Just as Unix is designed as a multi-user operating system, it is also designed as a true multitasking system. Many personal computer users are accustomed to running multiple programs at one time with an operating system like MacOS or Windows, but Unix multitasking is a different matter. In this chapter, you will learn the difference between the two methods and how to work with jobs and processes under Unix.

Personal operating systems use a style of multitasking called *task switching*. Task switching involves allocating the computer's processor cycles to each running program, allowing any given program to take all the time it needs to accomplish a particular task. This is why Windows and Macintosh computers sometimes "hang"; the processor is locked up by a certain job, and cannot do any other work until that job is finished. Since the process may be a background task, you might have no idea what is causing the system to lock up.

Given that Unix machines may have dozens of users logged in at any given time, each generating a different set of demands on the processor, task switching is not practical. Instead, Unix uses a style of multitasking called *time slicing*. With time slices, processor cycles are allocated to each running program. When a program's designated cycles are finished, the next program starts to work with the

processor even if the previous program is unfinished. Each program goes to the end of the line when its slice is over, waiting to resume work when it rises to the top of the list again. With this method, a Unix system may slow down when the system load is high, but it is rare to see a complete lock up because of processor overload.

Keeping Track of Running Processes

On a typical Unix system, there may be dozens of processes running at any given time. Many of these will be programs run by individual users, but other processes will be programs run by the system itself to perform various automatic functions. View the processes running on your machine by issuing the command

```
top
```

The command is an acronym for "table of processes." The output for this command will resemble Figure 5.1.

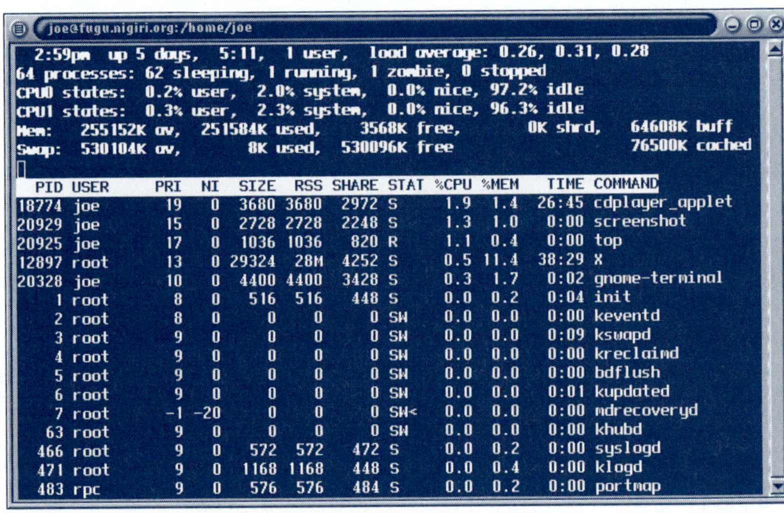

FIGURE 5.1 Output from the "top" program shows active processes in real time.

The "top" program output shows the processes as they work, in more or less real time. That is, the display is refreshed at regular intervals, usually once a second. If a new program is started, it will appear automatically on the list when the list is refreshed.

In Figure 5.1, you don't see the entire list of processes running on that machine because the output is longer than the monitor's capacity, and is limited to the size of the terminal screen. Some systems use a graphical front-end interface for top, which allows the user to scroll back and forth in order to view all processes. Figure 5.2 shows such an interface, using the program **gtop**.

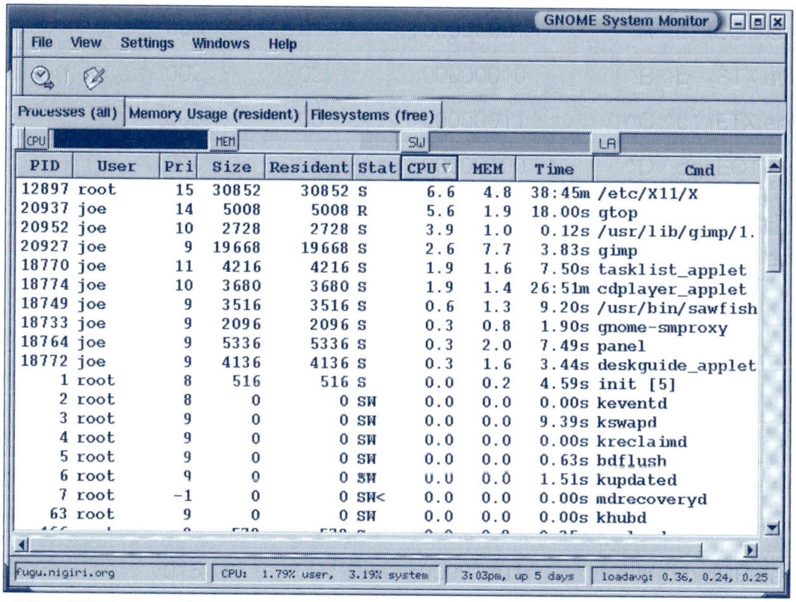

FIGURE 5.2 **The "gtop" program shows active processes sorted by their use of the computer's processor.**

With **gtop**, the display ranks processes by the percentage of processor time they are using, shown in the column headed %CPU. In the listing shown, note that the program "X" is taking up the majority of processor time on this system. The X Window System is the mechanism used to create a graphical user interface in the Unix environment. X provides the tools necessary to translate text commands and programs into graphical representations. Chapter 18, The X Window System, covers this system in more detail. Since graphics-related programs require more processor power than text programs, it's not surprising that X tops this list.

Foreground and Background Processes

In this era of graphical user interfaces, most people never stop to wonder how a person using only a text prompt can run more than one program at the same time. Normally, when you run a program from the shell, the system prompt disappears until the program has finished. Where this is the case, it should not be possible even to start another program—much less work with one—while the original program is running.

This problem is solved with the concept of foreground and background processes. When you give a shell command or start a program, the program is run in the *foreground*. It is your primary task, and takes over the terminal and system resources until it is finished. A program run in the *background* works differently. When you run a program in the background, the shell prompt returns as soon as the command is issued, allowing you to perform other tasks or use other programs while you are waiting for the background process to finish.

The shell offers the ability to switch back and forth between foreground and background processes, to bring a background process to the foreground for interactive work, and to move a foreground process to the background if it is going to take a while to finish. This process manipulation is possible in several shells, but is a particular feature of the bash shell used in this book. With a bit of practice, it is easy to become adept at moving processes.

To start a process in the background, simply issue the ampersand character at the end of the command line when you issue the command that invokes your desired program. That is, issue the command as

```
command &
```

The resulting output will look a bit different than what happens when you issue the command without the ampersand. The shell prompt will return immediately, and you should see the message

```
[1] 29098
```

Messages like this are described in the next section of this chapter.

The ability to run programs in the background, while useful, also brings up some issues which must be resolved in order to avoid future problems. The first issue is simply the problem of getting access to the background processes. In order to work with background processes, you must be able to move processes between the foreground and background. You must also be able to identify all running processes so you know which process should be moved. The **top** command, described earlier, is useful for monitoring active processes but is not particularly helpful for ongoing process administration.

The second issue involves handling output of foreground and background processes. If you run a program which produces output to the terminal screen, that output will print to the monitor whether or not the process is running in the foreground. The output from a background process can therefore interfere with, or interrupt, the output of a foreground process. Fortunately, this problem is easily managed.

Managing Processes

In order to manage processes effectively, you need to know which processes are running and how to identify each of them. There are two Unix commands which are particularly useful for this job. Earlier, you learned about the **top** program, which provides a range of useful data but which is not always the best administrative choice. Another command which generates similar output, but in a better format, is the **ps** command, an acronym for "process status."

The **ps** command provides a view of the running processes, as does **top**. The difference is that the **ps** output is static, while **top**'s output constantly refreshes itself. The **ps** output is a snapshot of system performance at the moment when you issued the command. The advantage of **ps** is that it has a number of options which can modify its behavior in various useful ways.

The default behavior of **ps** is to list only processes running in the terminal where **ps** is invoked. That is, if you issue the **ps** command in your personal user account, only processes running in your account will be listed. If you issue **top** in your user account, however, the output will show processes running in all accounts across the machine. If you have more than one terminal window running, as with the **screen** program described later in this chapter, **ps** will list only the programs running in the terminal window where it is invoked. The default output of **ps** looks like this:

```
PID    TTY          TIME      CMD
939   pts/0      00:00:00  bash
1127  pts/0      00:00:00  ps
```

The two processes shown in this output are the **bash** shell process and the **ps** process itself.

If you invoke this command in a particular terminal window and don't see all the processes that you know are running, however, issue the command with the -x option to force **ps** to report any processes running in your account. Output for the **ps -x** command looks like the output shown in Figure 5.3.

Many of the programs listed in the Figure 5.3 output are programs spawned by the graphical user interface, not by the user. They are still contained within the user's account, though, so they are listed. See the various **ps** options in Table 5.1.

A key part of ps output is the number in the far left column. This is the *process identification number.* Every process running on the system is assigned a unique identification number. When a command is invoked with the ampersand character, forcing the program into the background, the process number of the background process will print to the screen, as in

```
[1] 1179
```

FIGURE 5.3 The command ps -x results in output showing the processes running in your personal account.

TABLE 5.1: The "ps" Command and Selected Arguments

Argument	Function
-a	Shows all processes on the machine, including those started by other users (similar to **top**)
-u	Shows all processes on the machine, including those started by other users, sorted by user identification
-j	Includes job numbers in output
-r	Lists only actively running processes
-x	Shows all processes, including those not directly started by you, such as shell processes or other system activity

The number within brackets is the *job number*. The job number is similar to the process number, but refers only to processes which you start in your account. Job numbers are assigned sequentially to each process you start.

View all the jobs which you have started with the **jobs** command. Output from **jobs** will look something like this:

```
[1]    Stopped (tty output)        pine
[2]    Done                        emacs
[3]-   Stopped (tty output)        pico
[4]+   Stopped (tty output)        vi
```

Each line of the output contains the job number, the status of the job, and the name of each job that is running. Note that **jobs** prints only the jobs running in the current terminal; jobs running in other terminals will not appear, nor will processes running without an assigned terminal. The status of three of the four jobs listed here is "Stopped." These are interactive programs which must be halted before they are taken to the background. The job which is listed as "Done" was closed just before running the **jobs** command; had the command been issued a few seconds later, job 2 probably wouldn't appear at all. The third possible status is "Running," which you might see if you have a non-interactive process working in the background.

Managing Output

Managing output from multiple processes is not usually an issue for interactive programs. In those cases, the program halts until the user provides the necessary response to restart the program. With non-interactive processes, however, the program does not rely on continuing information from the user. When background non-interactive processes generate output, that output may interfere with output from the foreground process.

The easiest way to solve this process is to redirect the output from the background process. As explained in Chapter 3, Understanding Unix Commands, output can be redirected to a text file where it may be read or worked with at a later time. In order to redirect output from a background process, use the redirection operators described in Chapter 3 along with the ampersand character, used to force a program into background operation. That is, issue the command as

```
command > redirected-output-file &
```

Moving Jobs between Foreground and Background

Identifying jobs and processes is the key skill needed to work with multiple processes at once. Using the **top**, **ps**, and **jobs** commands provides the information necessary to move active processes between the foreground, where they can be worked with interactively, and the background, where they can run without interruption. While many programs move themselves between foreground and background, especially those programs which require user input before continuing with their work, administrators must move processes as well during their routine tasks.

In order to move a process from the foreground to the background, you must stop the process so that the shell prompt will return. To stop the foreground process, press the key combination <Ctrl>+<z>. This combination signals the foreground process to halt, but not to exit. When <Ctrl>+<z> is pressed, you should see a message like

```
[6]+   Stopped        vi
```

print to the screen. The shell prompt will also appear on the monitor.

Once the prompt has returned, issue the command **bg**, for "background". The halted foreground process will be sent to the background. If you now issue the **jobs** command, that process will be listed with its current status; the process will begin running again when it is moved.

Processes which have been moved to the background may never need to be accessed again, especially if they are non-interactive or will complete their work quickly. Other processes may be shifted frequently between foreground and background as they are needed. In order to pull a process from background to foreground, you must know the job number of the process; you can learn this with the **jobs** command, selecting the appropriate job from the complete listing.

Determine the correct job number and issue the **fg**, or "foreground," command with this syntax:

```
fg jobnumber
```

Tech Tip

Tip: **bg** takes the same syntax as **fg**.

The process will appear on the screen. If the process is interactive, like a mail or news reader, it will appear at the last point where user input was necessary. If the process is non-interactive, you may simply see the shell prompt disappear until the process is completed.

nice and renice

If necessary, you can change the priority level of running processes with the **nice** and **renice** commands. These commands define the order in which processes have access to system resources. Processes with a nice level of 19 are the "nicest" processes on the machine, as they permit all other processes to take precedence; processes with a nice level of –20 are the least nice processes, since they command all available resources until they are finished.

To start a job with a defined nice level, issue the command

```
nice level command
```

as in

```
nice 19 filename
```

If the job is already running, you must use the **renice** command to change its priority level. To use renice, identify the process ID number of the process you wish to change and issue the command

```
renice level PID
```

Consult the **nice** and **renice** manual pages if you want more information about priority levels or how to manage them.

Warning: Many systems do not permit users to change their processes' nice levels without permission. A user who habitually sets nice levels lower than 18 or 19 may find her processes shut down by the administrators without warning. Be aware of any system policies about priority and renicing before you begin to change the nice levels of your own jobs.

The /proc Directory

Those using Linux have an additional element which helps in managing active jobs and processes. The /proc directory contains a large number of virtual files which show the current state of the kernel as it runs and works with active processes. Files in /proc can be used by administrators to see specific data about a particular aspect of the kernel, or can be used by other programs to get up-to-date information which can be used as input for a particular task.

View files in /proc with the **cat**, **less**, or **more** commands. They cannot be opened or edited in text editors, but can be viewed easily with one of these programs. /proc files provide a vast amount of information about how the kernel is working, though some of the files can be hard to understand. For more information about your Linux system's /proc directory, consult your documentation or visit the Red Hat Web site and see their related documents: http://www.redhat.com/docs/manuals/linux/RHL-7.2-Manual/ref-guide/ch-proc.html.

The Screen Program

Foreground and background processes form an important part of the Unix operating system. As a practical matter, though, it can be cumbersome to work with processes in this way, especially with multiple programs that send large amounts of output to the monitor. Many administrators and users prefer a more streamlined way of dealing with multiple processes.

One of these streamlined methods is the program **screen**. **screen** is installed by default on some Unix variants, and is added by administrators on many more. This program allows the user to create any number of *virtual terminals*, each of which can run a separate job or multiple jobs. A virtual terminal is an additional shell process which, for text-based interfaces, works like multiple windows in a graphical user interface. It is possible to run background processes in **screen** terminals, and is even possible to nest other **screen** processes within existing **screen** terminal windows.

To start this program, or to determine whether or not it is installed on your system, issue the command

```
screen
```

at the system prompt. If the program is not installed, you will see a failure message. If the program is installed, however, it may seem as if nothing happened since the shell prompt will return. In fact, **screen** is now running. The shell prompt you see is running in a virtual terminal window. You can do anything with this shell prompt that you would do with the initial shell prompt.

To create a second virtual terminal, press the key combination <Ctrl>+<a> and then the combination <Ctrl>+<c>. Another shell prompt will appear; you are now in the second virtual terminal. To move between the two virtual terminals, press the key combination <Ctrl>+<a> and the number of the virtual terminal you want to move to. Note that **screen**, like many Unix programs, begins counting from zero instead of one. Therefore, to move back to the first virtual terminal, issue the command as

```
<Ctrl>+<a> 0
```

When you are done with a particular virtual terminal, return to its shell prompt and issue the command

```
exit
```

This command stops the shell process associated with that virtual terminal and exits. When you have exited all virtual terminals, **screen** will also exit.

Note:

The manual page for the **screen** program is quite well-written as manual pages go. There are far more features of this program than those described here. Issue the command **man screen** to learn more.

Summary

Like other modern operating systems, Unix is multitasking. The method used to manage multiple processes under Unix is called time slicing, which allocates a specific period of processor use to each active process in sequence. Other operating systems use the task switching method, which allows one program to use the processor until its work is finished. Each program run on a Unix system accounts for one or more processes, individual actions which require processor cycles. These processes can be monitored with several shell commands. Most processes run in the background and do not require user input, while one process at a time can be run in the foreground. Interactive programs are usually run as foreground processes; if an interactive program is run in the background, it must be pulled regularly to the foreground so that the user can provide input.

Each active process has a unique process identification number, which can be used to move the process between foreground and background. In addition, each process is identified by a unique job number, assigned according to the user who started the process. The **ps** and **jobs** commands are used to find these numbers. Process and job numbers are also used to manage the output of background processes, which might otherwise disrupt the activity in the foreground. While it is relatively simple to move

processes between background and foreground, it is time-consuming. Many administrators choose to use the screen program, which spawns virtual terminals. Each virtual terminal may be used to run a different program, making process management simpler and easier to manage.

Review Questions

1. What is the difference between task switching and time slicing? What are the advantages and disadvantages of each method?
2. Describe the **top** command and its function.
3. What are the advantages of a graphical table of processes program?
4. Explain how a user can run multiple programs while using a text-based shell.
5. Define an interactive program and provide several examples.
6. Describe the shell's role in process management.
7. How can a user gain access to background processes?
8. How can a user move a foreground process to the background?
9. What is the difference between **ps** and **top**, and when is it best to use each one?
10. Define "process identification number" and "job number."
11. Define the three possible statuses of the **jobs** command.
12. What keystroke combinations are used to manage processes and move them between foreground and background?
13. Explain the function of the **nice** and **renice** commands.
14. What is the function of the /proc directory?
15. What is a virtual terminal?
16. Explain how to manage multiple virtual terminals.

Exercises

1. Issue the **top** command on your machine. Pipe the output to a text file. What processes are running? Print the file or list the running processes, and identify each and its owner. Define each process; what does it do, and why is it important for the smooth running of a Unix system?
2. Select a command likely to produce a great deal of output (consult Appendix A for ideas). Run this program as a foreground process, noting how much output is produced. Next, start an interactive program like a text editor in the foreground, and then run the first command in the background. Describe what happens. Does the output disrupt your foreground process? Finally, run the first command in the background again, but redirect the output in any manner you like.
3. Run the **ps** program in your home directory. Describe each program that is running. Do you have a number of unfamiliar processes? How can you access them or remove them? (Hint: see the Appendix A entry for **kill**.) Explain why it is beneficial to the system for users to run as few programs as possible and to track their processes. Do the same with the **jobs** command.
4. Using the **cat** program, which prints output to a text file as it appears on the screen, track your process in this exercise. Run the **ps** program to show active processes. Identify the foreground and background processes, and move each active process between the foreground and background. Can you move all processes? What processes do not move? You may need to start several programs in order to have enough processes to move.
5. Start the **screen** program. Create several virtual terminals and start a program in each. Now, run the **top** and **ps** programs. How does the output differ from the output when you were not using **screen**? Issue the **w** command to get a listing of active users on the system. How many times do you appear? Can you tell what programs you have running in each screen?

seems like inserting text, the text in the file will not change until the editor is in insert mode. Think of every key on the board as having two functions; switching modes grants access to the alternate function. Table 7.2 shows the four basic keyboard commands that move the cursor.

There are more complex navigational commands available as well. In many of these keystroke combinations, shown in Table 7.3, you will see the value *n*.

TABLE 7.2: vi Cursor Movement Commands

[illegible]	[illegible]
h	Moves cursor one character to the left
j	Moves cursor one line down
k	Moves cursor one line up
l	Moves cursor one character to the right

TABLE 7.3: Additional Edit Mode Navigational Commands

Command	[illegible]
n+	Moves the cursor down *n* lines
n-	Moves the cursor up *n* lines
0	Moves the cursor to the beginning of the current line
$	Moves the cursor to the end of the current line
n$	Moves the cursor to the end of the line which is *n* lines below the current line
w	Moves the cursor to the beginning of the next word
*n*w	Moves the cursor to the beginning of the word *n* words from the current location
*n*G	Moves the cursor to the beginning of line *n*
[illegible]	Moves the cursor to the beginning of column *n*
G	Moves the cursor to the last line of the file
^B (Ctrl+B)	Scrolls file back one page
^D (Ctrl+D)	Scrolls file forward 1/2 page
^F (Ctrl+F)	Scrolls file forward one page
^U (Ctrl+U)	Scrolls file back 1/2 page

CHAPTER 6

The Shell Environment

IN THIS CHAPTER

1. Major Unix shells
2. Other Unix shells
3. Environment variables
4. Changing environment variables
5. System-level control files
6. Personal run control files

The shell environment is the primary method of interaction between user and operating system. Though the shell has a very small interface—the system prompt—it is part of every operation the user requests from the machine. There are a number of shells available to the Unix user, regardless of variant. Individual shells may be tailored to the programmer, to the user, or for some other reason. Several of these shells are profiled in this chapter.

Users can configure the shell to fit their particular desires or needs. These configurations are managed with environment variables, a construct which allows the user to change the value of a particular variable without having to change any programs or scripts which make use of the variable itself. Many of these variables are embedded in the shell's run control files, text files which are parsed when the shell starts up at boot. Configurations are generally stored in run control files, and many programs other than the shell use these files to manage user preferences.

Major Unix Shells

Although it may be difficult to see the range of options which differentiate one shell from another, significant differences do exist. The primary reason is to provide particular functions for shell programming, especially functions which utilize common constructs in a particular programming language. Despite the emphasis on programming flexibility, user-level functions and configurability provide yet another way to distinguish one shell from another.

This section introduces several of the major Unix shells, in terms of popularity and widespread use. These shells are available on almost all Unix variant installations, whether as the default shell or as an alternative which can be accessed by invoking the shell as a command at the prompt. While other shells may be downloaded and installed for a particular need or preference, one of these major shells will probably be available as a back-up or in an emergency with a less developed shell.

The Bourne (Again) Shell

We use the Bourne (Again) shell as the primary shell in this text. However, if you do not have the bash shell available, you can use the Bourne shell in almost all cases. The Bourne (Again) shell is a near-clone of the Bourne shell, and most bash commands should work equally well in sh (the Bourne shell).

The Bourne (Again) shell was originally developed as a Free Software alternative to the proprietary Bourne shell, and intended to be as close a copy as possible without violating the existing shell's copyrights. However, while working on the new shell, programmers decided to add some new features and to streamline some of the Bourne functions that were not as elegant as they could be. The resulting bash shell offers some options which are not possible in Bourne:

- ability to move the cursor with GNU Emacs key combinations
- ability to remember previous commands with a history log file navigable with the arrow keys
- ability to complete file names from a truncated text string and the Tab key
- improved script writing tools and functions

Many systems have bash installed as the default shell, or have installed it as an alternative. It is more likely to be found on systems running the FreeBSD or Linux Unix variants which emphasize the use of Free Software, but bash is installed on a number of commercial Unix variants as well.

The Bourne Shell

If the Bourne (Again) Shell is a derivative of the Bourne Shell, why not use the Bourne Shell itself? In fact, many people still do. The Bourne Shell is usually installed as the default shell on commercial Unix variants like HP-UX and earlier versions of Solaris. It is also installed by many users who learned Unix on a commercial variant and who find it to be a good blend of power and ease of use.

This ease of use comes from the Bourne Shell's limited array of commands. Bourne was the first Unix shell, and it has not been aggressively developed since then; therefore, not much functionality has been added since those early days. Those who come to Bourne from later shells with more capability may be frustrated, especially in working on the command line.

Despite its limited features, the Bourne Shell is favored by those who want a lean machine and dislike running software that offers too many unused functions. It is also useful to know the Bourne Shell if you plan to do much work on commercial Unix variants or if you plan to use graphical user interfaces exclusively. Users who plan to work primarily from the command line will probably want to upgrade to the Bourne (Again) Shell, which feels like Bourne but offers many more options. In general, any program written for the Bourne shell will run on the Bourne (Again) shell, but the reverse is not always true.

The Korn Shell

Like the Bourne (Again) Shell, the Korn Shell offers a range of functions beyond those of the initial Unix Bourne Shell environment. In fact, the Korn Shell is second in popularity only to the Bourne shell, since it is a powerful shell that fixes some of the problems which Bourne has with editing work directly on the command line. Users also appreciate the ability to configure the Korn Shell so that it emulates their favorite text editor, either vi or emacs.

Chapter 5, Jobs and Processes, introduced the concept of foreground and background processes, and the techniques of process management. These operations, now standard in many shells, were first developed as part of the Korn Shell. Other Korn features include the use of a second type of variable (array variables), an easy-to-program menu system, and integer arithmetic usable from the command line. Programmers also like the Korn Shell for quick, small shell scripts.

The C Shells

Two popular shells are based on the C programming language: csh and tcsh. While the most casual user may not notice a great deal of difference between the C shells and the Bourne shells, there are some significant differences once more complex tasks are started. Many Unix variants provide one of the C shells as an alternative to the Bourne or Bourne (Again) default; users familiar with C may want to change their default shell for a more familiar environment.

One of the major differences between the Bourne family and the C family is the way in which the C shells handle environment variables. Instead of editing each variable separately, the C shells use the "setenv" command to define values for a number of variables. setenv is issued at the command prompt, with the variable name and new value as arguments. This command is covered more thoroughly in the "Environment Variables" section of this chapter. The C shells also provide a C-based command structure for shell scripts. Users who are familiar with programming in C will find that shell scripting uses the same constructs.

In addition to environment variables and programming functions, the C shells offer a number of options not found in the Bourne family of shells, or which differ greatly from the Bourne family versions of the same concept. For example, the C shells provide file name completion, where the user can issue a partial file name as a command. The shell then searches for file names which contain that text string, and return the results to the screen. Other options include spellcheck for variables and commands, read-only variables, timestamps for entries in the history file, extended use of timed events and logs, and useful programming features like improved directory stack-handling commands.

The Z Shell

The final shell in this list is the Z shell, or "zsh." The Z Shell is a blend of features and operations from the Bourne Shell, the C Shell, and the Korn Shell. It is quite complex and offers its users the ability to make tiny configuration changes or call a small and unusual function in a shell script.

Because the Z Shell is such a complicated program, it is recommended for those who are confident and comfortable in the shell environment. Its complexity offers great rewards, but it does require some time and attention to detail to use this shell to its potential. The Z Shell uses a number of configuration files for each option, where other shells usually have only one. In fact, even the Z Shell manual page is unusually lengthy and complex. The Z Shell is not a beginner's shell, but for those who want to use the shell's power to manage their machines, it is an excellent choice.

Other Unix Shells

In addition to the shells listed above, there are several other shells in more limited use. Some of these shells were designed for specific functions or situations, while others are still under development. It is unlikely that the average user will find one of these shells installed as the default on any given system, but it is possible that one of these shells might be installed as an alternative shell.

scsh

The scsh shell is based on the Scheme programming language. Scheme is a very powerful and elegant language which is not used widely, but which has a vocal and dedicated user community. Those users who program in Scheme will find the scsh shell intuitive and useful.

rc and es

The rc and es shells do not implement the specific features of any one programming language. Rather, they attempt to bring modern programming techniques and abilities into the world of Unix shells, which are based on programming techniques more than 30 years old. The major difference between most Unix shells and the rc and es shells is in the number of shell operations which are represented as *function calls*, programming constructs which exist in all languages but which are not used for many operations in older Unix shells.

The Perl Shell

Over the past few years, the Perl programming language has become quite popular among programmers and administrators. The Perl programming syntax is not that different from the syntax used with bash, but there are significant differences. The Perl shell is an attempt to integrate Perl syntax with necessary shell functions. This shell is in an early stage of development.

Environment Variables

The shell itself is a very basic program. Its primary function is to interact with the operating system, not to provide a comfortable user environment. However, shell developers have recognized that users do need some consideration in order to make the shell easier to use and less difficult to work with.

As a result, every shell is configurable to some extent. Some shells offer more options than others, but all shells provide some level of user configurability. Options range from the appearance of the shell prompt to technical tricks which make shell programming easier. The common element of all these options is that they are controlled by *environment variables.*

Variables

What is a variable? A variable is a text string, or name, which is used to associate a particular setting with a specific value. The variable is an abstraction. It allows a program to use a piece of information without knowing what the actual information is. A programmer can write a general program, using variables, which will execute in different ways depending on the variable values set by the individuals running the program.

Variables can be named anything, whether or not the name makes sense to a human reader, as long as the name is constructed of letters; while numbers can be used in variable names, those numbers often have particular effect in a programming situation and can cause unexpected results. If numbers must be used in a variable name, keep them to the end of the name as in VARIABLE3, rather than 3VARIABLE. Shell variable names are traditionally written in capital letters to distinguish them from values, which are traditionally written in lower-case, as in this example:

```
EDITOR="vi"
```

This environment variable defines the default text editor as the vi editor. When an editor is needed for a particular command, the vi editor will be opened unless a different editor is specified.

The variables used in shell environment settings are *string variables.* That is, the value of the variable is always interpreted as a text string. In more complicated shell scripts and programs, two other variable types are used as well. An *array variable* is a variable which accepts more than one value at a time, as in

```
BREAKFAST=(eggs,oatmeal,steak)
```

The individual values are accessed by using an index number corresponding to the value's place in the list. An *integer variable* is a variable which takes a number as its value. The number can be positive or negative as long as it does not have a fractional component. Zero is also a valid integer value.

Common bash Environment Variables

To explain user environment variables, we provide some common variables used in the bash shell. Other bash variables are shown in Table 6.1. Similar variables are found in every shell, though their names may be slightly different. The values for many variables are set when a user account is created, while others are set by system-wide default. Most user-oriented variables are fine to change, but it is best to ask before changing path-related variables or other settings which may affect the system beyond your personal account.

USER

The USER variable contains your login identification, or user name. This variable identifies you in a number of places on the system, from the simple **w** command to complicated administration scripts that pull information about particular users.

TABLE 6.1: bash Environment Variables

Variable	Function
AUTO_RESUME	Defines method of process management for stopped jobs
BASH	The full path name of the bash shell
BASH_ENV	A variable used in scripting which defines a configuration file
BASH_VERSION	The current version of bash
BASH_VERSINFO	Several subvariables which identify the major and minor version numbers, the patch level, build version, and release status
CDPATH	A list of directories, separated by colons, which the **cd** command uses
DIRSTACK	An array variable containing the current contents of the directory stack
EUID	The effective user ID of the current user
FCEDIT	The default editor for the **fc** shell command
FIGNORE	A list of suffixes which will be ignored in file name completion
GLOBIGNORE	A list of text string patterns which will be ignored in file name completion
GROUPS	A list of the user groups to which the current user belongs
HISTCHARS	Defines characters used in history file management and use
HISTCMD	The identification number of the current command in the history file
HISTCONTROL	Toggles whether commands beginning with a space will be saved in the history file
HISTFILE	The file where previous commands are stored sequentially
HISTFILESIZE	The maximum number of lines which can be stored in the history file
HISTIGNORE	A list of patterns defining commands to be saved in the history file
HISTSIZE	The number of commands which can be stored in the history file
HOME	The home directory of the current user
HOSTFILE	A file like /etc/hosts used to complete hostnames
HOSTNAME	The machine name of the current host
HOSTTYPE	The type of system on which bash is running
IGNOREEOF	Toggles whether or not the shell responds to end of field characters or how many EOF characters must be issued before bash exits
IFS	Defines the internal field separators used to denote various data entries
INPUTRC	Defines a configuration file for the **input** shell command
LANG	Defines language for any variable beginning with LC
LC_ALL	Overrides the value of LANG for specific uses
LC_COLLATE	Specifies the order used in pattern matching

Continued

TABLE 6.1: bash Environment Variables (continued)

Variable	Function
LC_CTYPE	Specifies how characters will be interpreted in pattern matching
LC_MESSAGES	Specifies how pattern matching will manage double-quoted text strings
LINENO	The current line number in an executing script or program
MACHTYPE	The type of system on which bash is running, expressed in standard GNU format
MAIL	The file where bash checks for incoming electronic mail
MAILCHECK	The time interval at which bash checks for new electronic mail
MAILPATH	A list, separated by colons, where bash checks for electronic mail; may also be used to define a new mail message printed to the screen
OLDPWD	The previous working directory
OPTARG	The value of the last argument passed through the **getopts** command
OPTERR	Toggles error messages resulting from a **getopts** command
OPTIND	The index number of the next argument to be passed through **getopts**
OSTYPE	The operating system within which bash is running
PATH	The search path used when a command is given at the prompt
PIPESTATUS	An array variable containing the exit status values of the most recently completed processes
PPID	The process identification number associated with the shell's parent process
PROMPT_COMMAND	A command which executes each time the prompt appears on the screen
PS1	The prompt text string
PS2	The secondary prompt text string
PS3	The prompt for the **select** command
PS4	The text label used during an execution trace
PWD	The current working directory
RANDOM	A random number generator
REPLY	Default value for the **read** command used in shell scripts
SECONDS	The number of seconds since this shell process was started
SHELLOPTS	A list, separated by colons, of enabled shell options
SHLVL	An integer whose value increases each time a new shell process starts
TIMEFORMAT	Defines how timing information for pipelines will be displayed
TMOUT	The number of seconds which bash waits for input before exiting
UID	The current user's user identification number

MAIL

The MAIL variable defines the location where electronic mail is stored. This variable is used by your mail program and by the shell; the mail program uses this location to identify the file which contains incoming messages, while the shell uses this variable if you have asked the shell to notify you when new mail arrives. The value of the MAIL variable is a path name, usually something like

```
/var/spool/mail/$USER
```

Note that the path name uses the USER variable so that the entry can be the same for each person on the system. Each time this variable is invoked, the shell will look in your configuration for the value of USER.

Note: The bash shell prefaces variables with the $ character to draw a distinction between the variable named VARIABLE and the text string "variable."

PS1

The PS1 variable contains the format of the bash system prompt. In addition to simple text strings, the bash prompt can use *escape sequences* to represent particular information. Escape sequences are a way of representing generalized information: a type of sub-variable, in a sense. For example, the escape sequence **\u** represents the variable $USER, so the command

```
export $PS1 = "\u"
```

causes your user name to appear as the system prompt. Table 6.2 shows the various escape sequences which are valid for the PS1 variable's value.

HOSTNAME

This variable contains the name of the computer. The machine name is usually assigned when the operating system is installed, and is especially useful when working on a network which keeps different segments of the operating system on different machines.

PATH

The PATH variable tells the shell where to look for executable programs when you type a command. For example, when you use the **ls** command to get a directory listing, you are actually running a program which might have the full path name of /bin/ls. The shell knows to look in the /bin directory because that directory is part of the PATH variable's value. To see the current value of PATH on your system, issue the command

```
echo $PATH
```

You will get an output that is quite long, containing a number of paths separated by colons.

TABLE 6.2: bash Escape Sequences

Sequence	Value
\d	The current date in Weekday Month Date format
\h	The machine host name
\n	A new line
nnn	The character corresponding to the octal number *nnn*
\s	The name of the shell
\t	The current time, expressed in HH:MM:SS format
\u	The current user's user name
\w	The working directory
\W	The base name of the working directory
\#	This command's command identification number
\!	This command's history identification number
\\	A backslash character
\[	Initial character of a sequence of nonprinting characters
\]	Terminal character of a sequence of nonprinting characters

The basic value of PATH will be the same for all users, and is probably configured by the system administrator depending on where certain directories are kept on that system. Individual users might want to add other directories to PATH, especially if you run programs stored in non-standard directories. To change the value of PATH, you must define the new variable so that it includes both the previous value and the new value:

```
export PATH = "$PATH:/directory/subdirectory/"
```

With this method, you won't lose the original directories stored as the value of PATH.

Changing Environment Variables

All shells use environment variables to manage individual preferences, but the manner in which those variables are managed changes from shell to shell. The Bourne shells use the **export** command to change the value of an environment variable. While you can change the value of a variable simply by changing the value, as in

```
PS1="This is my new prompt:"
```

the value will not be carried over to any new subshells or kept when the session ends. In order to make the changed value permanent, use the export command to set the value:

```
export PS1 = "This is my new prompt:"
```

Now, when you log out or start a new shell, the new value will be used automatically. The **export** command changes the behavior of all instances of the shell from the point at which it is given; existing subshells or shell processes will not be affected.

The C shells manage environment variables differently. They use the **setenv** command, which takes the syntax

```
setenv NAME value
```

Place a line using this syntax into the appropriate run control file for your shell: .cshrc for the C shell, and .tchsrc for the tcsh shell. If you look at one of these files in a text editor, you will see a number of entries using **setenv**. The C shells offer a wide range of variables both for users and programmers. The C shell environment variables are shown in Table 6.3.

Note: Although shown here in capital letters to make the distinction clear between environment variable and other text, variables under the C shell are written in lower case letters.

TABLE 6.3: C Shell Environment Variables

Variable	Function
argv	Controls the list of command-line arguments supplied to the shell session
cdpath	A list of directories searched automatically by the **cd**, **chdir**, and **popd** shell commands
cwd	The complete path name of the current directory
echo	Causes the shell to print commands to the standard output before executing the program invoked
fignore	A list of file name suffixes to be ignored by the shell when using file name completion; the value of this variable is usually ".o".
filec	Switches the file name completion mechanism off and on; if the variable is on, typing a partial filename at the prompt will cause the shell to generate a list of all file names which match the supplied text string
hardpaths	Switches symbolic link usage on and off; when off, no symbolic links used in directory path names will work

Continued

TABLE 6.3: C Shell Environment Variables (continued)

Variable	Function
histchars	A two-character variable which defines the characters used for history substitution (! by default) and for quick substitution (^ by default)
history	The number of lines saved in the command history list; if no value supplied, the shell remembers only the most recent command
home	Defines the user's home directory; the character ~ may be used instead of the actual path name
ignoreeof	Determines whether the shell recognizes end-of-field characters; if on, the Ctrl+D key combination will shut down the active C shell process
mail	A list of directories checked by the shell for incoming electronic mail, and a number specifying how often the shell will check for mail
nobeep	Toggles a system beep when a file name completion operation is completed
noclobber	Manages output redirection to keep files from unplanned deletion
noglob	Modifier for file name completion, causing the shell to stop searching when one match to the supplied text string has been found
nonomatch	Modifier for file name completion, causing an echo of the initial text string request rather than an error message when no matching file is found
notify	Switches on and off shell messages announcing that a job has been completed
path	A list of directories automatically searched for a program or command invoked at the prompt
prompt	The text string which serves as the shell prompt
savehist	The number of lines in the command history list saved at logout
shell	The complete path name of the C Shell program
status	The status code of the most recently completed process
time	Sets the automatic timing of commands: either the reporting period in CPU seconds, or the resources being used

Run Control Files

While environment variables provide an excellent way to manage the shell environment in an individual session, the changes will not be permanent until they are made in the shell's *run control files* as described in the previous section. The values of environment variables are reset to the system defaults when the shell session ends, and those defaults are found in the run control files.

Run control files are configuration files which are always read at start-up. They usually have the file suffix .rc or use the "rc" component in the file name, and can be read and managed with a text editor. There are two types of run control files: system-wide and individual.

System-wide Run Control Files

System-wide run control files are configured by the system administrator. These files set the default behavior for the specified program, which defines how the program will appear to any user on the system (unless the user modifies her own run control files as described in the next section). The default behavior is the baseline from which any other configuration will stem, and there are some elements of program behavior which can only be controlled in a system-wide configuration file. These files should have permissions set so that users can view, but not modify, them.

The system-wide run control file for a normal bash installation is the file /etc/profile. An /etc/profile taken from a Linux system might look like this:

```
# /etc/profile
# System wide environment and startup programs
# Functions and aliases go in /etc/bashrc

if ! echo $PATH | /bin/grep -q "/usr/X11R6/bin" ; then
  PATH="$PATH:/usr/X11R6/bin"
fi
ulimit -S 0c 1000000 > /dev/null 2>&1
if [ 'id -gn' = 'id -um' -a 'id -u' -gt 14 ]; then
  umask 002
else
  umask 022
fi

USER='id -un'
LOGNAME=$USER
MAIL="/var/spool/mail/$USER"

HOSTNAME='/bin/hostname'
HISTSIZE=1000

if [ -z "$INPUTRC" -a ! -f "$HOME/.inputrc" ]; then
  INPUTRC=/etc/inputrc
fi

export PATH USER LOGNAME MAIL HOSTNAME HISTSIZE INPUTRC
```

```
for i in /etc/profile.d/*.sh ; do
  if [ -x $I ]; then
    . $I
  fi
done

unset i
```

Note: The hashmark character, #, is used to denote a *comment*. A comment is a line in the file which is not parsed as a command; the hashmark indicates to the shell that it should ignore anything following the # on that line. Comments are used to explain elements of the script or file to the user or to programmers who will work with the file long after it was written.

Clearly, there are many components in this file which have not yet been introduced. For the purposes of this chapter, however, consider this section of the file:

```
USER='id -un'
LOGNAME=$USER
MAIL="/var/spool/mail/$USER"

HOSTNAME='/bin/hostname'
HISTSIZE=1000

if [ -z "$INPUTRC" -a ! -f "$HOME/.inputrc" ]; then
  INPUTRC=/etc/inputrc
fi

export PATH USER LOGNAME MAIL HOSTNAME HISTSIZE INPUTRC
```

Disregard the actual constructs used to set up the file and look at the various components of this section. The upper-case words are all environment variables, and this section of the file is used to define those variables. Since this file is read each time a new bash session is started, these variables will take these values in every bash session.

Note the type of variables being defined. These are global variables which are not configurable by the user: user name, host name, size of the history file, and other system-related functions. A personal run control file might have more specific configurations that affect the look and feel of the bash shell; system-wide configurations tend to affect the operation of the shell more than the user environment.

Personal Run Control Files

Users who do not like the system-wide default shell settings can define their own environment variables. In some cases, these may be variables which are already defined in the system-wide files, such as the default text editor or prompt text string. In other cases, the user may add variables which are not defined system-wide in order to configure his personal environment as carefully as possible.

Personal run control files are stored in the user's home directory. The personal run control files for the bash shell are called .bash_profile and .bashrc. Run control file names usually begin with the dot character, so that they do not appear in a regular **ls** listing and overwhelm the user-created file names. You can view these *dot files* by adding the –a argument to the **ls** command, as in

```
ls -a
```

Personal configuration files are read after system-wide run control files are parsed at start-up. If the system file sets a variable's value and the personal file also sets a value for that variable, the personal value will override the system-wide setting. (This is not the case for read-only values like user name, host name, and other administrative variables.)

Environment variables for bash are usually kept in the .bash_profile personal run control file. A sample .bash_profile might resemble this:

```
# .bash_profile

# Get the aliases and functions
if [ -f ~/.bashrc ]; then
   . ~/.bashrc
fi

# User specific environment and startup programs

PATH=$PATH:$HOME/bin:/sbin:/usr/sbin
BASH_ENV=$HOME/.bashrc
USERNAME=""

export USERNAME BASH_ENV PATH

JAZZ=/usr/local/jazz
export JAZZ
```

This is a basic .bash_profile. The user has added two directories to the default PATH variable, and has defined a new variable called JAZZ to identify a new program running in the /usr/local directory. Should the user want to define other variables, such as the PS1 variable used to define the prompt text string, those settings would be placed in this file.

The .bashrc file, on the other hand, is generally used for defining *aliases*. An alias is a way to set a command which will be carried out with a command word that is not the normal invocation. That is, an extensive command or a command with a number of arguments might be aliased to the standard command word so that every time the command is invoked, that particular set of arguments is used.

One common alias is

```
alias rm='rm -i'
```

This alias means that every time someone on the system invokes the **rm** command to delete a file, **rm** will run with the –i flag. This flag causes **rm** to prompt for confirmation that the file really should be deleted, and is a common safety precaution. This alias can be found in many system-wide run control files. Aliases may be set system-wide or in personal run control files. To see a list of all aliases active on your system, issue the command **alias** at the shell prompt.

Run Control Files In Other Shells

In shells other than bash, configurations are handled in much the same manner but the file names are different. However, the configuration files are still edited with text editors, and they still run when the shell is booted up. Under the Korn Shell, there are three important run control files:

- **.kshrc** This file works much like .bashrc, and contains variable definitions and other commands which affect the shell environment.
- **.profile** Like bash's .profile document, this file controls the login environment for the Korn shell.
- **.sh_history** The .sh_history file contains a list of the most recently issued commands in the shell. It normally contains the 100 most recent commands, but can be configured to display fewer or more depending on your needs.

In editing these files, you will need to use a different set of environment variables than those used under bash. Table 6.4 shows some of the Korn shell environment variables.

Those who use the C shells (csh and tcsh), as explained above, will find it helpful to know something of the C language's syntax. There are four major run control files used with the C Shells:

- **.cshrc** Like .bashrc or .kshrc, this file is used to control the user environment while the C shell is running.
- **.tcshrc** For those using the tcsh shell, this file is used in place of .cshrc.
- **.login** This file controls the login environment and is similar to the .profile file used under bash or in the Korn shell.
- **.logout** When the shell process exits, any commands contained in this file are executed.

TABLE 6.4: Korn Shell Environment Variables

CDPATH	Defines the search path used in the cd command
COLUMNS	Sets the width of the edit window used in shell edit modes
EDITOR	Defines the default text editor
ENV	If this variable is defined, a path is generated by performing parameter substitution on this variable's value
ERRNO	The value is defined by the most recently failed subroutine
FCEDIT	Defines the default editor used with the **fc** command
FPATH	Sets the search path for function definitions
HISTFILE	Sets the path name of the file used to store command history; the default setting is .sh_history
HISTSIZE	Determines how many commands will be stored in the history file
HOME	The path name of the user's home directory, which will be entered on login and which is used as default with the **cd** command
IFS	Defines the characters which are used as internal field separators in this shell
LANG	A location value to be used as default when the variable LC_ALL does not specify a location
LC_ALL	Defines a location which is used to override any previously set values
LC_COLLATE	Sets the sequence to be used when sorting data
LC_CTYPE	Sets the location for an interpretation of any specified sequence of bytes
LC_MESSAGES	Defines the language in which messages are written
LINENO	The value is the line number of the line in a shell program currently being executed
LINES	Sets the column length when printing select lists
MAIL	Sets the path name of the file where new incoming mail is stored
MAILCHECK	Defines the number of seconds between shell checks for new mail
MAILMSG	The value of this variable is sent as a message when new mail is found
MAILPATH	A list of programs, separated by semicolons; if new mail is found and you are working in one of these programs, the shell will interrupt you with a message
OLDPWD	The previous working directory, set by the **cd** command
OPTARG	The last argument processed by the **getopts** command
OPTIND	The index of the last argument processed by the **getopts** command
PATH	A list of directories, separated by colons, which the shell will search when a command is issued

Continued

TABLE 6.4: Korn Shell Environment Variables (continued)

CDPATH	Defines the search path used in the cd command
PPID	The process number of the parent of the current shell process
PS1	The text string used as the primary system prompt
PS2	The text string used as the secondary system prompt
PS3	The text string used as a prompt within a select loop
PS4	The value which precedes each line of an execution trace
PWD	The present working directory
RANDOM	Generates a random number whose value is between 0 and 32767
REPLY	Defined by the select and read commands when no arguments are given to those commands
SECONDS	The number of seconds since the current shell process was invoked
SHELL	The path name of the current shell; the value is usually exported by the .profile file at login
TMEOUT	The number of minutes which the shell will remain idle before exiting

Summary

The shell environment is the program which allows users to interact with the operating system. The shell provides a shell prompt, where commands may be entered by the user, and then interprets those commands so that the operating system can respond appropriately. There are a large number of shells available to the Unix user, each with a different range of functions and features. Some shells emphasize particular programming constructs, while others focus on ease of use or administration. Selecting a shell is a matter of balancing personal taste with required functions.

The Bourne shell is the original shell environment and is still the most frequently used shell. The Bourne (Again) shell was developed as a Free Software alternative to the Bourne shell, and includes some upgraded navigation and programming functions. The C shells, csh and tcsh, are designed to use programming constructs from the C language; while the individual user may not notice much difference, those who program for the C shells write scripts differently than those who program for Bourne. The Korn and Z shells are also popular choices. There are many other shell options, ranging from newly developed programs to those with very limited focus.

Shells are configured with environment variables, which are maintained in run control files. These files are parsed every time a new shell session starts, and the values of the variables are implemented for that session. System-wide run control files are parsed first, and many administrative variables are set at that time. Personal run control files are parsed next. Any variables which a user has defined will supersede the system default setting, giving users the ability to configure their own shell sessions for specific needs. Run control files also allow users and administrators to define aliases, a way to configure the operation of a given command so that it runs with the same optional arguments each time it is invoked.

Review Questions

1. What is the shell environment?
2. What mechanisms are used to configure the shell environment?
3. Explain why there are different shells for different uses.
4. What is the difference between the Bourne and the Bourne (Again) shell?
5. Explain some of the features found in the Korn or C shells and how they differ from the features found in the Bourne family of shells.
6. When is it useful to run a shell in early development or limited use? What are the disadvantages?
7. Define a variable.
8. Define, and provide an example, of the three variable types.
9. What is contained in the PATH variable? What are the advantages of such a variable?
10. Explain the method used to change environment variables in the Bourne shell family.
11. Explain the method used to change environment variables in the C shell family.
12. What is a run control file?
13. What is the difference between a system-wide and an individual run control file? What are the effects of each?
14. What permissions should be set on a system-wide configuration file?
15. Explain the use of the hashmark character in a script.
16. Define an alias and explain its advantages and disadvantages.

Exercises

1. Search your system and list the shell environments which are installed and usable. Describe each shell and define a user community which might prefer that environment. Do a Web search and find some other shells; describe each and define a user community.
2. Issue the command **set** to get a list of all environment variables defined in your user account. Pipe this output to a text file. Compare this list to the complete list of variables provided for your shell, if your shell is one covered in this chapter; consult the shell's manual page if you are using a different one. What variables are available that are not defined? How would your environment change if you configured new variables? Configure several new variables and describe the effects.
3. View the system-wide run control files for your shell. Copy them to text files in your user account. What are the system-wide environment variables? How do the settings in these files affect your user experience? If you have access to the system administrator, ask why certain variables and settings are used as defaults and record the answers.
4. Copy your personal run control files to new text files. What are the personal environment variables defined in these files? How do they affect the system-wide default settings? From what you can tell (assuming little knowledge of scripting), what functions are included in your personal configuration files? What could you add to this file to affect your user experience?
5. Issue the **alias** command to see the aliases configured on your system. Pipe the output to a text file. What options are included in these aliases? How do the commands work differently from the basic command function? Create five to ten more aliases and add them to your printed list, explaining why each is a useful addition to the list.

CHAPTER 7

The vi Editor

IN THIS CHAPTER

1. What is text?
2. Text editors
3. Line editors vs. visual editors
4. The vi text editor
5. vi's modes
6. Editing in vi
7. Abbreviations and macros
8. vi run control files
9. Saving and exiting vi

Most of the work done on a Unix system is handled through various text files. Administrative tasks and system configuration commands are controlled by the data kept in particular types of data files. Even the operating system itself is usually configured with basic text files. Many of the programs which administrators write to solve a particular problem or situation are simple text strings contained in text files, which are readable by humans as well as by machines.

Why is text so important in the Unix world, and why don't many of these techniques use graphical interfaces? As described in previous chapters, Unix was developed long before graphical windowed interfaces. While there are graphical front ends for a wide range of Unix tasks, not every Unix system is capable of using them. Every Unix system can use plain text files, though, and the skills needed to work with text are critical for anyone planning to use Unix, no matter how infrequently.

Text files are usually created and managed with a specialized program called a *text editor*. Text editors are simpler than word processors since they are not designed to format text, but simply to manage it. There are a number of text editors available for Unix systems. One of the most widely used editors is called vi, and it is introduced in this chapter. Other text editors are covered in Chapter 8, Other Text Editors.

What Is Text?

The concept of "text" is more specific in the Unix world than it is in general conversation. You may be familiar with a number of definitions for text in everyday usage: the printed material on a page, a particular book (often one assigned for a course), or a sentence or two used as the basis for a speech or essay. In the Unix context, however, text is a specific technical term.

Text is a visual display which complies with a particular standard. In the United States, the standard is the American Standard Code for Information Interchange, or ASCII. This code assigns specific binary codes to individual letters, numbers, punctuation marks, and keyboard combinations.

The operating system parses keystroke input according to this code, and translates it into the binary information which is used to perform the requested action. For example, when you type the Unix command ls at the command prompt, the operating system must translate the letters l and s into the binary codes 01101100 and 01110011. The operating system then determines the appropriate response, recodes the resulting output according to the ASCII standard, and delivers a listing of files in the current directory to the standard output.

There are different codes for different character sets. Pictographic languages like Chinese or Korean do not use ASCII. Even European languages like French or German have characters which are not found in the English language, so they have their own codes as well. In order to display non-English languages on a given system, the correct fonts must be installed and configured appropriately.

As with other computer standards, the ASCII standard means that a particular block of text will be displayed identically on any computer which recognizes that standard. In the case of ASCII, all computers and operating systems recognize this code, with the single exception of very old IBM mainframes. You are unlikely to run into one of these machines, since most of them have been scrapped or turned over to museums. ASCII is one of the true common standards in the Unix world, even more than the graphical windowing system described in Chapter 18, The X Window System.

Table 7.1 shows the various keyboard characters and combinations, and the codes assigned to them. The decimal number identifies the character, while

TABLE 7.1: The ASCII Character Map

Decimal	Octal	Hex	Binary	Description
000	000	00	00000000	^@ ^` (NULL)
001	001	01	00000001	^A ^a (SOH start-of-heading)
002	002	02	00000010	^B ^b (STX start-of-text)
003	003	03	00000011	^C ^c (ETX end-of-text)
004	004	04	00000100	^D ^d (EOT end-of-transmission)
005	005	05	00000101	^E ^e (ENQ enquiry)
006	006	06	00000110	^F ^f (ACK acknowledge)
007	007	07	00000111	^G ^g (BELL)
008	010	08	00001000	^H ^h (BS backspace)
009	011	09	00001001	^I ^i (TAB)
010	012	0A	00001010	^J ^j (LF linefeed)
011	013	0B	00001011	^K ^k (VT vertical-tab)
012	014	0C	00001100	^L ^l (FF formfeed)
013	015	0D	00001101	^M ^m (CR carriage-return)
014	016	0E	00001110	^N ^n (SO shift-out)
015	017	0F	00001111	^O ^o (SI shift-in)
016	020	10	00010000	^P ^p (DLE data-link-escape)
017	021	11	00010001	^Q ^q (DC1 XON x)
018	022	12	00010010	^R ^r (DC2 c-R c-r)
019	023	13	00010011	^S ^s (DC3 xoff)
020	024	14	00010100	^T ^t (DC4 DCL)
021	025	15	00010101	^U ^u (NAK negative-acknowledge)
022	026	16	00010110	^V ^v (SYN synchronous-idle)
023	027	17	00010111	^W ^w (ETB end-of-transmission-block)
024	030	18	00011000	^X ^x (CAN cancel)
025	031	19	00011001	^Y ^y (EM end-of-medium)
026	032	1A	00011010	^Z ^z (SUB substitute)
027	033	1B	00011011	^[^{ (ESC escape)
028	034	1C	00011100	^\ ^| (FS field-separator)

Continued

TABLE 7.1: The ASCII Character Map (continued)

Decimal	Octal	Hex	Binary	Description
029	035	1D	00011101	^] ^} (GS group-separator)
030	036	1E	00011110	^^ ^~ (RS record-separator)
031	037	1F	00011111	^_ ^DEL (unit-separator)
032	040	20	00100000	SPC space
033	041	21	00100001	! exclamation-point
034	042	22	00100010	“ straight-double-quotation-mark
035	043	23	00100011	# number-sign or crosshatch
036	044	24	00100100	$ dollar-sign
037	045	25	00100101	% percent-sign
038	046	26	00100110	& ampersand
039	047	27	00100111	’ apostrophe
040	050	28	00101000	(left-parenthesis
041	051	29	00101001	) right-parenthesis
042	052	2A	00101010	* asterisk
043	053	2B	00101011	+ addition-sign
044	054	2C	00101100	, comma
045	055	2D	00101101	- subtraction-sign
046	056	2E	00101110	. period, dot, or decimal point
047	057	2F	00101111	/ right-slash or forward-slash
048	060	30	00110000	0 Numeral zero
049	061	31	00110001	1 Numeral one
050	062	32	00110010	2 Numeral two
051	063	33	00110011	3 Numeral three
052	064	34	00110100	4 Numeral four
053	065	35	00110101	5 Numeral five
054	066	36	00110110	6 Numeral six
055	067	37	00110111	7 Numeral seven
056	070	38	00111000	8 Numeral eight
057	071	39	00111001	9 Numeral nine

Continued

TABLE 7.1: The ASCII Character Map (continued)

Decimal	Octal	Hex	Binary	Description
058	072	3A	00111010	: colon
059	073	3B	00111011	; semicolon
060	074	3C	00111100	< less-than or left-angle bracket
061	075	3D	00111101	= equals sign
062	076	3E	00111110	> greater-than or right-angle-bracket
063	077	3F	00111111	? question-mark
064	100	40	01000000	@ at-symbol
065	101	41	01000001	A (Upper-case letters)
066	102	42	01000010	B
067	103	43	01000011	C
068	104	44	01000100	D
069	105	45	01000101	E
070	106	46	01000110	F
071	107	47	01000111	G
072	110	48	01001000	H
073	111	49	01001001	I
074	112	4A	01001010	J
075	113	4B	01001011	K
076	114	4C	01001100	L
077	115	4D	01001101	M
078	116	4E	01001110	N
079	117	4F	01001111	O
080	120	50	01010000	P
081	121	51	01010001	Q
082	122	52	01010010	R
083	123	53	01010011	S
084	124	54	01010100	T
085	125	55	01010101	U
086	126	56	01010110	V

Continued

TABLE 7.1: The ASCII Character Map (continued)

Decimal	Octal	Hex	Binary	Description
087	127	57	01010111	W
088	130	58	01011000	X
089	131	59	01011001	Y
090	132	5A	01011010	Z
091	133	5B	01011011	[left-bracket
092	134	5C	01011100	\ backslash
093	135	5D	01011101	] right-bracket
094	136	5E	01011110	^ circumflex or caret
095	137	5F	01011111	_ underscore
096	140	60	01100000	` accent-grave, backquote, or backtick
097	141	61	01100001	a (Lower-case letters)
098	142	62	01100010	b
099	143	63	01100011	c
100	144	64	01100100	d
101	145	65	01100101	e
102	146	66	01100110	f
103	147	67	01100111	g
104	150	68	01101000	h
105	151	69	01101001	i
106	152	6A	01101010	j
107	153	6B	01101011	k
108	154	6C	01101100	l
109	155	6D	01101101	m
110	156	6E	01101110	n
111	157	6F	01101111	o
112	160	70	01110000	p
113	161	71	01110001	q
114	162	72	01110010	r
115	163	73	01110011	s

Continued

TABLE 7.1: The ASCII Character Map (continued)

Decimal	Octal	Hex	Binary	Description
116	164	74	01110100	t
117	165	75	01110101	u
118	166	76	01110110	v
119	167	77	01110111	w
120	170	78	01111000	x
121	171	79	01111001	y
122	172	7A	01111010	z
123	173	7B	01111011	{ left-brace
124	174	7C	01111100	| vertical-bar or pipe
125	175	7D	01111101	} right-brace
126	176	7E	01111110	~ tilde
127	177	7F	01111111	^? delete

the octal (base 8), hexadecimal (base 16), and binary numbers are equivalents of the decimal. Note that upper-case and lower-case numbers have different identifiers, and that the first 31 characters are actually control characters, which control the action of a printer or a terminal window.

While there is no reason to memorize this table, it is important to understand that the processor inside your computer doesn't speak English (or Japanese, Faroese, or Portuguese). It only speaks binary; individual language standards make it possible for us to communicate with our machines, each using the language we prefer. Even systems in non-English-speaking countries use the ASCII standard. For example, though operating systems may offer Chinese users a Mandarin user interface, the configuration files and scripts will still be written in ASCII text. Except for the ancient IBM mainframes mentioned earlier, there isn't a computer running on this planet that runs without ASCII text.

Text Editors

A particular type of program, called a *text editor*, is used to create and edit text files. Text editors are relatively simple programs which allow the user to work with text directly, but which do not provide a great deal of formatting. Formatting is not particularly necessary in a Unix environment, since most text files are read in a terminal window or directly at the command prompt and do not need to be attractive to the reader.

Text editors are similar to word processors, but there are some important differences. A word processor, like Microsoft's Word or Corel's WordPerfect, is a WYSIWYG program. WYSIWYG is an acronym for What You See Is What You Get, and it means that the document or file will print exactly as it is displayed on the screen. The word processor program applies a number of invisible formatting directions to the text in order to create a visually appealing document. Opening a word-processed file in a text editor generally produces a screen of nonsense characters, which is how the formatting codes translate into pure ASCII. Because of these formatting codes, word processors must run in a graphical user environment which can translate the codes into visual representation. There are no word processors for text-mode shell environments.

Note: The original word processors were intended for professional publishers. They worked in text mode, and the formatting codes were inserted into the text by hand. Users couldn't see the result until the page was printed. WYSIWYG editors were developed in response to these programs, so that users could see what effect each formatting code had on the document. If you'd like to see a version of one of these early typesetting programs, take a look at LaTeX. LaTeX is still used widely in academic circles, as it's particularly effective at scientific and mathematical equations.

Line Editors vs. Visual Editors

As with any type of program, text editors have evolved through the years. The earliest text editors were line editors, which permitted the user to work on one line of a file at a time. Since there are obvious drawbacks to such a program, the next generation of text editors permitted the user to work on an entire file at once. These editors are called visual editors, and most of the text editors used today fall into this category.

The first Unix text editor was called **ed**, short for "editor." Due to the technical limitations of that era's monitors, **ed** was a line editor. To use **ed** and other line editors, the user must enter each line of a file as a separate action. The same method is used to edit an existing file, and the user must know each particular line number in order to work on that line of the file. The longer the file, the more troublesome it is to work with a line editor.

Surprisingly, **ed** is still around. In fact, it may be installed on the system you're using for this course. While it is difficult to use, **ed** is extremely useful in situations where only the most basic functions are available, such as a devastating system crash which has damaged your terminal. Basic **ed** skills are included in Chapter 8, Other Text Editors.

As monitor technology advanced through the years, programmers took advantage of the new capabilities to build more advanced text editors. One of the first full-screen, or visual, text editors to be released was **vi**. Visual editors like **vi** take advantage of the full monitor screen. Instead of working line by line, a user can display an entire file, or as much of it will fit on the screen at once. Visual editors allow the user to scroll through the file, move between lines, and even cut and paste material from line to line. None of this was possible with plain line editors.

While it may seem a strange thing to get excited about, choosing a text editor is something about which many people have strong opinions. Whether or not most people use **vi**, most will agree that it's one of the most important text editors available to Unix users. **vi** is available on a vast number of systems, since it's usually installed by default. This means that, if your system crashes or you need to use a system that doesn't have your favorite text editor installed, every Unix user should know the basics of **vi**. Even if you choose another text editor as your favorite, learn enough **vi** to use it in an emergency.

Note: Throughout this book, we assume that you will use a text editor to create or edit any text files which are required for a particular operation. Do not use a word processor to edit these files; even if you save them as plain text and import the files into your Unix account, they may not work properly.

The vi Text Editor

The **vi** text editor offers a number of features not found in earlier-generation line editors, but it may seem difficult or unintuitive for those users who are accustomed to modern word processors. With **vi**, all commands are entered on the keyboard instead of using a mouse for some work, and there is no menu system to help select the appropriate action. Despite these differences, most users find that **vi** runs much faster than their regular word processor, and that the files are much smaller.

Note: vi is pronounced "vee eye," not "vye" or "vee."

Tech Tip

Your system may have a version of **vi** called **vim**. This clone of **vi** works in much the same way. It uses the .vimrc file as its configuration, not the .exrc file described in this chapter. If you are using **vim** and find differences between what you read here or learn in class and how the **vim** editor works, consult its documentation for help.

To start the **vi** text editor, log into your Unix shell account and type **vi** at the system prompt. The text editor will open on your screen, as shown in Figure 7.1. To work with a particular file in **vi**, use the file's name as part of the command:

```
vi filename
```

Whether you open an existing file or a new file, you will not be able to enter new text immediately. One of the unusual aspects of **vi** is that it has two separate modes: insert mode and edit mode.

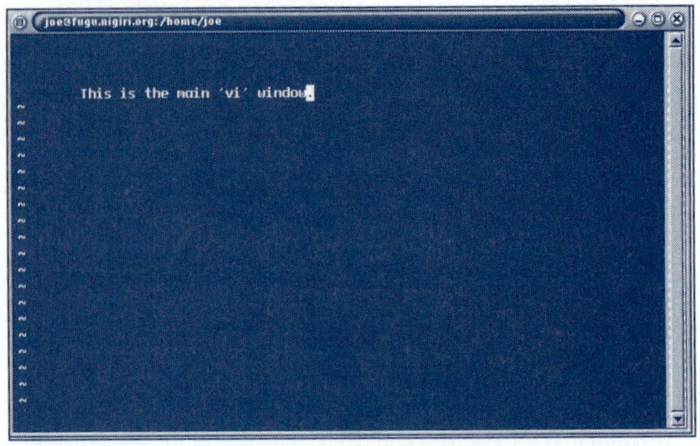

FIGURE 7.1 The vi text editor running in a terminal window.

vi's Modes

The **vi** modes make a clear distinction between editing commands and the actual text contained in the file. Depending on the mode in operation, keystrokes are interpreted by the editor in different ways. Users must be conscious of the current mode so that they can issue the correct commands or enter appropriate text.

When **vi** first starts, it opens in edit mode. Edit mode is used for commands to the text editor, not for new text. If new text is entered while in edit mode, **vi** will respond with a flurry of error messages since there is no text for the commands to work with. There are a number of text management possibilities available in edit mode, shown in the tables throughout the chapter.

Insert Mode

Insert mode is used to add new text to a file. The first action usually taken upon starting **vi** is to switch to insert mode, by typing the character **i**. A cursor will appear at the start of the first line, indicating that the mode has changed. Whenever the cursor is visible, the editor is in insert mode. If the cursor disappears, the editor has changed to edit mode.

As soon as the cursor appears, you can begin typing. Note that the cursor moves with the entered text. Should you want to move the cursor yourself, so that you can add words or letters, use the arrow keys on the keyboard. Although its tools are limited, insert mode does offer some editing capabilities. The BACKSPACE key erases the character directly to the left of the cursor, while the DELETE key erases the character directly above the cursor.

Edit Mode

While insert mode is necessary to get the basic text into a file, it is edit mode where the bulk of text file work happens. Once you have entered your text, switch back to edit mode by pressing the ESC key. The cursor will disappear, indicating that the mode has changed. Some of the basic edit mode operations are described in the "Using Edit Mode" section of this chapter. Edit mode allows the user to navigate the file, cut and paste blocks of text, find and replace text strings, and other useful activities.

Using Insert Mode

Using insert mode is simple. Once you have entered insert mode by pressing the "i" key, enter the text needed for that file. To work on a file that already has some text, enter insert mode before adding additional text to the file. Anytime you want to add more text, you need to be in insert mode. Entering text in edit mode causes **vi** to treat the text as a lengthy string of editing commands. The editor will return a mix of error messages and unintentional edits.

In addition to using the arrow keys to move through a file while in insert mode, other navigational keys are functional in **vi** as well. The PAGE UP and PAGE DOWN keys scroll the document, while the END key moves the cursor to the end of the line where it is currently located. Use the HOME key to move the cursor to the end of its current line. Most **vi** cursor movement, as well as a number of commands in edit mode, uses relative locations. That is, the cursor's current location is always considered home base even if the cursor is at the bottom of the document or buried deep in the middle.

Using Edit Mode

To enter edit mode, press the ESC key. In order to use most of the edit commands, you must locate the cursor at the text which is to be edited. The various keys used to navigate in insert mode also work in edit mode, but edit mode offers an additional set of navigational commands managed with multiple keystroke combinations.

Why use keystroke combinations instead of keyboard keys? Some older keyboards don't have the full array of navigational keys. However, the better reason is that it will make you a faster typist. If you don't have to move your hands to find the appropriate navigational key, you will maintain a steadier stream of input. Most people use a blend of navigational keys and keystroke combinations.

Since every keystroke in edit mode is interpreted as a command, there are a number of keystrokes which move the cursor. Though using these keystrokes seems like inserting text, the text in the file will not change until the editor is in insert mode. Think of every key on the board as having two functions; switching modes grants access to the alternate function. Table 7.2 shows the four basic keyboard commands that move the cursor.

There are more complex navigational commands available as well. In many of these keystroke combinations, shown in Table 7.3, you will see the value *n*.

TABLE 7.2: vi Cursor Movement Commands

Keystroke	Function
h	Moves cursor one character to the left
j	Moves cursor one line down
k	Moves cursor one line up
l	Moves cursor one character to the right

TABLE 7.3: Additional Edit Mode Navigational Commands

Command	Function
n+	Moves the cursor down *n* lines
n-	Moves the cursor up *n* lines
0	Moves the cursor to the beginning of the current line
$	Moves the cursor to the end of the current line
n$	Moves the cursor to the end of the line which is *n* lines below the current line
w	Moves the cursor to the beginning of the next word
nw	Moves the cursor to the beginning of the word *n* words from the current location
nG	Moves the cursor to the beginning of line *n*
n|	Moves the cursor to the beginning of column *n*
G	Moves the cursor to the last line of the file
^B (Ctrl+B)	Scrolls file back one page
^D (Ctrl+D)	Scrolls file forward 1/2 page
^F (Ctrl+F)	Scrolls file forward one page
^U (Ctrl+U)	Scrolls file back 1/2 page

Replace *n* with an actual number. For example, the command "*n*h" moves the cursor *n* spaces to the left in a single action. The only limitation is that the cursor cannot be moved beyond the beginning or end of its current line with left or right movement. To move away from the current line, the cursor must move up or down.

With these complex commands, it is nearly as easy to navigate a text file in **vi** as it is to navigate a document in a word processor. Many users find that working with keystroke commands is actually faster, since their hands never have to leave the keys to reach for a mouse. Many word processors use keystroke combinations as well, and some people find themselves using keystrokes instead of mouse clicks, even in other operating systems.

Editing in vi

Copying and Pasting

One of the most common editing tasks is to copy and paste. In this action, the user selects a chunk of text, copies it from the screen, and reinserts it at another location. In **vi**'s specialized terminology, copy and paste is known as "yank and put." The concept behind this name is that, when a user removes (or yanks) a chunk of text from the file, the chunk is put into a register. The register is **vi**'s name for temporary storage. When the user has found the new location for the text block, the block is copied from the register and put in the correct place.

To yank and put, place the cursor at the start of the text block you want to move. Determine the number of lines to yank and enter the command **nY**, where *n* equals the number of lines to be yanked. The text on the screen will not change, but the specified lines have been copied into the register. Next, move the cursor to the location where the text will be inserted and issue the command **p**. The text appears to the right of the cursor location. This is the most basic way to use yank and put. Table 7.4 shows some additional commands to use with this process.

Deleting Text

In the yank and put process described in the previous section, the yanked text does not disappear. With **vi**, yanking text and deleting text are separate actions, and each action must be performed in order to complete your edit. Deleted text does not go into a register, so you will lose any text which is deleted. Deleted text cannot be placed back into the file except with the restore option, which will restore the most recently deleted text string. Therefore, be sure that you have edited the file with yank and put to save any text you want to move before you begin deleting. Table 7.5 shows the deletion commands.

TABLE 7.4: Yank and Put Commands

Command	Function
*n*Y	Yank *n* lines into a register
*n*yy	Yank *n* lines into a register (same as *n*Y)
*n*p	Place a register after the cursor position for *n* characters
*n*P	Place a register before the cursor position for *n* characters
n]p	Place a register after the cursor position for *n* characters, adjusting indent to current line
n[p	Place a register before the cursor position for *n* characters, adjusting indent to current line
*n*gp	Place a register after the cursor position for *n* characters, but leave the cursor position after the new text

TABLE 7.5: Edit Mode Deletion Commands

Command	Function
x	Deletes character under cursor
dd	Deletes the line in which the cursor is currently located
d	Deletes everything from the cursor location to the end of the current line
:d	Deletes the current line (same as dd)
:d$	Deletes everything from the cursor location to the end of the current line (same as D)
:u	Undoes the last deletion

Search and Replace

One of **vi**'s more powerful aspects is the ability to match patterns in edit mode. Pattern matching means that **vi** searches throughout the file for a text string which matches one entered as a command. When the string is located, the user can either enter insert mode and continue to enter new text or stay in edit mode and replace the text string with a different string.

Suppose that you have written an essay about Unix, but to save time you have typed "un" throughout the file instead. After you finish the essay, use **vi**'s search and replace functions to find each occurrence of the string "un" and replace it with the string "Unix." This is much faster than reading through the entire essay, hoping to catch every abbreviation, and it is far more accurate. Table 7.6 contains the search and replace commands.

TABLE 7.6: Search and Replace Commands

Command	Function
/<*pattern*>	Searches forward from the cursor for the defined pattern
?< *pattern*>	Searches backward from the cursor for the defined pattern
:s/<*pattern*1>/<*pattern*2>	Replaces the first instance of <*pattern*1> with the string <*pattern*2>
:s/<*pattern*1>/<*pattern*2>/g	Replaces all instances of <*pattern*1> with the string <*pattern*2>

It is easy to construct the appropriate command for a search and replace operation. In the essay example in the previous paragraph, issue the command

```
:o/os/un/Unix/g
```

to change all the instances of "un" to the appropriately capitalized name.

Abbreviations and Macros

While the yank, cut, search, and replace tools are valuable **vi** functions, they may not be enough when working with long and complex files. **vi** offers two features which help to automate even the most tedious of documents, such as a lengthy shell script or configuration file. This section introduces abbreviations and macros, two **vi** tools which streamline work with text files.

An abbreviation is a shortcut which represents a longer character string. Just as the nickname "Sue" is a representation of the longer name "Susannah," a **vi** abbreviation allows the user to type a shorter phrase to represent a longer word or combination of words. In the same way, a macro is a short command which stands in for a longer command or string of commands. Instead of typing the same sequence of command strokes over and over, create a macro which will handle the entire sequence with one command.

How to Create an Abbreviation

To create an abbreviation in **vi**, use the **:abbr** command. This command uses the syntax

```
:abbr abbreviation complete-phrase
```

Assume that you attend Midvale Community College and that you must write a set of minutes about the Midvale student council's meeting. To save time, you would like to abbreviate Midvale Community College as "mcc" and Midvale Community College Student Council as "sc". To make these abbreviations, issue the two commands

```
:abbr mcc Midvale Community College
:abbr sc Midvale Community College Student Council
```

In insert mode, these abbreviations can be entered as you type the full text for the file. For example, the sentence "At the sc meeting today, a motion was approved to invite mcc President Angela Bonpensiaro to the annual holiday party" saves several keystrokes. **vi** notices the abbreviations and replaces them with the correct terms, so that the sentence reads "At the Midvale Community College Student Council meeting today, a motion was approved to invite Midvale Community College President Angela Bonpensiaro to the annual holiday party."

The judicious use of abbreviations can save time and keystrokes, but using abbreviations requires some thought. **vi** cannot tell the difference between the intentional use of a word and an abbreviation, so choosing a common word as an abbreviation may cause inadvertent error. For example, the command

```
:abbr an Angela Bonpensiaro
```

would set the word "an" as an abbreviation. Any time the word "an" was typed in a text file, **vi** would substitute the text string "Angela Bonpensiaro." Such an abbreviation might cause a sentence like this: "It was Angela Bonpensiaro unusually rainy day, so I went to Angela Bonpensiaro ATM to get some cash so I could buy Angela Bonpensiaro umbrella."

How to Create a Macro

Just as an abbreviation is shorthand for a longer word or phrase, a macro is shorthand for a longer command or string of commands. Suppose that you want to edit a series of old letters to use them for a new purpose. Because the letters are long and there are a number of them, it would be a bad use of time to retype them all. However, to make the letters applicable, a number of text strings must be found and replaced. For example, every instance of "boys" must be replaced with "children" to make the letters more inclusive.

Instead of issuing the command

```
:o/os/boys/children/g
```

for each letter, create a macro to simplify the process. Assign a particular keystroke combination to that macro, such as "kids". When vi recognizes this combination, the associated command executes.

Create this macro using the **:map!** command, which takes the syntax

:map! *keystroke-combination replacement-text*

as in

```
:map! kids boys/children/g
```

For each letter, you need only type the word "kids" to have **vi** instantly make the substitution throughout the document. To see a list of all current **map!** macros, enter command mode and type the letter Q. Then, enter the word **map!** to see the list.

Note: The **:map!** command works for substitutions done in insert mode. In order to make keystroke combinations that work in insert mode, especially for chains of commands that produce complex behavior, you will need to use the **map** command. **map** takes the same syntax as map!:

```
:map keystroke-combination command-string
```

As with **:map!**, you can see a list of currently active mapped macros by entering command mode, typing the letter Q, and then entering the word **map** to see the list.

The set Command

vi has a number of parameters that control its default behavior. Use these parameters to configure **vi** so that it works most efficiently by setting the value for the parameters using the **set** command. **set** takes the syntax

```
:set argument=value
```

where *argument* is the name of the parameter and *value* is the setting you want that parameter to have.

Some **vi** parameters have only two values: on and off. For these parameters, usually formatting options like autoindent or autowrite, use the syntax

```
set argument
```

or

```
set noargument
```

where *argument* is the name of the parameter. Adding the prefix "no" turns off the parameter, and issuing the name of the parameter turns it on. Table 7.7 shows some of the common user parameters.

vi Run Control Files

While the **:set** command can be used to change the value of a particular parameter during a given **vi** session, it is possible to set parameter values so that they will provide the chosen settings every time **vi** is started. For many formatting parameters, this is extremely useful and will save time in changing user settings each time you use the editor.

Chapter 6: The Shell Environment introduced the concept of run control files, files which manage the way in which a particular program operates. **vi**

TABLE 7.7: vi User Parameters

Parameter	Function
autoindent	Indents each line to match the previous line's left margin
autowrite	Automatically saves the file after certain commands
directory	Specifies the directory which holds the edit buffer (register)
ignorecase	Ignores upper and lower case in pattern matching
list	Displays tabs as ^I and end-of-line characters as $
mesg	Toggles e-mail write permission
number	Shows line numbers
shell	Specifies the Unix shell which appears when the escape sequence :! is used
shiftwidth	Sets tab width
wrapmargin	Sets the maximum line length

uses a run control file to manage parameter settings, including the values of abbreviations and macros which the user has already defined. Using the run control file to manage the **vi** environment is a good way to make using the editor more comfortable and familiar.

Setting Your Preferences in vi

The **vi** run control file is called .exrc, and should be located in your home directory. Should .exrc still not exist after you have started and exited **vi**, you can make the file yourself. Simply open a new file in **vi** and save it with the name .exrc.

Use the .exrc file to contain any commands that you want **vi** to execute automatically when the program starts up. Set commands are stored in this file, as well as any macros or abbreviations that you may have configured. A sample .exrc file might look like this:

```
set list
set noautoindent
set wrapmargin=80
abbr ms microsoft
map ^z :s/boys/children
```

Note that, in the .exrc file, commands are not preceded by the colon. The colon is reserved for commands which are issued in edit mode.

View the .exrc file as you would any other text file. If you want to view the file without making any edits, use the shell commands "less" or "more" to page through the file. If you want to edit the file, open it in a text editor. Be sure to save the file with the same name after you make changes; if the file is saved with a different name, **vi** will not use it at start-up. Saving a copy of the file under a different name is a good idea, though, since you will have a version of your configurations in case of a system crash or a problem with **vi**.

Make a habit of checking your .exrc on a regular basis. Clean out any macros or abbreviations that you no longer use. This frees up those keystroke combinations and abbreviations for use in other situations. It also makes **vi** start faster, since the editor must parse every line of .exrc when it starts, even if there are unused entries.

Saving and Exiting vi

vi's exit command is not particularly intuitive until you've worked with **vi** long enough to understand how its command syntax works. The simplest way to quit **vi** is to get into edit mode and issue the command **:q** (note the colon).

However, using **:q** is not the safest way to exit **vi**. That command forces **vi** to quit immediately without saving its work, which is a good way to lose the results of your labors. Luckily, most installations of **vi** will show a warning message before quitting on an unsaved file, giving you the opportunity to save the document. Should you have a nonstandard installation, though, you may suffer the consequences.

A better habit to establish includes the use of a save command before exiting the editor. The **vi** save command is **:w**, which causes the editor to write the file to the disk. In fact, you can combine the save and quit commands into one keystroke combination which will handle both actions. Simply issue the command **:wq** in edit mode when finished with your **vi** session. **vi** will write the current file to the disk, prompting if a filename is needed, and then close down. A good way to remember this command is "w for write, q for quit." Table 7.8 contains some other commonly-used commands for saving files and exiting **vi**.

TABLE 7.8: Save and Exit Commands

Command	Function
:w	Saves file by writing it to the disk
:q	Quits vi
:wq	Saves the file, then quits vi
:q!	Forces a quit, allowing you to leave vi without saving the current file
ZZ	Saves and quits (same as :wq)

Summary

On machines running Unix, the appearance of text is controlled by the ASCII standard, which determines how individual characters are displayed and processed. In order to work with text under Unix, you need to use a text editor. There are two major types of text editors: line editors and visual editors. The vi text editor is a visual editor, and is the most widely-found editor on Unix systems regardless of the Unix variant being used.

The vi editor operates in two modes: insert and edit. Each mode has its own set of commands which allows you to perform common text management tasks. With vi, you can cut and paste sections of text, replace or identify particular strings of text, or move through a given file rapidly and accurately. Even though vi may seem confusing at first, knowing the basics of the editor is a critical skill. Should your system crash or should you need to use a rescue diskette, vi will probably be the only editor available to fix the text files which control your computer's operation.

Review Questions

1. What is the definition of "text" in a Unix context? Why are text standards important?
2. What is the difference between a text editor and a word processor? What are the strengths and weaknesses of each program?
3. How does a visual text editor differ from a line text editor? What does "visual" mean in this context?
4. Explain the difference between **vi**'s two modes, and the advantages to the editor's mode system.
5. Why does **vi**'s edit mode include cursor movement commands when the keyboard arrow keys produce the same result? What are the advantages of keystroke combinations?
6. Define "register." How do **vi**'s edit commands make use of the register?
7. Why does **vi** use five different delete commands? In what situation is each command most useful?
8. Explain how to use **vi**'s pattern search functions to identify a particular line of text somewhere in the file.
9. What is the difference between an abbreviation and a macro? Provide several examples of each function.
10. What mechanism is used to alter **vi**'s behavior and user environment? What are some commonly used parameters?
11. How would you save two different versions of the same file? What is the safest way to exit **vi**?

Exercises

1. Start **vi** with an empty file. Type a letter to your instructor, explaining your motivation for learning Unix. Make sure that the letter has at least three paragraphs. Save this letter as unix-letter and exit **vi**.
2. Open the unix-letter file. Use **vi**'s yank and put commands to move the second paragraph above the first paragraph. Delete the third paragraph. Save the file as edited-unix-letter and exit.
3. Open the unix-letter file again. Use **vi**'s search and replace tools to find every occurrence of the word "Unix" in your letter. Replace it with "Linux," save the file as linux-letter, and exit **vi**. Open the linux-letter file, and use search and replace to change "Linux" to "BSD." Save the file as bsd-letter and exit.
4. Open a new file and save it as sample-exrc. Using your account's existing .exrc file as a model, add or edit at least five environment or behavior parameters to the file. Next, create several abbreviations and macros directly in the sample-exrc file.

CHAPTER 8

Other Text Editors

IN THIS CHAPTER

1. GNU Emacs
2. Pico
3. joe
4. NEdit

The **vi** text editor, introduced in Chapter 7, is found on almost every Unix variant by default. Because of this widespread availability, it is important for every Unix user to have at least basic familiarity with the editor in case it is the only editor available in a stripped-down environment or in an emergency. Minimal **vi** skills allow users to repair damaged files in order to get back to their normal user environment.

Although **vi** skills are important, many users find the editor to be unintuitive or difficult to use. Luckily for these users, there are a number of other text editors available as well. These editors range from those nearly as popular as **vi** to some which are sparsely used or in new development. Some people use one editor for programming tasks and another editor to work with text files.

Four text editors are introduced in this chapter. These editors appeal to different audiences and have different command and function sets. However, they are all accessible to an average user and can be utilized both for programming and for regular text work. The GNU Emacs text editor is the most complex of these four, and the Pico editor the simplest. The **joe** editor feels like a blend of Pico and Emacs, while NEdit represents the growing selection of graphical text editors.

Even more than shell environments, the selection of a text editor is a personal choice. The "look and feel" of different editors varies widely, so it is useful to try as many editors as possible to find the one that is most comfortable. If any of these editors are unavailable on your system, you can download them from a Unix file archive and install the programs in your user account.

GNU Emacs

As its name suggests, the GNU Emacs text editor is an integral part of the GNU operating system described in Chapter 1, What Is Unix? In fact, Emacs was the first part of the GNU system to be created. If any text editor can make a legitimate challenge to **vi** as the most important editor, Emacs is it. GNU Emacs is not installed by default on all Unix systems, but those who would like to try it can download it from http://www.gnu.org.

Note: The proper name of the editor is GNU Emacs, though the first component is often dropped in casual conversation.

The main attraction of Emacs is its raw power. Emacs allows the user to edit several files at the same time, move back and forth between files, cut and paste text between files, use shell commands from within the Emacs environment, and a host of other actions not possible in most text editors released before Emacs (and many others released after it). In fact, if a user is so inclined, Emacs can be used as an entire user environment, nearly replacing a regular shell environment. This is managed by running a regular shell session within an Emacs buffer; though such a method is not really more useful than running a separate shell process outside Emacs, this capability could be used in certain programs.

Unfortunately, the price of this power is a rather steep learning curve. In addition to being a powerful program, Emacs is complicated and has a somewhat obscure user interface. Emacs is also a large program, both in terms of the disk space it occupies and the memory it requires. This is generally not much of a problem, but users on old or limited hardware may experience problems with this editor. Figure 8.1 shows output from the **top** command, with an Emacs process consuming a significant portion of processor cycles.

Starting GNU Emacs

Start Emacs as you would any other program, by issuing the command

```
emacs
```

at the system prompt. The editor will open with a blank screen, as shown in Figure 8.2. To open Emacs for work on a previously saved text file, issue the command as

```
emacs filename
```

Despite having been developed as a text-based program, GNU Emacs has also been modified to run under the X Window System, which allows Unix variants to run graphical user interfaces. (X is introduced in Chapter 18, The X Window System.) In this chapter, Emacs is described in its text form; therefore, if you are working on a system that uses graphical interfaces, you will need to invoke Emacs without its X modifications. Do so with the command

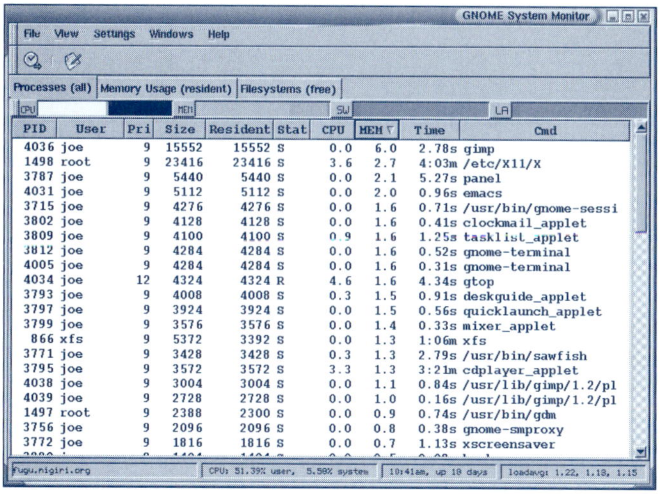

FIGURE 8.1 GNU Emacs consumes a large portion of processor resources.

FIGURE 8.2 The GNU Emacs text editor.

```
emacs --no-windows
```

Unlike **vi**, users of Emacs do not have to shift between separate insert and edit modes. Instead, all commands are issued as keystrokes or keystroke combinations, and the program then determines the appropriate mode for the command. That is, each time you press a key in Emacs, you are sending a command. This is actually how all programs work; when you press the A key, your keyboard sends a command to print the A character on the screen. It is particularly important to remember this concept in Emacs, however, since keystrokes can be interpreted both as text and as command at the same time. For simple cursor movement and text editing, the arrow keys and backspace key work normally. Other functions require specific commands, described in the following sections.

The GNU Emacs Screen

The Emacs screen is divided into three parts. The biggest part of the screen is the text area. At the bottom of the screen are the *mode line* and the *mini-buffer*. These areas provide important information about Emacs and about the file being worked on.

The *mode line* is the line highlighted in reverse color. If your terminal displays in black and white, the mode line will be black text on white background, rather than the normal white text on black background. The mode line displays information about the current buffer, such as its name and the segment of the file that is currently being displayed. The information in the mode line changes according to what work is being done in the window.

Directly below the mode line is the *mini-buffer*. The mini-buffer stores an echo of the most recent commands. Prompts will appear in the mini-buffer, as will other information and messages from the editor. Track your recent actions by keeping an eye on the mini-buffer.

Control and Meta Sequences

The use of control and meta sequences is the main difference between Emacs and other text editors. These sequences are managed with the Ctrl and Alt (or Esc) keys. Ctrl is called the control key because it is used in combination with other keystrokes and does not have functions assigned to it alone. The meta key is Alt on most keyboards; some older terminal keyboards may use the Esc key as the meta key.

In Emacs documentation style, keystroke combinations using these keys take a particular format: *X-x*. The Ctrl key is abbreviated as C, and the meta key as M. Thus, the keystroke combination of Ctrl and a, sometimes expressed as Ctrl+a, is expressed under Emacs as C-a. The keystroke combination of Alt and c is expressed as M-c. Tables 8.1 and 8.2 show common control and meta sequences used to maneuver through text files and manage the Emacs screen.

Buffers

Another difference between Emacs and other text editors is that most other programs hide much of their work behind the user interface. Emacs leaves everything out in the open, which adds extra elements to the user experience. One of these elements is the *buffer*, a concept common to all text editors but which is hidden in every editor but Emacs.

The buffer is a safety valve. When a user works on a file in an editor, she is not working directly on the file as it was last saved to the disk. Rather the file has been copied into the editor's memory. The file in memory is called the buffer, using a programming term which refers to any area of memory which is set aside for a program's working data. When the file is saved, the contents of the buffer replace the data previously saved on the hard disk under that file name.

TABLE 8.1: GNU Emacs Cursor Movement Commands

Sequence	Function
C-b	Cursor moves back one character
C-f	Cursor moves forward one character
M-b	Cursor moves back one word
M-f	Cursor moves forward one word
M-a	Cursor moves to beginning of current sentence
M-e	Cursor moves to end of current sentence
M-‘	Cursor moves to beginning of current paragraph
M-”	Cursor moves to end of current paragraph
C-v	Window scrolls to next screen of document
M-v	Window scrolls to previous screen of document
M-<	Cursor moves to beginning of buffer
M->	Cursor moves to end of buffer

TABLE 8.2: GNU Emacs Window Management Commands

Sequence	Function
C-x 0	Current window closes
C-x 1	Current window remains open but all other windows close
C-M-v	Other window scrolls to next screen of buffer
M-x shrink-window	Current window shrinks vertically
C-x ^	Current window grows vertically
C-x -	Current window shrinks horizontally
C-x "	Current window grows horizontally
C-x 4 b	Other window selects buffer
C-x 4 C-o	Other window displays buffer
C-x 4 f	Locates a file in other window

To read the contents of a saved file into an Emacs buffer, issue the control sequence

```
C-x C-f
```

A prompt will appear, asking for the file name. Enter the file name and press Enter. The contents of that file will appear in the Emacs buffer.

It is possible to work with several Emacs buffers at the same time. Use the same C-x C-f command to open a second file, then switch between the buffers with the command

```
C-x b
```

If you have more than two buffers open, you will need to use the buffer name to move between the buffers. The buffer name is the same as that of the file open in that buffer. You can see a list of all open buffers at any time by issuing the command

```
C-x C-b
```

Windows

Using buffers in the manner just described will move sequentially from buffer to buffer, but displays only one buffer at a time. It is also possible to show multiple buffers at one time, using the Emacs window function. "Windows," in this sense, does not refer to the type of windows found in graphical user interfaces, but rather to a simple division of the screen into multiple work areas.

Windows can be useful in several situations. One of the most common uses is for a side-by-side comparison of two files, or even of two parts of the same file. The window can be split vertically, as in Figure 8.3, or horizontally, as in Figure 8.4.

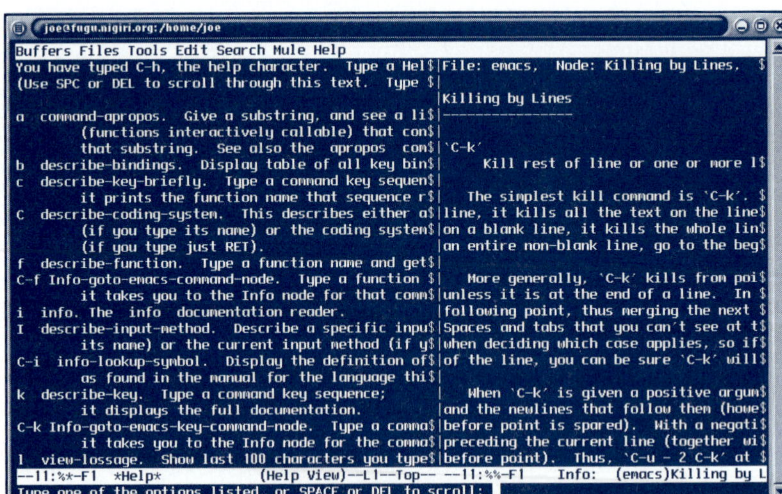

FIGURE 8.3 The GNU Emacs text editor split vertically.

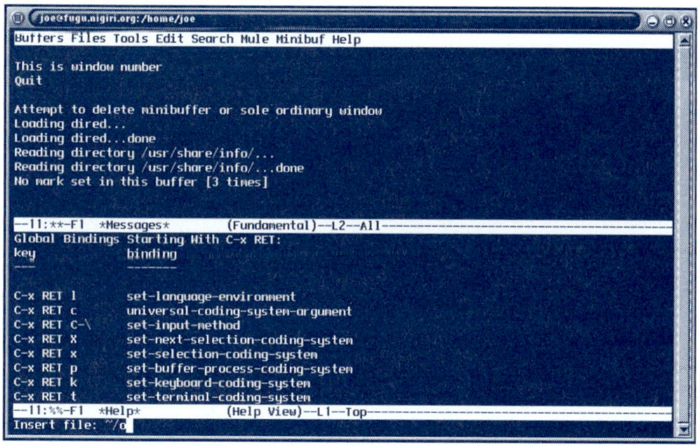

FIGURE 8.4 The GNU Emacs text editor split horizontally.

Once split, you can work within each window as if it is running a separate Emacs process. Move the cursor between windows with the command

```
C-x o
```

Saving and Exiting

Saving a file and exiting Emacs are usually separate processes. To save an Emacs text file, issue the command

```
C-x C-s
```

To save multiple buffers simultaneously, issue the command as

```
C-x s
```

Once all the files have saved, exit the editor with the command

```
C-x C-c
```

However, if you forget to save before you issue the exit command, Emacs will prompt you to save the file(s) first.

Note: The GNU Emacs tutorial, accessed with the command C-h t, is helpful for those who want to learn more about working with this editor.

Pico

For users who find both **vi** and Emacs to be confusing or unintuitive, there are a number of other text editors available. Many of these users find the Pico editor much more to their liking. Pico is an editor developed for use with the

Pine electronic mail program, which is introduced in Chapter 9: Internet Applications.

While Pico lacks some of the features that make **vi** and Emacs so good for programming and other types of heavy-duty editing, it is simple to use and doesn't place much of a strain on system resources. If you work mostly with simple text files, Pico might be a good choice for you.

To start the Pico text editor, simply issue the command

```
pico
```

at the system prompt. To open Pico for work on a specified saved file, issue the command as

pico *filename*

The editor opens, as shown in Figure 8.5. Pico has only one mode, so it is ready for new text or editing as soon as the program opens.

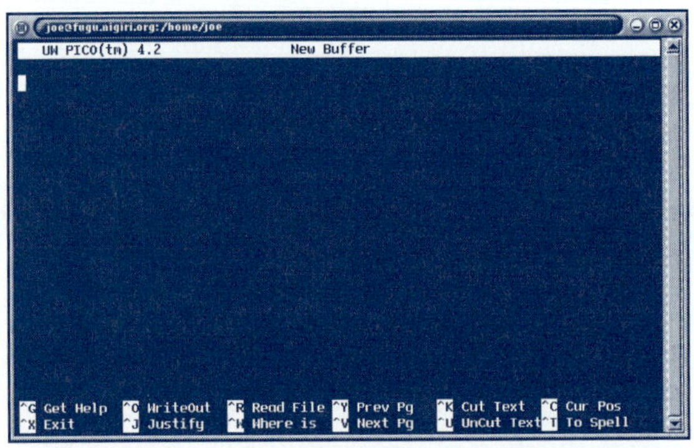

FIGURE 8.5 The Pico text editor.

Pico commands, like those in Emacs, are invoked with a keystroke combination. Unlike Emacs, though, all Pico commands use the Ctrl key, abbreviated with the caret character ^. That is, the command ^x is the same as Ctrl+x or C-x. Use the arrow keys to move the cursor around the file. The backspace key deletes the character immediately to the left of the cursor position.

Along the bottom of the Pico window, there are two rows of text. These rows show the most frequently used commands. Table 8.3 shows all Pico cursor movement and text editing commands.

Note: Users who enjoy working with Pico should try the Pine e-mail reader. Pine is described in Chapter 9, and can be configured both as a mail reader and a news reader. It uses Pico as its native editor, so the user need only learn one set of commands to manage multiple programs.

TABLE 8.3: Pico Commands

Command	Function
^a	Cursor moves to beginning of current line
^e	Cursor moves to end of current line
^f	Cursor moves forward one character
^b	Cursor moves back one character
^n	Cursor moves to next line
^p	Cursor moves to previous line
^v	Window scrolls forward one screen
^y	Window scrolls back one screen
^k	Kills (deletes) current line of text
^u	Restores the last deletion at current cursor location
^j	Justifies current paragraph
^w	Prompts for a text string, then searches for it
^r	Reads contents of another file into current file at current cursor location
^o	Saves (outputs) buffer to a specified text file
^x	Exits Pico
^g	Pico help files
^t	Invokes **ispell**, if installed (a Unix spellchecker)

joe

The **joe** editor is like a cross between Emacs and Pico. Like Emacs, you can use **joe** to work with multiple buffers in multiple windows. Also like Emacs, **joe** has a wide variety of commands which are given in the same sequences as Emacs commands and which are written in the same shorthand. Like Pico, **joe** has only one mode, and has no mode line or mini-buffer.

Open **joe** by issuing the command

```
joe
```

at the system prompt. The editor will appear, as in Figure 8.6. To open **joe** with an existing file, issue the command as

```
joe filename
```

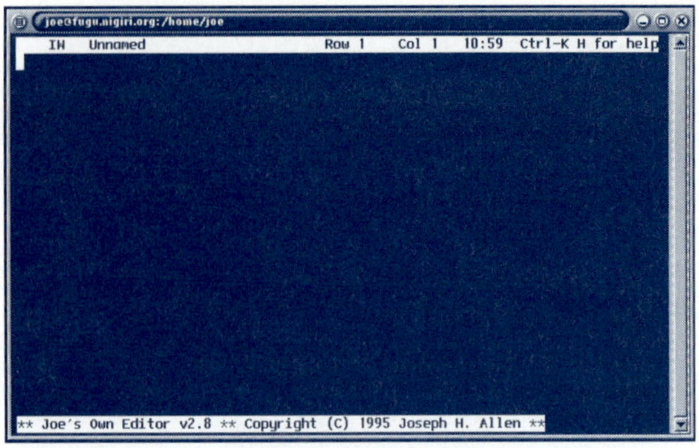

FIGURE 8.6 The joe text editor.

Use the arrow keys to move through the document. **joe** offers more control key sequences than Pico, many of which are shown in Table 8.4.

TABLE 8.4: joe Commands

Command	Function
C-b	Cursor moves one character back
C-f	Cursor moves one character forward
C-p	Cursor moves to previous line
C-n	Cursor moves to next line
C-z	Cursor moves to previous word
C-a	Cursor moves to beginning of line
C-e	Cursor moves to end of line
C-u	Window scrolls back one screen
C-v	Window scrolls forward one screen
C-k u	Cursor moves to beginning of file
C-k v	Cursor moves to end of file
C-d	Delete character at cursor location
C-y	Delete current line
C-w	Delete word to right of cursor
C-o	Delete word to left of cursor
C-j	Delete all text from cursor to end of line
C-_	Undo last text deletion

Continued

TABLE 8.4: joe Commands (continued)

Command	Function
C-^	Redelete last restored deletion
C-k f	Prompts for a text string, then finds it
C-|	Searches for next occurrence of previously searched text string
C-k o	Divides current window in half
C-k g	Current window grows
C-k t	Current window shrinks
C-k n	Cursor moves to window below current window
C-k p	Cursor moves to window above current window
C-c	Current window killed
C-k e	Prompts for file name, then displays specified file in current window
C-k |	Toggles window display between "show all windows" and "show current window"
Esc-y	Restores (yanks) previously deleted text into buffer at current cursor position
C-k'	Shell prompt
C-k !	Executes specified shell command
C-k j	Justifies current paragraph
C-k r	Prompts for file name, then reads file content into current buffer at cursor location
C-k h	**joe** help files
C-k x	Saves file with specified name
C-c	Exits **joe** (kills current window if multiple windows open)

NEdit

For users who work with a Unix variant with a graphical user interface, there are a number of graphical text editors available for installation. One of the best graphical editors is NEdit, which has a clean appearance that does not clutter the desktop and uses relatively little system resources. The main advantage of using a graphical text editor is that the mouse can be used to move the cursor and select text, and also to navigate through a dropdown menu system.

If your graphical user interface offers an icon or an entry in the Start menu for NEdit, click it to start the editor. Otherwise, open a terminal window and issue the command

```
nedit
```

at the system prompt. Like the other editors introduced in this chapter, you can open NEdit with a specific file by issuing the command as

```
nedit filename
```

The editor will open as shown in Figure 8.7.

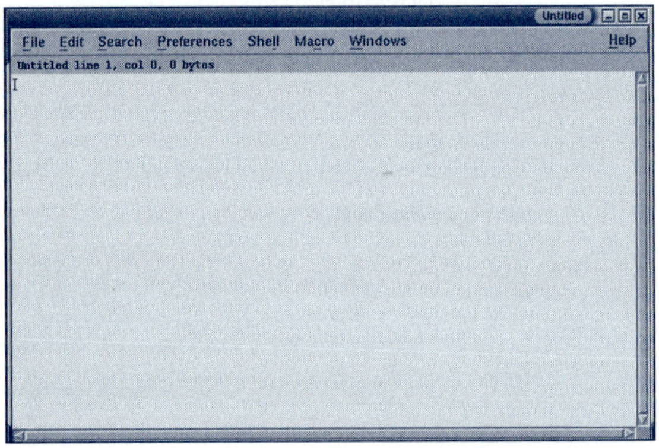

FIGURE 8.7 The NEdit text editor.

The NEdit window is primarily devoted to the text areas. Above the text area is a single-line menu bar. The NEdit menu works like any other graphical menu, and provides better access to more commands than most text-mode editors. The ability to sort commands into individual dropdown menus allowed NEdit's developers to include commands especially useful to programmers, as well as those commands necessary for regular text file work. Tables 8.5 through 8.11 describe the commands available in NEdit's menus.

TABLE 8.5: NEdit File Menu Commands

Command	Function
Close	Closes current buffer
Save	Saves current buffer to specified file
Save As	Saves current buffer to newly specified file
Revert to Saved	Restores buffer to previously saved file contents
Include File	Reads a specified file into buffer at current locaton
Load Macro File	Loads a specified macro file
Load Tags File	Loads a specified index file of tags for programming
Unload Tags File	Removes tags file from program memory
Print	Sends current document to printer
Print Selection	Sends selected text to printer
Exit	Shuts down NEdit process

TABLE 8.6: NEdit Edit Menu Commands

Command	Function
Undo	Deletes previous edit
Redo	Restores previously deleted exit
Cut	Removes selected text, storing it in the cut-buffer
Copy	Copies selected text to the cut-buffer without deletion
Paste	Takes removed text from the cut-buffer and restores it at current cursor location
Paste Column	Formats pasted text as a vertical column
Delete	Removes selected text permanently
Select All	Selects all text in document
Shift Left	Moves entire line one space to the left
Shift Right	Moves entire line one space to the right
Lower Case	Formats selected text in lower case
Upper Case	Formats selected text in upper case
Fill Paragraph	Removes all hidden new-line characters from current paragraph
Insert Form Feed	Inserts hidden form-feed character which serves as a page break for printing, at current cursor location
Insert Control Code	Inserts defined ASCII character at cursor location

TABLE 8.7: NEdit Search Menu Commands

Command	Function
Find	Locate a specified text string
Find Again	Repeat previous search
Find Selection	Finds next occurrence of selected text
Find Incremental	Prompts for a text string and begins searching as soon as the first character is entered; as the string is entered, the search is refined
Replace	Replace one specified text string with another
Replace Again	Repeat previous replace operation
Goto Line Number	Cursor moves to the specified line
Goto Selected	Cursor moves to selected text
Mark	Sets a hidden marker in the text
Goto Mark	Cursor moves to the next marker
Goto Matching ()	Cursor moves to the starting or closing parenthesis in an expression
Find Definition	Searches an associated tags file for the definition of a selected function

TABLE 8.8: NEdit Preferences Menu Commands

Command	Function
Default Settings	User-defined defaults
Save Defaults	Saves current file settings as default
Statistics Line	Displays file information on separate line
Show Line Numbers	Displays line numbers
Language Mode	Offers syntactic assistance for specified programming language
Auto-indent	Defines the method of text indentation
Wrap	Defines the method used to wrap lines
Tabs	Defines width and style of tabs
Text Font	Defines font used to display content
Highlight Syntax	Based on programming syntax, determines programming language being used and highlights syntax errors
Make Backup Copy (.bck)	Toggles automatic backup saving to a file with the .bck suffix and the current file name

Continued

TABLE 8.8: NEdit Preferences Menu Commands (continued)

Command	Function
Incremental Backup	Toggles buffer backup at defined intervals
Show Matching (..)	Toggles colored parentheses when cursor is at a parenthesis, to help find the paired character
Overtype	Toggles overtype and insert mode
Read Only	Will not use or save buffer contents

TABLE 8.9: NEdit Shell Menu Commands

Command	Function
Execute Command	Invokes defined shell command
Execute Command Line	Invokes defined shell command with arguments
Filter Selection	Invokes defined shell command using selected text as target, replacing selected text with output
Cancel Shell Command	Cancels running shell command

TABLE 8.10: NEdit Macro Menu Commands

Command	Function
Learn Keystrokes	Copies user input to save as a macro or as input for the Replay Keystrokes command
Finish Learn	Stop recording keystrokes
Cancel Learn	Delete recorded keystrokes
Replay Keystrokes	Repeat stored keystrokes
Repeat	Repeat last replay
Complete Word	Fills in remaining characters based on initial characters
Fill Sel. W/char	Fills selected area with specified ASCII character
Quote Mail Reply	Adds the > character at start of each selected line
Unquote Mail Reply	Strips > characters

TABLE 8.11: NEdit Windows Menu Commands

Command	Function
Split Window	Divides current window into two panes, permitting two simultaneous views of the buffer
Close Pane	Closes the buffer of the active window, thus closing the pane

Note: Even though NEdit takes advantage of the graphical user interface, it is still only a text editor. It is not a word processor, so fancy formatting, fonts, and other visual and graphical options are not available. If you need a word processor for a Unix machine, investigate StarOffice for multiple platforms or WordPerfect for Linux, which has all the features found in WordPerfect for Windows or Macintosh.

Summary

Although users need basic familiarity with the **vi** text editor in the event of an emergency or the lack of any other installed editor, many find **vi** to be too complicated or unintuitive for daily use. There are a number of other text editors which these users may prefer. These other editors have a range of functions and commands which make them suitable for various situations and user bases.

GNU Emacs and **vi** are roughly equal in popularity. Emacs is a large and complicated program that can actually be used as a shell environment since it has so many internal functions. Although Emacs is difficult to learn, users appreciate its power when working on complicated documents. The editor can work on multiple files at one time, or can display different sections of the same file in adjacent windows.

Pico and **joe** are text editors which are simpler than either Emacs or **vi**. The Pico editor was developed as part of a simplified e-mail reader, Pine. It uses a small set of commands and has a single user mode, and is best suited for simple scripts and text work. The **joe** editor is a bit more complex than Pico, but also has a single mode and a limited set of commands. Both offer friendly user interfaces.

Graphical text editors are increasingly popular, as they blend basic editor functions with an interface which uses familiar dropdown menus and allows mouse input. The NEdit graphical editor includes a range of commands especially helpful to programmers. A graphical editor is usually included in a graphical desktop interface like KDE or Gnome.

Review Questions

1. What are the main features of the GNU Emacs text editor?
2. Why does Emacs consume so many system resources?
3. What is the function of the mode line and the mini-buffer?
4. Define the control and meta keys and their purpose.
5. Explain the structure of Emacs commands.
6. Explain the buffer concept.
7. How is the buffer handled in Emacs? How is it managed in other editors and word processors?
8. Explain the difference between windows in Emacs and windows in a graphical user environment.
9. What are the features of the Pico text editor?
10. Who is the intended user base of Pico?
11. What are the features of the **joe** text editor?
12. How does **joe** differ from Pico?
13. What are the advantages of a graphical text editor?
14. What features does NEdit offer programmers?
15. What is the difference between a text editor and a word processor?

Exercises

1. Open the GNU Emacs text editor and enter several screens of text. Using the commands in Tables 8.1 and 8.2, move the cursor through the document, open new buffers, and split the screen into windows. What are your impressions of the editor? What are the disadvantages and advantages of Emacs? Would you choose Emacs as your regular editor?
2. Open the GNU Emacs tutorial with the command C-h t and follow the steps. Describe each step of the tutorial and the skills that you learned. Did the tutorial help familiarize you with additional Emacs commands? Has it changed your opinion about the editor?
3. Open the Pico text editor and enter several screens of text. Using the commands described in Table 8.3, navigate through the document and work with the various editor functions. What is your impression of Pico, and what do you see as its advantages and disadvantages? Would you select this editor as your regular program?
4. Open the **joe** text editor and enter several screens of text. Using the commands described in Table 8.4, navigate through the document and work with the various editor functions. What is your impression of **joe**, and what do you see as its advantages and disadvantages? Would you select this editor as your regular program?
5. If you have access to a graphical user environment with a text editor installed, click the editor's icon or select its entry in the Start menu. Enter several screens of text. If you have opened NEdit, use the commands described in Tables 8.5 through 8.11 to navigate through the document and work with the various editor functions. If you are working with a different graphical editor, what are the differences between it and NEdit as described in this chapter? What is your impression of the editor, and what do you see as its advantages and disadvantages? Would you select this editor as your regular program?
6. Write a comparison of the text editors you have tested in this chapter, as well as **vi**. Describe the functions and user environments which are most appealing to you or which you think to be the most important, and those which you do not like. Provide a description of the ideal user base for each editor.

Ethernet has two generations [illegible]

Hubs

[illegible]

Routers

Routers are another [illegible] piece of equipment. The purpose of a router is to connect between [illegible] network and an external network such as the Internet. [illegible]

Routers also often have [illegible]

Cable and DSL

[illegible]

Cable modems are small routers that connect an Ethernet network [illegible]

CHAPTER 9

Internet Applications

IN THIS CHAPTER

1. Electronic Mail
2. Electronic mail clients
3. The World Wide Web
4. Web browsers
5. USENET News
6. News readers

The first eight chapters of this text provided an introduction to Unix itself and to the basic commands and programs which allow the user to begin work on a Unix machine. The next three chapters introduce Unix networking, the element that makes Unix so powerful and seamless across groups of computers, whether a small network of two or three machines or the countless machines that make up the Internet.

Much of the software that contributed to the development of the Internet was developed on Unix machines. Because of this, Unix's networking features have been an integral part of the operating system for many years. In contrast, Windows95 was the first version of Microsoft Windows to contain integrated networking functions. At their core, personal operating systems are just that: personal. Networking is an adjunct to their normal single-user focus. Under Unix, however, networking is an essential component of the operating system. Many of the same mechanisms are used to work on a single machine as are used to work on machines across a room or across the country; whether you are logged in remotely or while sitting at the machine, the same commands are used to move through directories, use text-based applications, and other regular tasks.

To introduce these networking concepts, we begin with the most popular use of networking: Internet applications. These applications are designed to transport and view particular data types. Some Internet applications are user-oriented, like Web browsers; others are administrative, like fetchmail. In Chapter 10, Networking I and Chapter 11, Networking II, you will learn more about the concepts and mechanisms which underlie these popular applications and other Unix network use.

Electronic Mail

Since the Internet was first developed (as DARPAnet), electronic mail has been the most popular application. The concept of sending a text message from one machine to another is not limited to electronic mail; there is a native messaging function under many Unix variants, but those messages print immediately to the recipient's screen and require that the recipient be there to get the message. Electronic mail, however, will wait patiently until it is opened and read.

Electronic Mail Protocols

Like everything else in the world of computer networking, the exchange of electronic mail between computers is governed by a *protocol.* A protocol is an exact description of the way in which a particular exchange of information must take place. The protocol specifies the type of information which one computer must send to another machine, and the exact format in which that information must be given.

The Post Office Protocol, or POP, and the Internet Message Access Protocol, or IMAP, are the two most popular protocols governing the way in which electronic mail clients and servers communicate with each other. The *client* program is the user access program, while the *server* is the administrative program which collects and distributes all mail messages for a given system. A third protocol, the Simple Mail Transport Protocol, or SMTP, manages the manner in which servers communicate directly.

fetchmail

Although some Unix mail applications allow users to retrieve mail directly from a remote mail server, others do not. These readers can access mail only from a *local* mail directory, one located on the same machine as the mail reader. If a system administrator has installed such a reader on his system, he—or the individual user—must also run a program which retrieves mail messages from a remote mail server and makes them available on the local machine for local use.

The program used to manage remote mail retrieval is called **fetchmail**. **fetchmail** was introduced in Chapter 1, What Is Unix?, as it was Eric Raymond's experiment in writing open source software. The **fetchmail** program retrieves mail messages from a remote POP or IMAP server and brings them back to its home machine, delivering the messages to the local mail directory where users can access them. If you are not sure whether your mail client requires you to run **fetchmail**, ask your system administrator.

To run **fetchmail**, you must know four pieces of information:

- the name of your remote mail server
- your user name on the mail server machine
- your password on the mail server machine
- the e-mail protocol in use

Once you know this data, create a file in your home directory called **.fetchmailrc**. Enter the information in this format:

```
poll <mail.server.name>
proto <protocol>
user <yourusername>
pass <yourserverpassword>
```

A typical .fetchmailrc file might look like this:

```
poll mail.bigcc.edu
proto pop3
user criswilson
pass bAttl3sh1p
```

Save the file and exit your text editor.

You must set a specific set of permissions on this file. Because your mail server password is saved in plain text, leaving the file accessible means that anyone who reads it will be able to access the server and intercept your mail. Issue this set of commands to restrict access as tightly as possible:

```
chmod a-rwx .fetchmailrc
chmod u+rw .fetchmailrc
chmod ug+x .fetchmailrc
```

Consult Chapter 4, The File System, if you need to refresh your understanding of file permissions.

Once .fetchmailrc is properly defined, you can run the program by issuing the command

```
fetchmail
```

at the system prompt. You will need to issue this command every time you want to check your mail.

If this seems onerous to you, **fetchmail** has an automation option which causes the program to run silently in the background, accessing the mail server at regular intervals and downloading any new messages. This option is set with the –d flag, which takes a numeric argument expressing the number of seconds between "gets." For example, the command

```
fetchmail -d 360
```

causes **fetchmail** to contact the mail server every six minutes, or 360 seconds. Issuing the command in this way means that **fetchmail** will run constantly in the background until you stop it with the command

```
fetchmail -q
```

or until the process is killed by some other means.

The $MAIL Variable

Your electronic mail delivery should now be working properly, whether through your system administrator's method of mail management or your own installation of **fetchmail**. No matter how it got there, your mail messages should be stored in a local mail directory. To find the correct location, check the value of the $MAIL environment variable with the command

```
echo $MAIL
```

The output will look something like this:

```
/var/spool/mail/username
```

If you don't get a response from the echo command, ask your system administrator where your mail *spool* is located. A spool is a directory where incoming messages are stored. Assign that path name as the value for your personal $MAIL variable by placing an appropriate line in your shell's run control file. For the bash shell, issue the command

```
export MAIL="/var/spool/mail/username"
```

replacing *username* with your actual user ID. It is important to have this variable properly defined so that your personal mail client will look in the appropriate location for your mail. If the value is not correct, you won't know that you have mail.

Electronic Mail Clients

While mail can be read directly from the spool, it is not the preferred solution. Electronic mail clients offer a text editor, easy save options including nested folders, and other basic functions which make mail management much easier than reading the straight data feed. Reading mail from the spool may also cause the message format to be corrupted, so that messages cannot be displayed later in a mail client if desired.

Most Unix installations include the very basic program **mail**. **mail** can either be used interactively or run as a standalone program. The **mail** program is not particularly user-friendly and it does not have a wide array of features, so most system administrators install other programs to make mail management easier. These electronic mail readers come in both text-based and graphical formats.

MAIL

Should you find yourself in a situation where **mail** is the only mail client available to you, you can use this basic program to manage incoming and outgoing mail. However, this program is not widely used as a primary mail client, with most users preferring one of the more advanced clients described below. As with the text editor **vi**, though, it is good to know the basics of **mail** so that you can still access your e-mail if you are on a machine with limited software and have no access to other mail clients.

To check mail with the **mail** program, issue the command

```
mail
```

at the shell prompt. The program will either display a "no new mail" message, as shown in Figure 9.1, or will show a list of messages in your incoming mail folder. You can read a message by entering the message number.

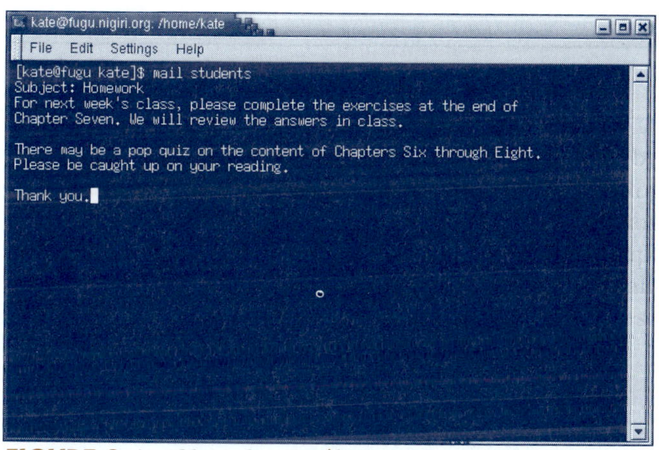

FIGURE 9.1 Use the mail command to check for new incoming messages.

To compose a new message, you must start at the shell prompt. Issue the command

```
mail recipient@address
```

The mail program opens, and a Subject: line appears. Enter the subject of your message and press Enter. The cursor then moves to a blank line. Compose your message, as shown in Figure 9.2, pressing Enter at the end of each line. When you have finished the body of the message, press Enter to get a new line, then press the keystroke combination Ctrl+d to send the message.

FIGURE 9.2 Composing a message in mail is quite simple.

ELM

One of the oldest mail clients is called Elm. Elm is an acronym for ELectronic Mail. To start Elm, issue the command

```
elm
```

at the system prompt. The mail reader appears, as in Figure 9.3.

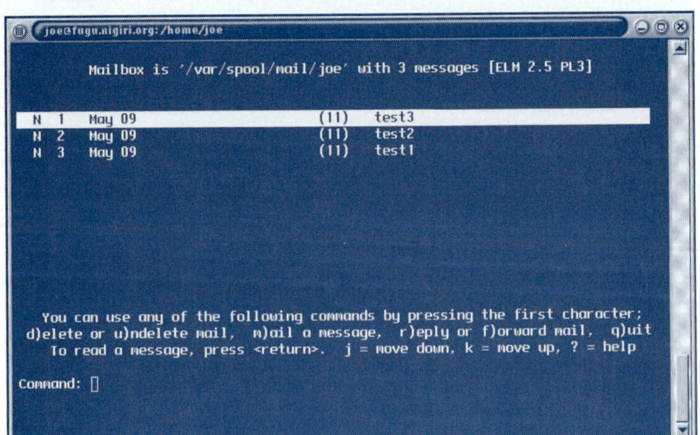

FIGURE 9.3 The ELM e-mail client is an excellent way to manage incoming mail.

Configuring Elm

Elm has a large number of configuration options which modify its behavior. To set the most basic options, press the **o** key at the main Elm prompt to invoke the **options** command. A list of options, with associated values, appears. Type the letter associated with the parameter you want to change; the cursor will move to the appropriate entry, where you can change the value.

For example, you can change the default Elm editor from this screen. Changes made here will not affect your general shell environment variables, so you could select Pico as your Elm editor but use vi in your normal shell work. Replace the path name of the current editor with the path name of the editor you want to use. Press the Enter key to set the value and return to the options prompt. Edit as many values as you like, then press the **>** key to save your changes. Press the **i** key to leave the options menu and return to the main Elm screen.

If you wish to do more advanced configurations, you must edit the Elm run control file. This file is stored in a subdirectory of your home directory, using the path /.elm/.elmrc. The .elm directory is created when you run Elm for the first time. If you have not made changes in the Elm option menu, you may not have an .elmrc file yet. This means that Elm is using the systemwide configuration file, usually stored at /usr/lib/elm/elmrc-info, but possibly at another location depending on your Unix variant. Locate the file with the command

```
whereis elmrc-info
```

The path name will print to the screen. When you make changes on the Elm options menu, Elm copies this file into your .elm subdirectory and renames it .elmrc.

Once the .elmrc file exists in your user account, you can edit it with a text editor. The file is too long to reproduce here, but it is well commented and easy to understand. A sample from the file looks like this:

```
# Would you like to be asked for Carbon-Copy addresses #
when sending a message?
### askcc = ON
```

The hashmarks at the beginning of the line indicate that the line is a comment and is not to be interpreted as program data when the .elmrc file is parsed at start-up. Because the actual option line is also preceded by three hashmarks, the option itself is not active and Elm will not prompt for cc: addresses when a new message is sent. Make the value active by removing the hashmarks and change the value if desired, as in:

```
# Would you like to be asked for Carbon-Copy addresses
# when sending a message?
askcc = OFF
```

Save the file and exit the editor. The next time you run Elm, it will parse your personal .elmrc and adopt any settings you have changed.

PINE

Another popular Unix electronic mail client is called PINE. Although the documentation does not confirm this, the general assumption is that PINE is an acronym for "Pine Is Not Elm." PINE is integrated with the Pico text editor. Though PINE will work with other editors if the configuration is changed, users who are comfortable with Pico will find PINE very easy to learn and use.

Start PINE by issuing the command

```
pine
```

at the shell prompt. The client opens, as shown in Figure 9.4. The opening PINE screen contains a menu of options; move up and down the list with the arrow keys, and press Enter to select a particular option. The L key opens the mail folders screen, which shows the default program folders as well as any folders which you have created to store saved messages. The Inbox folder contains incoming mail.

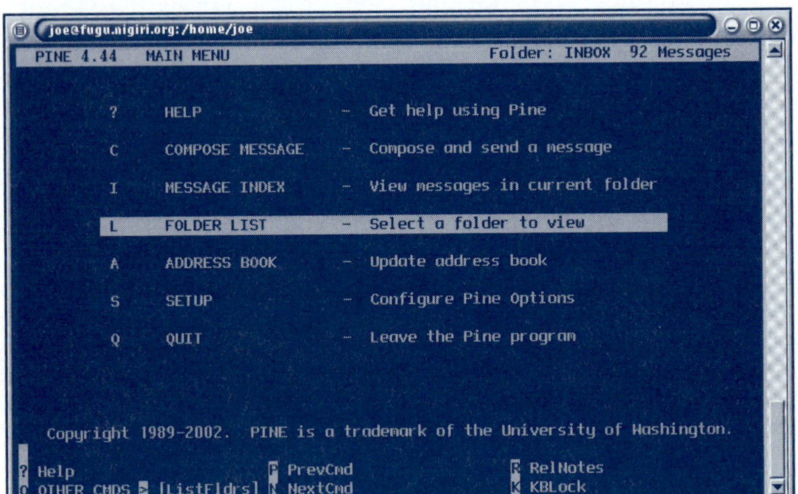

FIGURE 9.4 The PINE e-mail client offers a range of editing tools, as well as an integrated news reader, and uses the Pico text editor.

The Inbox folder contains a list of messages stored in the mail spool. Both read and unread messages are listed here; new messages have an N next to their subject. Move up and down the list with the arrow keys, and press Enter to open a selected message.

At the bottom of the screen, there are two rows which contain several commands. These rows are *context-sensitive*, meaning that the commands shown will change depending on the current task you are doing. Commands shown while you are reading messages will be different from commands shown while you compose a new message or when you are working with the Address Book. PINE commands are usually issued as keystroke combinations using the Ctrl key, just as commands are issued in the Pico text editor.

To compose a new message, issue the c command. This opens the Pico editor, unless you have defined another editor in your PINE run control files. The commands across the bottom of the screen will change to reflect basic Pico commands. When you have finished entering the text of your message, issue the ^x command. PINE asks whether you want to send the message or not; press the Enter key to send the message.

There are extensive help and tutorial files available from the main PINE menu. PINE can also be configured as a news reader, and offers an excellent folder-based method of organizing saved messages. The Address Book function both saves messages and allows you to create address groups to send messages to a large group of recipients with one address, rather than typing each address individually.

Configuring PINE

Although PINE has a set of run control files like most other programs, you should never need to access these files directly. The integrated configuration utility in PINE contains almost every user-configurable variable in the run control files, and is easy to use.

To configure PINE, select the Setup option from the main PINE menu. Enter an addition command, chosen from the rows at the bottom of the screen, to define the task you want to perform. Usually, this is the C, or "Config," option. This command opens a screen containing the various parameters available for definition. Use the arrow keys to scroll through the list until you find the desired option. Press the Enter key to select the variable, and then enter the value you want the variable to have. If the variable is an ON/OFF choice, pressing Enter will automatically change the value to its opposite.

Graphical Electronic Mail Programs

A number of programs are available to manage electronic mail within graphical user environments. PINE or Elm will work just as well within a graphical environment as within a text environment, run within a terminal window, but some users prefer a mail reader written specifically for graphical use. If you prefer a text mail reader, though, there is no reason to change when you change your user environment.

Graphical electronic mail clients provide point-and-click mouse access to messages, and offer functions which eliminate the need to memorize commands.

In addition, it is often possible to configure these programs with mail server information so that there is no need for a program like fetchmail. Of course, these programs can also be configured to read mail from a local mail directory which is supplied by fetchmail.

Most graphical mail clients operate in more or less the same way, so only one program is described here. Should you have access to a different graphical mail client, take this description as an example and use the program's documentation and help files to learn how to work with your specific software. If you have ever used a graphical mail client under Windows or on a Macintosh, you already know the basics of the analogous program under Unix. Graphical mail clients include KMail, Balsa, Netscape Mail, and Ximian Evolution, though there are many others in Unix software archives.

The graphical mail client described in this chapter is KMail, which is the native mail client provided with the KDE graphical desktop environment. The current version at the time this book was written is 1.0.29, but the program is under active development; future versions may differ in the specifics of their commands or operation.

We assume that you are using the KDE desktop and that KMail is installed. KMail can be started in one of three ways: click the KMail icon on the desktop, select the KMail entry in the Start menu, or open a terminal window and issue the command

```
kmail
```

at the system prompt. The editor appears, as shown in Figure 9.5.

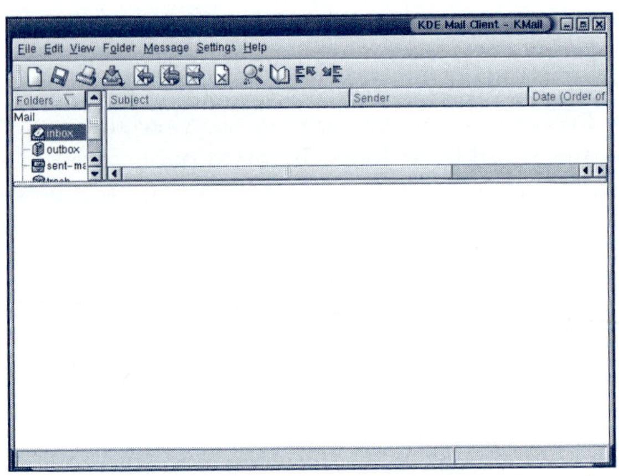

FIGURE 9.5 Most window managers and graphical desktop systems offer a graphical e-mail client, such as KDE's Kmail.

The KMail screen has a menu bar, an icon bar, and three *panes*, or distinct window areas. The upper left pane provides access to KMail's sub-folders. These folders include the Inbox, the Outbox, a sent-mail folder, and the Local folder used to store messages that you want to save. This pane also contains the Trash Can, where deleted messages are stored in case you need to recover them. Select a folder by clicking on it; the name of the current folder is highlighted.

The pane to the right displays the messages stored in the highlighted folder. If the highlighted folder is the Inbox, then the messages displayed will be those in the mail spool. The largest pane, below the message pane, displays the body of the current message selected in the message pane.

To compose a new message, click on the "Compose New Message" icon in the icon bar or select the "New Composer" option from the File menu. The KMail composer window opens, showing the message headers and a large text entry window. Fill in the headers and enter your message. To send the message, click the "Send" icon or select the "Send" entry from the File menu.

The World Wide Web

In the past ten years, the World Wide Web has exploded in popularity. The Web was developed by Tim Berners-Lee in the late 1980s as a way to share files and data without having to download individual files or use a primitive file-sharing program called **archie**. In addition, the Web made it possible to share photos, sound files, and other file types integrated into a single document.

Although the Web and the software which supports it were developed in a Unix environment, the development of a graphical Web browser for Unix lagged behind the development of similar programs for Windows and Macintosh. In recent years, programmers have focused on Unix graphical browsers, and now Unix users have several choices, some of which are the same programs used on Windows and Macintosh platforms.

Lynx

It might seem strange to think it possible to browse the Web with a text-based program. After all, most people think, the Web is a graphics-intensive environment, and a text-based browser can't show those elements of each Web page visited. This is actually something of a misunderstanding. While the Web integrates a large amount of graphics, it is usually not necessary to see the graphics in order to use a particular page. This is especially true if the page's authors have followed the HTML protocol and have labeled each image with text tags ("ALT tags," for those familiar with HTML).

Unix offers a powerful, yet small, text-based browser called Lynx. Lynx displays the textual content of any Web page, along with any text tags attached to the image and sound files. Lynx also presents hyperlinks and form fields. As long as the page is programmed properly, Lynx should display it.

Note: Pages which are not programmed according to the HTML protocol will display badly or will not come up at all in Lynx. This is unfortunate, since the same restrictions found in Lynx also apply to adaptive browsers used by people with physical restrictions, including blindness.

Start Lynx by issuing the command

```
lynx
```

at the shell prompt. It will appear, as shown in Figure 9.6. You can also open Lynx to a specific Web page, by issuing the command with the URL as an argument, as in

```
lynx http://www.mcgraw-hill.com
```

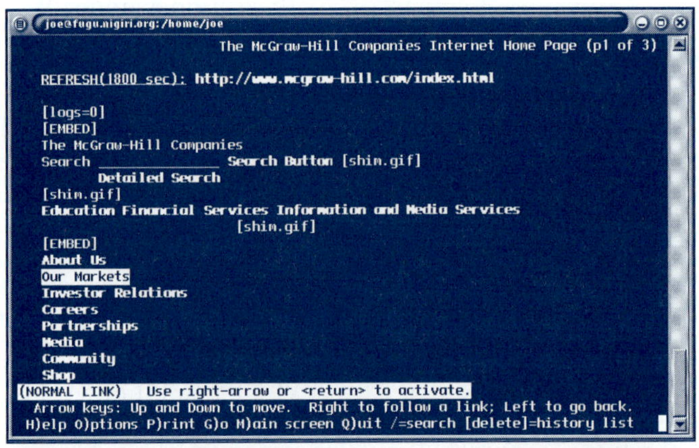

FIGURE 9.6 **The lynx Web browser is text-only, but offers fast and efficient Web browsing and can also be used to incorporate Web data into shell programs.**

Obviously, since Lynx is limited to the single font available to the terminal, it cannot reproduce all the formatting found in the average Web page. Nevertheless, Lynx attempts to convey the sense of the page as accurately as possible by using bold type, underlined type, and different colors (if the terminal is enabled for color). Hyperlinks usually appear in bold. Use the arrow keys to jump from hyperlink to hyperlink; the right arrow activates the link, moving to the new page, and the left arrow returns the browser to the previously viewed page. The **g** key opens a prompt where you can enter a new URL, and the **q** key exits the program.

Netscape

If you have a graphical user environment available on your Unix machine, you have more Web browsing options. Unix users have been rather fortunate, because the Netscape development team has always produced a Unix version of their product from the earliest release. In fact, Netscape's predecessor Mosaic was originally developed only for Unix. It wasn't until Mosaic was absorbed into the Netscape project and the Netscape browser itself was written that versions were also released for Windows and Macintosh.

Although Netscape is lagging behind Microsoft Internet Explorer in general use, primarily because Explorer is the default Windows browser, that competition does not exist in the Unix world. Netscape has remained consistently popular until very recently, when other development teams released new graphical browsers for the platform. The Netscape team is committed to Unix and to making their products consistent across all platforms.

Netscape looks and works under Unix exactly as it does under Windows and Macintosh. Start Netscape either by selecting its entry from your graphical environment's Start menu, by clicking its icon on the desktop, or by opening a terminal window and issuing the command

```
netscape
```

Mozilla

One of the reasons behind Netscape's decline in popularity, even among Unix enthusiasts, is the development of Mozilla. The Mozilla project began when Netscape, influenced by Eric Raymond's writings, made the Netscape Web browser source code available to the public. Netscape hoped that the Free Software and Open Source communities would use this code to create a better browser that would compete with Internet Explorer on the Windows platform.

From Netscape's perspective, this effort has met with limited success. While Mozilla is indeed an improvement over its Netscape predecessors, the process took much longer than Netscape anticipated at code release. In fact, at the time this text was written, Mozilla 1.0 had not yet been released; it is planned for release in 2002, and the second beta version has been available for some time.

From the Free Software and Open Source point of view, the Mozilla project has been a tremendous success. The resulting browser is nimble, streamlined, highly configurable, appealing to the eye, and above all, it is free in all senses of the word. Mozilla is a major accomplishment for the open development process.

Download Mozilla from the Netscape Web site at http://www.netscape.com or from the project site at http://www.mozilla.org. Once installed, it works much like Netscape, and is shown in Figure 9.7. It also has an associated mail client and news reader, should you want to use those integrated functions rather than a stand-alone program for each.

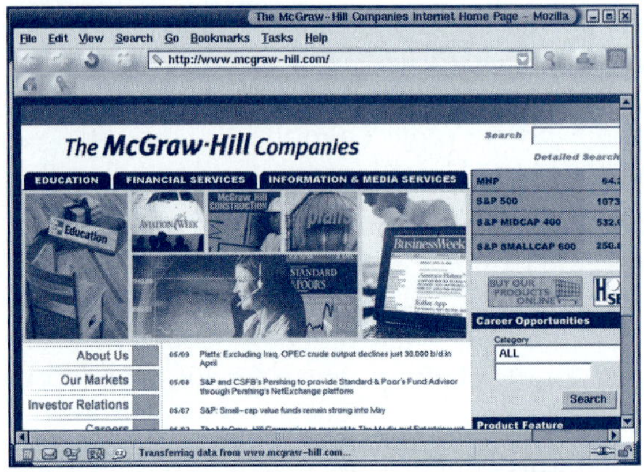

FIGURE 9.7 **The Mozilla Web browser is part of an Open Source Netscape initiative, and is increasingly popular.**

Opera

For those users who consider themselves purists, the Opera browser is a relatively new alternative to Netscape and Lynx. Opera is a streamlined browser that does not provide extra programs for mail or news. It is available free of charge for those who are willing to accept small advertisements within the program frame, or at a reasonable price for those who prefer to run software that is ad-free.

Download Opera at http://www.opera.com. The browser can be started in any of the normal ways, including issuing the command

```
opera
```

at the shell prompt in a terminal window. Figure 9.8 shows the browser. Most browser commands are the same, but Opera has some special features. Use the Preferences feature to select what types of files can display on your computer; you can toggle animated files, sound files, pop-up windows, JavaScript, and many other items which irritate some users.

The reason many have switched to Opera has little to do with turning off pop-up windows, though. Opera is a *compliant browser*, which means that it displays only HTML code which is compliant with the current version of the HTML

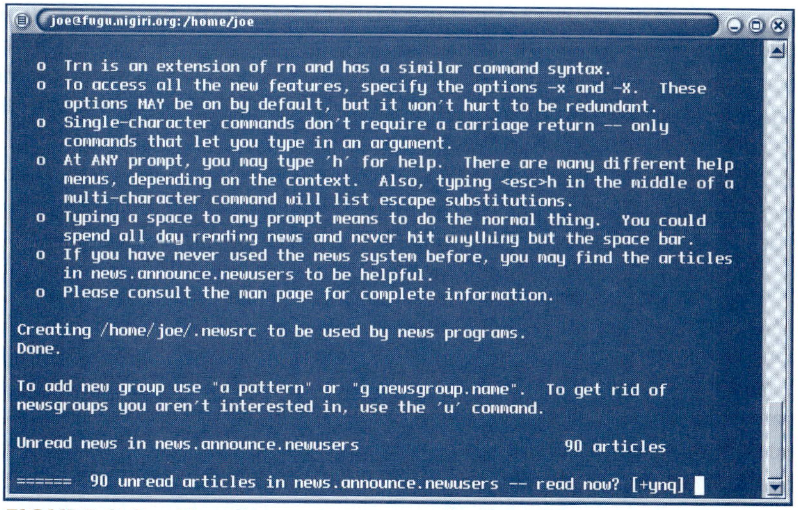

FIGURE 9.8 **The Opera browser displays HTML-compliant Web pages, and offers many user configuration options.**

protocol. This means that some pages will not display in Opera, or will only partially load. Pages written using Microsoft's Front Page extensions, which are noncompliant, are especially affected by this restriction. While using Opera does mean that some parts of the Web are not available to its users, perhaps wider use of this browser will encourage more compliant coding.

USENET News

In the days before the Web was invented, USENET news was the primary nonmail method of communication on the Internet. USENET can be compared to a large network of bulletin boards. Each USENET news server sends the messages posted to it locally out to other servers, to be made available for anyone on those servers to read and respond. A typical news server communicates with several other servers, trading messages in a number of groups, and this exchange means that a single message can be copied to thousands of servers all over the world in a matter of hours.

As Web-based bulletin boards have become more popular, USENET's popularity has waned. USENET's biggest detriment is also the source of its greatest appeal: nobody controls it. While one person or institution might control a single news server, or even several servers, nobody owns the system as a whole. Consequently, there are no rules governing its use or administration other than what is accepted as common practice among news server administrators.

In the days when the Internet was confined primarily to universities, government institutions, and technological corporations, this system promoted a refreshingly free exchange of ideas among users and a strong sense of community. Many USENET users developed deep friendships beyond the computer screen, and hundreds of marriages resulted from online conversations. Because nobody controlled the system, censorship was all but impossible and the community vocally endorsed freedom of speech.

Unfortunately, the explosive growth of the Internet due to commercial online services led to an influx of new USENET users who did not care for the community ethos which had developed over the years. The number of people who abuse newsgroups has, on many groups, overwhelmed the responsible posters. Because there is nobody in control, it is hard to stop abusers. This is not to say that USENET is altogether useless—not at all. There is still a vast amount of useful conversation taking place on USENET, especially on technical groups devoted to a myriad of software and programming languages. However, the strong sense of community that once prevailed is long gone.

With that said, USENET is still worth investigation. You may find a group which discusses your favorite hobby or collectible, in which you can join a raging debate, or where you can trade jokes and participate in an ongoing conversation. USENET groups are organized by hierarchy. There are nine major hierarchies, shown in Table 9.1. These are generally called the "Big 8 plus alt" since the alt.* hierarchy was created as an alternative to the more stringent group-creation process in the Big 8. There are, however, hundreds

TABLE 9.1: The Nine Major USENET Hierarchies

Hierarchy	Subject
alt.*	Wide variety of topics; hierarchy conceived as an alternative to the Big 8
comp.*	Computer and technical issues
humanities.*	Discussion of literature, language, and other humanities topics
misc.*	Any topic which doesn't fit in other existing Big 8 hierarchies
news.*	Discussion of issues relating to USENET news (current events falls under misc.* or soc.*)
rec.*	Recreational topics, such as hobbies, exercise, pets, and travel
sci.*	Scientific topics, excluding computer-related subjects
soc.*	Social sciences, including psychology, cultural issues, gender and relationship topics, and language
talk.*	Topics which tend to spark intense debate; groups in the talk.* hierarchy are traditionally unmoderated, allowing completely free discourse

of other hierarchies devoted to everything from local issues in a particular small town to scientific research, individual countries, Christian issues, and K–12 education.

trn

To view news messages, you must use a news client. There are a number of news readers available for the Unix platform, both graphical and text-based. The text-based news readers are more powerful, and many users prefer to use a text-based reader even if they use graphical programs for all other Internet applications. However, if you use an integrated Internet application like Netscape, which offers both an e-mail client and a news reader, you may choose to stay with the single program rather than learn an additional application.

The **trn** news reader is very popular, and is easy to learn. Start it by issuing the command

```
trn
```

at the shell prompt; the program appears as shown in Figure 9.9. The first time you run the program, it will show you the groups selected by your system administrator. If your administrator has not configured a list of groups, **trn** will either show you no groups or all groups to which your news server subscribes. Those groups are all listed in the file .trnrc, contained in your home directory. Go to a group, such as news.newusers.questions, by issuing the command

```
g news.newusers.questions
```

trn pulls all articles in that group from the local news spool and displays them.

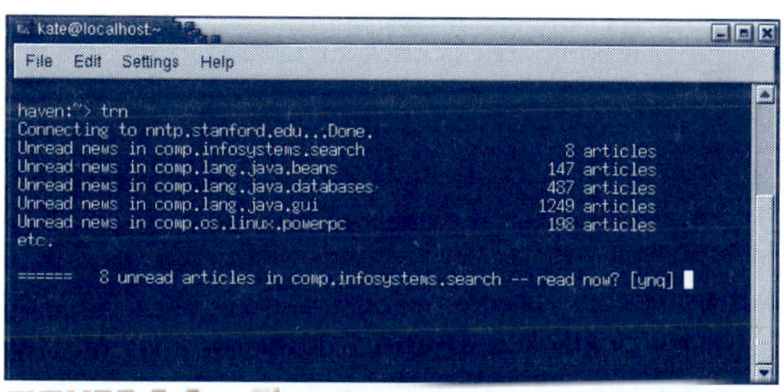

FIGURE 9.9 **The threaded news reader trn makes it simple to keep track of newsgroup posts.**

The advantage of **trn** is that it is a threaded news reader. As you move through the list of messages in a particular newsgroup, **trn** displays all the messages in one thread (under one subject line and its related messages) before moving to the next thread. This makes the often dizzying number of posts and topics in most groups more comprehensible. **trn** has an excellent set of help files, which act as a basic tutorial.

Summary

The concept of networking is integral to the Unix operating system. Some of the most popular user applications are actually networking applications, targeted specifically at Internet file transfer and display. Unix offers powerful applications to manage electronic mail, the World Wide Web, and USENET news. (Other Internet applications, used for file transfer and remote access, are described in Chapter 10, Networking I.)

Electronic mail messages are transferred over network connections between the originating machine and the receiving machine. The end recipient reads the messages through a mail reader client program, which usually accesses the messages from a local file. A second program is used to get the messages from a remote mail server and transfer them to the local mail spool, where they are accessible to the user's client program. Typical Unix mail readers include Elm and PINE.

The World Wide Web is a method of sharing various file types without requiring the file components to be downloaded or sent by mail. The Web requires a particular user client called a browser, which translates the file types into a single page displayed for the user. Unix users can view the Web in both text and graphical modes. The text browser Lynx uses character formatting to denote various aspects of Web design. Graphical browsers available for the Unix platform include Netscape, Opera, and Mozilla.

USENET News, once as popular among Internet users as the Web is today, has become less well known with the rise of the Web. It is still a valuable method of sharing messages, however, and sustains vigorous conversations on a wide range of topics. USENET messages are viewed with a news reader client, which may sort messages by topic, allow the user to score other posters so that highly scored posts are read first, or offer a friendly interface. Common text news readers include trn, rn, and tin.

Review Questions

1. How does the concept of networking differ between Unix and personal operating systems?
2. What is an Internet application?
3. Define electronic mail, and why it is preferable to other forms of text messaging.
4. What is a protocol?
5. Why are protocols important?
6. Describe the difference between client programs and server programs.
7. How do electronic mail clients obtain new mail messages?
8. How does the **fetchmail** program work?
9. Why should .fetchmailrc have restrictive permissions?
10. Why is a user's mailbox path name stored in the $MAIL variable?
11. Define a spool.
12. What is the difference between the elmrc-info file and the .elmrc file?
13. PINE's command lines are context sensitive. Why is this considered beneficial?
14. What is the basic purpose of the World Wide Web?
15. How can a text-based browser convey the sense of a graphically intensive Web page?
16. What is the difference between the Netscape browser and the Mozilla browser?
17. What are the features and drawbacks of the Opera browser?
18. How are USENET messages propagated across the Internet?
19. How are USENET messages organized?

1. Find copies of the POP and IMAP protocols on the Web. Although they are dense technical documents, read the introduction and skim the contents. What do these documents define? How specific are the recommendations? How would you handle these requirements if you were a programmer?
2. Try the various mail readers installed on your system. Which do you prefer? What features does it offer? Write a comparison of the clients you tried, and make an argument for your favorite one.
3. Open the Opera browser and visit some of your favorite Web sites. Do the pages appear differently than in your regular browser? Are there pages that do not display at all because they use bad HTML? Try altering some of the preference options, such as turning off animated files or pop-ups, and describe the results. Do you like the Opera experience? Describe the ideal user for this browser.
4. Spend some time reading through various USENET newsgroups. The group news.newusers.questions is a good place to start. Compare the user experience you have with the news reader to the experience you have when working with a Web-based bulletin board. Both are message-based communication; how do they differ? Which do you prefer, and why? Make an argument for one form over the other.

   Note: If you decide to post to a newsgroup or Web board, or are assigned to do so, post an on-topic message to an appropriate group. It is bad etiquette to post random messages to a group you just happen to enter. Your instructor or system administrator may set up a local newsgroup for you to practice with.

CHAPTER 10

Networking I: Introduction to Unix Networking

IN THIS CHAPTER

1. Remote access and file transfer
2. telnet and rlogin
3. rcp and rsh
4. Secure tools
5. Basic networking concepts
6. TCP/IP
7. Networking hardware

The previous chapter introduced some common Internet applications used on the Unix platform. The Internet is the most commonly understood network, as most people comprehend how information travels between computers around the world along a number of pathways. In this chapter, you will learn the concepts behind the networks themselves.

With this chapter, we move from personal user experience with Unix to the area of *system administration*. In the first nine chapters, you learned how to manipulate files and programs with simple commands. In the remainder of the text, you will learn to look at these files and programs as they affect the Unix machine and network as a whole. Once network connections are configured and established on a single machine, any user on that network can use the software installed on that single computer as long as she has been granted permission to do so.

Because many of the functions involved with networking require superuser privileges, you will either need access to a machine on which you have root (e.g., a personal computer running FreeBSD, Linux, or a similar variant) or your instructor will need to make arrangements for you to have these functions demonstrated. If

you are using a personal Unix variant and have root, you will also need to have access to a network: preferably, one connected to the Internet so that you can download new software as needed or consult online documentation.

Remote Access and File Transfer

Although the applications used to manage access to remote machines and to transfer files are user-level applications, they differ from the user applications described in Chapter 9, Internet Applications, because they do not involve the services with which casual Internet users are familiar. Rather, these applications involve tools which make it possible to work with machines across a networked environment. Often, working with these other machines is exactly like using the local machine at which you are sitting.

Specifically, these applications involve remote access and file transfer. *Remote access* programs allow a user to log into a machine on the network and use that machine just as if it were the computer on her desk, no matter where that remote machine is located. For example, one of the authors of this text routinely works on a machine in Palo Alto, California, from her desk in Boston. Other users of that machine log in from European countries, Japan, and at least eight U.S. states. In the same way, it is possible to log into a machine at home while travelling, to get electronic mail or check system function. Note that this means an actual login to the computer, as if it were right in front of the user, as opposed to remote retrieval of electronic mail or viewing files through the Web.

File transfer is a function which allows users to download or upload files from one machine to another across a network. While this capability is built into all Web browsers, its function is not as explicit in a browser as it is when handled by normal Unix methods and software. File transfer programs are usually called FTP clients, an acronym for File Transfer Protocol.

telnet, rlogin, rsh, and rcp: Why Nobody Uses Them Anymore

The programs described in this section are rapidly becoming obsolete. Nonetheless, they are included here because they are still in use on many machines. The programs which have replaced them are built on these programs and their code, rather than being completely new inventions.

The reason that these programs are becoming obsolete has to do with network security. These programs were written at a time when the practice of *cracking*, or breaking into networks without authorization, was less advanced and popular than it is today. These programs are used to establish a simple connection between individual machines, and allow the user to perform whatever tasks are needed on the remote machine.

Note: The term "hacker" has been adopted by the media to describe people who attempt illegal entry to a network. This is a misuse of the term, which is an old nickname for someone who enjoys working on source code to improve a piece of software. The correct term for those who try to break into systems for which they have no permission is "cracker." Such illegal conduct is abhorred by hackers.

The simple nature of the connection created by these programs means that sensitive information, such as a password, is sent in clear text. The system crackers working today have access to a class of tools called *packet sniffers* which make it a relatively simple matter to intercept these communications and to capture passwords in the process. A packet sniffer works by trapping the individual packets of information that make up the data stream and sending those packets to the cracker for further investigation.

Another reason the "r" commands are dangerous is that it is possible to use them *without* passwords. As irresponsible as it may seem, a user can define a set of user and machine names which can be granted "trusted" access to the local machine. This is done by creating a file in the /etc/ directory called hosts.equiv. In that file one places the name of a remote machine along with an optional user name and a plus or minus sign. For example, the entry

```
+ flerbnert.com sam
```

will allow the user "sam" to login from the domain "flerbnert.com". If any of these elements are left out, it is assumed that all values will satisfy the condition. Thus

```
+ sam
```

will allow user "sam" to log in without a password from any remote machine, and the line

```
+ flerbnert.com
```

will allow any user to log in without a password from the "flerbnert.com" domain. This begins to get *really* dangerous when you introduce this line:

```
+
```

as this will allow any user to log in without a password from anywhere.

Note: /etc/hosts.equiv cannot be used to provide passwordless access to the "root" account.

Tech Tip

The /etc/hosts.equiv file can also be used to deny access from a certain machine. The line

```
- flerbnert.com
```

will deny access to any login attempts from the flerbnert.com address.

Despite the security flaws in these programs, they still exist on most Unix machines and are actively used on many. There are several reasons for this. First, these programs are still quite useful, especially for programs which require a machine to connect to itself for various purposes. Second, the programs are useful in networks of trusted machines, or networks which do not connect to the Internet. Finally, these programs are often part of shell scripts or other administrative programs which were written in the years before security was such a critical concern. It will be many years before these programs completely fade from regular use.

telnet and rlogin

The telnet and rlogin programs are used to establish a simple interactive connection between a single local machine and a single remote machine. The command is issued with a full machine name as the argument, as in

```
telnet somemachine.bigcc.edu
```

or

```
rlogin somemachine.bigcc.edu
```

The program returns with a login prompt, just as if the user were logging into the machine locally; of course, this assumes that the remote machine accepts telnet connections and that the user has an account on the remote machine. Should the remote machine not accept telnet connections, the process will hang without completion or the program will return a "Connection denied" message.

After the user enters his user name and password, he will be taken to a shell prompt. At this point, working with the remote machine is no different from working locally. The same commands and programs can be used, assuming they are installed on the remote machine, and files can be managed in the same way. Commands issued at this shell prompt affect the remote machine, not the local machine. To affect the local machine, the user must suspend the **telnet** or **rlogin** process and get a local prompt.

The only difference between a task on the local machine and one on the remote machine is that commands given to the remote machine must travel along the electronic pathway between the two computers. Depending on how far apart these machines are, the amount of traffic on the network, and how many *hops* (intermediate machines) the data must take, the connection may be nearly instantaneous or may lag by several seconds. The connection will persist until the user logs out of the remote machine. Upon logout, the telnet or rlogin process exits, and the user is returned to the local shell prompt.

Note: For almost all purposes, **telnet** and **rlogin** are synonymous.

rsh

The **rsh** program allows the execution of a single shell command on a remote machine. **rsh** is an acronym for *remote shell.* Unlike a telnet or rlogin process, an **rsh** process is not interactive. Therefore, the command invoked by **rsh** cannot be an interactive process: for example, a text editor or Lynx Web search. Any noninteractive shell command can be used, though.

To invoke **rsh** and execute a command remotely, you must construct a complex command. **rsh** takes the syntax

```
rsh remote.machine.name -l username command
```

as in

```
rsh somemachine.bigcc.edu -l bjones w
```

The user is prompted for a password. If the correct password is provided, then the command is executed. In this case, the command produces a list of users logged into the remote machine. It does not log the user bjones into that machine, as the connection closes as soon as the command has been sent and the output received on the local machine's standard output.

Note: If a remote machine does not accept **telnet** or **rlogin** connections, it is unlikely that it will accept **rsh** connections.

rcp

The **rcp** program is a file transfer utility. With **rcp**, a user can copy a single file from one machine to another without actually logging into the other machine. The command takes the syntax

```
rcp remote.machine:/path/remote-file /path/local-file
```

to copy a file from the remote machine to the local machine, and the syntax

```
rcp /path/local-file remote.machine:/path/remote-file
```

to copy a file from the local machine to the remote machine.

Thus, the command

```
rcp pub.bigcc.edu:/home/bjones/.elmrc /home/bob/.elmrc
```

copies the .elmrc file from the bjones user account on the machine pub.bigcc.edu to the bob user account on the local machine. Note that the user must know the bjones account password to transfer this file, and must have permission to write files to the bob account in order to complete this command. The command

```
rcp /home/bob/.elmrc pub.bigcc.edu:/home/bjones/.elmrc
```

would do the opposite, moving bob's .elmrc into the bjones account.

A Security Note

Despite developer attempts to add security features to these programs, they have fallen out of favor on most networks. These days, it is difficult to find machines that permit incoming connections from these four programs. You should not be surprised if attempts to connect with these programs fail. On those machines that do accept remote connections with one of these programs, the program may not work exactly as described here due to some security patch which has been added. If either situation is the case, you may have better luck with the commands described in the next section.

Secure Tools

In response to the security problems posed by **telnet** and the "r commands," many system administrators have begun to use a replacement suite of tools. These tools are collectively known as SSH (or SSH's Free Software counterpart, OpenSSH). SSH stands for Secure Shell.

The SSH tools **ssh** and **scp** operate in much the same way as **telnet**, **rsh**, and **rcp**, but with one crucial difference: these tools use encrypted connections. In other words, when one machine connects to another using SSH, a piece of information called a *key* is the first data bit exchanged. This key is used to scramble all of the information passing between the two machines, and is the code used to unscramble the data when it arrives at the other location.

When the user is prompted for a password, the password is also sent in this encrypted form. A cracker lurking on the connection with a packet sniffer may be able to grab the encoded password but, because he does not have the appropriate key, will not be able to decode it. For the encryption scheme to work properly, compatible SSH software must be running on both the local and remote machines. SSH has become so popular, though, that a healthy percentage of machines are now running the program suite.

ssh

The **ssh** command can mimic either **telnet** or **rsh**, depending on how the command is given. For an interactive session like that started with **telnet**, **ssh** takes the syntax

```
ssh -l login remote.machine.name
```

as in

```
ssh -l plee pub.bigcc.edu
```

The "-l *login*" component of the command can be omitted if the user's login name is the same on the remote machine as it is on the local machine. If the user has accounts under the name plee on both machines, she can use

```
ssh pub.bigcc.edu
```

instead of the longer command. An alternative form of the long command is

```
ssh loginremote.machine.name
```

as in

```
ssh plee pub.bigcc.edu
```

The **ssh** program can also be used noninteractively, to mimic the **rsh** program and issue single commands to the remote machine. For this result, the command takes the syntax

```
ssh -l login remote.machine.name command
```

or

```
ssh loginremote.machine.name command
```

As in the previous operation, the login name can be omitted if it is the same on both machines.

These two commands make up the bulk of common SSH operations. Be aware, however, that SSH is a robust program with many options and modes not described here. If you want to learn more about the Secure Shell suite of tools, consult the online manual page with the command

```
man ssh
```

scp

The **scp** program is a replacement for the **rcp** program. Like **rcp**, **scp** is used to copy files between a local and a remote machine, but uses a secure connection to transfer the data. **scp** commands are constructed like rcp commands, and take the syntax

```
scp loginremote:/path/remote-file /path/local-file
```

to transfer a file from the remote account to the local account. The syntax

```
scp /path/local-file loginremote:/path/remote-file
```

is used to transfer a file from the local machine to the remote machine. scp will prompt for a password before beginning the file transfer.

Basic Networking Concepts

The programs described in the previous section of the chapter illustrate the most basic concepts of intermachine networking. With those concepts in mind, we can turn to a larger view of the network. This view helps to demonstrate the basic infrastructure of a network, and how each individual computer fits into the picture.

How Networks Operate

At the most basic level, a network works by transmitting bits of information between machines. These bits, or *packets,* are encoded into electrical signals by an *interface:* a modem or network card. The encoded packets are then sent, usually over a physical wire but sometimes through the air like a radio signal, to another interface, where they are decoded. The resulting information is then passed to the intended recipient. Typically, a large chunk of information, such as an electronic mail message or a Web page, is broken up into many small packets which are then reassembled at the receiving end. This is the case whether the network is a simple connection between two machines on the same table, or between many machines all over the world connected through the Internet.

It is not necessary to understand the mechanics of each of these actions to understand the basic networking concepts. The way in which messages are broken apart and reassembled, the way in which packets are constructed, the way in which information is converted into transmittable signals, and other mechanisms are beyond the scope of this text. Fortunately, these are not activities in which the average user must participate in order to use the network. Instead, they are functions of the operating system and of the computer's hardware. For most work involving networks, you need only know how to manipulate network connections on the macro level.

As noted previously, networks are controlled by various protocols. These protocols govern the format of information exchange. The precise way in which a piece of hardware or software handles information is not particularly important, as long as that information is formatted in compliance with the protocol **at the time the information is presented to another machine**. How the machine handles that data in its own space is irrelevant as long as it is properly organized when it arrives at another location.

With the reassurance of protocol compliance, any number of programs responsible for network functions can interact freely without having to know how each of the other programs works. As long as all of the programs are protocol-compliant, they can pass data back and forth without problems. This is how messages and packets can be passed among a net of machines with different hardware, different operating systems, and different kinds of software which handle network traffic: in short, a network exactly like the Internet.

TCP/IP

The common language for networks connected to the Internet is a combination of protocols known as TCP/IP. TCP/IP stands for Transmission Control Protocol/Internet Protocol. It is not the only way in which network information can be shared, but because it is the standard for the Internet, it is by far the most popular protocol for network transmission. Most people and institutions want their networks to be connected to the Internet, and so it seems appropriate to construct their private networks in compliance with TCP/IP.

The TCP protocol governs how packets are created, and how they are transmitted across the networks. It is extremely technical, and is not generally of concern to individual users. The IP protocol, on the other hand, is much more relevant to average users. The IP protocol governs how machines are connected to the network, and how those machines are identified. In order for a connection to find the machine to which it is directed, there must be some way to identify that machine, and that machine alone. The IP protocol defines how those identifications are assigned.

IP Numbers

Every computer on a network must have a unique identifier attached to it. Under the Internet Protocol, these identifiers are numerical. Specifically, the machine identifier is made up of a set of four numbers, with each set of numbers separated by a dot. Each set must be a number between 0 and 255. A typical IP number might be

```
122.12.0.41
```

Why are the numbers limited to those between 0 and 255? These numbers are the decimal translation of a binary number having eight digits. Thus, the binary number 00000000 is equal to the decimal number 0, and the binary number 11111111 is equal to the decimal number 255. All other possibilities fall between these two extremes. The lowest possible IP address, in binary form, is

```
00000000.00000000.00000000.00000000
```

and the highest is

```
11111111.11111111.11111111.11111111
```

Because these numbers contain 32 binary digits in total, they are known as *32 bit* numbers; a *bit* is a binary digit.

Note: In binary code, the only possible characters are 0 and 1. Combining strings of zeros and ones creates commands which the computer's processor can understand.

Under this system of assignment, there are 4,294,967,000 possible IP addresses available for computers attached to a single network. It may seem surprising, but even with nearly 4.3 billion addresses, the supply is running out. This shortage is due to the way that addresses are allocated. In the early days of the Internet, when an organization applied to have a particular slice of network space allocated for its exclusive use, it was given a large range of numbers—some of which it may never use. Although the slices are smaller today, the practice continues. It seems wasteful, but there are technical reasons behind the allocation, and the system worked reasonably well until the Internet explosion a few years ago.

Another reason for the IP address shortage is that some ranges of addresses are reserved for special uses,and cannot be allocated to networks which want to attach to the Internet. Note that a network may use any IP addresses it likes within its own net, but if that network ever connects to the Internet as a whole, each machine must have a unique identifier. It is simpler to start out with appropriate IP numbers than it is to reconfigure every IP number on the local network when the network is eventually attached to the Internet.

Regardless of the reasons behind the shortage, however, it is no longer the threat it once was. At the time this text was written, a new version of the Internet Protocol, called "IP version 6," had been drafted and is under revision. This new version expands the address space to 128 bits, doubling the length of the IP number. The expansion means that the pool of possible addresses will explode from 4.3 billion to 3.4×10^{38} IP addresses, a number with 37 zeros. That pool should not be exhausted anytime soon.

Name Resolution

Clearly, it would be difficult to remember every set of numbers that identify the various computers attached to the Internet. Computers can easily track these numbers, but humans tend to make mistakes. Humans remember words and names much better, and for this reason, naming machines and networks is now common practice. Indeed, such names have become so popular that they are now in common conversation. Amazon.com, Yahoo.com, and the like are not only the designated names of actual networks but are legal trademarks and brand names.

How do these names get associated with the corresponding IP numbers? This is the job of the Domain Name Service, or DNS. DNS is a network of *name servers* spread throughout the Internet. These servers maintain a database of network and machine names and their associated IP numbers. When an individual or organization registers a domain name, she must tell the registering authority the address of one or more name servers which will maintain that domain name's DNS entry. Usually, two name servers are registered: a primary server and a backup. Likewise, when a new computer is connected to the Internet, a particular DNS server must be specified in its networking configuration so that the computer will know where to look when it tries to resolve an Internet address.

Networking Hardware and Software

There is a huge variety of networking hardware available in catalogs and stores. From basic modems to common network interface adapters and hubs, to heavy-duty interfaces which allow a machine to be connected to a major network artery like a T-1 line, the choice is nearly overwhelming. Likewise, there is a plethora of software available for almost any task from simple mail, news, and Web servers to software that turns a basic PC into a *router*, a dedicated switchboard for Internet connections.

In this section, you will learn about some of these hardware items. The descriptions provide a basic introduction to their function and the common network technologies they employ and represent. However, it is only a survey because individual manufacturers build components which require different software drivers or commands to operate. If you work with networking hardware devices, consult that device's manual for specific information on how best to use it in your situation.

Modems

Most people have either used or seen a modem. A modem is the piece of hardware that allows network connections to be made over telephone lines. The word *modem* is a contraction of the term "modulator/demodulator." The first modems were called *acoustic couplers* because they translated the computer's information into audible tones. The modem was a cradle into which a telephone receiver was nestled, and the tones would play into the mouthpiece.

As modems evolved, it became more common to simply plug the phone line into the modem itself, rather than rely on the handset. Today's modems are usually internal, installed directly into the computer case. If the modem is external, like a cable modem, it plugs into a socket on the back of the case.

While significantly faster than the acoustic couplers of old, today's modems still function in more or less the same way. Modems convert outgoing packets of information into electrical signals that are sent over telephone wires to a corresponding modem on the receiving end. The receiving modem decodes these signals, converting them back into data packets.

The advantage of modems is that they can be used anywhere. As long as you have a phone line and the telephone number of a receiving modem, you can make a connection. The disadvantage of modems is that they are slow. The fastest modems are capable of transmitting data at a rate of 56,000 bits per second, whereas other methods of connection can easily be ten times that or more.

Note: While the term "modem" is used to describe other connection devices, like the cable modem, that device works differently from the telephone modem.

Ethernet

Another common way to network computers is with *Ethernet*. Ethernet is a fanciful name given to a system in which computers on a network are connected with a web of dedicated wires. The most common form of Ethernet today is the 10baseT or 100baseT type. These types use cables with ends that resemble outsized phone jacks and are called RJ-45 connectors. These cables plug into Network Interface Cards, or NICs, which are installed in the computers and are connected to network hubs.

Ethernet has two advantages over dial-up networking. First, it's much faster; second, it's always on. Unlike modems, which have to be dialed into the receiving machine in order to work, machines connected by Ethernet are always connected. Ethernet's disadvantage is that it only works over fairly short distances, about 100 meters. You must run Ethernet cable anywhere you want to put network machines if you choose this method of networking.

Hubs

Hubs are network switchboards designed to be used with 10/100baseT-type Ethernet. A *hub* is a fairly small and simple piece of equipment. It has a number of sockets, anywhere from four to twenty-four or more. Each computer on the network is plugged into the hub. The hub then serves as a switchboard, effectively connecting every computer on the network to every other computer on the network.

Routers

Routers are another specialized piece of equipment. The purpose of a router is to connect between a local network, such as an Ethernet network, and an external network such as the Internet. Like hubs, routers act as switchboards but on a much greater level. Most routers are machines specifically designed and built for this task, but it is also possible to convert a general-purpose computer into a router.

Routers also often have the secondary task of physically connecting Ethernet networks to the heavy-duty networks that are used to transport information across cities, states, and ultimately the world. This is done through heavy dedicated lines like T-1 or T-3 lines, which are large lines usually provided and maintained by the local telephone company or its partners. These lines can carry huge amounts of data and often cost thousands of dollars each month. These connections require specialized interface hardware devices that are installed in the routers.

Cable and DSL

One of the big problems facing Internet providers is how to provide their customers with the speed and convenience of Ethernet while maintaining the low cost and universality of access that modems bring. Two technologies have emerged to bridge this gap: cable "modems" and DSL.

Cable modems are small routers that connect an Ethernet NIC or a PC's USB port with the same sort of cable that is used to transmit cable television signals. Because this cable is already installed in many areas, it is easy to connect private residences to the Internet with this technology. Although the technology is still available in somewhat limited areas, cable companies are expanding their service rapidly.

Along similar lines, Digital Subscriber Lines (DSL) use phone lines to accomplish the same task. While using the same infrastructure as dial-up modems, DSL uses them in a different way. With the DSL technology, users get higher speeds and always-on connections. They can also use the telephone and DSL connection at the same time, unlike a regular modem. Like cable modems, DSL technology is spreading as local telephone companies invest in the required hardware.

Summary

Native networking functions in the Unix operating system allow a user to work on a machine across the network as if they were working directly on a keyboard plugged into that machine. Remote access and file transfer programs allow users to log into these remote machines, execute commands remotely, or transfer files between machines. The initial forms of these commands are still used, but have security issues which make them an unwise choice. More secure versions are increasingly popular, and offer a better solution for remote activity.

Networks operate by transmitting packets of information between machines connected by wires or other interfaces. These packets are constructed according to the guidelines of the TCP protocol. The other major Internet protocol, the Internet Protocol, defines how machines are named and identified on the Internet. These machine names are composed of four sets of numbers between 0 and 255. However, because humans remember words better than numbers, the Domain Name Service allows letter-based machine names to be translated into the IP numbers which the network recognizes.

Network hardware ranges from simple modems to complex routers. These devices enable multiple computers to communicate, either by dialing in across a telephone line or connecting through a cable. Most people join a network by connecting their single computer for a temporary link to a larger web of machines, a portion of which may be machines which are permanently wired to each other and which have a constant link.

Review Questions

1. How does a network operate?
2. Define a remote access program.
3. How does remote access differ from viewing a Web page hosted on a remote machine?
4. Define a file transfer program.
5. What is the difference between hacking and cracking?
6. What are packet sniffers, and how can they be defeated?
7. Although they are security risks, why are programs like telnet and rlogin still used?
8. What is the function of the **telnet** and **rlogin** programs?
9. How can a user execute commands on the local machine when logged in remotely to another machine?
10. What factors affect how long a command will take to execute when given remotely?
11. What is the function of the **rsh** program?

12. How is **rsh** different from **telnet** and **rlogin**?
13. What is the function of the **rcp** command?
14. What is the advantage of the Secure Shell programs over other programs which perform the same functions?
15. Explain the process which computers use to transfer information between themselves?
16. Define the TCP and IP protocols.
17. Explain the structure of an IP number.
18. How are text names like amazon.com translated into IP numbers?
19. What is a modem?
20. How is an Ethernet network constructed?
21. What is the difference between a hub and a router?
22. What is the difference between a cable modem and DSL?

Exercises

1. Investigate the software installed on your system. Are **telnet**, **rlogin**, **rcp**, or **rsh** available? Does the system accept these connections from outside machines? What is the system policy on remote access? Write an essay arguing the advantages of either traditional programs or the Secure Shell programs.
2. Find the TCP and IP protocol documents on the Web. Read at least the introduction and skim the actual protocols. What do these protocols define? What parts of the protocol can ordinary system administrators use, and what parts are intended for programmers' use?
3. Using a Web catalog or a print catalog from a computer parts store, identify ten different network hardware devices. Describe the capacity and function of each device. What is the ideal user base for each device? How does price factor into your description of an idea user? What devices are available for single users or administrators of very small networks, taking price and capacity into account?

CHAPTER 11

Networking II: Fundamentals of Unix Networking

IN THIS CHAPTER

1. LANs, WANs, and internets
2. Network topology
3. Ethernet networking
4. Routers, gateways, and DNS
5. Dial-up networking
6. Case study: Setting up a simple network

In the previous chapter, you learned some of the basic constructs which underlie Unix networking. In this chapter, you will learn more about the mechanics of Unix networks: how networks are constructed and the procedures used under the Unix operating system to build and maintain the nets. Compared to the programs introduced in Chapter 10, the concepts explained here are much less transparent to the average user. While a user will take advantage of many programs which utilize functions like FTP or HTTP, most users do not know—or care—where their routers are located or how those machines work.

If you want to try the mechanical or software configurations described here, you will need to have root access to a computer with appropriate networking hardware: a modem, a phone line, a dial-up account, and a Network Interface Card, as well as some sort of network connection for the Ethernet section. Since most people who have these items are using a personal-computer Unix variant, the examples in this section assume a Linux environment. Should you be using a machine that runs another Unix variant, consult your documentation or instructor for any commands or syntax which may differ from what is given here.

LANs, WANs, and Internets

The terms LAN, WAN, and internet are used quite casually in information technology conversations. Anyone who participates, no matter how marginally, in popular culture knows about "the Internet," and may also have heard of LANs or WANs. It is important to understand the difference between these three types of networks before moving further into specific construction details. Each of these terms refers to a particular network type, which manages data flow in a certain manner. Though the types are distinct, they are also interrelated, and any given large network may have sub-networks of a different type.

Local Area Networks

The term *LAN* is an acronym for *local area network.* A LAN is any group of computers which are directly connected to each other, usually with wires. In common use, the term usually refers to an Ethernet network which occupies a single building or office. A LAN can be built from as few as two machines to as many as can fit into the physical area. However, many system administrators opt to run several smaller LANs rather than wire together hundreds of computers into the same network. Practical considerations form the outer limit, rather than technical barriers.

Wide Area Networks

WAN is an acronym for *wide area networks,* and refers to groups of machines which are networked across some distance. Typically, a WAN is comprised of several geographically dispersed LANs. These LANs may connect to each other through dial-up connections, or by dedicated data lines. In addition, the VLAN, or Virtual LAN, is a WAN that uses secure connections over the Internet. WANs are often used to link separate offices within a company. For example, a corporation with offices in New York, Hong Kong, Paris, and Tangiers would have a LAN in each office; those LANs, when hooked together, form the company-wide WAN.

Internets

Finally, there are *internets.* You are no doubt used to hearing about the Internet, with a capital I, usage which implies that there can be only one. However, in a purely technical sense, the term "internet" is somewhat looser. An internet is somewhat like a supersized WAN. In fact, a WAN itself could be considered an internet since it manages data flowing between, or "inter," individual networks. However, an internet connotes greater disparity than merely geographical distance. For example, an internet may bridge networks owned by different institutions which use different operating systems and local network configuration. Several universities might link their LANs and WANs together so that faculty members could work together more easily. The resulting network is an internet.

Today, most people talk about THE Internet, not AN internet, as if the Internet were a single monolithic network that every computer will eventually become part of. The Internet, however, is really a mesh of smaller networks that interconnect in the most public and open ways possible. It is a network of LANs and WANs, owned by diverse individuals, companies, and other institutions that hook together to create an infrastructure as universally available as possible. Individual networks join and detach from the larger mesh every minute, so the Internet is an internet in constant flux.

The phrase "Information Superhighway" is now a cliché, but the analogy of networks to physical roads is a useful one. Think of the individual computer as a house. The house is connected to the road by a driveway, which is just a very small road. The road connects many driveways together, and connects to other roads to make up a neighborhood, or LAN. The neighborhoods, in turn, connect to larger roads which carry more traffic throughout the city, or WAN. Cities are connected to each other through large state or interstate highways, building an internet. Your driveway in El Paso thus has a connection—however indirect—to anyone else's individual driveway anywhere on the continent of North America. Each of these roads belongs to a different person or organization; driveways are personal property, roads belong to cities, highways belong to states or the federal government, yet they all connect to each other to carry drivers where they want to go. This is the essence of the Internet.

Network Topology

Networks can be differentiated by type, as described above, or by topology. The network type does not necessarily dictate a particular topology, though some topologies are more common to certain network types than others. A *topology* is a mapped shape; network topologies usually have descriptive names like ring, star, or hub. Some topologies are most effective in small networks, while others work equally well with very large numbers of machines. The hardware required for building each kind of topology will differ, though all require cable to connect the machines on the network.

The Bus Topology

Under a bus topology, each machine is connected to a central cable. This cable, or *bus*, transfers data down its length until the data reaches the machine to which it is addressed. Figure 11.1 shows a schematic of a bus topology network.

Bus topologies are most efficient for small networks. Because incoming data must pass through the cable searching for the correct destination, data destined for the last machines attached to the bus will arrive more slowly than

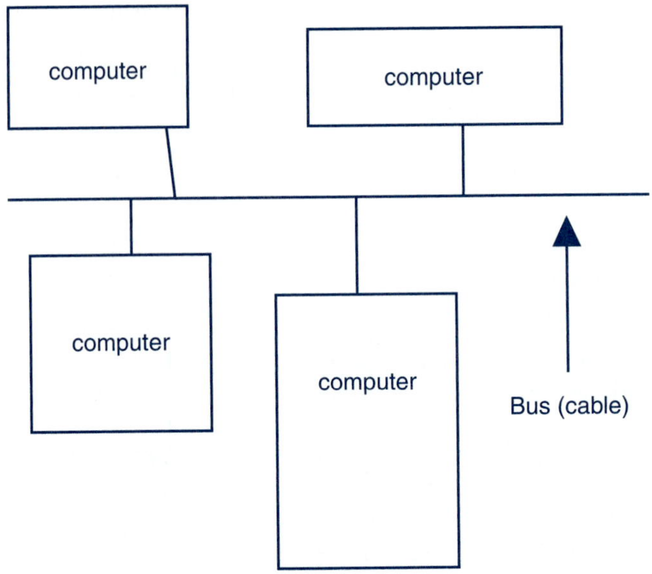

FIGURE 11.1 The layout of a bus topology network.

data destined for the first few machines hooked to the bus. While these are easy networks to build, they are becoming increasingly uncommon as low-cost networking equipment has arrived on the market.

The Ring Topology

Ring topology is similar to bus topology, except that the central cable loops around in a circle instead of ending at the terminus of the cable length. It is a slightly more efficient method of delivering data than a straight bus network. Figure 11.2 shows the schematic of a typical ring topology network.

Most ring networks have one machine, usually the computer into which the beginning and end of the ring cable is plugged, which manages ring traffic. The *token ring network*, a variant of this topology, does not have a permanent network management machine. Rather, a discrete piece of data called a *token* is passed along the ring. Whatever machine has the token is the machine which controls the network. Like bus topologies, though, the ring topology is most effective for smaller networks and is passing out of favor.

The Hub Topology

Most Ethernet networks use the hub topology, also known as the *Star topology*. In a hub network, each machine connects directly to a piece of hardware called a *hub*. The hub acts as a switchboard, receiving incoming data, determining the intended recipient, and distributing the data to that machine. Figure 11.3 shows the schematic of a typical hub network.

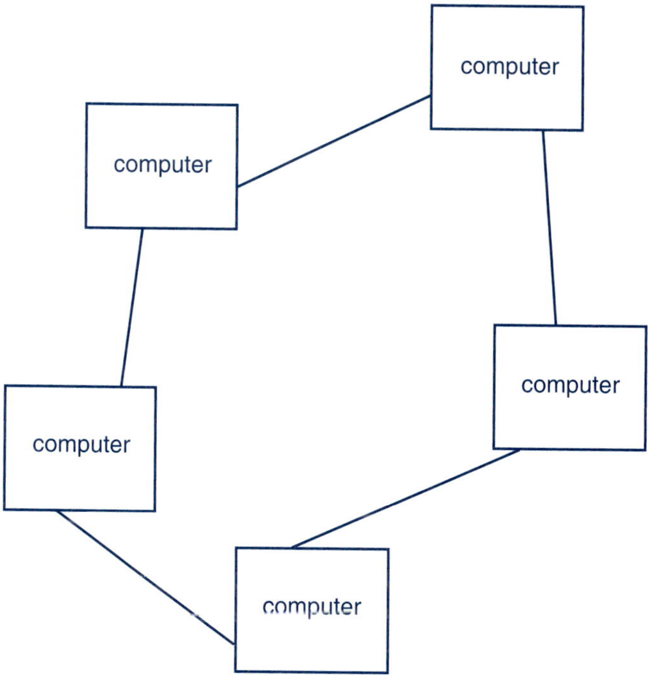

FIGURE 11.2 The layout of a ring topology network.

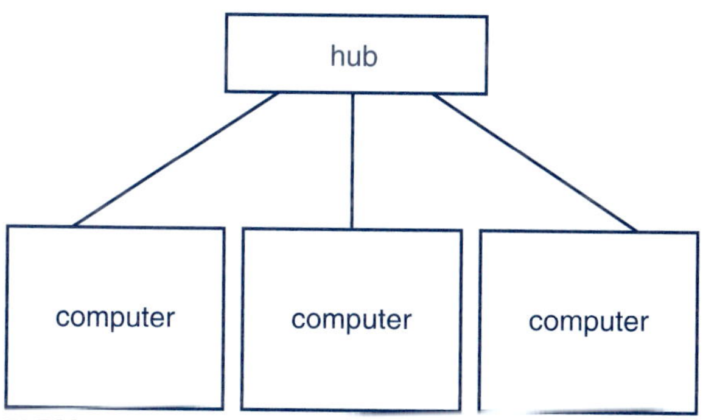

FIGURE 11.3 The layout of a hub topology network.

As Ethernet hardware has become cheaper and is more easily purchased, hub networks have become increasingly popular regardless of network size. Many small home networks now operate on Ethernet hubs, as do very large networks in corporations or academic institutions. One of the reasons that hub topology is so attractive is that it is easy to add or remove machines from the network simply by adding or removing a single cable from that machine to the hub. Under a ring or bus topology, the entire network may be affected as the central cable is rerouted.

Ethernet Networking

Most modern LANs are built around the *ethernet* concept. Ethernet is a term which was coined in 1972 at the Xerox research center in Palo Alto, California. The term refers to a network of machines connected by dedicated wires that carry nothing but network data. Signals sent over an ethernet network are sent to all machines on the network; those signals are ignored by machines to which the signals are not addressed.

These signals are coded with the individual machine's *hardware address*, a unique number which identifies that machine alone. The hardware address, also sometimes called the MAC, or *Media Access Control*, is not the same thing as an IP number. The hardware address is coded into the network interface hardware by the manufacturer and cannot be edited or changed by the end user. The developers of Ethernet thought that this method of data propagation resembled the Victorian idea of a "luminiferous ether" which was thought to carry electromagnetic waves throughout the cosmos; thus the name "ethernet."

Today, for a network of dedicated wires to be considered ethernet, it must conform to the standard codified as IEEE Standard Number 802.3. This standard protocol governs the way in which information is carried over the network. As long as the network conforms to that standard, it is considered to be an ethernet network regardless of the actual hardware involved. Indeed, ethernet networks may use a variety of physical media, including thin coaxial cable, thick coaxial cable, *twisted pair* cable (similar to telephone cable), and fiber optic cable. Of these options, twisted pair cable is both most affordable and widely used.

Twisted pair cable comes in many varieties, but two types are most popular: Category 3 cable and Category 5 cable. The two types are basically the same, except that Category 5 cable is thicker and can carry data farther before the signal begins to degrade. Each end of a twisted pair cable terminates in a modular plug that looks like the modular plug used for a telephone jack, but slightly larger. This plug is called an RJ-45 plug. Most ethernet Network Interface Cards sold today have a compatible RJ-45 jack. One end of the cable plugs into the card, and the other into a hub which also has RJ-45 jacks.

In contrast, ethernet networks which use coaxial cable do not use hubs. Such networks connect all the computers together in a bus configuration, using the thicker coaxial's capability to handle vast amounts of data in a relatively rapid manner. Coaxial cable is the same wire used to bring cable television programming into your home. It is relatively cheap, but is less flexible than twisted pair and is harder to conceal under carpets or inside walls.

Fiber optic networks do use a hub, like a twisted pair network, but it must be a hub specially designed for fiber optic use. Fiber optic cable uses pulses of light, rather than electrical signals, to carry data through the network. This technology is still quite new, and anyone wanting to build a fiber optic network must invest large sums in specialized hardware. Because coaxial or twisted pair ethernet hardware is so affordable, there is no real incentive to switch to fiber optic technology for the vast majority of networks.

In addition to hubs and routers, there are a couple of other pieces of specialized hardware that are used with ethernet networks. *Bridges* are used to connect two segments of a network together and transmit data between them. *Repeaters* do much the same thing. The difference is that a bridge is slightly "smarter" and can decide if a given signal should be allowed to cross the bridge or not, whereas a repeater sends the signal across regardless. In terms of decision-making power, a bridge is somewhat "dumber" that a router but somewhat "smarter" than a repeater.

Ethernet can carry data at very high speeds. The slowest type of ethernet carries data at a maximum rate of ten megabits (10 million bits) of data per second. By contrast, the fastest dial-up modem carries data at a maximum rate of 56 kilobits (56 thousand bits) per second. However, there are also varieties of ethernet that can carry data at rates up to ten gigabits, or 10 billion bits, per second. The 10 gigabit ethernet is a new standard, and operates only over fiber optic hardware, but most conventional hardware can be used to transmit and receive data at 100 megabits or even 1 gigabit per second.

Though these numbers are impressive, most networks will operate more slowly than the maximum rating for their hardware. Network speed is very closely tied to network traffic. Like a busy road at rush hour, the more bits that are flying around the network, the more they tend to collide and slow each other down. Even though effective speed is always lower than maximum rated speed, faster network hardware on a congested network will still result in a faster user experience than slow hardware on a relatively clear network.

Configuring Ethernet under Unix

Building an ethernet network on a set of Unix machines is straightforward. Assume that you have an existing network and want to add a new machine. This new machine already has an appropriate network identification card installed, and has been attached to the network hub with a Category 5 twisted pair cable. All that remains to do is to "turn on the ethernet" by configuring the machine and hub to recognize each other.

This configuration is done with the **ifconfig** command. Although the syntax used with **ifconfig** differs from Unix variant to variant, the command works in the same way on all machines. **ifconfig** is a powerful command with a myriad of uses. For the purposes of this chapter, only a few functions of **ifconfig** are used. To learn more, consult Appendix A or see the **ifconfig** manual page by issuing the command

```
man ifconfig
```

at the shell prompt.

Issue the command **ifconfig** without any arguments to see the current status of all configured network interfaces. On a machine without any active network connections, like the new machine being added to this example network, the output will look somewhat like this:

```
lo      Link encap:Local Loopback
inet addrs:127.0.0.1   Mask:255.0.0.0
UP  LOOPBACK RUNNING   MTU:16436  Metric:1
RX packets:20163 errors:0 dropped:0 overruns:0 frame:0
TX packets:20163 errors:0 dropped:0 overruns:0 carrier:0
collisions:0 txqueuelen:0
```

"lo" is a network interface which the Unix operating system uses to talk to itself. The IP address visible in the second line, 127.0.0.1, is a special IP number that always refers to the current machine itself. In other words, regardless of what an individual machine's assigned IP number may be, it also always has a second IP number of 127.0.0.1 and thinks of itself in those terms.

In order to use the **ifconfig** program to bring up an ethernet connection, you must have superuser privileges. You must also know the new IP number which is to be assigned to that machine. With both those conditions met, you can connect the new machine to the network with the command

```
ifconfig eth0 192.168.1.111 up
```

The argument eth0 refers to the interface. The first ethernet network interface card is always referred to as eth0; should you have a second NIC, which is rare, it would be called eth1. The command, as issued above, tells the computer to assign the IP address 192.168.1.111 to the first ethernet device, and then to activate that device. To deactivate an active ethernet device, issue the command

```
ifconfig eth0 down
```

Note: The "eth*X*" designation is Linux-specific. Other Unix variants use different designations. For example, FreeBSD uses the designation "ep*X*" as in the command **ifconfig ep0 192.168.1.111 up**. Sun's Solaris variant uses the designation "le*X*." Before you attempt to bring up an interface on your particular Unix variant, be sure to check the documentation to see how ethernet interfaces should be named in the command.

At this point, if you issue the **ifconfig** command without arguments again, you will see a different output than you did before the new interface was configured. The new output will resemble this:

```
eth0   Link encap:Ethernet   HWaddrs 00:60:8C:BB:D0:7E
inet addr:192.168.1.111  Bcast:192.168.0.255
Mask:255.255.255.0
UP  BROADCAST  RUNNING  MULTICAST  MTU:1500 Metric:1
RX packets:1480424 errors:217 dropped:0 overruns:213
frame:217
```

```
TX packets:1371779 errors:0 dropped:0 overruns:0 carrier:0
collisions:19662 txqueuelen:100
Interrupt:9 Base address:0x300
lo        Link encap:Local Loopback
inet addr:127.0.0.1  Mask:255.0.0.0
UP LOOPBACK RUNNING   MTU:16436   Metric:1
RX packets:20163 errors:0 dropped:0 overruns:0 frame:0
TX packets:20163 errors:0 dropped:0 overruns:0 carrier:0
collisions:0 txqueuelen:0
```

The loopback device reports in the same manner that it did in the first execution of this command, but now the newly configured ethernet device is also included in the output with the settings you provided.

The new machine is now connected to the network, and should be able to exchange information with any other machine on the network, including electronic mail messages and file transfer between network machines. This machine will not, however, be able to reach machines across the Internet or anywhere outside the local network, because it has not been configured for external access. These configurations are the topic of the next section of this chapter.

Routers, Gateways, and DNS

Computers have little skill in independent thought or analysis. Although the machines can calculate vast amounts of data very quickly, they are limited to performing those tasks which are ultimately requested by an operator and none other. When a computer is added to a network and the interface is appropriately configured, the computer can identify the network to which it is attached because of the physical link at the network interface card. However, the computer cannot find its way to any other network even if the physical connections exist, because it has not been told how to get outside its own limited net.

Providing these directions and maps for a given network is called *routing*. Routing is usually the job of a single dedicated computer called a *router*. It is a fairly simple task but is very intensive in its use of machine CPU cycles. Using a regular user or administrative machine to handle routing would probably overwhelm that machine's capability, so a separate machine is used. The router must examine each individual packet that travels through it, and determine where that packet should be sent. On a busy LAN, the data volume may be so high that even a mid-performance machine would be swamped.

Because of these performance requirements, routers are typically specialized pieces of equipment. The most popular routers are those made by the Cisco corporation. Cisco routers have a specialized operating system which is designed so that administrators can configure new network routes quickly and easily. Cisco router administration is specialized enough that there is a complete series of certifications which guarantee a minimum level of competence, and Cisco-certified administrators often find it easier to get new work than those with no formal recognition of their abilities.

Though Cisco and other commercial hardware companies offer an array of machines with varying capabilities, ordinary personal computers can also be made into routers. This is a much cheaper option, since specialized hardware is quite expensive. Homemade routers are less likely to be able to handle vast volumes of data and would not be the best choice for a high-volume network but can be sufficient for small networks. Indeed, for a very small network like those found in homes or small businesses, routing can be handled by a single non-dedicated personal computer which may also hold other elements of the operating system.

Note: Those who want to know more about the use of converted personal computers as routers might be interested in the Linux Router Project. LRP software fits on a single diskette, and can be used to turn any Linux PC into a router. Once running, the LRP software allows the administrator to configure network interfaces and new routes with a menu-driven user interface. Learn more about the Linux Router Project at http://www.linuxrouter.org.

From the point of view of a single computer on a network, the router acts as a *gateway* to the outside world and other networks. The machines on the network must be told that any packets not destined for machines on the immediate network should be sent to the router/gateway. From that point, the router takes over and distributes the packets to their external destination. These instructions are known as setting up the *default route* and are given with the **route** command.

Note: Like the **ifconfig** command, **route** is a powerful and complex command. See Appendix A and the **route** manual page for more information on its capabilities.

Defining Network Default Routes

Before setting up a default route, examine the current status of routing on the new machine. Issue the command

```
netstat -r
```

at the command prompt. This command generates output which should resemble this:

```
Kernel IP routing table
Destination Gateway    Genmask     Flags MSS Window irtt Iface
192.168.1.0    *    255.255.255.0   U    40    0     0   eth0
127.0.0.0      *      255.0.0.0     U    40    0     0    lo
```

Two routes are shown here. The first, 192.168.1.0, refers to the network to which this computer is physically connected. In order for any network connection to function, this route must exist. Otherwise, the machine would not know how to send any packets outside itself. This route was created when the ifconfig command was issued.

Note that the route ends in .0 rather than the computer's individual .111 address. Any IP number that ends in 0 is a special one, and refers to the network as a whole rather than to a particular machine. This route is also associated with the interface eth0, which is the identity of the Network Interface Card as defined when the computer was added to the network.

The second route in this output is the route for the loopback device. While it might seem strange that a machine needs a network designation in order to talk to itself, the loopback connection operates like any other connection in keeping with the "consistency" element of the Unix design philosophy. Therefore, loopback routes are as essential as network routes.

To add a new route, you must know the IP address of the gateway machine (router). For this example, assume that the IP address is 192.168.1.99. Issue the command

```
route add default gw 192.168.1.99
```

This command defines 192.168.1.99 as the default route. Any packets that are not destined for a machine on the local network will be sent to 192.168.1.99 and then redirected to the outside world. To see how this is reflected in the routing table for this machine, reissue the command

```
netstat -r
```

at the command prompt. The output will look something like this:

```
Kernel IP routing table
Destination  Gateway      Genmask     Flags MSS Window irtt Iface
192.168.1.0     *      255.255.255.0  U    40    0      0  eth0
127.0.0.0       *        255.0.0.0    U    40    0      0   lo
default    192.168.1.99 0.0.0.0       UG   40    0      0  eth0
```

The new route has been added and is reflected in the output. Instead of a specific network designation, the new route is named "default" and the gateway machine is defined in its entry. Like the local interface, the new "default" route is associated with the eth0 network interface. This makes sense because, even if network traffic is destined for the Internet or some other external network and not a machine on the local network, the packets will still be sent and received through the interface eth0.

DNS

Once the machine has been configured and the routing set up properly, the network connection is fully functional. The machine can exchange data with any local machine as well as with machines on external networks through the gateway. Before the machine can access the Internet and use it properly, though, there is one last task to be done.

In the previous chapter, you learned about *domain name resolution*. Recall that Domain Name Servers are required so that computers can translate alphabetical machine names into IP numbers. To move across the Internet, the new machine must know how to locate the Domain Name Servers used by the network. These instructions are given by editing a configuration file.

Note: Domain Name Servers are usually mentioned in the plural, though only one DNS machine is used for any given reconciliation. It is common practice for networks to have multiple servers, usually 2. This extra machine acts as a backup. If the primary server is down, the secondary machine will be consulted automatically.

In order to specify the addresses of the name servers, edit the configuration file /etc/resolv.conf (or whatever the appropriate file name is for your particular Unix variant, found by consulting the documentation). If no network configurations have yet been made on this machine, the file may not exist. You can create it by issuing the command

```
touch /etc/resolv.conf
```

Open the file in a text editor and place two lines in it:

```
nameserver 192.168.100.101
nameserver 192.168.100.102
```

replacing these IP numbers with whatever IP numbers are the actual DNS addresses you must use. Save the file, exit the text editor, and ensure that the file permissions are set so that the file is world readable by issuing the command

```
chmod a+r /etc/resolv.conf
```

The machine is now fully connected to the network and is able to make connections to machines on the Internet as well as on the local network.

Dial-up Networking

If you are using Unix in a school or business setting, it is most likely that you will connect to the Internet or other external networks through an ethernet connection. With the increasing popularity of Linux and FreeBSD for small home Unix networks, however, many people must rely on dial-up connections for their Internet access. Dial-up networking is never an optimal solution, but has additional complications for the Unix user.

Most dial-up connections are made through a commercial Internet service. Before you attempt to use a Unix machine for a dial-up connection, be sure that such a connection is compatible with Unix networking. Under Unix, a standard PPP (Point to Point Protocol) connection is used for dial-up networking. Provided that the Internet service offers a compliant connection, there should be no problem dialing up and establishing a connection. However, some Internet companies—notably America Online and the Microsoft Network—use modified versions of the protocol that require specialized software not available for the Unix platform.

Note that it may be difficult to find out whether or not your Internet service provider is Unix-compatible. Most ISP technical service departments provide little training about Unix, and most customer service operators will say that Unix is not supported on their ISP. "Not supported," however, does not necessarily mean that Unix is banned; it just means that you probably won't be able to rely on tech support for help if you run into a problem. The important element is that you sign up with an ISP that uses a standard unmodified PPP connection.

If you are using Linux to connect via dial-up, the procedure is fairly simple. Most Linux distributions provide a graphical tool to assist with configuring the connection. Simply open the tool and follow the instructions to set up the connection.

Under other forms of Unix, the process can be more complicated. Under FreeBSD, for example, you will need to edit the configuration file /etc/ppp/ppp.conf by adding a new section. Open the file in a text editor and add these lines:

```
LOCALISP:
set phone phone number
set authname login name
set authkey password
```

where the terms in italic are replaced with the actual information. You could also change the name LOCALISP to any value you prefer, which is especially useful if you have more than one ISP. Save the file and exit the editor.

Now, restart the PPP daemon so that it takes the new information into account. Issue the command

```
ppp -auto LOCALISP
```

(or whatever value you used to name the new entry). PPP is now configured and will be deployed automatically as soon as you issue any commands that require a network connection. FreeBSD will connect to the ISP defined in the named entry.

Although this may seem relatively simple, other Unix variants use more complex methods to configure dial-up access. Like Linux, some variants may provide a configuration tool, while others will require work with configuration files. Your variant's documentation will provide appropriate information about setting up dial-up networking on your machine.

Case Study: Setting Up a Simple Network

In this section, you will work through the process of setting up a small network of linked machines. Once the machines are all hooked together, you will connect the entire network to a larger network by using one of the computers as a simple router/gateway. While it is not necessary to perform this project in order to understand it, doing so may help you gain some hands-on experience with building networks.

In order to complete this project, the following equipment is necessary:

- 4 personal computers running Linux
- 5 Ethernet Network Interface Cards (one PC should have two NICs)
- 5 segments of Category 5 twisted-pair cable with RJ-45 jacks
- 1 Ethernet mini-hub having at least five ports

In addition to the hardware, you will also need the following items:

- An available connection to an ethernet network, preferably one with access to the Internet, and all IP numbers associated with that network
- The IP numbers of two available DNS servers

Set aside the computer with two NICs for now. It will serve as the gateway machine, but it is best to construct the rest of the network first.

Connect each of the three remaining machines to the hub with a length of Category 5 cable. Use the shortest length of cable that will span the distance between machine and hub without being too tight. Make sure that the hub is plugged into an electrical source and is running properly. Check all the RJ-45 jacks to ensure that they are securely in place.

Assign each machine an IP number beginning with 192.168.1. IP numbers in the 192.168 range are reserved for use on any private internal network. No machine with a direct connection to the Internet may use these numbers. In this project, only the gateway machine will have an IP number outside this range since it is the only machine which has a direct connection outside the network. For example, the first PC might be 192.168.1.1, the second 192.168.1.2, and the third 192.168.1.3.

In addition to the IP number, give each machine a name. While machine names can be thematic, for this project you can select simple names like PC1, PC2, and PC3. The machine name is stored as the value of the HOSTNAME environment variable. You should also create a file at /etc/hostname that contains the machine name, so that the computer will automatically check for its name at bootup.

On each machine, configure and activate the ethernet interface. For example, on PC1 you would issue the command

```
ifconfig eth0 192.168.1.1 up
```

On PC2, the command would be

```
ifconfig eth0 192.168.1.2 up
```

and on PC3,

```
ifconfig eth0 192.168.1.3 up
```

Once you have connected, named, and numbered the machines, they should all be able to talk to each other. To verify this, do a "ping test." On PC1, issue the command

```
ping 192.168.1.2
```

You should see output like this:

```
PING 192.168.1.2 from 192.168.1.1 : 56(84) bytes of data.
64 bytes from 192.168.1.2: icmp_seq=0 ttl=225 time=5.785 msec
64 bytes from 192.168.1.2: icmp_seq=0 ttl=225 time=415 usec
64 bytes from 192.168.1.2: icmp_seq=0 ttl=225 time=412 usec
64 bytes from 192.168.1.2: icmp_seq=0 ttl=225 time=426 usec
64 bytes from 192.168.1.2: icmp_seq=0 ttl=225 time=412 usec
```

This output continues until you press Ctrl+c to stop it.

ping is a utility which sends a data packet to the designated address at regular intervals. When the packet arrives at its destination, it is echoed back to the originating machine. If you get an error message or there is no output, there is a problem with your connection. Ping each machine from the other two machines to make sure that all the connections are working in both directions.

At this point, it is useful to set up some basic name resolution so that you don't have to continue typing nearly identical IP numbers. Though this network does not yet have access to a name server, there is a workaround for very small networks. On each machine, create a file called /etc/hosts that contains these lines:

```
127.0.0.1 localhost.localdomain   localhost
192.168.1.1   PC1
192.168.1.2   PC2
192.168.1.3   PC3
```

Save the file and exit the editor. Now, issue the command

```
ping PC2
```

instead of

```
ping 192.168.1.2
```

You should get the same output that you got the first time you pinged that machine.

You now have a fully functional LAN. If your needs were as simple as sharing data among the three computers, you could stop working. However, most people want to connect their small networks to the Internet. This is where the fourth machine comes into play.

Connect one of the NICs in the fourth computer to the hub with a length of Category 5 twisted-pair cable. Connect the other NIC to whatever is being used for the Internet connection: a modem, a cable modem, an Ethernet wall jack, etc. Designate the eth0 interface as the interface used to connect to the external network and assign it the "real" IP number given to you at the start of the project:

```
ifconfig eth0 xx.xxx.xxx.xxx
```

The other NIC, which is attached to the hub, receives the designation eth1. You can assign this NIC an internal IP number in the 192.168 range:

```
ifconfig eth1 192.168.1.100
```

Ending the IP number with 100 distinguishes the gateway machine from the other regular machines on the network.

Now that all machine interfaces are configured and IP numbers assigned, you can set up basic routing. On the gateway machine, issue the command

```
route add default eth0
```

This is somewhat different from the routing command discussed earlier in the chapter. In this instance, since this machine is intended to function only as a gateway, the default route identifies the ethernet device connected to the external network. The device connected to the internal network should have had its own route created when the interface was configured.

Because this is a Linux-based network, you can now set up IP masquerading. This is a useful function which allows the PCs on the network—even though they don't have "real" IP numbers—to use the Internet. To the outside world, it will appear that all the signals from this LAN are coming only from the gateway machine, but the gateway will know which internal computer sent which signal and route the appropriate response to the correct computer. Issue the command

```
modprobe iptable_nat
```

at the shell prompt. This command loads the kernel module that enables IP masquerading. Next, issue the command

```
iptables -t nat -A POSTROUTING -o ppp0 -j MASQUERADE
```

This command sets up the networking rules for masquerading on the gateway machine. Finally, issue the command

```
echo 1 > /proc/sys/net/ipv4/ip_forward
```

to turn on IP forwarding, which is a necessary component of IP masquerading.

Now, at each of the PCs on the network, issue the command

```
route add default gw 192.168.1.100
```

Open the file /etc/resolv.conf (or create it) on each PC. Add two lines to the file, containing the two IP numbers used for your primary and secondary DNS servers. Save and exit the files.

At this point, the network should be fully operational. As long as the Internet connection on the gateway machine is live, you can connect to the Internet from any of the local PCs. Obviously, mail and news clients will need to be configured appropriately before they will work, but Web browsers and direct commands like ping should function properly.

Summary

Although Unix can be used on a stand-alone computer, it is particularly effective used on a network. A network of computers can manage data flow in one of several ways: a local area network, a wide area network, or an internet. LANs are small groups of machines directly wired to each other; a WAN is usually a network of LANs connected through intermittent connection or dedicated connections; an internet is a network of WANs. The ultimate internet is the Internet, which is a constantly-changing assortment of various networks around the world.

Networks are built with particular topologies. The type of hardware available, and the space in which the network must be built, determine the topology selected. Topologies have descriptive names like bus, ring, or hub. The hub topology is most common, especially since the development of ethernet networks, which join machines with standards-compliant cable which can carry vast amounts of data at high speeds. Ethernet networks are easy to configure under all Unix variants. Most networks, especially if they connect to larger networks like WANs or internets, also have specialized hardware called a router, which distributes incoming and outgoing data to the appropriate destination. Network administrators may also need to configure domain name resolution, dial-up connections, or other network elements depending on the ultimate use and function of the network.

Review Questions

1. Define a local area network.
2. How is a local area network constructed?
3. Define a wide area network.
4. How is a wide area network constructed?
5. Define an internet.
6. How is an internet different from a WAN?
7. What is the difference between an internet and the Internet?
8. What is the difference between network type and topology?
9. Name several topologies and draw a picture of each.
10. When is a bus topology most appropriate?
11. What are the advantages and disadvantages of the ring topology?
12. Why would an administrator prefer a hub topology over other kinds of networks?
13. Define Ethernet.

14. What is a hardware address?
15. What makes a network an ethernet network?
16. What kind of networking hardware can be used to construct an ethernet network?
17. What are the advantages and disadvantages of coaxial cable? Fiber optics?
18. How can a network's effective speed be evaluated most accurately?
19. Describe the **ifconfig** command and its use.
20. What are the components of **ifconfig** output?
21. What is a loopback device?
22. Define a router and explain its function.
23. Why is routing CPU intensive?
24. What is a gateway?
25. Why do networks need default routes?
26. Define domain name resolution and explain how it works.
27. What is the Point-to-Point Protocol?
28. How can you determine whether an ISP is Unix-compatible?
29. Why are two DNS IP numbers required when setting up a network connection?
30. What is **ping**? How does it work?
31. What is IP masquerading?
32. How can you test a network to see if it is working properly?

Exercises

1. Investigate the various networks at your school, workplace, and home. Describe each type of network by both its type and its topology, as best you can. Can you tell the difference between the network used in your computer lab and the network provided by your Internet service provider? What about computer access at your job? Who manages each of these networks, and what kind of functions are available to end users like you?
2. Using the roadway analogy as a starting point, construct three or four other analogies for various types of networks. What kind of example would you use to illustrate how a WAN operates? A LAN? Provide better analogies for the Internet than the roadway example. Illustrate your answers if diagrams or pictures will help the reader understand the analogy more clearly.
3. Consult a networking hardware catalog, either in print or online. Given what you know about the various kinds of hardware required to set up a network, design three different networks using the items sold in your catalog. The networks should each have at least eight user machines, a router, and a connection to the Internet. The first network has no price limit, and should incorporate top-of-the-line components. The second network must be as inexpensive as possible; you might investigate used parts or local shops for component prices as well. The third network should be a reasonably priced network using mostly new components. Write a description of each network, including the technical specifications of the components included in each.
4. Identify several Internet service providers in your area, including both local and national providers if possible. If your school offers dial-up access to students, add it to the list. Call each provider or visit their Web sites to ascertain if the provider is Unix-compatible or Unix-friendly. What kind of software is required for users to connect to the service? Is it PPP compatible? How easy would it be for you to use this service if you only had a Unix machine? Create a table showing the results of your research, and recommend one particular ISP for Unix users, giving your reasons.

5. Consult the documentation for your Unix variant, either in printed material or on the Web. Describe the mechanism used to configure dial-up services on this variant. How do you define the ISP? What method is used to establish the connection? Are there specific configuration tools required with this variant? Write a report showing what you did at each step.
6. Assume that you have a network of eight computers. Invent a domain name to be associated with this network (or use one assigned to you by your instructor). Create at least six different sets of machine names. Which would be easiest for you to remember? Which would be easiest for users? Which would be hard to administer? Avoid obscenity or private jokes, and assume that you built this network for business use.

CHAPTER 12

Shell Programming I: Introduction to Shell Programming

IN THIS CHAPTER

1. What is shell programming?
2. Programs vs. scripts
3. Anatomy of a shell program

In the previous sections of this book, you have learned to use the shell to execute single commands, and to chain commands together with redirections and pipes. In this section of the text, you will learn to create entire programs from individual shell commands. These programs are in a repeatable format which does not need to be retyped each time you want to run that sequence of commands.

Such programming of the shell is called, appropriately enough, *shell programming*. It is also sometimes known as *system programming*, especially when the programs serve an administrative function. However, system programming is a broader term which can also refer to programs which affect the running of the system but which are not necessarily composed of shell commands. For example, it is possible to do system programming in the Perl language. For this reason, we do not use the term "system programming" to refer to work done within the shell.

What Is Shell Programming?

Shell programming is where the real power of Unix is unleashed. Because the shell's command language is also a fully featured programming language, complete with the ability to handle data in complex ways, a very high degree of automation is within reach. For the system administrator, shell programs can increase efficiency and save large amounts of time formerly spent on repetitive tasks.

Automating Repetitive Tasks

When system administrators think of the benefits of shell programming, one of the first areas is that of automating repetitive tasks. System administrators are often called upon to perform certain tasks at regular intervals. The classic example of this kind of task is the system backup. Most organizations that rely upon their Unix machines require their system administrators to make regular backups of all files housed on those computers. These backups are critical, since they are often the only thing that stands between the organization and the loss of all its crucial data in the event of a system crash, disk failure, crack attack, or any other catastrophic event that might damage the system. Most networks have some version of a *tiered backup schedule.* That is, the entire system might be backed up once a month, but certain directories would be backed up weekly or even daily, due to the importance of the data stored in those directories.

Clearly, running backups on a frequent basis represents a large time investment for network administrators. Fortunately, doing backups is a fairly mechanical operation, and can be successfully automated with shell programs. Those shell programs can then be run automatically with the Unix scheduling utility **cron**. With these simple tools, almost all of the labor involved with regular backups can be eliminated. Once the programs have been written and the automatic scheduler configured, the administrator's work is reduced to double-checking that backups were performed as scheduled.

Similar solutions can be applied to the myriad of other repetitive tasks found on most networks: disk space inventories, security audits, file type management, and the like. The automation of these tasks leaves the administrator free to concentrate on unique problems that inevitably appear in the course of daily network operations. What were once time-intensive tasks now require only regular checks.

Making the Complex Simple

While shell programming can eliminate or sharply reduce time spent on repetitive tasks, it can also help simplify complex jobs. There are a number of tasks that have lengthy command chains and may warrant time spent on streamlining the effort required. For some of these tasks, the effort put into the job may be significantly greater than the time it would require to create a programmed solution.

For example, assume that you are the administrator of a large Unix network with hundreds of users. In reading your daily logs, you notice that the network is running out of disk space. You suspect that many users are keeping too much data in their home directories. To solve this problem, you could examine the amount of disk space in each home directory and, if necessary, e-mail each user asking them to reduce the number of files. With hundreds of users, however, this might take hours or days. The other solution would be to create a program that does the same thing. Writing the program would take less than an hour, and it can then run in the background while you go on to other work.

Programs and Scripts

Many people refer to shell programs as *scripts*. For most purposes, these terms are synonymous. However, there is some controversy surrounding this usage. Some people believe that shell programming is not "real" programming because the native shell language does not have as many features as do actual programming languages like C. Others draw a distinction by defining a *program* as something which must be compiled, or converted into binary code before running, and a *script* as something which is interpreted, or converted into binary code while running. Still others think of shell programs as scripts because they learned the terminology many years ago when native shell languages were much less developed than they are now.

Whatever the reason for the terms, it is less than precise to use the term *script* for shell programming. "Script" implies a rote series of steps that are repeated, more or less verbatim, each time the program is run. Shell programs are more complex than that. Shell programs can evaluate data and make decisions about how to execute themselves, and they can change their behavior in response to their circumstances. The term "script" is too restrictive for such complex behavior. Nevertheless, the word is commonly used and you will see it frequently, even in this book.

Anatomy of a Shell Program

A shell program is a simple text file. It can be read by humans and by machines. There are several components common to shell programs, no matter what their function. These components are fairly broad concepts which make up the overall framework of the program. In the remaining chapters of this section of the text, these general ideas will be broken down into more specific constructs and program components.

Invoking the Shell

Like most other elements in the Unix operating system, shell programs are stored as text files. There is nothing particular about a shell program that appears different from a letter, a configuration file, or a journal entry. The computer cannot tell that a file is a shell program simply by looking at the file and any designations it may carry. In order to let the operating system know that the file is a shell program, the program must invoke the shell as its first action.

To invoke the shell, the first working line of the shell program must contain a line like this:

```
#!path/to/shell
```

where the string *path/to/shell* is replaced with the full path name of the shell you want to execute this script. Should there be a number of shells installed on the system, any one of them may be used to run a particular script, even if it is not the shell currently active in the user environment.

Note: The "first working line" of the program is the first line which will be parsed by the shell as a command. The first working line is not necessarily the initial line of the program. It may be preceded by comments, as explained below, which are intended for human readers and not for the shell.

Thus, any shell program which is intended to invoke the bash shell would have the first working line of

```
#!/bin/bash
```

since /bin/bash is the traditional location of the bash executable file. The construct #!, known as a *hash-bang* or *shebang* in Unix slang, indicates to the operating system that the specified shell must be started in order to run the program.

Comments

Comments do not affect the operation of the shell program. Instead, they are notes written by the program's creator and are intended for human users of the program. Comments may explain a particular construct or might warn the user of a potential problem.

Many people, including programmers, underestimate the importance of comments. Comments serve to keep a program understandable, regardless of its complexity. Every program should have a comment at its beginning which explains the function of the program, and comments in each section of the program explaining what that particular segment of the program is designed to do.

When you are writing shell programs, and if you move on to write more complex programs, you should add comments even if you never plan to share your programs with anyone else. Over the course of time, it is very easy to forget how a given program works, especially if it was only used a few times. Revising an old program can be a frustrating experience if it was not properly commented at the start.

To insert a comment into the program, simply start the comment line with the hashmark character, #, as in

```
# This line is a comment.
```

Comments which occupy more than one line must have a hashmark at the beginning of each line, as in

```
# This is a comment

# which spans two lines.
```

Note that the hashmark alone and the hashbang, #!, are two different things. The shell invocation is not a comment even though its initial character is the hashmark.

Commands

Commands are the heart of a shell program. The central idea of shell programming involves chaining shell commands together to create complex behavior. In a shell program, you can use any command that might be issued at the shell prompt, provided that it operates non-interactively or can be configured to do so. For example, you could use the **ls** command, but not the **pico** command, because the Pico text editor requires interactive data entry.

It is important to remember that many Unix programs which normally run interactively do have options which allow them to run non-interactively, thus allowing their use in a shell program. One such program is the text-based Web browser **lynx**, which has the –dump and –source options. These options allow a Web page or remote file to be grabbed by the shell and sent to the standard output without any intervention from the user. Such actions can be quite handy, perhaps to pull a local weather report or a set of sports scores at regular intervals. To learn more about changing the default behavior of a given Unix command, consult the program's manual page or any other program documentation you might find.

Data

If a program consists of a set of actions, the data is the object upon which those actions are performed. Data can be anything: numbers, words, expressions, or even other commands. A program might draw data from a text file, a system log, a random number generator, or any other source on the machine.

Data used by shell programs are stored in variables. In earlier chapters, you learned about environment variables, which store settings for the user environment. Program variables work in the same way, except that they are not exported to the system as a whole. Instead, they remain specific to the shell program in which they were created. This does not mean that you cannot use environment variables in a shell program; they are valid entries and types of data. However, a variable only needs to be defined as an environment variable if it is going to be used by more than one program.

Flow Control

Flow control is a concept which does not have a good analog outside of programming. Flow control is a set of constructs which allow the shell program to make decisions about how to execute itself. These constructs can allow a section of a given program to be executed repeatedly as long as conditions permit, or executed conditionally when a specified set of parameters exists.

Flow control constructs are almost always used in conjunction with data variables. In this way, the program can respond to different types of data in different ways. If the datum represented by a variable says one thing, the program will behave in a particular manner. If the datum says something else, the program will behave differently. Quite often, the "art of programming" is the creative use of flow control.

Summary

Although most users' primary interaction with the shell is to issue single commands at the command prompt, the shell is actually a fully-featured and powerful environment. Using the various tools included in the shell, users and administrators can link complex sequences of commands and data interpretation to produce functional programs. These programs can be used for a myriad of tasks within the shell, but the most common uses of shell programs are to automate repetitive tasks and to simplify complex operations.

Shell programs always begin with a line which invokes the shell itself. If the shell is not invoked, there will be no program to interpret the commands within the program. Any shell can run a program written specifically for it, but most shells have difficulty running scripts written for other shells. After the shell is invoked, the program continues with the commands required for its operation. These commands may be accompanied by comments, notes from the programmer which are intended for user help. Because they are set off with the hashmark character, comments are not parsed as part of the program. Some programs also identify data which is to be used as input for the program's commands. Other programs make use of flow control, which is a programming construct permitting the program to make decisions about its behavior depending on input data or other elements.

Review Questions

1. Define shell programming.
2. What are some uses of shell programs?
3. Why is automating repetitive tasks beneficial?
4. How can shell programs help to simplify complex jobs?
5. What is the difference between a program and a script?
6. What features do shell programs have that scripts do not have?
7. What are the benefits of storing shell programs as text files?
8. Define "invoking the shell." How is it done?
9. Why are comments beneficial?
10. How are comments incorporated into a program?
11. What is the difference between "#" and "#!"?
12. What types of commands can be invoked in a shell program?
13. What can be used as the data set for a shell program command?
14. What is the difference between a program variable and an environment variable?
15. Define flow control.

Exercises

1. Through experience, external reading, or conversation with network administrators, compile a list of repetitive tasks which are part of an administrator's regular routine. Which of these tasks could be automated or simplified with a shell program? What elements would the program need to accomplish each task?
2. Visit a script archive on the Web. (URLs for such archives can be found in the Internet resources appendix, or through a search engine.) Make a table showing some of the administrative scripts contained in the archive. What are the functions of these scripts? Is the script a general-purpose program or is it designed for a somewhat unusual situation? Recommend any scripts that you think provide an essential function for a network administrator.
3. Look through a few scripts and configuration files, either on your machine or that you find in an archive. Some configuration files are also found in the appendices of this book. Do these files have comments? Do the comments help you understand the function of the program? Identify places where additional comments might be useful, and identify comments that are particularly helpful. How do the comments affect your experience in reading the file?

CHAPTER 13

Shell Programming II: Variables and Flow Control

IN THIS CHAPTER

1. Shell program basics
2. What is a variable?
3. Assigning variables
4. Special variables
5. Conditional flow control
6. Iterative flow control

In this chapter, we introduce the basic techniques of shell programming. The chapter begins with a discussion of variables, explaining how to assign values to variables and how to manipulate those values. It concludes with a discussion of flow control, with a specific emphasis on using variables in flow control constructs.

Shell Program Basics

In Chapter 12, you learned that a shell program is composed of individual shell commands. A simple shell program might look like this:

```
#!/bin/bash
# Program to set up basic networking functions – must be
run as "root"
/sbin/ifconfig eth0 192.168.1.21
/sbin/route add default gw 192.168.1.1
```

You might recognize these commands from the networking section of this book as the commands used to connect a Linux machine to an ethernet network and to the Internet. Such a program could be saved, for example, under the file name /usr/local/net-up. By doing this, you need only invoke the command

```
/usr/local/net-up
```

in order to start the machine's network functions.

This type of shell program fulfills the basic components needed to be a "program," but is overly simple. In particular, the program doesn't make decisions about how to execute itself, and decisions of many kinds are the core of what programs are meant to do. In order to make decisions, the program needs two elements: first, a means of storing and manipulating data, and second, a means of evaluating that data and taking action on it.

The first of these elements is done with variables. As you have learned earlier in this book, variables are a means by which the meaning of a piece of data can be separated from its function in the program. In this way, we can make grammatical use of data without needing to know the actual value of that data. The second element is represented by the various flow control structures. Flow control structures are specific instructions that the programmer gives to the computer about how to evaluate data, and what actions to take if the data meets certain criteria.

What Is a Variable?

In the most basic sense, a variable is a name given to a piece of information. Consider the algebraic expression

```
x=1
```

In this expression, the name of the variable is *x* and the value of that variable is 1. The fact that the variable's value is 1 has no real value; we simply selected that as the value. It could easily have been 2, 385, or 38920573. The equal sign is used to define the variable.

In a sense, you can think of the variable's name as a container, like a box. The variable's name is written on the side of the box: in this case, *x*. Inside the box is the value: in this case, 1. The box and its contents are separate from each other. If you want, you can replace the contents of the box with a different value. The variable will still have the same name, and will function in the same way within a program.

Variable Names

In order to create a variable, you must name it. Under Unix, the name of a variable can be almost anything. The only restrictions on variable names are that they must begin with a letter or with the underscore symbol _. Names may contain only alphanumeric characters or the underscore. No other symbols may be used; in fact, even the underscore is only used in special circumstances.

Although these are the basic rules for variable names, there are other conditions which are common practice. Variables are usually named with uppercase letters, as in VARIABLE. This makes the variables easy to see when scanning a large chunk of program code. Also, variable names are usually descriptive. That is, the variable's name indicates the variable's function, as in LENGTH or NAME. A variable named FILESIZE is generally considered better than a variable named EJSLKE438.

Variable Types

The most common type of variable used in shell programming is the *scalar variable*. A scalar variable is a single discrete piece of information. Scalar variable values can be a number, a letter, a word, or a group of words (a text string). The key to understanding a scalar variable is to understand that the entire value of the variable—no matter how many characters or words it may contain—is interpreted as a single datum. If you use a text string containing several words as the value of a scalar variable, you cannot treat each individual word as a separate element within the program. The string, as a whole, is the value of the variable.

In contrast to the scalar variable, another common variable type is the *array variable*. An array is a variable type that can hold a number of different values. These values are identified by an index number, which can be part of the variable name. For example, the array variable ANIMALS might hold the values "dog," "fish," and "horse." To refer to any single one of these values within a program, you need to refer to its index number, which is assigned when a value is added to the array. Thus, the values

```
ANIMALS[0]="dog"
ANIMALS[1]="fish"
ANIMALS[2]="horse"
```

would be used to define the set of values which make up the total value of the ANIMALS array variable (Remember that, under Unix, counting always begins with zero.)

Before an array variable can be used for the first time or can be given values like the ones above, it must be *declared*. In other words, you must tell the shell explicitly that you are creating an array variable. Do so with the **declare** command and the –a option, as in

```
declare -a ANIMALS
```

You can then assign values to this variable name.

Note:

Array variables have only been available in the bash shell environment since bash version 2.0. If you are using an earlier version of bash, you cannot use array variables. Check the version of bash installed on your system by issuing the command

```
bash -version
```

Arrays are also unavailable under the regular Bourne shell.

Assigning Variables

As mentioned above, a variable cannot be used until it has been *assigned*. Assigning a variable involves giving it an initial value. This is done through the use of an *assignment operator*, which is the equal sign =. In the case of a scalar variable, the command is simple:

```
ANIMAL = "horse"
```

In the case of an array variable, the format is slightly more complex:

```
ANIMALS = ("dog" "fish" "horse")
```

The format of an assignment for an array variable must be a list of elements contained in quotation marks and separated by a space, with the entire list enclosed in parentheses. If one of these elements is missing, the variable's value will not be set correctly.

When you assign a variable, you create the variable name and also provide the initial variable value. The value of the variable can change throughout the course of a program, as value definition is a valid command within such a script. However, when you initially assign the variable, you should provide the value that it will use first. The name of the variable remains constant and cannot be changed; if you give an improper name to the variable, misspell it, or use an unintuitive name, simply edit the program to reflect the appropriate name.

The $ Operator

When using variables, it is important to distinguish between use of the variable itself and the use of the variable's value. This is done with the $ operator. When this operator is placed at the start of a variable name, it provides a specific instruction to any program using the variable: "Use the value of this variable whenever it is invoked."

A program may contain both a definition of the variable's value and a statement using the $ operator, as in these lines:

```
ANIMAL=horse
echo $ANIMAL
```

When these lines run, the output of the program is the word **horse**. However, if the second line of this example were changed to

```
echo ANIMAL
```

the program would always output the word ANIMAL, no matter what the actual value of the ANIMAL variable might have been.

Both the plain VARIABLE and $VARIABLE expressions have a place in a shell program. In general, the plain variable name is used to declare or assign a particular variable. The $ operator is used anytime the program needs to use the variable's value as part of its operation.

Earlier in this book, we discussed the PATH variable. This environment variable defines the various directories which are to be searched automatically for a specified program file when it is invoked. To define new PATH values, the command

```
PATH=$PATH:/usr/bin/directory-name
```

is issued. This expression is particularly useful with a variable like PATH, which may have a lengthy string of values. With the syntax shown in this example, the new directory is appended to the existing value instead of replacing it. This is done by using the old value, expressed as $PATH, and then adding the new value after the colon character, :.

Note: Remember that you can change the value of any variable at any time, simply by reassigning it at the command line. This is true both for environment variables and for variables used only in shell programs.

Variable Interpolation

The PATH variable example in the previous section provides an example of *variable interpolation.* Interpolation is the process which happens when one uses the variable with the $ operator to designate a place where the value of the variable is to be used. For example,

```
ANIMAL="horse"
echo "My favorite animal is the $ANIMAL."
```

The output of these two lines would be

```
My favorite animal is the horse.
```

In this instance, the word "horse" has been *interpolated* in place of the variable name. This is fairly common in interactive scripts, and will be discussed in more detail later in this chapter.

Special Variables

As mentioned earlier in this chapter, there are some restrictions on the characters which can be used in variable names. The reasons for some of these restrictions are obvious. For example, the mathematical operators (+, −, and the like) are reserved for mathematical operations within the shell program. Likewise, comparison operators such as <, >, and = are restricted because they indicate particular operations which take place within the shell program.

However, there is an additional set of symbols which cannot be used in variable names because they are already used as a set of existing variables. These variables have pre-defined meanings which can be useful shorthand when writing shell programs. For example, the $ variable represents the process identification number of the current shell. If you wanted to see the value of the $ variable within the program, you could insert the line

```
echo $$
```

As with any other variable, to use its value the variable name must be prepended with the $ operator. The $ operator is distinct from the $ variable. Table 13.1 shows the special variables which exist under the bash shell.

Conditional Flow Control

With this understanding of variable construction, it is time to turn to variable use within shell programs. Apart from the simple interpolation shown above, the other main option for variables is to evaluate them. The program can

TABLE 13.1: Special Variables Under the bash Shell

Variable	Function
?	Returns the exit status of the previous command
$	Returns the process identification number of the current shell process
-	Returns the options given to the current shell process on start-up
!	Returns the process identification number of the last background command
0	Returns the file name of the current script
1-9	Returns the first through ninth command-line arguments given when invoking the current script; $1 is the first argument, $2 the second, etc.
_	Returns the last argument given with the previous command

compare a given variable's value with values that were selected before the script was run, or with the values of other variables. The result of this comparison can then direct the way in which the program executes. Such a procedure is called *flow control* because it is designed to control the path which the program takes while it executes: that is, the way in which the program "flows."

There are two types of flow control. *Conditional flow control*, the subject of this section, is the type of construct which directs the computer to execute a certain section of code only if a certain condition is met. The other type of flow control is *iterative flow control*. Iterative flow control directs the computer to execute a section of code repeatedly, or to iterate the section, unless or until a certain condition is met.

At this point, you might be confused. How is it that both conditional and iterative flow control have conditions which must be met? This is an unfortunate piece of linguistic overlap. The important thing to keep in mind is that conditional flow control is designed to execute a given section only once, whereas iterative flow control is designed to repeat a given section of code over and over until the specified condition is met.

The if-then Construct

The main feature of conditional flow control is the *if statement*. "if" is a command that informs the shell of a decision which must be made. An if construct takes the general form of

```
if <some condition>
then
  <something happens>
fi
```

The term "fi" at the end of the section is simply the word "if" spelled backward. It denotes the end of the conditional section.

This sample illustrates how a conditional flow control statement works. It says "If <*some condition*> is met, execute all the commands between the words "then" and "fi." If the condition is not met, the commands between "then" and "fi" will be skipped, and the program will jump to the command immediately following the word "fi" and continue to execute.

A more concrete example of an if statement would include actual conditions and consequences, as in

```
ANIMAL="dog"


if [ $ANIMAL = "dog" ]
then
  echo "The condition has been met."
fi
```

Here, the line "The condition has been met" will only be printed to the standard output if the value of the variable ANIMAL is equal to "dog."

However, if the variable's value is "horse," for example, the line will not echo:

```
ANIMAL="horse"
if [ $ANIMAL = "dog" ]
then
  echo "The condition has been met"
fi
```

The value of ANIMAL does not match the conditional value defined in the program, so the program ignores the conditional action and moves to whatever command follows the "fi" entry at the end of this conditional section.

These examples share several features which may be confusing or unusual to someone not used to reading program scripts. The first element, and perhaps the most obvious, is the indentation of the conditional line. This indentation is not strictly necessary for technical purposes; the program would run equally well if the lines were all flush with the left margin. However, it is a matter of programming style to indent lines within the same enclosing construct: in this case, the construct enclosed between the "if" and "fi" statements.

This indentation is primarily a matter of readability for human programmers. The indented subordinate lines provide a visual sense of which instructions are subordinate to others. In other words, the physical layout of the script shows the overall structure of the program. This is particularly important when constructs are nested inside other constructs.

For example, it is common to nest two if statements, as in this example:

```
if <condition 1>
then
  if <condition 2>
  then
    <some action>
  fi
<some other action>
fi
```

In such a scenario, <*some action*> only happens if both conditions 1 and 2 are met, whereas <*some other action*> happens if condition 1 is met, whether or not condition 2 is also met. Just by reading the sample and considering the indentations, you can see the two separate constructs with one nested inside the other.

The second feature of written shell programs that requires explanation is the use of square brackets, [and], to enclose the complete conditional phrase.

These brackets constitute an implicit command. In fact, using brackets is the same as using the **test** command. The example used in the previous paragraph,

```
ANIMAL="dog"

if [ $ANIMAL = "dog" ]
then
  echo "The condition has been met"
fi
```

could also be written to use the **test** command explicitly rather than using the square bracket shorthand, as in

```
ANIMAL="dog"

if (test $ANIMAL = "dog")
then
  echo "The condition has been met"
fi
```

The two programs are identical. The parentheses are used in the second script to set the if command apart from the **test** command.

The final component of program scripts with special utility is the equal sign, =. Its purpose may seem obvious, but there are some subtleties unique to its use in programs. First, in the context of a **test** statement (whether explicit or not), the equal sign functions as a comparison operator, and not as an assignment operator as it was shown earlier in this chapter. Second, the equal sign functions only as a comparison for textual values. If you want to compare numerical values, you must use the numerical comparison operator, −eq. The −eq operator is used in the same way, as in

```
if [ $VAR -eq 1 ]
```

or

```
if (test $VAR -eq 1)
```

Tables 13.2 and 13.3 contain complete lists of the textual and mathematical comparison operators available under the bash shell.

The if-then-else Construct

Often, programmers find that the simple if-then construct is too limited for their needs because they want to set up an either/or situation. For such purposes, the if then construct can be extended with the **else** statement. The general form of an if-then-else construct looks like this:

```
if <condition>
then
  <something>
```

TABLE 13.2: bash Textual Comparison Operators

Operator	Function
string A = *string B*	Alphanumeric text string A is the same as text string B
string A != *string B*	Alphanumeric text string A is not the same as text string B
string A > *string B*	Alphanumeric text string A is greater than text string B
string A < *string B*	Alphanumeric text string B is lesser than text string B

TABLE 13.3: bash Mathematical Comparison Operators

Operator	Function
A –eq *B*	*A* is equal to *B*
A –ne *B*	*A* is not equal to *B*
A –gt *B*	*A* is greater than *B*
A –ge *B*	*A* is greater than or equal to *B*
A –lt *B*	*A* is less than *B*
A –le *B*	*A* is less than or equal to *B*

```
else
  <something else>
fi
```

In this situation, if the <*condition*> is met, <*something*> will result. If the condition is not met, <*something else*> will happen. Either <*something*> or <*something else*> will always happen, but <*something*> and <*something else*> will never happen together.

As with the simpler if-then programs, an if-then-else construct can be expressed in different ways. The construct allows for shorter programs than the use of multiple if-then constructs. The program

```
ANIMAL="horse"

if [ $ANIMAL = "horse" ]
then
  echo "The condition has been met"
else
```

```
    echo "The condition has not been met"
fi
```

is the same as the program

```
ANIMAL= "horse"

if [ $ANIMAL = "horse" ]
then
  echo "The condition has been met"
fi
if [ $ANIMAL != "horse" ]
then
  echo "The condition has not been met"
fi
```

The != expression means "does not equal." The if-then-else construct is simply a shorter way of expressing the same outcome as the two sequential if-then statements.

The if-then-elif-then Construct

If there are more than two possibilities for a given scenario, there is another construct which allows for simpler programs. Of course, the programmer can stack multiple if-then or if-then-else constructs, but an unspoken goal of many programmers is to find the most elegant solution and the briefest program possible. The **elif** statement adds another layer of complexity to the conditional flow control construct.

The elif statement provides an alternative possible value for the variable. In a program, it extends the range of outcomes; if Condition A is not met, the elif statement defines a possible Condition B which has its own outcome. If neither Condition A or B is met, the program provides the outcome defined in the then statement. In action, the elif statement looks like this:

```
ANIMAL="horse"

if [ $ANIMAL = "horse" ]
then
  echo "The horse condition has been met"
elif [ $ANIMAL = "dog" ]
then
  echo "The dog condition has been met"
else
  echo "The condition has not been met"
fi
```

The programmer can include as many elif statements as are needed to manage the possible desired values. The else statement is not required, but provides a neat result for values which are not pre-defined in the elif statements. If no else statement is provided, the program will simply fail if an unexpected value is provided.

The case Construct

The last main construct used in conditional flow control is the **case** construct. This is the only conditional construct that is not part of the if family. The case construct is a useful way to manage a list of alternative values, especially where a chain of elif statements would be too long or cumbersome.

The case statement uses a number of possible values, indented and on separate lines following the same layout principles of the rest of the program. Each value has an associated outcome. The program in the previous section, rewritten to use the case construct rather than the elif statement, would look like this:

```
ANIMAL="horse"

case $ANIMAL in
  "horse" )
    echo "The horse condition has been met"
  ;;
  "dog" )
    echo "The dog condition has been met"
  ;;
  * )
    echo "The condition has not been met"
  ;;
esac
```

There are several items of note in this script. The right parenthesis character is used to define each option in the case, and the double semi-colon is used to end each option's entry. The asterisk, which is an optional entry, stands for "any other value." Finally, the complete case construct ends with the term **esac**, "case" spelled backward. This mirrors the if/fi expression used in an if-then construct.

A script written with the case construct works in almost the same way as a script written with stacked elif constructs. The difference is primarily one of organization. Some people find case constructs clearer to read, or easier to write, than stacked elif constructs. It is a personal choice.

Iterative Flow Control

As described earlier, *iterative flow control* is used to repeat a specified section of code until or unless a certain condition is met. Consider this program:

```
#!/bin/bash

#Program that asks the user to guess the animal I have
#in mind

MY_ANIMAL = "horse"
USER_ANIMAL="nothing"

while [ $USER_ANIMAL != $MY_ANIMAL ]
do
echo "Input an animal: "
read USER_ANIMAL    # the 'read' command takes input
                    # from the keyboard
  if [ $USER_ANIMAL != $MY_ANIMAL ]
  then
    echo "Sorry, please try again "
  fi
done

echo "That is correct. "
```

In this example, the code between the words "do" and "done" is executed over and over again, as long as the value of the MY_ANIMAL variable is not the same as the user-supplied value of the USER_ANIMAL variable. As soon as the two values are the same, the program exits the loop and continues with whatever command is on the line immediately following the word "done."

This script has a conditional construct inside the iterative construct, which is perfectly valid. The conditional construct will be executed each time the loop iterates. It is also valid to embed an iterative loop inside another iterative loop, or a conditional loop inside another conditional loop. You must open and close each complete construct appropriately so they execute as individual operations.

Caution: Whenever you use an iterative construct, you should be reasonably certain that the proper condition will arise at some point and stop the iteration. Creating an *infinite loop* is not usually dangerous, but does represent a type of program failure. It can also consume a disproportionate amount of system resources while it is running.

The while Loop

The script in the previous section showed an example of a "while" loop, which causes the subordinate code to execute repeatedly as long as the condition is met. When the condition becomes false, the loop exits and the program continues to execute the commands following the "done" statement. In the example above, the *inequality comparison operator* != was used to set up a double negative: the condition is true as long as the two variables are not equal. This may seem counterintuitive, but it is valid both technically and as a matter of programming style.

The until Loop

If using a double negative is unappealing or difficult to write, try the "until" construct, which iterates the code section as long as the condition remains false. The sample script can be rewritten like this to use the until loop:

```
#!/bin/bash

#Program that asks the user to guess the animal I have
#in mind

MY_ANIMAL = "horse"
USER_ANIMAL="nothing"

until [ $USER_ANIMAL = $MY_ANIMAL ]
do
  echo "Input an animal: " #
  read USER_ANIMAL    # the 'read' command takes
                      # input from the keyboard
  if [ $USER_ANIMAL != $MY_ANIMAL ]
  then
    echo "Sorry, please try again"
  fi
done

echo "That is correct. "
```

The only differences are that the while command has been changed to an until command, and the inequality comparison has been changed to an equality comparison operator. The until construct takes the same do/done enclosure as the while loop. This syntax holds for all iterative flow control constructs.

The for Loop

The "for" loop is most commonly used to iterate a block of code one time for each element in a specified set of values. Consider this program:

```
#!/bin/bash

declare -a ANIMALS

ANIMALS=(horse dog cow fish whale)

for ANIMAL in "${ANIMALS[@]}"
do
  echo $ANIMAL

done
```

This program sets up one array variable with a list of values. Then, the for loop iterates once for each value in the array. Note that ANIMAL and ANIMALS are two separate variables; ANIMALS is the array variable, and ANIMAL is a scalar variable to which each element of the array is the assigned within the loop.

Note in particular the way in which the array is rendered in the for statement. This format is required in order to use an array in this manner. The quotation marks and curly braces, { and }, are required in order to access the value of a particular element. The character in square brackets is the *positional parameter* which is used to track the element currently being used. The parameter's value starts at 0, and increments by 1 each time the loop repeats.

The select Statement

The "select" statement, though technically considered part of iterative flow control, is actually a somewhat different concept. It is used to create a menu of items from which the user can select. Consider this program:

```
#!/bin/bash

declare -a ANIMALS

ANIMALS=(horse dog cow fish whale)

select ANIMAL in "${ANIMALS[@]}"
do
  echo "The animal you selected is $ANIMAL"
done

1) horse
2) dog
3) cow
4) fish
5) whale
#?
```

At the prompt #?, the user must enter a number from the list. When the number is entered, the code inside the do/done enclosure is executed. If the user were to enter 1, for example, she would see this output:

```
The animal you chose is horse.
1) horse
2) dog
3) cow
4) fish
5) whale
#?
```

The process will repeat over and over again because no exit has been built into the program. To end the program, the user must press the Ctrl+c keystroke combination. An easier solution is to add an end into the program, as in

```
#!/bin/bash

declare -a ANIMALS

ANIMALS=(horse dog cow fish whale)

select ANIMAL in “${ANIMALS[@]}”
do
  echo “The animal you selected is $ANIMAL”
  exit
done
```

The exit command causes the program to end. Obviously, if the exit command is included in the program, the select loop will only iterate once.

There is another way to improve this program. The prompt is not particularly user-friendly and does not indicate what the user should do with the list presented on the screen. To change the prompt, you must change the value of the PS3 variable. PS3 is a special environment variable which controls the value of the prompt. A script incorporating this change might look like this:

```
#!/bin/bash

declare -a ANIMALS

ANIMALS=(horse dog cow fish whale)
PS3="Select the number of your favorite animal: "

select ANIMAL in "${ANIMALS[@]}"
do
  echo "The animal you selected is $ANIMAL"
  exit
done
```

Now the user will see this on the standard output device:

```
1) horse
2) dog
3) cow
4) fish
5) whale
Select the number of your favorite animal:
```

When the user selects an entry, the program will output the line

```
Your favorite animal is <the entry selected>
```

and then exit.

Summary

Shell programs are composed of variables and commands, along with other structural details. The variables used in shell programs can be environmental variables defined outside the program as regular shell values, or can be program variables constructed specifically for the program being written. Variables can be either scalar variables, containing a single piece of information, or array variables, taking several data points as the value. Variables must be named and their initial value declared before they can be used in a program operation.

Once variables have been constructed, both the variables and their values can be used in program sections. The concept of flow control underlies most program scripts, defining how the program runs. There are two types of flow control: conditional and iterative. Conditional flow control causes a particular code block to run only if a specified condition is met, while iterative flow control causes a particular code block to repeat until a specified condition is achieved. There are a number of code constructs which can be used to manage both types of flow control.

Review Questions

1. What are the necessary components for a shell program?
2. What components are required for a shell program which makes decisions about how to execute itself?
3. Define a variable.
4. What restrictions does Unix place on variable names?
5. Why are descriptive variable names preferred?
6. Define a scalar variable.
7. What kinds of values may a scalar variable have?
8. Define an array variable.
9. What types of values may an array variable have?
10. How is an array variable's value defined?
11. Define an assignment operator.
12. What is the function of the $ operator?
13. What is the difference between ADDRESS and $ADDRESS?
14. How can a new value be appended to an existing variable's value?
15. Define variable interpolation.
16. Why are some characters barred from variable names?
17. What is the difference between a mathematical operator and a comparison operator?
18. What is flow control?
19. Define conditional flow control.
20. Define iterative flow control.
21. What is the purpose behind indenting program lines and sections?
22. Why are square brackets used in shell programming?
23. Explain the different functions of the = character.
24. What is an infinite loop?
25. How is the text of the shell prompt defined?

Exercises

1. Write a short program that defines one scalar variable and its value and one array variable and its values. The program should print, to the standard output, the value of the scalar variable, the first value of the array variable, the value of the scalar variable, the second value of the array variable, and so on. The array variable should have at least five values.
2. Write a program which asks the user for his or her favorite flavor of ice cream. The program should print the response "Your favorite flavor of ice cream is <*response*>." For one reasonable response, however, the program should return the response "I hate <*flavor*>."
3. Using the program from exercise #2, rewrite it so that the implicit test becomes an explicit test. If you used an explicit test in constructing the program, convert it to an implicit test.
4. Write a program which queries the user about her favorite automobiles. Using an if-then-elif statement, provide customized responses for at least four makes of automobile and a response for unidentified cars.
5. Using the program from exercise #4, rewrite it to add iterative flow control so that the program will not exit until the user enters "Audi TT." Hint: A nested structure may be necessary.

CHAPTER 14

Shell Programming III: Regular Expressions

IN THIS CHAPTER

1. What is a regular expression?
2. grep
3. sed
4. awk

One of the more common tasks found in shell programs is the parsing of text. *Parsing* is the act of analyzing text for certain specified words, phrases, or patterns. Obviously, a computer cannot understand the meaning of words or phrases in the same way that a human can. However, there are mechanisms which can be incorporated into a program that can identify and match particular strings of characters or other patterns in the text.

Pattern matching, in shell programs, is done with *regular expressions*. A regular expression, also known as *regex* or *regexp*, is a symbol which stands in for particular textual strings. Using these pattern-matching operators, you can specify the kinds of characters to be matched, the number of characters to be matched, their position in the text string, and so on.

For example, assume that you want to print out a list of all the files in your home directory that have the suffix **.txt**. This is a simple pattern-matching operation used in conjunction with the ls command. At the shell prompt, issue the command

```
ls *.txt
```

The command returns, as output, a list of all files with the **.txt** extension. The asterisk used in this command is a pattern-matching operator which means "any combination of zero or more characters."

In such situations, the pattern-matching operator can be called a *metacharacter*, because it is a character which refers to other characters rather than acting as itself. That is, the asterisk used in the

```
ls *.txt
```

command is not a literal asterisk; instead, it represents any other string of characters that fits its definition. Just as GNU Emacs uses the *metakey* in constructing keystroke combinations, the metacharacter used in regular expressions is a symbolic representation of actual values.

The ***.txt** component of the example command is a regular expression. The full value of this expression could be described as "any combination of zero or more characters, followed by the specific string '.txt'". This expression can match any file name from the bare **.txt** to **123456789.abcdefghijkl.txt** and beyond. As long as the file name contains at least the '.txt' component, it will match this regular expression. Such an expression is very broad, and may match a large portion of the searched dataset, but it is still useful for quick searches or in situations where you might know the type of filename but not the specific name.

In addition to the asterisk, there are a number of other pattern-matching operators. The specific function of these metacharacters depends on the program in which they are used. However, many of these metacharacters function in much the same way, regardless of the program. This is due to common practice among those who develop regular expression processing programs, and to the rise of the POSIX standard. This standard governs a number of programming conventions, including the use of regular expressions. In the sections that follow, which introduce various programs utilizing regular expressions, individual metacharacter behavior is described for each program.

grep, sed, and awk

Most metacharacters, unlike the asterisk, are not used directly at the shell prompt. Instead, they are used within programs which have been written specifically for the purpose of processing regular expressions with a standard syntax. The most important of these programs are the Unix utilities **grep**, **sed**, and **awk**. Each of these programs is distinct, but together the trio works to accomplish a wide range of text-processing tasks.

Commands using these utilities, and their related metacharacters, can be issued at the shell prompt or used within a shell program. They are particularly useful when searching through a lengthy file for a specific entry or value. For example, you might write a system administration program that requires a particular value taken from a lengthy log file. Using a regular expression is the easiest way to automate the search.

Note: In recent years, a number of programming languages have been developed. These languages include the regular expression processing functions of **grep**, **sed**, and **awk**. In particular, the Perl programming language has a powerful and flexible regular expression engine. Many system administrators have come to prefer the fully integrated Perl language as an alternative to the somewhat fragmented Unix utilities. Perl is outside the scope of this book, but those who are interested in programming might enjoy investigating it. Certainly, administrative scripts written in Perl are rapidly approaching the popularity of native shell programs.

grep

The term "grep" is an acronym for "Get Regular Expression Print." It is pronounced as a single syllable, rather than as individual letters or as "gee-repp." In fact, **grep** is used as a conversational verb in many situations. As the name implies, the **grep** program is designed to identify strings which match a specified regular expression, and then to print those strings to the standard output.

The **grep** program takes the basic syntax

```
grep pattern filename
```

For example, if you wanted to search a log file named **mail_log** for the user name **mstern**, you would issue the **grep** command as

```
grep mstern mail_log
```

Any entries in the mail_log file which contain the text string **mstern** will print to the standard output, usually the monitor.

The **grep** command can also be issued without a specified input file. This allows you to pipe the output of an initial command into **grep** as the input source. For example, the command

```
ls *.txt
```

could be rewritten as

```
ls | grep *.txt
```

This particular example is not very useful, but the concept can be used to construct more elaborate regular expressions within a shell program or at the command prompt. If, for example, you needed to identify the process ID number of a given running process, you could use **grep** to find the appropriate process. If you were looking for a Netscape process, the command might look like this:

```
ps -x | grep netscape
```

The command would return only processes with the string **netscape**, limiting the time needed to scan all running processes.

grep Metacharacters

The first regular expression metacharacter introduced in this chapter was the asterisk. The asterisk, *, represents "any combination of zero or more characters." In fact, the asterisk literally matches any value. The regular expression *.txt can match the values **.txt**, **a.txt**, **b.txt**, **ab.txt**, **a.b.txt**, **ab15.txt**, **ab.15.txt.log**, and any other value that contains the .txt string somewhere in the name even if it is not the final element of the file name.

Where the asterisk is used to match any value, regardless of its length, the dot character, ., is used to match any single character. Thus, the expression .txt will match **atxt**, **btxt**, **3txt**, and so on. It will not match **abtxt** or **13.txt**.

A group or range of characters contained within square brackets will match any single character which matches one of the specified characters. The expression

```
[aeiou]
```

will match any single lower-case vowel if it is a unique string (not contained within a longer string). The expression

```
[a-z]
```

matches any single lower-case letter.

With these commands, you could create a regular expression pattern that resembles this:

```
[A-Za-z][aeiou].[1-9]*
```

This pattern would identify any upper or lower-case letter, followed by a lowercase vowel, followed by any single character, followed by any group of zero or more characters. Possible matches for the expression include

```
Rod2

ao23CCCCC
Bix99999.txt
```

and many, many other possible strings. However, this pattern is not limitless. Strings that would be ignored include

- 89b4 (does not begin with a letter)
- aba2.c (second character is not a vowel)
- letter.txt (fourth character is not a number)

grep Meta-"noncharacters"

In addition to the various metacharacters, there are a group of pattern-matching operators that do not represent characters. Rather, they represent additional conditions on the expression that are not character-oriented. Such characters can be used to specify the location of the text string within the file.

This is particularly useful when searching for an entry in a file that may contain many iterations of the same text string, perhaps a user name.

The circumflex character, ^, matches the beginning of a line. Thus, when you use the circumflex at the start of a regular expression, it limits the match only to strings which appear at the beginning of a line in the file. Even if the exact string is matched elsewhere in the input dataset, **grep** will not return a valid match unless the string is at the beginning of a line. The expression

```
^[Hh]orse
```

will match the strings **horse** or **Horse** only if they are at the start of a line. Any other horse strings within the text will be ignored.

Likewise, the dollar sign character, $, represents the end of a line. Thus, the expression

```
[Hh]orse$
```

will match the strings **horse** or **Horse** only if the string is the final string at the end of a line. Other matching strings will be ignored, as with the circumflex character. While the circumflex is more useful than the dollar sign in matching strings, the $ can be helpful in particular situations. Imagine, for example, that you had created a user group with the group ID 2834. Because this was the last group you had created, it would be at the end of every group listing for individual users. Simply search for that value with the dollar sign to identify users with that associated value.

The two meta-noncharacters can also be combined. If you issue the expression as

```
^[Hh]orse$
```

grep searches for this string, but will return a positive match only if the string appears both at the beginning and end of the same line. That is, the pattern matches only when **horse** or **Horse** is the only value on a given line.

"Anti-meta-noncharacters"

The final pattern matching operator used with the **grep** command is the backslash, \. The backslash is used to turn off the pattern-matching behavior of whatever character directly follows the \. This is necessary for any pattern which requires the literal value of a character which is normally used as a pattern-matching operator. For example, if you wanted to match a value which contained a literal dollar sign, as in the price value **$24.99**, you would need to use the combination of \ and $ to represent the dollar sign. (Otherwise, the expression would mean "find the text string **24.99** at the end of a line.")

To list all the lines with dollar values in a file named **price.txt**, you might issue the command

```
grep \$[0-9][0-9]\.[0-9][0-9] price.txt
```

This command uses backslashes to define the actual meaning of the $ and . characters, rather than their pattern-matching behavior. In addition, the possible return values are limited to prices that are and no more than $99.99. To get prices in other ranges, the command must be altered.

The Pluralizer

As noted in the previous section, the command given would limit possible returns to those with two digits on either side of the dot. What happens if a price in the document is greater than $99.99? The command, as given, cannot add those prices to the output. However, unless you already know the values in the document, you might not know that there are values in excess of $100. In such situations, you might choose an alternative method of repeating a pattern and seeking matches.

The expression \{**n,m**\} causes the pattern immediately preceding this string to repeat at least *n* times, but no more than *m* times. This allows a more elegant manner of writing the expression without requiring multiple repetitions of the same elements, which is both boring to write and more open to error. Using this expression, the previous command could be rewritten as

```
grep \$[0-9]\{1,\}\.[0-9]\{2\} price.txt
```

In this revised command, the element immediately to the left of the decimal place, **[0-9]**, will be repeated at least one time. Because the expression uses the comma but provides no upper boundary, there is no ceiling. The expression can repeat as many times as there are eligible values. To the right of the decimal, the expression **{2\}** indicates that the expression **[0-9]** will repeat only twice. Because there is no comma between the curly brackets, the program cannot repeat the [0-9] expression fewer or more than twice.

Note: The backslashes before the curly braces in this example do not mean that the curly braces have some specific pattern-matching function that is being turned off. Rather, the backslashes are used to indicate that the curly braces should not be interpreted as literal curly braces used to enclose particular strings of text. In other words, you can think of the curly brace operators as being the entire combination of backslashes and curly braces. Think of it as \{ and \} rather than as the individual elements of \ and { }.

sed

Now that you have learned how to construct regular expressions, and how to use **grep** to find matching strings, you can use both the expressions and the **grep** commands to process information. However, **grep** is not the tool best suited to working with strings once they have been identified. Rather, the *stream editor* **sed** is the appropriate tool.

Not unlike **vi** or GNU Emacs, **sed** is a text editor of sorts. In fact, **sed** is based on one of the original single-line text editors, **ed**. The main difference between **vi**, **ed** or similar text editors and an editor like **sed** is that **sed** is intended to edit data as it is generated; thus the description of **sed** as a *stream editor*, since it edits the stream of data as it flows past.

In practical terms, this means that, with a single command, you can use a range of editing commands on a particular file or data source. These commands are noninteractive, which makes them ideal for shell programs and other scripting or programming needs. A program like **sed** works almost seamlessly with **grep**. Where **grep** identifies strings which match the specified patterns, **sed** can then edit those strings in accordance with predefined needs. Adding **sed** to **grep** increases the potential of a program, and allows additional complexity for each individual command within the script.

The **sed** syntax places individual editing commands as arguments to the sed command itself. These editing commands are specific to **sed**; regular shell-based editing commands will not work within the **sed** construct and will cause the command to fail. Perhaps the most common **sed** operation is a simple search-and-replace. Suppose that you have a document called chip.txt, which contains a block of plain text. In this file, you have made multiple references to **IPC**. In order to replace this acronym with its full expanded value, you can use sed to identify and replace the specified text with a command like

```
sed 's/IPC/Intel Pentium chip/g' chip.txt
```

sed searches the file, identifies any strings of IPC, and replaces them with the correct value.

Note: This may seem uninteresting or obvious, given that almost every text editor and all word processors do the same thing. However, **sed** works directly on text files without having to open an editor, pull in the file buffer, identify and change text strings, save the file, and exit. **sed** can work noninteractively within a shell program, which a normal interactive text editor cannot do.

sed takes the syntax

```
sed 's/target/replacement/options' source
```

where *target* and *replacement* are specified text strings, and *source* is the file or dataset upon which **sed** should work. The *options* are not required elements of the command, but can force **sed** to work in more complex ways. In the previous example, the *g* option forced **sed** to search the entire file for every occurrence of the IPC target. Had the *g*, or "global," option not been included, **sed** would have stopped searching after the first iteration of the string was found and replaced.

Line Addresses

Any **sed** command can take, as a prefix, a line number or range of line numbers. For example, if you want to restrict the editing action to a particular line in the file, just issue the command with that line number. In the command given above, the replacement could be limited to the fourth line of the file by changing the command to

```
sed '4s/IPC/Intel Pentium chip/g' chip.txt
```

In this case, the **sed** command would go directly to the fourth line of the file, execute the substitution, and exit. To execute on multiple lines, issue the command as

```
sed '4,14s/IPC/Intel Pentium chip/g' chip.txt
```

The substitution will be executed on lines 4 through 14 of the file.

It is also possible to group several commands and associate them with a range of line numbers, as in the complex command

```
sed '4,22 {
  s/IBM/International Business Machines/g
  s/Sun/Sun Microsystems/g
  s/DEC/Digital Equipment Corporation/g
}' unix.txt
```

Obviously, this command is not something to be issued at the command line. However, complex **sed** commands like this are commonly found in shell programs.

sed Scripts

Once you start constructing complex **sed** commands, it becomes much easier to work with the commands when they are contained in separate files. When each complex construction is kept in its own file, the file can be invoked as part of the **sed** command. If the complex command above was saved to a file named **sedcommands**, for example, it could be invoked with a command like

```
sed -f sedcommands unix.txt
```

Note that, when saving the command to its own file, a target text file should not be specified. The target is specified when the actual **sed** command is constructed. This permits use of a given complex **sed** command on multiple text files without having to reconstruct the command for each individual target file.

sed Commands

In addition to the search-and-replace substitution command, **sed** offers editing commands which allow specified strings to be deleted, appended, or inserted into the target text file. Unlike the substitution command, these other editing commands are usually given at the end of the pattern being matched. For example, to delete a piece of text, you might issue the command

```
sed '/target/d' input.file
```

This command matches all occurrences of the text string *target* and deletes them when found. Like the substitution command, you can restrict the deletion to a line or range of lines by prepending the command with a line number or range, as in

```
sed '22,25/target/d' input.file
```

The append command inserts text into the file after the point specified in the invocation. The append command takes the syntax

```
sed '/target/a\
This is the text that will be appended. It may\
span several lines.' input.file
```

Note the backslash after the **a** command, and that the backslash is repeated at the end of each incomplete line of input text.

The insert command is similar, except that it inserts the text immediately before the specified point. That is, the command

```
sed '/target/i'\
This is the text that will be inserted, which\
can span several lines.' input.file
```

will insert the new text immediately before the string specified as the target. Should the text be placed at the incorrect spot, as when append is used when insert was intended, the delete command can take multiple lines of text as well.

awk

Like **sed**, **awk** is a program that operates line-by-line on its input. The difference between **sed** and **awk** lies in what each program was designed to do. Where **sed** is concerned primarily with editing, **awk** is more concerned with formatting output. The primary concept to keep in mind when using **awk** is that of the *field*.

A *field* is a particular section of an input line. Each field is separated from the other fields in the line by a specific character called a *delimiter*. The default delimiter is any "whitespace" character: that is, a space or tab character. In other words, a typical line of text would be broken up into individual words, and the spaces between each word would be interpreted as delimiters. Each field in a line is identified by the dollar sign character and a field number. Fields are numbered from left to right.

To illustrate this concept, assume that the input consists of the sentence

```
I have a pet dog.
```

The fields are assigned in this manner:

```
$1 = I
$2 = have
$3 = a
$4 = pet
$5 = dog
```

If you were to issue the command

```
echo "I have a pet dog" | awk '{print $3}'
```

the output would consist of the word "a." The command elicits the third field in the line.

Like **sed**, **awk** commands are usually used on a specified input file. Assume that the example sentence has been saved to a file named **dog.txt**. The **awk** command can then be issued with the syntax

```
awk '{print $3}' dog.txt
```

to get the same output value.

Note: When using **awk**, especially in the context of shell programs, make sure that you do not confuse **awk** fields with shell variables. It is easy to mistake one for the other since they both use the $ character as identification. Always be aware of which elements are inside the **awk** command structure and which are not.

The pet dog example may seem excessively simple for what is, after all, a powerful formatting program. In practical use, **awk** can be invoked to make administrative tasks easier by stripping unnecessary elements from standard output. To show how this works, consider the output of the command

```
ps aux
```

as invoked on a Linux machine also running the KDE desktop environment:

```
USER   PID  %CPU  %MEM  VSZ   RSS  TTY  STAT  START  TIME  COMMAND
root   1    0.1   0.3   1368  476  ?    S     14:45  0:03  init
root   2    0.0   0.0   0     0    ?    SW    14:45  0:00  [keventd]
root   3    0.0   0.0   0     0    ?    SW    14:45  0:00  [kapmd]
root   4    0.0   0.0   0     0    ?    SWN   14:45  0:00  [ksoftirqd_CPU0]
root   5    0.0   0.0   0     0    ?    SW    14:45  0:00  [kswapd]
root   6    0.0   0.0   0     0    ?    SW    14:45  0:00  [bdflush]
root   7    0.0   0.0   0     0    ?    SW    14:45  0:00  [kupdated]
root   8    0.0   0.0   0     0    ?    SW    14:45  0:00  [mdrecoveryd]
root   12   0.0   0.0   0     0    ?    SW    14:45  0:00  [kjournald]
root   91   0.0   0.0   0     0    ?    SW    14:45  0:00  [khubd]
root   184  0.0   0.0   0     0    ?    SW    14:45  0:00  [kjournald]
root   504  0.0   0.4   1428  560  ?    S     14:46  0:00  syslogd -m 0
```

```
root      509  0.0  0.3   1364   436  ?      S   14:46  0:00  klogd -x
rpc       529  0.0  0.4   1508   540  ?      S   14:46  0:00  portmap
rpcuser   557  0.0  0.5   1560   720  ?      S   14:46  0:00  rpc.statd
root      642  0.0  0.5   1496   648  ?      S   14:46  0:00  /sbin/cardmgr
root      697  0.0  0.3   1360   480  ?      S   14:46  0:00  /usr/sbin/apmd -p
root      777  0.0  0.7   2200   908  ?      S   14:46  0:00  xinetd -stayalive
root      818  0.0  1.2   4600  1604  ?      S   14:46  0:00  sendmail: accepti
root      837  0.0  0.3   1400   440  ?      S   14:46  0:00  gpm -t ps/2 -m /d
root      855  0.0  0.4   1544   620  ?      S   14:46  0:00  crond
root      883  0.0  0.2   1344   292  ?      S   14:46  0:00  /usr/bin/vmnet-br
root      906  0.0  0.2   1344   292  ?      S   14:46  0:00  /usr/bin/vmnet-ne
root      932  0.0  0.3   1432   464  ?      S   14:46  0:00  /usr/bin/vmnet-na
root      999  0.0  0.5   1708   648  ?      S   14:46  0:00  /usr/bin/vmnet-dh
xfs      1236  0.0  3.6   6088  4680  ?      S   14:46  0:00  xfs -droppriv -da
daemon   1272  0.0  0.4   1404   516  ?      S   14:46  0:00  /usr/sbin/atd
root     1298  0.0  0.3   1344   400  tty1   S   14:46  0:00  /sbin/mingetty tt
root     1299  0.0  0.3   1344   400  tty2   S   14:46  0:00  /sbin/mingetty tt
root     1300  0.0  0.3   1344   400  tty3   S   14:46  0:00  /sbin/mingetty tt
root     1301  0.0  0.3   1344   400  tty4   S   14:46  0:00  /sbin/mingetty tt
root     1302  0.0  0.3   1344   400  tty5   S   14:46  0:00  /sbin/mingetty tt
root     1303  0.0  0.3   1344   400  tty6   S   14:46  0:00  /sbin/mingetty tt
root     1304  0.0  1.3   6144  1668  ?      S   14:46  0:00  /usr/bin/gdm -nod
root     1312  0.0  1.7   6688  2248  ?      S   14:46  0:00  /usr/bin/gdm -nod
root     1313  0.9 10.7  26248 13608  ?      S   14:46  0:35  /usr/bin/X11/X :0
joe      1322  0.0  0.8   2244  1052  ?      S   14:46  0:00  /bin/sh /usr/bin/
joe      1428  0.0  5.4  19460  6860  ?      S   14:46  0:00  kdeinit: Running.
joe      1431  0.0  5.5  19400  7076  ?      S   14:46  0:00  kdeinit: dcopserv
joe      1434  0.0  6.5  20484  8352  ?      S   14:46  0:00  kdeinit: klaunche
joe      1436  0.0  7.4  20472  9420  ?      S   14:46  0:00  kdeinit: kded
joe      1447  0.1  7.9  20784 10012  ?      S   14:46  0:04  kdeinit: klaptopd
joe      1448  0.0  2.8   6124  3632  ?      S   14:46  0:00  /usr/bin/artsd -F
joe      1458  0.0  8.4  23240 10716  ?      S   14:46  0:00  kdeinit: knotify
joe      1463  0.0  0.2   1416   316  ?      S   14:47  0:00  kwrapper ksmserve
joe      1465  0.0  7.2  20436  9144  ?      S   14:47  0:00  kdeinit: ksmserve
joe      1466  0.0  8.5  21476 10844  ?      S   14:47  0:01  kdeinit: kwin -se
joe      1468  0.0  9.6  21996 12228  ?      S   14:47  0:02  kdeinit: kdesktop
joe      1471  0.0  0.5   1804   652  ?      S   14:47  0:00  autorun -l --inte
joe      1472  0.0 10.4  23552 13208  ?      S   14:47  0:01  kdeinit: kicker
joe      1480  0.0  8.0  21292 10156  ?      S   14:47  0:00  kdeinit: klipper
joe      1482  0.0  7.8  20484  9972  ?      S   14:47  0:00  korgac -miniicon
joe      1484  0.0  7.8  21184  9968  ?      S   14:47  0:00  kdeinit: kwrited
joe      1487  1.9 10.0  24260 12780  ?      R   14:47  1:14  kasteroids -session
joe      1488  0.0  8.9  21464 11300  ?      S   14:47  0:01  ktron -session 11
joe      1491  0.0  7.0  20260  8940  ?      S   14:47  0:00  kalarmd -login
joe      1495  0.3 10.4  24420 13212  ?      S   14:47  0:14  kdeinit: kwrite -
joe      6625  0.0  9.2  22568 11716  ?      S   15:31  0:01  kdeinit: konsole
joe      6627  0.0  1.0   2520  1348  pts/1  S   15:31  0:00  /bin/bash
joe      6665  0.0  0.5   2632   716  pts/1  R   15:49  0:00  ps aux
```

This is lengthy output which contains a number of fields on each line. While it is relatively easy to read, it would be faster to strip away the fields which are not needed at the moment. In order to strip out every field except process ID number and command invoked, issue the command

```
ps aux | awk '{print $2 "\t" $11}'
```

Note some unusual elements of this command syntax. First, **awk** elements are enclosed in curly braces. When used in a shell context, the commands must also be enclosed in single quotes to prevent the curly braces from being interpreted by the shell. Second, the command includes an **awk**-specific metacharacter, "\t". This metacharacter stands for a tab character, which is inserted between the two desired fields. The metacharacter is enclosed in quotation marks so that it will be interpreted as such by **awk**. Other **awk** metacharacters include "\b" for a backspace, and "\n" for a new line.

With those syntactical elements in place, this revised command results in the output

```
PID         COMMAND
1           init
2           [keventd]
3           [kapmd]
4           [ksoftirqd_CPU0]
5           [kswapd]
6           [bdflush]
7           [kupdated]
8           [mdrecoveryd]
12          [kjournald]
91          [khubd]
184         [kjournald]
504         syslogd
509         klogd
529         portmap
557         rpc.statd
642         /sbin/cardmgr
697         /usr/sbin/apmd
777         xinetd
818         sendmail:
837         gpm
855         crond
883         /usr/bin/vmnet-br
906         /usr/bin/vmnet-ne
932         /usr/bin/vmnet-na
999         /usr/bin/vmnet-dh
1236        xfs
1272        /usr/sbin/ard
1298        /sbin/mgetty
```

```
1299        /sbin/mgetty
1300        /sbin/mingetty
1301        /sbin/mingetty
1302        /sbin/mingetty
1303        /sbin/mingetty
1304        /usr/bin/gdm
1312        /usr/bin/gdm
1313        /usr/bin/X11/X
1322        /bin/sh
1428        kdeinit:
1431        kdeinit:
1434        kdeinit:
1436        kdeinit:
1447        kdeinit:
1448        /usr/sbin/artsd
1458        kdeinit:
1463        kwrapper
1465        kdeinit:
1466        kdeinit:
1468        kdeinit:
1471        autorun
1472        kdeinit:
1480        kdeinit:
1482        korgac
1484        kdeinit:
1487        kasteroids
1488        ktron
1491        kalarmd
1495        kdeinit:
6625        kdeinit:
6627        /bin/bash
6685        ps
6686        awk
```

The pared-down output is much easier to read, and allows the administrator to check individual processes more quickly.

Changing the Field Separator

If whitespace is an inappropriate selection as delimiter for certain field types, it is easy to change. Suppose that you want to work with the /etc/passwd field, which stores its information in fields separated by colons. Do this with the –F flag, specifying the character that you would prefer **awk** recognize as a delimiter. For example, if you want to take the first and third fields from /etc/passwd, issue the **awk** command as

```
awk -F: '{print $1 "\t" $3}' /etc/passwd
```

Using Pattern Matching with awk

When constructing **awk** commands, you can also use the same kind of pattern-matching operations you would use in other regular expression constructions. **awk** has its own set of pattern-matching constructions, which offer the same type of flexibility.

In the previous example using the lengthy output from the **ps aux** command, it is possible to use pattern-matching to pull out only the processes which have an associated terminal, indicated by entries in the TTY column. To do so, issue the command as

```
ps aux | awk '/tty/ {print $2 "\t" $11}'
```

With this syntax, the print command is limited to only those lines which match the pattern "/tty/".

awk Scripts

As with **sed**, you can also place complex **awk** commands in a separate file. That file can then be invoked as part of a scripted program and execute its operations on a variety of input files. Were you to save a complex **awk** command to a file named **awkcommands**, you would then invoke that file with a command like

```
awk -f awkcommands input.file
```

Summary

Shell programs often require that text be parsed in order to obtain data used as input for another process. Since computers do not have human minds, they rely on pattern-matching to analyze text input. Pattern-matching is done with regular expressions, or sets of symbols which stand for particular types of text strings. These expressions can result in very broad matches with many results, or limited searches with few but specific returns. Pattern-matching is a feature of several Unix programs and other programming languages.

Three of the most common Unix programs which use pattern-matching are **grep**, **sed**, and **awk**. **grep** is a program which searches an identified data source for a specified text string, and prints matching strings to the standard output. The **sed** program is a stream editor, which edits data as it is generated. Unlike text editors or word processors, **sed** is noninteractive and can run without user intervention. The **awk** program, like **sed**, works on data as it is generated; rather than editing it, however, **awk** formats it according to specified instructions. Of these programs, only **grep** is regularly run at the command line. All three are integral parts of shell programs, however, and can add a level of complexity to shell work that rivals that possible in dedicated programming languages.

Review Questions

1. What is parsing?
2. Define a regular expression.
3. How does pattern matching work?
4. How does the asterisk function as a pattern-matching operator?
5. What is a metacharacter? Give examples.
6. What is the POSIX standard?
7. What are the advantages of regular expressions in shell programs?
8. Explain the function of the **grep** program.
9. What metacharacters are specific to **grep**?
10. What are the functions of ^ and $ under **grep**?
11. What is the difference between using a character as a pattern-matching operator and using it with \?
12. What is a pluralizer, and how is it constructed?
13. Explain the function of the **sed** program.
14. How does **sed** differ from a text editor or word processor?
15. What is the **sed** syntax?
16. Why might it be advantageous to store **sed** or **awk** commands in separate files?
17. Explain the function of the **awk** program.
18. What is a field?
19. Define a delimiter, and provide examples.
20. What is the **awk** syntax?

Exercises

1. Create a regular expression that matches the words ablate, agate, palmate, and attend, but does not match material. Write this expression three different ways.
2. Create a short text file containing a letter to your instructor which outlines the way in which **grep**, **sed**, and **awk** can be used together in a shell program. Using **sed**, replace all occurrences of grep with GREP, sed with SED, and awk with AWK.
3. Using the text file generated in the previous example, use **awk** to print the first, fourth, and eighth word of any line which contains the words GREP, SED, or AWK.
4. Create a shell program which performs the operations found in exercises 2 and 3 using the letter as the data source. Be sure that it runs properly.
5. (For students with some programming experience) Locate or install Perl on your machine. Visit the Perl Web site at http://www.perl.org to learn the basics of the language. How can you write Perl scripts to duplicate the work done earlier with **grep**, **sed**, and **awk**?

CHAPTER 15

Shell Programming IV: Signals and Status

IN THIS CHAPTER

1. Exit status
2. Signals
3. Signal traps
4. Pulling together shell program concepts
5. Selecting techniques

In the previous chapters of this section, you have learned the basic structures of shell programs. In this chapter, the concepts of exit status and signals are introduced. While these are easy concepts to understand, they have significant implications for the complexity of any programs that contain them.

With exit status and signal functions in your programs, you can create chains of programs that perform complicated sequences of actions. These actions are determined by the success or failure of individual elements within each script, or by the success or failure of a program itself. While these functions may be a bit complex for the types of administrative scripts that are written quickly to solve an immediate need, they do show up in more extensive programs that you download from an archive or that you may spend some time crafting.

Exit Status

Every command that is invoked in a Unix environment, whether it is given on the command line or in a shell program, generates an *exit status*. This status is a numerical value that corresponds with either the output of a program (if, for example, it was a mathematical operation) or with the success or failure of the command. The exit status is also sometimes called the *return value* because it is returned after the command is finished. By using this value, you can cause your programs to behave in different ways depending on the success or failure of a particular command embedded in the program.

Consider a simple flow control statement that looks like this:

```
if [ $VAR = 1 ]
then
  <some action>
fi
```

Embedded in the if statement of this fragment is an implicit use of exit status. Remember that the square brackets represent a **test** command. The example could be rewritten as

```
if (test $VAR = 1)
then
  <some action>
fi
```

The **test** command is a command like any other. As such, it returns an exit status. In this case, it returns a value of zero if the expression it is evaluating is true, and a value of 1 if it is false. This is consistent with the values that most commands return.

Zero is the value returned when a command succeeds; any other value represents failure. In most cases, the value for failure is 1, but in some situations failure may be represented by other numbers if the program distinguishes between different types of failure. These unusual values will usually be described in the command's manual page or other documentation.

In the example above, a return value of 0 from the **test** command is interpreted as a true condition by the if command. When the returned value is 0, the enclosed code will be executed. A return value of 1 from the **test** command would be interpreted as false, so the enclosed code would not be executed and the program would move to the next non-conditional block of code.

In other words, an if block written as

```
if (0)
then
<some action>
fi
```

would always execute. Since the value is always a positive result, the action will always be performed. Consider the code

```
if ( cd /<some_directory> )
then
  ls
```

```
else
  echo "Directory not found"
fi
```

Here, the program is instructed to change into the directory */some_directory*. If the command is successful, the program generates a directory listing from the ls command. If the program is not successful, then the program will print the error message.

This block works because the cd program returns a value of 0 for success and a value of 1 for failure. The success and failure values are contained in the cd manual page:

```
cd [-LP] [dir]
  Change the current directory to dir. The variable
  HOME is the default dir. The variable CDPATH
  defines the search path for the directory
  containing dir. Alternative directory names in
  CDPATH are separated by a colon (:). A null
  directory name in CDPATH is the same as the
  current directory, i.e. ".". If dir begins with a
  slash (/), then CDPATH is not used. The -P option
  says to use the physical directory structure
  instead of following symbolic links (see also the
  -P option to the set builtin command); the -L
  option forces symbolic links to be followed. An
  argument of - is equivalent to $OLD-PWD. The
  return value is true if the directory was
  successfully changed; false otherwise.
```

Note the final sentence. In shell terminology, "true" means 0 and "false" means 1.

The example above is an implicit test of the exit status of the **cd** command. To make the test explicit, you would need to use the special variable ?, which has as its value the exit status of the most recently executed command. To use this value, the code could be rewritten as

```
cd /<some_directory>
if [ $? -eq 0 ]
then
  ls
else
  echo "Directory not found"
fi
```

While this format is clearer, many programmers would prefer the previous version which combines the execution of the command and the test of its exit status in a single line. Many such decisions are made on the basis of elegance, a subjective consideration. What one programmer finds elegant may not seem so to another.

Creating Exit Status

These examples provide some insight into the importance and usefulness of exit status to the shell programmer. Exit status can also be produced within individual shell programs. Remember that, as described in Chapter 13, an exit statement can be added to a shell program to close a code loop. That exit statement can take an argument composed of a number which will become its exit status.

To illustrate this concept, consider the code block

```
if <normal execution>
then
  exit 0
else
  exit 1
fi
```

In this case, if the main action of the program executes as planned, the program will exit with the status of zero. If something happens and the program does not execute properly, it will have the exit status 1. The complexity of the example can be expanded, as in

```
if <normal execution>
then
  exit 0
elif <error_type_1>
  exit 1
elif <error_type_2>
  exit 2
elif <error_type_3>
  exit 3
elif <error_type_4>
  exit 4
else
  exit 5
fi
```

In this case, if the program failed, the exit status would identify the type of failure.

The value of such examples is in their implication for your programs. Your programs can use any command that can be issued at the shell prompt. This means that you can also use your programs as commands nested into other programs. Since your program can generate an exit value, that value can be used to carry information from one program to another in a chain of consequences.

Signals

The previous section touches on another issue central to shell programming. Using exit status so that one program can pass information to another program is a type of *interprocess communication.* In this case, that term is applied somewhat loosely as it is not necessarily diverse processes which are communication, but the concept behind the term is fairly accurate.

A more complete sort of interprocess communication is handled by *signals.* Signals are, as their name would suggest, flags with particular meaning. Unlike exit status, however, signals are a function of the operating system kernel and not of the shell. Signals are standardized across Unix variants, however, so a given signal will do the same thing on any Unix machine.

In order to use a signal, three elements must be present. First, there must be a way to identify the process which is to receive the signal. Second, there must be a way to send the signal. Third, a *signal trap* must be available; a signal trap is a set of instructions in the receiving process which describes what is to be done when the signal is received.

Unique Identifiers

The problem of identifying the receiving process has already been solved. Simply use the process identification number of the intended recipient process. How can this identification number be obtained if the recipient process has not yet started at the time the initial program runs? In particular, there must be a way in which the sending program can pull the receiving program's PID and incorporate it.

The shell has a function which can help in this situation. The special variable $ always stores the PID of its own process as its value. Thus, you can use this variable to store the PID in a place where the sending program can always find it, as in this code:

```
echo $$ > /var/run/program_name
```

In this example, the intended recipient process writes its PID to a file in the /var/run directory. Note that you don't have to use the /var/run directory for your programs; however, under some Unix variants like Linux, that is the purpose of the directory.

Once the PID has been written to that file, the sending process can access the file for the PID and use it to define a new program variable's value, as in

```
RECEIVERPID='cat /var/run/program_name'
```

Another option might be to place the PID into a shell environment variable, as in the command

```
export RECEIVERPID=$$
```

though many programmers would prefer the file approach.

Sending Signals

Identifying the process ID number of the recipient program is the first step. Next, you will need a way to send the signal between the two programs. This is done with the **kill** command. Because most signals are used to shut down the receiving process, kill is an intuitive name for this command.

kill offers a wide range of signals which can be incorporated into shell programs or issued at the command line. The various options for **kill** can be generated with the command

```
kill -l
```

which produces the output

```
 1) SIGHUP       2) SIGINT       3) SIGQUIT      4) SIGILL
 5) SIGTRAP      6) SIGABRT      7) SIGBUS       8) SIGFP
 9) SIGKILL     10) SIGUSR1     11) SIGSEGV     12) SIGUSR
13) SIGPIPE     14) SIGALRM     15) SIGTERM     17) SIGCHLD
18) SIGCONT     19) SIGSTOP     20) SIGTSTP     21) SIGTTIN
22) SIGTTOU     23) SIGURG      24) SIGXCPU     25) SIGXFSZ
26) SIGVTALRM   27) SIGPROF     28) SIGWINCH    29) SIGI
30) SIGPWR      31) SIGSYS      32) SIGRTMIN    33) SIGRTMIN+1
34) SIGRTMIN+2  35) SIGRTMIN+3  36) SIGRTMIN+4  37) SIGRTMIN+5
38) SIGRTMIN+6  39) SIGRTMIN+7  40) SIGRTMIN+8  41) SIGRTMIN+9
42) SIGRTMIN+10 43) SIGRTMIN+11 44) SIGRTMIN+12 45) SIGRTMIN+13
46) SIGRTMIN+14 47) SIGRTMIN+15 48) SIGRTMAX-15 49) SIGRTMAX-14
50) SIGRTMAX-13 51) SIGRTMAX-12 52) SIGRTMAX-11 53) SIGRTMAX-10
54) SIGRTMAX-9  55) SIGRTMAX-8  56) SIGRTMAX-7  57) SIGRTMAX-6
58) SIGRTMAX-5  59) SIGRTMAX-4  60) SIGRTMAX-3  61) SIGRTMAX-2
62) SIGRTMAX-1  63) SIGRTMAX
```

Note that each signal has a number and a name, and that all names begin with SIG. You can refer to any signal with either the name or the number. However, if you use the signal name, you must drop the SIG component in order to call the appropriate signal. For example, if you want to include a section in a program which terminates a process with signal 15, SIGTERM, you could write the section as

```
kill -15 <process_ID>
```

or as

```
kill -TERM <process_ID>
```

In fact, since signal 15 is the default value for the **kill** command, you could actually just write **kill** <***process_ID***>, but you must follow the syntax above for all other signal values.

Regardless of the method you choose, signal 15 will be sent to the process specified by the identification number. What happens at that point depends largely on how the receiving process has been configured to deal with that signal. The exception to this guideline is signal 9. No matter what code exists in the receiving process, signal 9 will always stop that process from running.

The most commonly used signals are SIGHUP (1), SIGINT (2), SIGKILL (9), SIGSEGV (11), and SIGTERM (15). However, given that signal 9 is the only signal that distinguishes itself in any significant way at a superficial level, you can usually use whatever signal you prefer as long as you only use signal 9 when you really want to kill a running process.

Note: Of course, each of these signals is slightly different. If they weren't, there would be no reason to have such a long list of signals. Most of these signals are used for interprocess communication within the kernel and in other low-level system functions. Unfortunately, there is little accessible documentation describing the function of each signal. If you understand the C language and are able to read C code, you can read the source code for the kernel in which the signals are defined, assuming that the source for your Unix variant is available. For most purposes in shell programs, however, you will probably settle for a small subset of signals that you use consistently.

Signal Traps

In order to use signals effectively, you must create a signal trap. To do this, you must anticipate the particular signal that will be received and decide what should happen when the signal appears. Not surprisingly, signals are trapped with the **trap** command. For example, the line

```
trap "exit 1" INT
```

would cause the program to exit with a status of 1 if a SIGINT (signal 2) is received.

An example of this process can be found in this code block:

```
#!/bin/bash
# program that keeps looping until it gets a SIGINT
trap "echo 'caught a SIGINT'; exit 1" INT
while 0
do
  echo "looping"
  sleep 10
done
```

This program prints the word "looping" until it receives a SIGINT, at which point it prints "caught a SIGINT" and exits with a status of 1.

Note that there are two commands on the trap line, separated with a semicolon. The shell interprets the semicolon as the end of a command line, so you can stack several commands on the same line of code. Thus,

```
echo 1; echo 2
```

is the same as

```
echo 1
echo 2
```

This construct is not usually used in shell programming except in cases where you need to put two commands inside a space designed for one. You may sometimes see this syntax used in flow control statements, as in

```
if <something> ; then
  <some action>
fi
```

This is not recommended for flow control, but do not be confused if it appears in a script which you are reading.

Pulling It All Together

In the chapters of this shell programming section of the text, you have been introduced to a number of programming tools and techniques. However, these varied tools have not been shown to you in one integrated program. To some extent, programming methodology is beyond the scope of this introductory book. However, this section contains a detailed example of a useful shell program, so that you can see how such programs are constructed and how the various tools you have seen in these chapters are actually used.

This shell program can be used to set up a network configuration, as described in Chapter 11. The program uses many of the techniques introduced in this section, and some others which may be unfamiliar to you. However, reading the program should be straightforward and its function apparent.

```
#!/bin/bash
################################################################
#
#  net-config: A program to configure network
#  interface and routing information interactively.
#  This is not a substitute for knowing how to
#  configure such information by hand.
#
#  This version only configures an eth0 interface. If
#  you want to configure a different interface, you
#  will have to change a particular line.
```

```
#
#################################################################
NAMESERVERS ()
{
  # This is a function. A function is a sort of
  # mini program within a program. This code will
  # not be executed here at the beginning. Rather,
  # it will be executed when the function is
  # called. The function will operate exactly as
  # any other command would.

  echo -n "Enter IP address of nameserver 1: "
  read DNS1
  echo -n "Enter IP address of nameserver 2: "
  read DNS2
  echo "nameserver $DNS1" >> /etc/resolv.conf
  echo "nameserver $DNS2" >> /etc/resolv.conf
}

# Set path info for 'ifconfig' and 'route' commands
# Change these if yours are stored somewhere else

IFCONFIG=/sbin/ifconfig
ROUTE=/sbin/route

# If an eth0 already appears in the 'ifconfig' output,
# you may have a conflict. Confirm that user wants to
# continue.

if ($IFCONFIG | grep eth0 )
then
echo -n "Found an eth0 device already. Do you want to
  continue? [Y/n]: "
if [ $CONT = "n" ]
then
  exit
    fi
fi

echo -n "Input IP number: "
read IP

echo -n "Input IP number of gateway: "
read GATEWAY

# Check to see if an /etc/resolv.conf file already
```

```
# exists. If it does, adding nameservers may not be
# necessary

if [ -s /etc/resolv.conf ]
then
echo -n "/etc/resolv.conf exists and is not empty. Do you
  want to add nameservers to it anyway? [Y/n]: "
    read CONT
    if [ $CONT = "Y" ]
  then
NAMESERVERS  # Here is the function from
             # the top of the file
    fi

else
  touch /etc/resolv.conf
NAMESERVERS  # Here it is again. This is why
             # such functions are useful.
fi

  # Go ahead and configure the network

  echo -n "Bringing up eth0 . . ."
  if ( $IFCONFIG eth0 $IP up )
  then
    echo "done."
  else
    echo "Couldn't do it. Program aborting"
    exit 1
  fi

  echo

  echo -n "Setting routing info . . ."
  if ($ROUTE add default gw $GATEWAY )
  then
    echo "done."
  else
    echo "Couldn't do it. Program aborting."
    exit 1
  fi

  echo -n "Shall I conduct a ping test? {y/n]: "
  read $PING
  if [ $PING != "n" ]
  then
```

```
        echo -n "Site to ping: "
        read PINGSITE
        if (ping -c 5 $PINGSITE)
        then
          echo
          echo "Network looks good."
        else
          echo "Seems to be a problem."
          exit 1
        fi
      fi
```

Before you do anything else, read the program carefully. Can you follow it? Aside from the function, which is explained in the comments, no unfamiliar techniques have been used.

First, consider the broad outline of the program's purpose. To begin, the program assigns two variables as the full path names of the **ifconfig** and **route** commands. This is primarily a precaution. On the off chance that the script might be used on a system where these commands are not located in the /sbin directory, there should be a quick way to change the path. Having assigned these variables, a user need only make a single quick edit to change their paths.

The next thing the program does is to check that there is not already a configured ethernet device on the system. That is done with the block

```
if ($IFCONFIG | grep eth0 )
then
echo -n "Found an eth0 device already. Do you want to
  continue? [Y/n]: "
if [ $CONT = "n" ]
then
  exit
    fi
fi
```

Note the construction of the if statement. The if statement depends on the success or failure of the **grep** command, which uses the output of the **ifconfig** command as its input. If the **grep** command finds the string "eth0" in the output of the **ifconfig** command, **grep** will return a value of 0 and the related warning is printed.

Next, the program solicits the IP numbers of the local machine and gateway. Then, the program checks to see if the /etc/resolv.conf file exists. This function uses a test that has not yet been introduced here. Note the line

```
if [ -s /etc/resolv.conf ]
```

In addition to making numerical or textual comparisons, the **test** command (implicit in the square brackets) can test the attributes of a file. The –s flag tests whether a file exists and whether it is empty (i.e., has a size greater than 0 bytes). Other file test flags are shown in Table 15.1.

If the /etc/resolv.conf file exists and is not empty, the program gives the user the opportunity to skip adding new nameserver values. This is because nameserver values may have already been configured with working nameserver addresses. However, if the user chooses to add values or if the /etc/resolv.conf file does not exist, the user is given the chance to supply nameserver addresses. The nameserver values are added to the /etc/resolv.conf file. This program uses a function to handle this action because the same code is used in two places. In such a circumstance, it makes more sense to use a function than to duplicate the code.

Once all of the information is in place, the program configures the network interface and routing information. Note the use of conditional blocks:

```
echo -n "Bringing up eth0 . . ."
  if ( $IFCONFIG eth0 $IP up )
  then
    echo "done."
  else
    echo "Couldn't do it. Program aborting"
    exit 1
  fi
```

If for some reason the **ifconfig** command fails, the program will abort and return an exit status of 1.

TABLE 15.1: Flags to the Test Command

Flag	Function
-e	The specified file exists
-d	The specified file exists and is a directory
-f	The specified file exists and is a normal file (not a directory)
-s	The specified file exists and has content
-r	The user has read permission for the specified file
-w	The user has write permission for the specified file
-x	The user has execute permission for the specified file
-O	The user is the owner of the specified file
-G	The group ID of the owner matches the file's ID
-nt	The file is newer than another specified file
-ot	The file is older than another specified file

Finally, the program gives the user an opportunity to ping a remote machine. This step is not necessary, but it is helpful in order to ensure that the procedure has gone smoothly. Note the "-c 5" argument to **ping**. This tells the **ping** command to send only five packets. If the packets are returned successfully, the **ping** command exits with a status of 0. If this is the case, the program is successful and exits with a status of 0. If not, the program reports an error and exits with a status of 1.

Selecting Techniques

This program did not use every technique presented in this section of the text. Techniques used in the program included

- assigning variables
- using functions
- conditional flow control
- nested control structures
- implicit test commands
- exit status
- output redirection
- pipes
- pattern matching

The techniques introduced which were not used in this program include

- signals
- iterative flow control
- input redirection

While these techniques could have been included in the program as examples, they were unnecessary for the function of the script. While it is good to know a number of programming functions, you do not need to use everything you know in a single program.

Summary

With each new technique added to a programmer's repertoire, that writer's programs can reach new levels of complexity and utility. The concepts of exit status and signals enable the programmer to incorporate interprocess communication into her scripts. Exit status is a value reported by a program as it exits. This value is usually 0 for success, and any other value (but usually 1) for failure. The exit value can be evaluated by a program and action taken or ignored based on the value.

Signals are flags used by the operating system kernel. Each signal has a slightly different meaning, most of which are too arcane for basic scripting. The signal SIGKILL (9) can be issued to stop any running pro-

gram. This signal, and a few others like it, can be incorporated into programs to stop running processes as part of the program's function. In order to work properly, signals must identify the process which is to be signaled, must have a sending mechanism, and must have a trap on the receiving end which will process the signal when it arrives.

With the various techniques introduced through this section of the text, students can write basic programs which will help them to manage Unix machines and networks. To write effective programs, the programmer should select the most appropriate mechanisms from the set of command structures which he knows. Good programs are not only functional but are clear, well-commented, and elegantly constructed.

Review Questions

1. Define an exit status.
2. How can return values affect the outcome of a program?
3. What are the common exit status values? What do they represent?
4. How can you learn the exit values used by a particular command?
5. What is the function of the special variable $?
6. What is the difference between an explicit and an implicit test?
7. How is an exit statement constructed?
8. Define interprocess communication.
9. What is a signal?
10. At what level of the machine do signals function?
11. Will BSD signals work on a Linux machine? Why?
12. What elements must be present for a signal to work?
13. Why is the process ID number valuable in shell programming?
14. Explain the two ways in which particular kill signals can be invoked.
15. What is a signal trap?
16. How can a single line of code contain more than one command?
17. Name at least two ways in which the test command can evaluate a file.
18. How should you select the techniques which you will use in writing a particular program?

Exercises

1. Select at least ten random commands from the command Appendix. Read the manual pages and other documentation for these commands to determine the exit status values used by each. How might you use these commands, and their return values, in shell programs?
2. Using the network configuration program at the end of this chapter, modify the code so that the exit status of each command is printed to the standard output. Be sure that the program works.
3. Write a program which stores its process identification number in a separate text file. The program must loop until it receives a signal 15. When the program receives a signal 15, it should exit and echo a message to the screen. Run this program in the background. Modify the network administration script so that, if at any point the script fails, it sends the signal 15 to the other process.
4. Modify the network configuration script to include a noninteractive mode which will take arguments from the command line for the IP numbers of the host and the gateway. Hint: you will have to use special shell variables to handle command line arguments.

5. Write a shell program which performs one of the functions listed below. Use as many (or as few) of the programming techniques you have learned as are necessary to accomplish the job. Make sure your script runs.

   a. Parses the /etc/passwd file for all users whose usernames begin with "b" or "o"; reports those names to the monitor along with the size of those users' home directories.

   b. Finds the date of last modification (timestamp) for all files in the /tmp directory; deletes all files more than a month old and reports those file names to the standard output. WARNING: be sure that nobody has any important files in the /tmp directory before you run this program.

   c. Reports the size of all users' home directories and automatically e-mails a message to any user whose directory is greater than 15 megabytes. WARNING: Do not actually run this program without permission from the system administrator.

CHAPTER 16

Basic System Administration: Part I

IN THIS CHAPTER

1. The system administrator
2. Managing users
3. Managing user groups
4. Disk management
5. The Unix filesystem
6. Mounting directories and devices
7. Backups
8. System security

Sooner or later, most people who use Unix will start to perform some administrative tasks. Whether or not you become a professional system administrator, or even whether you install a personal computer Unix variant on one of your computers, you will be exposed to tasks that are normally considered administrative. These tasks include dealing with user accounts, managing the disk and its allocation, and basic security control. Additional administrative jobs, primarily those that deal with software and print services, are introduced in Chapter 17: Basic System Administration, Part II.

In the Unix environment, system administration is a job that almost anyone can perform. While the person who holds the root account has final say over what can and cannot be done on the machine, individual users often invoke the same programs that administrators use. On some systems, users are responsible for functions that, on other systems, are the sole responsibility of the administrator. The differences are in part due to the culture of the organization which hosts the net-

work, and in part due to the willingness of the administrator to enlarge the scope of user abilities.

Note: In this chapter, we assume that you either have permission to perform certain tasks on your machine, or that you are the root account (having installed a personal computer Unix variant). On all well-configured systems, if you do not have permission to try one of these commands and you do it anyway, the command should fail. However, your attempt will be recorded in system logs and may cause some curiosity about what you are doing; ask permission if necessary.

The System Administrator

In most situations, the term *system administrator* refers to "the person or persons who have access to the root account." The concept of *root* has been introduced earlier in this book, but it is especially important to discuss it in the context of system administration. The root account is one of the hallmarks of Unix, differentiating it from personal operating systems.

Whoever has access to the root, or *superuser*, account, has total and complete control over the machine. The root user can add or delete users, software, system default settings, network connections, and any other activity which might be performed on the computer. Root can read any file in any directory, including files contained in personal user accounts. Root has no need for passwords, except for the root password, because the root account can assume the identity of any user account on the machine. Root, in short, is a dictator with absolute power.

Why does Unix hand so much power to one account? The root concept exists because someone needs to have the ultimate authority. Root can do all these things because they need to be done, but it would be chaos if every user could change administrative settings whenever they chose to do so. Instead, the ability to affect the entire machine is limited to those with access to the root account, and individual users are limited to administering their own home directories.

Obviously, with such power comes responsibility. The root holders may be tempted to snoop through user accounts, or to enforce rules based on how much they like a particular user. On a personal machine with only a few users, this might be more of an annoyance than a problem. On large networks, however, administrators must enforce system policies as even-handedly as possible. In general, no matter how large or small the system, it is best to set down certain rules and administer the machine according to those policies. The ethics of system administration are a legitimate concern, both for the administrator and for the users on the network.

Managing Users

One of the most time-consuming administrative activities is managing the user base. Users must be added, deleted, monitored, and educated on a regular basis. The larger the system, the more time must be spent on users. Even those who are simply running a personal Unix variant at home must manage users, since the most basic installation still has at least two users: root and the regular user account of the machine's owner. Since the root account should never be used for ordinary tasks, a separate personal account must be created.

Depending on the Unix variant in question, the administrator may be able to use a number of specialized user management tools to handle regular tasks. On many systems, these tools use appealing graphical interfaces that allow mouse or menu use. However, it is always good to know how to perform administrative tasks at the command line, since the graphical interface may be missing or corrupted for some reason. When working on your particular machine, consult its documentation to learn the intricacies of any specialized software available to root.

Adding Users

The most common user management task is adding new users. While most Unix variants now offer convenient front ends to this process, you can add a new user directly at the command line. The process is more complex than with a graphical management tool, but it is still a straightforward job. To add a new user, you must create an entry in the /etc/passwd file for that person and assign a password, build the user's home directory and all start-up files, and set any quotas or permissions necessary for that user.

Almost every Unix variant has the **useradd** or **adduser** program installed by default. This utility automates some of the tedium involved in building a new user account. The **useradd** program is discussed here, but **adduser** works in almost exactly the same way. (See the manual page for further information.) At its most basic, **useradd** takes the syntax

```
useradd [options] username
```

That is, to create a basic account for the username slynch, you would issue the command as

```
useradd slynch
```

The **useradd** program creates a home and mail directory. However, **useradd** cannot be used to define passwords. This is a good thing; password management should involve actual humans. You will have to define slynch's password by hand.

Adding a new user with the basic **useradd** syntax still means that you have work to do. That command won't assign slynch to any user groups, define system defaults, or provide any refinements to the account. Luckily, useradd options can be used to do all this. (In fact, you can use **useradd** options to define the initial password, but it must be one that you select. **useradd** will not supply an initial password value.) The command

```
useradd -g users -G alpha gamma -s /bin/bash slynch
```

does quite a bit more than the basic command. With this command, the user slynch has been assigned to the primary group "users," but has also been assigned as a member of the user groups "alpha" and "gamma." In addition, slynch's default shell environment has been defined as bash. Table 16.1 shows some other options that can be used with **adduser**.

Deleting Users

Removing users is even easier than adding them. Why would you want to remove a user? There are several reasons for this. The user may no longer work or study at the site which hosts the network; the user may have violated some system policy, causing her to be banned from the network; the account has had a security breach; or you may have misspelled the user's name when creating the new account. All of these, and many others, are valid reasons to remove a user account from the system.

Note: In the case of a security breach or a system policy violation, you may wish to disable the account instead of removing it. Disabling the account means that the user cannot access it, but all her files remain intact and all her group and user ID associations remain in force. E-mail sent to that user name will also be stored rather than having it bounce because the username no longer exists. The account can be re-enabled when the problem has been repaired or any punishment for the violation is complete.

TABLE 16.1: adduser Options

Option	Function
-d *homedirectory*	Defines the path for the user's home directory
-e *date*	Defines the date upon which the account will no longer be valid, taking the form YYYY-MM-DD
-g *groupname*	Defines the user's primary group
-G *groupname(s)*	Defines any other groups to which the user will belong, separated by a comma only
-p *password*	Defines the initial password assigned to the user
-s *shell*	Defines the default shell environment
-u *number*	Defines the user's login ID number; if this option is not used, the number is automatically assigned

If you used a graphical user management tool to add the user account, you can use the same tool to delete the account. Depending on the tool, you may need to remove associated files and directories by hand, or the program might handle the data for you. Some user management tools, like the **admintool** program found under Solaris, also offer an account-lock option. This is an easy way to disable access temporarily.

For users who were added with the **useradd** or **adduser** commands, there is another utility which removes accounts. The **userdel** program, as the name implies, is the opposite of **useradd**. It takes the syntax

```
userdel username
```

Unlike **useradd**, **userdel** does not have a range of options. It takes only one option, the –r flag. When **userdel** is issued with this flag, the program will remove the account's associated home directory and all its contents at the same time, as in

```
userdel -r slynch
```

If **userdel** is not available on your system, it is still quite simple to remove a user. In a text editor, open the file /etc/passwd. This file contains entries for all users on the system. To delete a user, simply remove the related entry from /etc/passwd, save the file, and exit. With this method, you will have to remove associated files and directories by hand.

Warning: Unless the user has explicitly granted you permission to do so, be careful about deleting personal files. Those files are the property of the user. In general, it's a good idea to ask departing users what they want to do with the files. You could offer to compress them and e-mail the compressed file, or you might grant a grace period during which they should move anything they need to a new account. It's also a good idea to ask the user's permission if you'd like to use their configuration files or any scripts they have stored in the home directory.

Managing User Groups

User groups are a Unix concept which makes it easier to organize sub-sets of users and the various files and programs that they need. Individuals are assigned to groups, which in turn are granted permissions on particular aspects of the system. Granting permissions on an administrative program, for example, is much faster when it is just the group that needs permission rather than the 50 users assigned to that group.

Groups can be assigned when the user account is first created, or at any point in the account's existence. There is no limit to the number of groups possible on the system, and any given user could theoretically belong to all possible groups. In common practice, most users belong to a group with the same name as their user name, and possibly to one or two other groups. A university department which runs its own server, for example, might have groups named "students," "faculty," and "staff." Each group would have different access to the software stored on the network.

Groups are handled differently under different Unix variants. Under Linux and FreeBSD, group information is stored in the /etc/groups file. Other variants use similar files or provide graphical administration tools to manage group identifications and assignments. To see what groups you belong to, issue the command

```
groups
```

at the shell prompt. The output will show the names of each group to which you have been assigned; each of these groups also has a unique group identification number, just as each user has a unique user identification number.

Earlier in this book, you learned about file permissions. One of the elements of file permissions is the ability to grant or revoke permissions to a specified user group. The file's owner sets permissions so that her group(s) can access a particular document or program. Only the file's owner can change either the permissions or ownership of a particular file. For some functions, the root account must make these changes.

Disk Management

Next to working with users, working with the system's hard disks takes up a great amount of administrators' time. Disks, like any other storage medium, must be regularly cleaned and organized in order to work most efficiently. This is as true of a desk or table as it is of a single computer or a network.

What Is a Disk?

A disk, at its simplest, is a storage device. There are removable disks, sometimes called *floppies*, which encase a thin flexible medium in a harder outside shell. Early floppies were quite large, but the 3.5" diskette is now the standard for removable disk media. *Hard disks* were originally rigid and very large; the earliest disk-based computers had little storage space in comparison with their size.

Today, the names for storage media bear less resemblance to their actual construction. A disk might be a diskette, a hard disk, a CD-ROM, a DVD, a MiniDisc, a Zip disk, or one of several other technologies. They are all recordable media, though, and may all be used on the same network. When discussing Unix disk management, the implied disk is the computer's hard disk.

Disk Partitions

Even if you have a large hard disk on your Unix computer, you may not want to devote the entire disk to a single purpose. Under Unix, you can divide the disk into a number of smaller disks. This is called *partitioning the drive*. Partitions go by different names, depending on the Unix variant you are using. Under Solaris, for example, a partition is called a "volume"; under FreeBSD, it's a "slice." No matter what it's called, the intention is clear. A partition is part of a larger whole.

Why partition the hard drive? One of the most common reasons to do this is to separate system files from user files. By placing user files on a separate partition, a curious user cannot wander into restricted areas and nose around in the system directories. It is also a security advantage, since access to the system files is restricted. Since users tend to take up as much space on the disk as they are allowed, segregating user files to a separate partition means that disk usage can be controlled more closely; a user who packs his account full of MP3 files will not take up space better suited for system logs or the mail spool.

Disk partitions are usually created when the operating system is installed. Most installation managers are interactive, and you will be prompted to define partitions at an early stage in the installation. If you don't create partitions during installation, it is possible to partition the disk at a later stage, but it is more difficult and more likely to cause fatal problems.

Warning: When you partition a disk, all data on that disk is destroyed. Back everything up before you start. Some commercial partitioning programs claim to be able to work without deleting existing data, but there are many treacherous steps in the process and such claims may not always be the case. Never partition a disk that is not backed up on a separate disk, and always assume that the disk will be completely wiped during the partition. You will be pleasantly surprised if that does not happen, but wasting the time required to secure your data is far better than the alternative.

The Unix Filesystem

Individual partitions are treated as separate drives by the operating system. They are defined as individual devices, and each has its own entry in the /dev directory. Under Unix, the hardware devices which store data are a concept separate from the concept of the *filesystem*. The filesystem is the way in which files and directories are organized.

In the Unix world, the filesystem is a top-down tree. The top directory is the / directory, and every other directory on the machine is stored under /. Thus, the /dev directory is actually a directory named "dev" which is stored in the / directory. When you write a path name for a particular file, you are providing a map to its location within the filesystem.

However, each of these directories might be stored on a different partition or even on another machine in the network. The idea of the directory is divorced from the actual location of the bits that make up its data. This is why path names look like this:

```
/home/programfiles/atillinghast.txt
```

and not like this:

```
/dev/hda1/home/programfiles/atillinghast.txt
```

To get to the file named atillinghast.txt, you do not need to know where it is stored. You simply need to know its location in the filesystem.

Mounting Directories and Devices

There is a conceptual hole in this explanation. If the user does not need to know where the file is located, but the file must be found in order to run, how does the operating system resolve the path name to the actual position of the data? After all, even if the user does not have to know where the file is stored, the operating system does.

Under Unix, this problem is solved through *mounting*. When a device or directory is mounted, it is made available to the network. Thus, if the device hda1 is not mounted, none of the data on that device can be used even if a user issues the correct pathname. The operating system will return a "File not found" error.

Local devices must be mounted just like remote devices. Most local devices are mounted during the boot-up process, as part of the ordinary configuration of the system. Remote devices, including disk partitions, can also be mounted automatically. If, for example, you store a frequently used database on a remote partition, you could configure the operating system to mount that partition automatically when the computer is started. Users would be able to access that database without having to mount the partition themselves.

Mounting Local Partitions

Unlike making disk partitions, a particular device can be mounted or unmounted repeatedly during an active session. It is an easy process, and many users and administrators choose to mount some devices only when they are needed and unmount them when they are done. This falls under the theory that the fewer running processes on the machine, the faster the machine and the fewer problems that might occur.

To mount a device, you must first create a *mount point* where that device will be placed within the filesystem. Mount points are empty directories, which take the name of the filesystem to be mounted. For example, assume that you store user directories on a separate hard drive which has the device name hda2, and you want to make these directories available with the path name /home. The empty directory /home is the mount point.

To create a mount point, use the same commands you would use to create an ordinary directory. As root, issue the command

```
mkdir /home
```

at the shell prompt. The directory will be created and is ready to have the filesystem mounted. Use the **mount** command to actually mount the directory. mount takes the syntax

```
mount [options] device mount-point
```

In this case, the command would be issued as

```
mount /dev/hda2 /home
```

Under some variants, you may have to provide an option which defines the filesystem type. Your variant's documentation, or the manual page, will explain the proper syntax for mount on your system, should it differ.

Once you have finished with the filesystem, you can unmount it without having to shut down the system. (There is rarely a reason to shut down a Unix system.) To remove a filesystem, use the **umount** command. Note that there is no "n" in **umount**, and that there is no "unnmount" Unix command. It is a simple command, taking the syntax

```
umount filesystem
```

In this example, you would issue the command as

```
umount /home
```

Once the filesystem has been unmounted, it disappears from the operating system. Files on that device can no longer be accessed unless the filesystem is remounted. If the device is a removable medium like a CD or a diskette, it can be removed from its drive once the unmounting is complete.

Warning: Never remove a mounted device. It could cause a fatal crash of the operating system or even cause physical damage to the drive.

Mounting Remote Devices

One of the attractive features of Unix is that a remote device can be mounted and used locally just as if it were attached to the local machine. For users on corporate WANs, this can be a cost-efficient way to share files and work documents without having to send removable media between offices. Simply mount the remote device and get the files necessary, then unmount it when you are finished.

Remote devices are managed with a service called the *Network File Service,* or NFS. Mounting a remote device is much like mounting a local device, but requires a few extra steps. First, you must make some configurations on the remote machine. Log into the remote machine as root, and open the file /etc/exports in a text editor. Entries in this file take the syntax

```
filesystem        permitted-machine
```

If the local machine is called fred and stores the directory /sports, for example, you'd make an entry in the remote /etc/exports file like this:

```
/sports        fred
```

Save the file and exit the editor. Make sure that the remote machine's NFS server is running, and issue the command

```
exportfs
```

at the remote machine's prompt. Log out and return to the local machine's shell prompt to mount the filesystem.

There are also extra steps to take when issuing the mount command. Specifically, mounting a filesystem over NFS requires that you specify the file type as NFS, and you must provide specific path names for both the remote machine where the filesystem is housed and for the filesystem itself. Assuming that the remote machine is named barney, you'd issue the command as

```
mount -t nfs barney:/sports /news
```

to mount the remote sports filesystem into the local mount point /news. Remote filesystems unmount in the same way as local devices, with the umount command:

```
umount /news
```

Note: NFS implementations vary according to the Unix variant you are using. FreeBSD, Linux, and similar Unix variants use the method described here. Users of other variants should consult their documentation.

Backups

One very common task of the system administrator is that of making backups of the data contained on a computer system. Backups preserve data in the case of some catastrophic event such as a disk failure or a crack attack. It is especially critical to backup data on large machines such as servers or mainframes, which may contain data that are critical to the operation of an organization.

There are quite a few methods available for doing backups. Large organizations sometimes make use of professionally written backup and recovery software.

Smaller organizations and personal systems can make use of common utilities. Backups should be done at regular intervals, with quickly changing data (e.g., databases, /home) being backed up more often than data that tends to be the same over long periods of time (e.g., system-wide configuration).

While it would be difficult to describe a procedure that would be appropriate for all situations, the following will make a simple compressed archive file of a given directory:

1. Create a directory where the backup archive will be stored. This directory should be on its own partition, and should have plenty of space, as archive files can be quite large. In this example, that directory is called /backup.
2. Identify the directory to be archived: in this example, /home.
3. Using the **tar** command and a compression utility (in this case, gzip), create an archive file that will be placed in the /backup directory, as in

   ```
   tar cvfz /backup/homedirs.tgz /home
   ```

   The archive file will be called backupdirs.tgz.
4. Make a copy of the archive file on a second medium. For example, if the archive is smaller than about 650 MB, you could burn it onto a CD-ROM. Larger archives might require media with more space, such as tape drives, or the hard drive of a separate machine. If at all possible, the backup copies should be stored in a building other than the building in which they were made. (If fire were to destroy the building, for example, the backups would still be available.)

System Security

Whether you are administering a large network with thousands of machines or a small Linux network in your home, you should be concerned about security. The news brings a new story of security breaches almost every week, from the relatively amusing re-design of someone else's Web pages to the technical and comprehensive spying on a competitor's network or in the government files of another nation. Security is big business, with hundreds of firms providing software and consulting aimed at making networks safer.

While it's possible to spend hundreds of thousands of dollars on security, there are some habits which even the smallest network can establish. Security is as much a mindset as it is a program or piece of hardware. Administrators who keep security in mind at all times make better decisions and run tighter networks. In these times, it's rare indeed to find an administrator who doesn't think about security at all.

However, different people have different security risks and different attitudes toward those risks. The administrator of a small home network with a dial-up connection to the Internet has much less to worry about than the person with a cable modem or DSL line, who in turn is relatively well off compared to the administrators at the U.S. Department of Defense or at Citibank. Some administrators get nervous if a file has been moved by a legitimate user, while others simply don't care unless the machines are actually stolen. As in all things, cultivate a middle ground approach unless you have an actual reason to upgrade or downgrade your security precautions.

Physical Security

Oddly enough, physical security is sometimes overlooked when the topic of network security comes up. While software is a very useful tool and works in the vast majority of security cases, physical security is another concern. If someone breaks into your apartment and takes your computer, that's a security breach. They have your machine, with all its data, and any communications hardware they may have taken. Such a theft could be as damaging to you as a crack or a virus from a downloaded file.

Physical security solutions are common sense. Lock your doors and windows. Carry homeowner's or rental insurance, and engrave your machines with your driver's license number. Keep an inventory of your hardware, with serial numbers and receipts if possible. This will help the police if your property is stolen. If you have a roommate or friend who is prone to stupid pranks, figure out how to lock up the machines. Even a simple knob lock on a spare bedroom may be enough to dissuade those who are just "trying to be funny" by tinkering with your network. At work, consider a separate server room if you have a number of machines to keep safe. Such a room should be well ventilated and may need extra cooling to deal with machine heat. Individual machines can be cabled to desks.

A persistent thief can overcome most physical security precautions, but it is the casual thief that causes the most trouble. If someone really wants your data, they can just open the case and take the hard drive. Someone who grabs your machine and runs is looking for an easily pawned or fenced item. Take the same precautions with your computer equipment that you would with an expensive bicycle or stereo components.

Internal Security

The more users on your network, the more security risks. Every new user is an additional potential breach. Administrators should make every attempt to get to know their user base. This doesn't necessarily mean taking each user to lunch, but rather familiarizing yourself with regular system behavior. Does user bfandahl log on from home every night at 11:00 P.M. to download files? Have you ever seen user jkatz log in on weekends? Once you know what regular behavior patterns are, you'll be able to spot unusual or strange patterns in your logs and regular system scans.

The most secure systems restrict the behavior of individual users as much as possible. Configure permissions so that each user has the most limited permissions possible, and expand each permission as needed rather than granting global permissions and then going back to crack down when there is a problem. Use user groups to sort your user base into segments which can be given access to certain programs but not to others.

Most internal security problems stem from bad user and administrative habits. Do your users routinely tape passwords to the monitor? Do they share passwords or user accounts? Do they dial in from home and let their kids surf the Web from behind the company firewall? Turning to administrative responsibilities, do you have strong and clear user policies explaining passwords, account usage, disk space limitations, and other important topics? Do you remind your users of these policies regularly and review them to make sure that new technology is still covered? Remember that it is always easy to make a policy looser, but it is nearly impossible to place new restrictions on people who are used to doing what they want.

External Security

Most people think of external security measures first when confronted with the idea of security behavior. External security software deals with intrusions into your network from outside. These are usually cracks from external networks like the Internet, which break into your system without proper authorization. The stories you see on the news are usually stories about external intrusion.

The problem with external security is that it is the hardest element to control. You don't know what the shadowy cracker halfway around the globe is planning to do, or what he's thinking. Your reaction must happen after the intrusion, because you do not know the person and cannot identify suspicious behavior before the problem occurs. This is why so many external security programs and consultants use names that evoke padlocks, barbed wire, lockdowns, and other physical images of barred entry. External security is focused on locking down as many points of entry as possible, rather than on the motivation of the unknown intruder.

There are some simple steps you can take to enhance external security without having to buy expensive proprietary software. First, shut down any services that you don't need. If you don't get a news feed, don't run a news server, and so on. Some services may be automatically configured when you install the operating system. You'll need to scan your active processes to see what's running and what can be stopped without affecting normal activity on the machine.

Next, require that secure connections be used for any external connection to the machine. Replace **telnet** and **rlogin** with SSH. Replace file transfer programs with secure versions. Make sure that users supply valid passwords to connect to the machine. Note that, at the time this book was written, cryptographic software like SSH was still banned for export outside the United States and Canada. If you are in another country, you will need to seek locally available cryptography for your security needs. In general, keep all your software upgraded. As soon as a security hole is found in any program, the news rushes across the Internet. Keep on top of patches and new releases.

Read your log files regularly. Look for unusual behavior or patterns, and see if you can figure out why they happened. Perhaps the strange entry is due to a cracker, or perhaps a user is logging in at an unusual hour because she can't sleep. Logs aren't infallible, since most savvy crackers now run *log scrubber* programs which delete any mention of their activity, but neophyte or stupid crackers can often be caught easily with log data.

Consider installing security software. Port scanners look at your network from outside, trying to find uncontrolled ports which are open and accepting connections. Trade port scans with an administrator at another network so you can both benefit. Then, shut down any unused ports that are hanging open. Open ports are the easiest way for someone to get access to your system, and they're the most common crack for people with cable modems or DSL. Intrusion detection software builds a database of your system's information in a kind of snapshot. Run the software regularly to compare the current situation to the snapshot, and if something is amiss, the program will report it to you.

More advanced solutions involve firewalls and proxies. A firewall is essentially a port block with a set of rules. Certain IP numbers can access machines on the other side of the firewall, which other IP numbers are not allowed to enter. Proxies are a way to transfer data between an internal machine and an external machine without ever actually connecting the two. Both are excellent solutions for the small-to-medium network, and mandatory for larger networks with millions of connections daily.

Password Security

Whether or not you ever become a system administrator, you can participate in one of the easiest security schemes by selecting an appropriate password and practicing good password management. Passwords are like car keys. If someone steals your car keys, they can unlock and drive your car wherever they like. The car doesn't know it's you; all the car knows is that the proper key was inserted into the steering column. Just like the car, your Unix account doesn't know that the person entering your password isn't you.

Passwords should be *strong passwords.* The best passwords are a mix of alphabetical and numeric characters, as well as a mix of upper and lower case. Passwords should never be plain dictionary words. Many crackers use a dictionary program called **crack** which runs an entire file of dictionary words against the password file. Therefore, the password

```
bumblebee
```

is a *weak password.* It can be changed to a strong password with a few simple tweaks:

```
bUmbL3B3e
```

In addition to selecting a strong password, change it frequently. Changing your password once a month is a good habit to establish. Don't change it so frequently or use such a difficult password that you have to write it down, though. Written passwords are an invitation to abuse.

Note: If you are a network administrator, you can download password management software. These programs can be configured to expire current passwords at regular intervals, and can also be set to reject dictionary words or passwords that do not meet particular local rules. While some users may balk at stringent password rules, it is one of the easiest ways to protect internal security on your network.

Summary

No matter how many users are on a particular Unix machine or network, the system administrator has responsibility for every account and activity that happens. The system administrator has access to the root, or superuser account, which has the ability to view any file or perform any action on the machine, even those activities which are not permitted in the administrator's normal user account. The superuser system gives control to a single person or small group of people in order to have a single point of authority for the machine or network. This authority keeps the system more secure and limits the ability of ordinary users to affect settings or documents which control how other users can use the system.

Managing users is one of the major administrative tasks on a Unix machine. Users can be added or deleted with certain shell programs, or with graphical user management tools found in many Unix variants with graphical user interfaces. User accounts can be configured to allow access to particular areas of the machine, through user permissions, or can be revoked or suspended should the user fail to adhere to system policies.

The other major component of system administration is disk management. Whether it is effective allocation of the disk space or the use of remote filesystems to bring additional files to local users, administrators must be aware of the various filesystems mounted on the machine and across the network. These filesystems may be on the local hard disk, whether partitioned or not, or may be on external devices or on other machines connected to the network. All can be used by a local user in the same way as long as the filesystem is mounted properly.

Finally, administrators must keep a close eye on the system's security. Network or machine security is divided into three general areas: physical, internal, and external. Physical security refers to the hardware itself, which can be stolen or otherwise compromised. Internal security involves user behavior and

effective administration, such as with the setting of appropriate permissions and using user groups effectively. External security is the first kind of security most people think of, since it involves attacks on the local machine or network from outside, such as across the Internet. The best security plan for any given machine or network requires an honest assessment of risk, and the implementation of both effective local policies and strong security-related software.

Review Questions

1. Define the term "system administrator."
2. What is the root account?
3. What powers does the superuser account have?
4. Why does Unix use a superuser system?
5. Can individual users perform some of the superuser's tasks? In what situations?
6. What are the drawbacks of a superuser system?
7. Name some activities involved in user management.
8. What is the function of /etc/passwd?
9. Why would an administrator prefer to use **useradd** instead of adding a user by hand?
10. Provide some reasons why a user might be removed from the user base.
11. Should an administrator automatically remove files associated with deleted accounts? Why or why not?
12. What is a user group?
13. Why are user groups useful constructs?
14. How can file permissions be used to affect groups instead of individuals?
15. What is a disk? Name several types.
16. What is a disk partition?
17. When are partitions useful?
18. Why might an administrator limit user account size?
19. How are partitions created?
20. Describe the Unix filesystem.
21. Define "mounting."
22. What are the benefits of the mounting mechanism?
23. What is the difference between mounting a device automatically and mounting it manually?
24. Define "mount point."
25. How do you remove a mounted filesystem?
26. What is NFS?
27. Why is security a concern?
28. Define physical security.
29. What is internal security? How can it be enhanced?
30. How can external security be strengthened?
31. Explain good password policies.

1. If you are using a graphical user interface, such as an integrated desktop environment, look through the menus to find the various system administration tools provided by the GUI. Read the documentation on the GUI's Web site, if necessary, to learn how each tool works. Compare each tool to its shell command counterpart. Which method do you find easier to use? Why? Does your opinion change from command to command?
2. Draw a diagram of your network's filesystem. If you can identify which filesystems are mounted remotely, label them on the drawing. Identify the function of each directory and whether or not users have permission to execute, write, or read files in that directory.
3. Write a brief essay in which you describe the security risks on two networks: your school or employer's network, and a small home network connected to the Internet with a cable modem. What are the security liabilities for each? Suggest a reasonable security program for both administrators. You may need to search the Web for particular software or hardware recommendations.
4. Review the user policies of your school or employer, including password policies. How do the policies affect your behavior as a user, from a system administration viewpoint? Do these policies place restrictions on users for security purposes? Are they reasonable restrictions, or are they either too harsh or too lenient? Write alternative policies which, in your opinion, provide better security or user environment for the network. If you can learn what external security mechanisms are in place, include those in your review.
5. Obtain documentation for the intrusion detection program AIDE, the port scanner PortSentry, and the proxy program Dante. (All are free on the Web.) Write an explanation of how each program works. Is this software you would recommend? What is the place of each program in a unified security approach?

CHAPTER 17

Basic System Administration: Part II

IN THIS CHAPTER

1. Managing software
2. Installing software from source code
3. Package management systems
4. Printer administration

In Chapter 16, you learned about some of the basic tasks of system administration: managing users, disk space, and security. In this chapter, you will learn about two other elements of most system administration jobs. Managing software is an ongoing process which involves reviewing software archives on a regular basis, reading Unix news sources, and talking with other administrators in order to learn about revisions to installed programs or new programs which may help your machine run better. Managing print processes used to be a chore under Unix, but new software has made it easier to handle.

Depending on your particular situation, you may not manage users or need to have extended experience with remote filesystems. However, anyone who works on a Unix machine will probably need to install software at some point, whether in a user account or on the system as a whole. Most users also expect to have access to a printer; while this chapter does not address the mechanics of an actual print job, it shows you how to add and configure new printers for your network. Printing is usually a function of the program which the user has used to make the document.

Managing Software

One of the most common things a system administrator must do is to install software. If you have ever installed software on a Macintosh or a Windows-based PC, you probably had a fairly simple experience. Software manufacturers tend to provide installation programs which greatly reduce the amount of user input into this process. This is possible because these operating systems were created by a single manufacturer—Microsoft and Apple—which can provide detailed specifications to the software companies. These specifications can, in turn, help the companies write simple installation programs.

In the Unix world, things are not always that simple. Some distributors do provide package management software that makes the job of installation much easier, but there is no guarantee that this will be the case when you download a new program. Software installation under Unix can be as simple as giving a single command, or as complicated a scenario as you can imagine. This should not scare you off, however. Even at its most complex, Unix software management is ultimately comprehensible. Most software packages, especially those which are professionally produced, come with detailed instructions for installation.

There are two general methods used for installing software. Software can be compiled from source code, or installed directly as binary packages. Installing from source code has the advantage that one can often install a single package on any one of a variety of Unix variants; the disadvantage is that it is a more complicated procedure. Binary packages offer simplicity, but are usually restricted to a single Unix variant; in the case of Linux, sometimes packages are restricted to a single Linux distribution.

Installing Software from Source Code

A great deal of Unix software is available as *source code*. Source code is the form in which the programmer wrote the program, which is human-readable and cannot be run directly as an executable file. This is especially true of packages which are released as Free or Open Source software. In order to install source code packages, the system administrator must run a compiler to convert the source code into an executable binary file which will run on her particular system.

In order for this conversion to work, you must have certain elements installed on your system. First, you must have a compiler. Most Unix systems install a compiler by default when the operating system is installed. Other systems have a compiler available, but it may not be available because the system administrator has never configured it properly.

Check to see whether or not you have a compiler available to you by issuing the command

```
which cc
```

at the shell prompt. **cc** stands for "C compiler." Even if you are using a different compiler, like the GNU C compiler called GCC, there should be a symbolic link which starts the actual compiler when the **cc** command is invoked. If a compiler exists on your system, its location will print to the screen.

If you get no output, no compiler is configured on your system. If you installed your own operating system, such as FreeBSD or Linux, you will probably have a compiler on the CDs or in the downloaded files which you used to install the operating system. Otherwise, you can download a current version of the GCC compiler from the GNU project at http://www.gnu.org/software/gcc/gcc.html. If at all possible, download a binary copy suitable for your platform since, in order to install the compiler from source code, you would need a working compiler.

Tech Tip

To install the compiler from a binary package, see the section of this chapter devoted to binary installations.

Once you have a functional compiler, you will also need the program **make**. This is a program which helps to automate the compilation process. Again, you can check for the program by issuing the command

```
which make
```

at the shell prompt. If there is no output, download **make** from any Unix software archive.

Most software also requires that certain *libraries* be installed on the system before the software is installed. Libraries are compilations of functions that programmers separate into individual files. These functions are commonly used, and segregating them in this way means that the function set can be reused by multiple programs without having to be written into each program. Unfortunately, there is no one ideal set of libraries which will allow you to install any program you like. Required libraries depend on the software package you want to install. The documentation that comes with the package should tell you what you need.

Getting and Unpacking the Package

The first step in the installation process is to obtain and unpack the software. Most software is obtained from a CD or from an online Web or FTP archive. Regardless of how you get the package, transfer it to your machine's hard drive. You should store the package in a directory which you have set aside for this procedure. Many people like to use the directories /tmp or /usr/src.

Note: Because the /tmp directory is, as its name implies, a temporary location, do not store important files or programs here. System administrators may wipe this directory regularly without checking to see what its contents are, assuming that users will store important files in their own home directories. Once you have installed the program, you can delete the downloaded package from the temporary directory.

The software package will usually come in the form of a *tarball.* A tarball is a collection of several files and/or subdirectories that has been archived into a single file. Tarballs are often compressed after they are archived, to make the file as small as possible. The filename of the tarball is usually given in a syntax which makes it easy to know what format the file is in. The filename

```
packagename.tar
```

indicates an uncompressed archive, while

```
packagename.tgz
```

or

```
packagename.tar.gz
```

indicates an archive which has been compressed with the **gzip** program. A filename of

```
packagename.tar.bz2
```

or

```
packagename.tar.bz
```

or

```
packagename.tbz2
```

or

```
packagename.tbz
```

indicates an archive which has been compressed with the **bzip2** program. **bzip2** is similar to the more widely used **gzip**, but creates a smaller compressed file. **bzip2** is usually used when the file being compressed is very large, and is a useful program to have on your system.

In order to unpack these files, you must use the **tar** program. **tar** is an abbreviation for "tape archive." The program was originally used to create backup files which were to be stored on tape drives. While it is still sometimes used for that purpose, **tar** is now also used routinely to create compressed packages for a variety of purposes. To unpack the downloaded package, issue the command

```
tar xvf filename
```

if the package is a *.tar file; use the command

```
tar xvfz filename
```

if the package is a *.tgz or *.tar.gz file; and the command

```
tar xvfj filename
```

if the package is a *.bz, *.bs2, *.tar.bz, or *.tar.bz2 file.

Depending on the size of the archive, this process could take some time. The "v" option produces *verbose output*, meaning that you will see the name of each individual file as it is extracted from the archive. Once the archive has been extracted, list the contents of the current directory with the **ls** command. You should see a new subdirectory with the same name as the package you just untarred. Move into that subdirectory with the **cd** command; you are now ready for the next step of the installation process.

Reading the Documentation

It may seem strange to think of reading the documentation as a step in the process of installing new software. When you are installing software from source code, however, reading the documentation is extremely important. In the directory created by extracting the archive, there should be various documentation files. In particular, you should have files named README and INSTALL. Read these files carefully and completely.

In addition to the README and INSTALL files, there may be other documentation available with the package. These files are often stored in a subsubdirectory named /doc, or will otherwise be obvious from their names. The README file may also indicate where the additional documentation is to be found. Note that, in some cases, the additional documentation is intended to be read from within the installed program and may be formatted unusually or be unreadable as text files.

Warning: Always read all of a package's documentation, or as much of it as you can, before proceeding with the installation. At the very least, you must read the README and the INSTALL files to learn whether there are unique requirements for this program.

Why is reading the documentation so important? Any idiosyncrasies of the installation procedure will be explained in the INSTALL and README files. These files also provide information that you may need to supply during the compilation, or warn you that certain external or system information will be needed. This gives you time to obtain the necessary information before you begin the compilation process, which cannot be stopped without aborting the installation. Any special considerations involved in compiling this software for your particular system will be explained in these files. Your chances of a successful installation, and the least amount of wasted time, are maximized by reading the documentation before you begin installing the package.

The following steps in this section are general procedures that are common to many software installations on many Unix variants. These steps are not universal, however, and you should always be on the lookout for any places where an individual package's installation procedure differs from what is described below. Wherever the two processes do not correspond, the procedure described in the package's documentation always takes precedence over these more general instructions.

Configuring the Installation

Many software programs come with a customized shell program called **configure**, **Configure**, **setup**, or something similar. The INSTALL document will tell you what the program is called. Be sure that you are in the package subdirectory and issue the command

```
./configure
```

If necessary, replace "configure" with the actual name of the program.

The configuration program does not usually require user input. However, some versions are interactive, and you should be prepared to supply required information if necessary. Also, some configure programs take arguments if you want to enable certain options that should be compiled into the program. Here again, the documentation will tell you what those options are. Most of the time, however, you can just run the program and it will handle itself appropriately. The configure program will check for your compiler, the required libraries, and other important elements needed for successful installation.

Compiling the Software

Once the configuration program has run (or if there is no configuration program for this package), you are ready to compile the program. This is normally a simple process. Issue the command

```
make
```

at the shell prompt. The **make** program uses the output of the configuration program, as stored in a new file called **Makefile**, to direct the action of the C compiler. At this point, the compiler will begin its work. You will probably see a number of messages scrolling up the screen as the program compiles.

Depending on the size of the software package and the speed of your computer, this process can take anywhere from a few seconds to a few hours or more. If the compilation seems to be taking a long time, there is little that you can do to speed the process. Some software packages go as far as to suggest that you go and have some coffee at this point.

Once the compilation is finished, you will have a working piece of software, provided that nothing has gone wrong. If some problem has occurred, you should see error messages generated by the compiler. These messages can give you various useful clues about what the problem might have been. You may be missing a library or have a necessary shell program installed in an unusual location. Make the necessary repairs or install the required libraries and try the installation procedure again.

All that remains at this point is to install the binaries and configuration files in the appropriate locations in the filesystem. Some packages can do this for you if you simply type

```
make install
```

at the shell prompt. Other packages will not. As always, the documentation is your guide. If you choose to take the **make install** route, remember that the files will be installed in the directories that the writers of the software thought most appropriate. If you want them installed someplace else, you will have to move them by hand.

Package Management Systems

Installing software from source code has its advantages and its disadvantages. On one hand, you get a lot of control over the process when you install from source code. Many source code packages offer a large number of *compile time options.* These options let you create a final binary that does exactly what you want, without wasting system resources on unnecessary functions. The price you pay for this flexibility is a level of complexity that can range from the merely tedious to the baffling and frustrating.

Package management systems reverse this situation. For most normal software installations, package management systems make installing software a simple process which is often just a matter of issuing a single command. The disadvantage of these systems is that you are often limited to installing a piece of software that has been preconfigured to fit as many situations as possible. In most cases and for most users, this is not a problem and a package management system may represent a significant time savings with little to no downside.

Another advantage of package management systems is that they often create and maintain a database of the software installed on your system. This database allows the manager to check and report on any possible dependency or conflict issues when you install a new package, or get required libraries before an installation. Some package management systems automatically check for new versions of your installed software and download updates when they are released.

Yet another advantage of these management systems is that some software which is not Open Source—that is, which is available only in a precompiled binary format—is available under certain package management systems. For example, the popular commercial program **vmware**, a PC hardware emulator, is available in packages that are compatible with the RPM package management system. Such programs are never available as source code.

There is no rule which decrees that a given system may have only software installed by a package manager or software compiled locally from source code. Most systems have both, and most administrators are equally fluent in the procedure required for both kinds of installation. The only caveat in this situation is that the package management system's database, if it has one, will not know about the programs you have compiled yourself. This is not a problem of vast proportions, and at its worst would probably be a minor annoyance rather than a legitimate reason to avoid source code.

Case In Point: RPM

Package management systems are often specific to the particular Unix variant with which they are released. Since there are several of these systems, each slightly different, it serves no purpose to describe each here. A review of one of the most popular package management systems, RPM, should give you a good idea of how similar programs work on other Unix variants.

RPM, a recursive acronym which means "RPM Package Manager," was originally developed for Red Hat Linux. Because RPM is Free software, however, the code was publicly released and has subsequently been adapted by several other Linux distributions. RPM variants can be found on Linux Mandrake and SuSE Linux, among others.

RPM is a simple program for almost all installations. To install a package, simply issue the command

```
rpm -i packagename
```

To uninstall a package, issue the command

```
rpm -e packagename
```

To upgrade an existing package, issue the command

```
rpm -U packagename
```

RPM, like all package management systems, only works with packages that are specially formatted for it. Such packages are usually called RPMs, and have a particular filename syntax:

```
name version-number build-number.architecture.rpm
```

The first three elements are the main identifying information in the package name. Name and version number are self-evident.

Build

Build number refers to the particular binary version of the package. For example, a package distributor may compile the software five times to get just the right mix of compile-time options. The final version would be referred to as "build number 5" and that number would be reflected in the package name.

Architecture

The architecture component of the package name refers to the type of system for which the software is compiled. For example, most personal computers are identified as "i386," for "Intel 386." Of course, the Intel 386 processor has not been state-of-the-art for many years. However, software compiled for a 386 will run on any later Intel PC processor or clone of an Intel processor. From time to time, you may see packages compiled for later Intel architectures, as in "i586" or "i686." Other common architecture designations include "ppc" for Macintosh, "alpha" for DEC Alpha processors, or "sparc" for Sun Sparc processors.

You may also come across two other architectural designations from time to time. The "noarch" designation denotes software that is not specific to a particular architecture. For example, programs written in interpreted languages such as Perl or Python will run on any architecture so long as the appropriate interpreter is installed properly. The "src" designation identifies packages which consist of software in source code form. RPM has the ability to invoke the local C compiler and to create binary programs from source code RPMs.

Note: Installing source code RPMs is an advanced skill and is not dealt with in this chapter. If you want to learn more about this process, visit the RPM Web site and read the documentation. The site is listed in Appendix D, Internet Resources.

These elements are all pulled together to create the actual package name. An RPM file might have a name like this:

```
dos2unix-3.1-3.i386.rpm
```

This name tells you the name of the package, **dos2unix**, the version number, **3.1**, and the build number, **3**. It also tells you the architecture required for this package, **i386**.

To install this file, issue the command

```
rpm -e dos2unix-3.1-3.i386.rpm
```

To uninstall this file, issue the command

```
rpm -i dos2unix-3.1-3
```

Note that the architecture and package suffix has been left out of the command. This is because once the package is installed, it is known to the RPM database only by the basic element of the package name. The architecture and .rpm suffix are a given at that point, since the software would not install on incorrect architecture and the RPM program would not work with a non-RPM-encoded package.

In addition to these functions, RPM is *network-aware*. That is, if your local machine is connected to a network or to the Internet, you can simultaneously download and install a package by issuing the command with a full URL as in the command

```
rpm -i ftp://some.server/rpms/dos2unix-3.1-3.i386.rpm
```

In this case, you must supply the complete file name since RPM needs to go to the appropriate FTP location and download the file. The last two elements are only ignored when the package is already downloaded and resident on your local hard drive.

Printer Administration

Administering printers used to be one of the more troublesome aspects of Unix system administration. However, this has changed with the recent maturation of the Common Unix Printing System, or CUPS. The problem with Unix printing is that no two variants handled print jobs in the same way. The configuration files were obscure, and could not be shared among machines. Even with the advent of graphical configuration tools for printers, it seemed that no two Unix variants could agree on how to run things.

CUPS, on the other hand, replaces all of these systems with a single consistent interface that works across many Unix variants. At the time this book was written, CUPS was supported under Linux, FreeBSD, and at least seven commercial Unix variants including IRIX, HP-UX, AIX, and Solaris. In addition, it is now the primary printing system on several of these variants.

In the real world of legacy networks, of course, you may find yourself using a system which does not have CUPS installed. In this case, you will need to roll up your sleeves and find the documentation which explains exactly how your system's print services work. However, if you are the person in charge of the system, consider replacing any non-CUPS printing system with a CUPS-enabled variant. It will save a lot of time in the long run.

Working with CUPS

If you have a Unix variant which will work with CUPS but do not have the CUPS software installed, obtain it at the CUPS Web site (see Appendix D: Internet Resources) and install it using the process described above. Once it is working, shut down any running print servers that were previously installed and configured.

One of the advantages of CUPS is that you can use a simple Web interface to manage and administer your print services. Open your Web browser and enter the address **http://localhost:631/** in the address box. You should see a page like the one in Figure 17.1.

Adding a Printer

To add a printer, click on the link labeled "Do Administrative Tasks." The "Admin" page will appear, as shown in Figure 17.2.

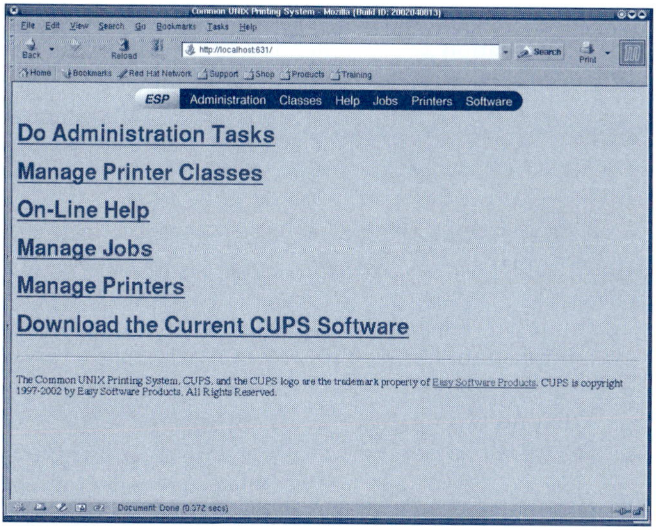

FIGURE 17.1 The main CUPS page.

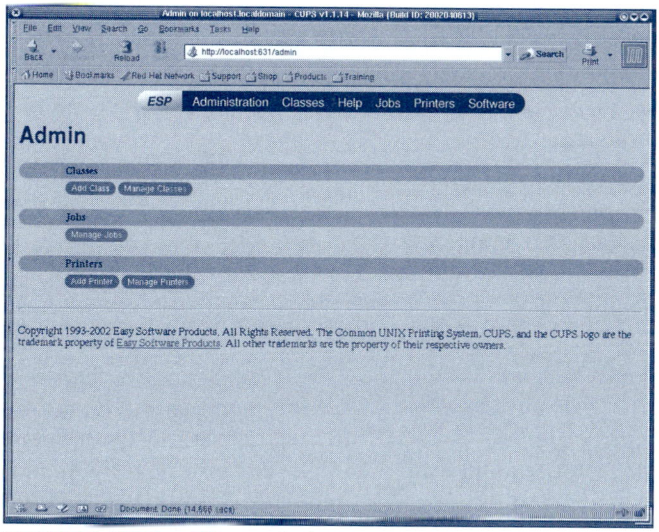

FIGURE 17.2 The Admin CUPS page.

Click the "Add Printer" link to bring up the "Add New Printer" page, as shown in Figure 17.3.

Assign a name to the new printer. This name should be something descriptive, perhaps the type of printer or the manufacturer's name. The name should also be distinctive. Though it may seem trivial, administering a number of printers with similar names can become tiresome and difficult.

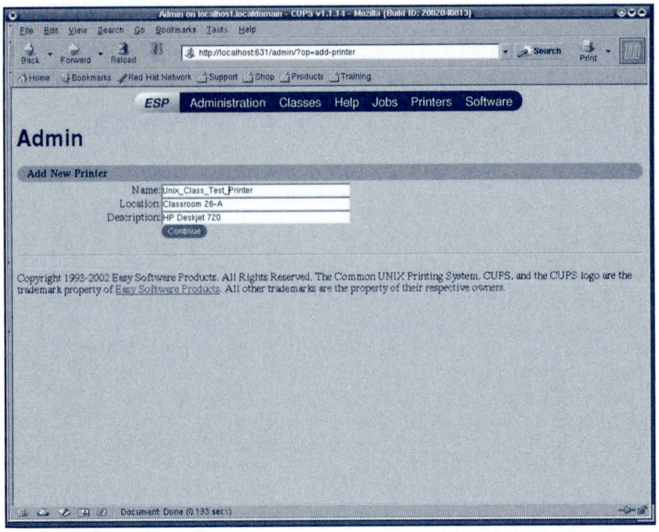

FIGURE 17.3 Adding a new printer with CUPS.

In the Location field, enter the printer's location. Use room numbers, workstation ID numbers, or any other designation which makes sense. Be wary of using the names of people who will use the printer; they may change locations or leave the job, but the printer will still be called **sarahlaser** long after nobody remembers Sarah.

Finally, you can enter a description if needed. If your employer assigns bar codes to identify hardware, this might be a good field for that code. You can also ignore the field. When you have finished, click the Continue link.

At this point, as shown in Figure 17.4, you will be asked to provide a device name. The device is the connection to which the printer is attached. This could be a parallel port, serial port, USB port, or other device. Enter the appropriate identification and press Continue.

Next, you must enter the make of your printer. Select the appropriate hardware manufacturer from the list and click Continue. On the next page, select the appropriate model from the list, and click Continue. The printer has now been added and is ready to receive print jobs. Figure 17.5 shows the newly added printer.

Controlling Printers

Once the new printer is added, you can add additional printers by using the same procedure. You can also use the Web interface to control the printer. Click on the "Printers" link in the navigation bar to see the printer control page.

On this page, your printer is represented by an icon and a legend containing some of its identifying information. Along the bottom of the page appear

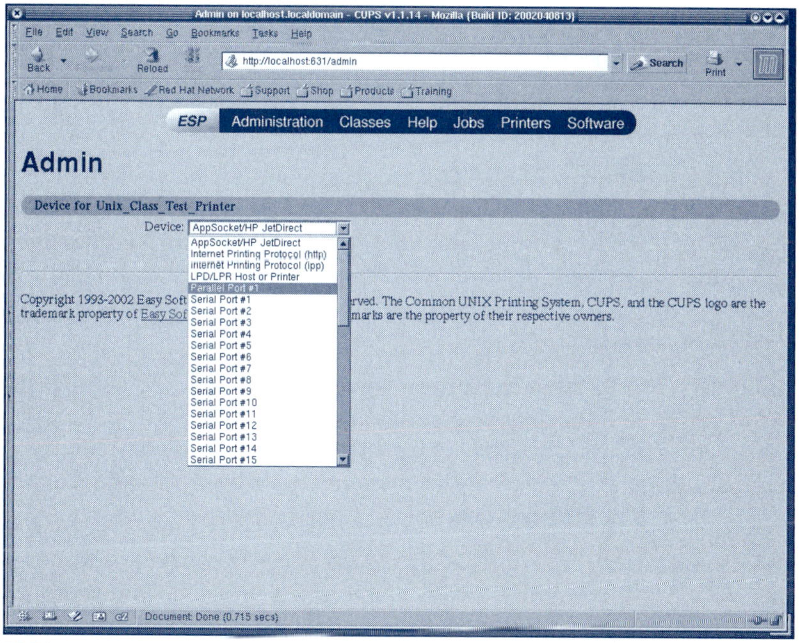

FIGURE 17.4 Selecting the new printer's device.

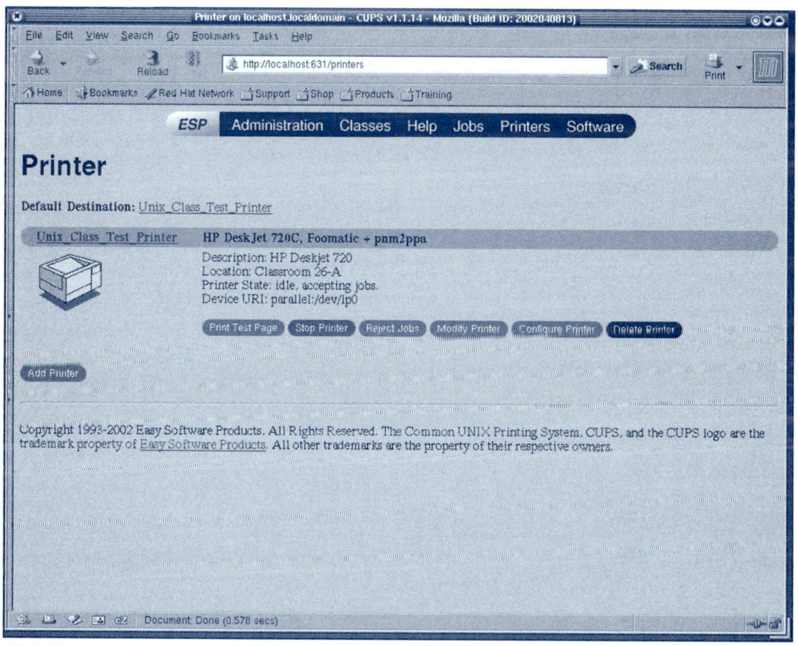

FIGURE 17.5 A newly configured printer.

links for several operations which you can perform on the selected printer. Table 17.1 shows the printer options.

Network Printing

One of the key features of the Unix environment is networkability. CUPS makes networking printers a much easier process than in the past. Some printers have built-in ethernet capability, while others can be attached to a machine which is, in turn, accessible to the network. No matter how the printer is networked, CUPS allows you to have a single printer which can be accessed and used from multiple points on the network.

To configure a printer to act as a print server on the network, simply add the printer as described above. Make sure that the machine to which it is connected is accessible via port 631. Once this setup is complete, clients on the network should be able to access this printer simply by sending print requests to port 631 on the target machine.

Tech Tip

If you look in the /etc/services file described in Chapter 19, you will see that port 631 is reserved for the Internet Printing Protocol.

The most basic method of configuring clients to use this service is to simply do nothing. CUPS will recognize any available print server on the same subnet within 30 seconds of its being brought online. For this to work, both the client and the server must be on the same subnet. That is, the first three numbers of each machine's IP address must be the same.

If you want to use a printer on a separate subnet, you will need to do some manual configuration. On the client machine, open the file /etc/cups/cupsd.conf file in a text editor. Locate the section, about two-thirds of the way down the file, which says

```
#
# BrowsePoll: poll the named server(s) for printers
#

#BrowsePoll address:port
```

TABLE 17.1: CUPS Printer Management Options

Option	Function
Print Test Page	Prints a test page
Stop/Start Printer	Toggles selected printer on or off
Accept/Reject Jobs	Allows or throttles new jobs in the print queue
Modify Printer	Opens printer information dialog
Configure Printer	Offers further configuration options
Delete Printer	Removes printer profile from configuration

Add the line

```
BrowsePoll <server.IP.number>:631
```

immediately after this section. Then, restart the CUPS server by issuing the command

```
kill -HUP <CUPS process ID number>
```

The client machine should now be able to see the new print server.

Summary

Although not all system administrators work directly with users or with security, almost everyone installs or removes software from their computers. In addition to managing software, many administrators must also manage printers. Over the past few years, both jobs have become easier as new technology has been introduced. Managing software and printers is now almost automated and can take up much less of an administrator's time than they would have ten years ago.

Software packages can be downloaded from the Web or taken from CD-ROMs. Packages intended for Unix come in two types: source code and precompiled binaries. Source code is the program as the programmer wrote it, and must be compiled into an executable binary before it is usable. Precompiled binaries are already compiled, but may not have the flexibility in options that source code packages offer. Source code is compiled and installed in a multi-step process. Binaries can be installed with a package management system which automates much of the process and requires little input from the user.

Printers have been an irritating part of the Unix universe for many years. Until recently, there was no standardization, and each Unix variant could have a different way of managing print jobs. With the development of CUPS, the Common Unix Printing System, print management has gotten easier and can now be done from a simple Web interface. Printers can be added, deleted, or configured from the CUPS software.

Review Questions

1. What is the difference between installing software under Unix and installing software under Windows or MacOS?
2. What is source code?
3. What are precompiled binary files?
4. What is a compiler?
5. Define *library*.
6. Why are software libraries used by programmers?
7. What is the function of the /tmp directory?
8. What should be stored in /tmp?
9. Define "tarball."
10. What is the difference between archiving and compression?
11. What is verbose output?
12. Which documentation files are critical to successful installations?
13. What information do these files contain?

14. What does the configure program do?
15. What is a Makefile?
16. What is a package management system?
17. Define "compile time options."
18. Explain the syntax of an RPM package name.
19. What is a build?
20. What is CUPS?
21. What types of device can be used for printer connections?
22. What is the function of port 631?

Exercises

1. Visit one of the Unix software archives listed in Appendix D, Internet Resources. Find a utility or other small program which you can install in your home directory. Download a source code package with the *.tar or *.tar.gz extension. Unpack and install the program in your home directory. Make sure that it runs.
2. Determine whether your system has a package management system available. If so, identify the system and the type of package needed. As in Exercise 1, visit a software archive and download a utility or other program. Note that many precompiled binaries are system-level programs, and you may need to have root access in order to install the program you have chosen. Using the package manager, install the program. Make sure that it runs.
3. Using the Web, research several different package management systems. Check different Linux, BSD, and Unix variants for their package management methods. What are the similarities? How do they differ? State a preference for one system and explain your choice.
4. Determine whether there are printers attached to your system or network. What operating system is used on this network? Is it CUPS-compatible? If CUPS is not used to manage these printers (hint: check for the CUPS configuration file or the output of **ps** to see if the CUPS daemon is running), how are printers managed?

CHAPTER 18

The X Window System

IN THIS CHAPTER

1. What is the X Window System?
2. How X Windows works
3. Features of X Windows
4. Window managers and desktop environments
5. Installing and starting X
6. X Windows and networks
7. Customizing the X environment
8. X Windows and security
9. X Windows and Adaptive user environments

In many situations throughout this book, you have had the opportunity to work with Unix in two ways: at the shell command prompt, and through a graphical user interface. While most modern computer users are most familiar with graphical interfaces and find text-based prompts to be unusual or difficult to work with, these interfaces are relatively new. In the first decades of Unix, users could only interact with the operating system through the shell prompt, and that is why so many programs and commands are still best issued within the shell.

In 1984, however, a new standard was issued that made graphical Unix interfaces possible. This was a landmark year for computer users, as it was also the year in which the first Macintosh was released, also with a graphical user interface. (The first release of Microsoft Windows was still some years away.) The Macintosh interface, Unix graphical display, and Windows all stem from the same research done at the Xerox Palo Alto Research Center in the 1970s, but implementation of that research took different paths over the intervening ten years.

Graphical display on a Unix system is possible because of the X Window System. This is a graphical interface which underlies any user-level graphical interfaces installed on the computer, such as the desktop programs KDE, Gnome, or Ximian. In this chapter, you will learn the theory behind the X Window System, how it works with user-level programs, and some administrative techniques for working with X.

What Is the X Window System?

The X Window System is both a system and a standard. More precisely, the term *X Window System* can be applied both to the standard and to any programs which implement it, which can be confusing in casual conversation. As with other standards discussed in this text, the X Window System standard is administered by an impartial body: the X Consortium. The standard defines the way in which Unix systems create and manage graphical images which display on the user's monitor.

Unix itself is not a graphical operating system and does not have the functions necessary to render visual images on the screen (except for text). If you were to install a graphical program directly on top of Unix, the operating system could not draw the pictures necessary to use the program. This is where X comes in. X is an intermediary which acts as an interpreter between the operating system and the graphical software, allowing the two to work together in displaying visual images. The standard defines the various rules which graphical software must obey in order to have images rendered.

Most Unix installations include an X Window System program as part of the default software. X is so critical to modern Unix software that it is difficult to find systems that do not run some version of X Windows. Commercial Unix variants probably run commercial X implementations or versions of X which have been written especially for that variant. The personal Unix variants designed for personal computers use the X implementation XFree86, which works with personal computer architecture rather than large servers and their specialized hardware. Although most versions of X Windows software are written for Unix, there are a few releases which can run under Windows as well.

Note: The current version of the X Window Standard is X11R6, the sixth revision of the eleventh version of the standard. Changes in X are slow, unlike some standards which are still under active development, and it is not likely that a new version will be released in the immediate future. Thus, any documentation you might find on the Web or in X-related books is probably valid as long as the book is relatively new.

How X Windows Works

The X Window System confuses many people because it is neither part of the operating system nor part of the user interface. Although X makes graphical user interfaces possible, it is not directly accessible for ordinary users. Because it holds this intermediary role, it is easy to forget about X when describing the way in which the computer and user interact.

X uses a *client-server architecture*, as shown in Figure 18.1. Client-server design is common in networking, as it reduces the overall system resource impact and allows machines across the network to share programs and hardware. In such a system, the server process is designed to provide a given array of functions for individual clients. These clients may be processes on the same machine as the server, or may be connections from external computers. For example, a Web server provides requested files for client browsers, which connect across the network or Internet to the server.

In the same way, the X server provides the tools needed for a particular graphical process to individual client requests, usually coming from various user-level programs. When you open an MP3 player on the desktop, for example, both the desktop and the player will call on the X server for assistance in rendering the new appearance of the screen to show the player on the desktop and the desired skin on the player.

Client-server architecture is remarkably stable. X uses this design even when running on a standalone machine, as it mimics the way in which a regular network operates. If the server crashes, it is unlikely that the whole machine will crash with it; compare this to Windows, where graphics rendering problems can cause the entire system to lock up. Under Unix, if the graphical interface crashes, you can solve the problem from a text prompt.

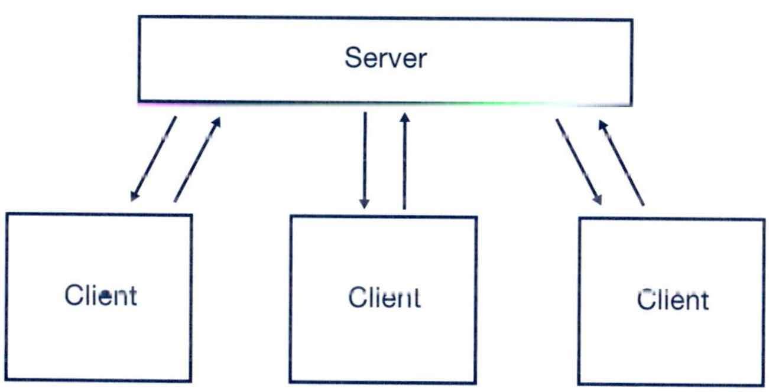

FIGURE 18.1 A schematic showing client-server architecture.

Features of X Windows

Separating X functions from the operating system has a number of benefits, as well as a number of features which are distinctly different from operating systems where the graphical interface is tightly enmeshed with the user experience. Because X is optional, it is self-sufficient and set apart from regular system operation. If a machine does not run graphical software, it doesn't need an X server. Thus, the administrator of that machine does not need to configure or administer X. Since X is resource-intensive, a machine without it will probably run faster and more efficiently than if the server runs even though it is unneeded.

When X is functional, it does require significant system resources. However, given that graphical functions are inherently resource-intensive, X Windows is remarkably streamlined. One reason for this elegance is that the X Window System is designed for networks. The system must be simple enough that a number of clients can make sophisticated requests of the server without overloading its capabilities, but powerful enough to respond to multiple requests at one time. Under networked X, for example, it is possible to display graphical programs running on one machine on the monitor of another machine, as long as they are both connected to the server and are properly configured. Although Windows NT now has this feature, and some Web-driven conferencing software touts this as a major breakthrough, X has had this capability for years.

Although X runs perfectly well on stand-alone computers, large networks may find it more efficient to run one X server and have individual client machines connect to it, rather than each machine running its own X server. In fact, many hardware vendors sell *X terminals* as part of large cluster installations. An X terminal is simply a stripped-down machine with a network connection, a monitor, and some memory. These terminals connect to the X server to get their graphical display, and to other machines on the network for user functions.

Another benefit of X is that, because it is a standard, individual interpretations of the standard should work well together. A heterogeneous network which has machines running several flavors of Unix, each with its own X client software, should still be able to use a single X server to manage displays on all the machines. As long as the individual variants' X software meets the X standard, problems are minimized.

Window Managers and Desktop Environments

If X is not user-level software, what is the software which provides the graphical user interface? There are three different program types that affect what you see on the screen: *display managers*, *window managers*, and *graphical desktop environments.* Some machines use all three, while others use only two and still others integrate all the functions into one program.

A display manager is the program which actually interacts with the X software on your machine. When you click an icon with your mouse, or open a new program, the display manager routes your request to the X client, which then makes a connection to the X server. The default X display manager is called, logically enough, **xdm**. (Depending on the graphical user interface installed on your machine, **xdm** may be replaced by a specialized program required by your GUI.) Display managers are not usually user-level programs. Although you can open the program, it is best to make configurations with specific tools rather than to edit any **xdm** files directly. All machines with graphical capabilities have a functional display manager.

A window manager is a form of graphical user interface. The window manager is a program which determines how various graphical elements appear on your screen: individual windows, icons, backgrounds or wallpaper, and so on. The window manager also controls the interaction between the items on the screen and any pointing devices installed on the computer, like a mouse or a tablet/pen pointing device. Some window managers are very basic, providing only a set of windows, each of which contains a shell prompt. Other window managers are quite elaborate and might as well be called graphical desktop environments.

Graphical desktop environments are complex user interfaces which offer a high level of configurability and which have a number of integrated programs. The most popular desktops are KDE, Gnome, and Ximian (an offshoot of Gnome). Figure 18.2 shows the Gnome desktop. These desktops work just like the user interfaces under Windows or Macintosh. They have Start buttons, icons on the desktop, status bars, various entertainment and configuration programs, and the ability to change appearance by applying new themes. If you are using a personal Unix variant, it probably installed a desktop by default.

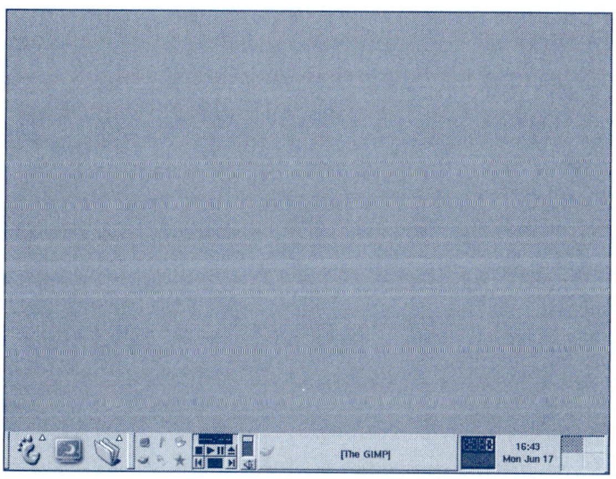

FIGURE 18.2 The Gnome integrated desktop environment.

What is the basic difference between a window manager and a graphical desktop? After all, both have multiple windowing and user-configurable appearance. The difference is that a window manager is simply a way to manage multiple individual shell sessions. You can open an infinite number of shell sessions, each in its own window, but you cannot drag and drop information between windows or use the mouse to move files between directories. These are not native X functions, so the window manager can't handle them. When using an integrated desktop, though, additional code allows these drag and drop actions. Although the two types of programs may look nearly identical, they offer very different approaches to programs and file management.

In general, people who have extensive experience with Windows or Macintosh computers will find an integrated desktop to be more familiar and easier to use. Because desktops offer so many graphical tools for common system tasks, it is possible to perform almost every Unix job through some desktop accessory. Window managers are better suited for users who are comfortable with the shell interface, and who don't do a lot of work with the mouse. Users who have slow computers or limited system resources may need a window manager; X already consumes a good portion of resources, and adding a system-intensive graphical desktop may overwhelm the machine.

Note: You don't have to run any sort of graphical interface at all. If the only work you want to do on your machine involves shell prompts and text files, then consider removing X client/server software completely.

Installing and Starting X

In the vast majority of cases, the X Window Server should install as part of the operating system. In fact, X is often the first component to install; most modern Unix variants use a graphical install interface, which requires X to run. If you see graphical elements on the screen, the X server/client software is working appropriately.

Should these elements not appear, however, there may be a problem with the X server. Most problems with X stem from hardware conflicts. If your machine uses a video card or other video hardware that X does not recognize, the server may refuse to cooperate with your machine. The only solution is to replace the offending piece of hardware. Luckily, this type of conflict is usually found only with cheap knock-offs, not with name-brand cards.

X runs without any need for user interaction. Should you see the monitor freeze while you are working, chances are that the X server process has failed. There are a number of reasons why the server might crash, and none of them are reasons for panic. Simply press the Ctrl+Alt+Backspace keystroke combination to stop and restart the server, and you should be able to continue without a problem. Because X runs independently of the operating system, you won't need to reboot.

X Windows and Networks

As explained earlier in this chapter, the X Window System was designed to be networkable. Because individual clients access the X server to obtain the tools they need to draw their graphical elements, the X processes can be spread across multiple machines without significant degradation. Whether the local client connects to an X server on the local machine or to a server running on another machine on the network makes no difference to the client program.

From an administrative point of view, this architecture is a benefit. A single machine could be dedicated as an X applications server, to which all the other machines on the network connect when in need of X applications. As you will see in the section on customizing X, such a dedicated machine could also act as a font server, taking even more strain off the local user machines. In fact, the user machines could all be X terminals with no significant hard drive of their own; since Unix allows remote file systems to be mounted as if they were local, an X terminal can display programs and files stored on a different machine.

The trick to using X successfully across a network is to ensure that the environment variable DISPLAY is configured appropriately. This variable must be defined on both the client machines and the X server machine. As with other environment variables, you can check the current value of the DISPLAY variable by issuing the command

```
echo $DISPLAY
```

at the shell prompt. It is likely that the output will either say

```
:0
```

or

```
localhost:0
```

Both of these values are fine, and will permit remote X use.

Next, log into the X applications server machine. You can do this directly if you have physical access to the computer, or remotely with one of the remote access programs described in the networking section of this book. Issue the command

```
export $DISPLAY="/local-machine-name\:0"
```

at the shell prompt, substituting the actual host name for *local-machine-name*. This command enables the local, or client, machine to display whatever output would normally be displayed on the monitor of the server machine. In short, it changes the standard output of the server machine from its own monitor to the monitor of the client machine.

In some cases, this simple export will not solve a miscommunication between the two machines. If you see an error message that says

```
cannot connect to X-server
```

then you must log out of the server machine. On the client machine, issue the command

```
xhost +remote-machine
```

where *remote-machine* is either the IP number or host name of the X server computer. This will identify the appropriate destination as an environment variable on the local machine, allowing X commands and output to flow between the two computers across the network. Reconnect to the X server machine, and reissue the command

```
export $DISPLAY="/local-machine\:0"
```

The connection should establish properly at this point.

X across the Internet

At this point, a question may occur to you. Since X can be displayed across networks, and since the Internet is essentially a very large network, can X be displayed across the Internet? The simple answer is yes, and it seems to happen all the time. If a person on a Unix machine opens a Web browser and views a remote page, she has an open X session. However, this is not a true X session since she has not configured her display to receive the standard output of the remote machine; her browser is simply drawing the appropriate elements on the local monitor through a normal X client/server connection.

Instead, consider a situation in which a Windows user is connected to the Internet. This person wants to work remotely with a program or set of files on a Unix network in another country. Under Unix, this would be simple. The user would configure the remote output as described above, Since Microsoft Windows does not use the X Window System to handle its graphical display, though, how can the user work with the remote data? The answer lies in Broadway.

Broadway is the code name for an element of the X Window System which has been fully incorporated into the latest versions. Broadway provides Web-based X sessions, regardless of the operating system on the client machine. This works because the X standard and the HTTP standard have been combined to create a new subprotocol which uses existing HTTP formats to deliver X content. The Windows user in this example can pull up the programs or files through her Web browser, run the X session, and log out without having to install new software, change her operating system, or waste time on tedious reconfigurations.

Customizing the X Environment

Configuring X software is something that is usually left to system or network administrators. Because the user experience with X is filtered through user-level software like graphical desktop environments or window managers, user configurations are made to those programs and not directly to X software itself. However, there are system-wide elements which the administrator can enhance or add, and which benefit all users on the network regardless of what end-user software they might prefer.

Fonts

Next to the basic ability to draw graphical elements on the monitor, one of the biggest advantages of the X Window System is the ability to use multiple fonts. Different fonts, or typefaces, serve different functions in an X environment. Some fonts are used to label individual windows, others to label icons on the desktop or to make entries in menus, and still others are user-selected within a program like a word processor. Fonts are used as elements of graphic images and as design components for Web pages, presentations, and other file types.

Unlike Windows or Macintosh computers, though, installing new fonts on a Unix system is not necessarily an easy task. Font installation is an administrative task, not an end-user job. Because fonts are a function of X, adding new ones or removing unused typefaces requires X configuration. Depending on your operating system, the individual steps required to install a new font will be different. The same general rules apply regardless of Unix variant, though:

1. Identify and download the compressed font package from a font archive or a CD.
2. Decompress the file. Read any documentation included in the package.
3. Convert the font format, if necessary, to a format recognized by X. This is usually done with the **bdftopcf** converter included with the X software package.
4. Create a new subdirectory of the fonts directory and move the new font to the new location.
5. Rebuild the fonts directory. This is done with the X command **mkfontdir**.
6. Define the new font's path name in the appropriate X server configuration file.
7. Configure the X server to recognize the new font path, by adding the path to the server's environment variables.

8. Save and exit any open text files.
9. Restart the X server process.

Obviously, these steps are too general to use as directions for a specific installation. If you are administering an X server and need to know how to add new fonts for your particular server software and operating system, consult the documentation to learn the appropriate method. In particular, Solaris users should follow their documentation closely; Solaris, Sun's personal Unix variant, uses a proprietary X server. Linux and FreeBSD use the XFree86 X server, for which documentation and assistance can easily be found on the Web.

Font Servers

Fonts take up a lot of space. Pictographic fonts, like those used for Chinese, Korean, and Japanese, take up even more space than character-based fonts like those used for English and other Western languages. Networks which provide a large range of fonts to users often face storage space concerns because of the intensive resource consumption. For networks running Linux, however, a new option has recently been developed: the font server.

The font server concept separates font management from the basic X tasks performed by the server and client software. Under a font server set-up, each individual machine on the Linux network could run its own X server and clients, but would house no fonts locally. Instead, when a new font was needed, the X server would connect to the network's font server and obtain the necessary files to produce the desired typeface. For networks where many users work in pictographic or ideographic languages, like Cyrillic, a font server can be an elegant solution in place of storing individual font files on each workstation where those fonts are needed.

The drawback to the font server concept is that the software is still somewhat unreliable. It is under active development, and continues to get better, but still is not an ideal and bug-free solution. For those administrators who need the help that a font server can provide, it is a workable option now. For others, who would like the flexibility of a font server but are not in immediate need, it may be best to wait until the software is more advanced and connections are more seamless. Regardless of the amount of work required to install and operate a font server, however, the concept is exciting and will surely be ported to other Unix variants in the near future.

Colors

Although desktop environments and window managers do not handle font configuration, they do a very good job at managing color configurations. In fact, managing system colors is so much easier with a desktop environment than it is by configuring X directly that most people prefer to use the software and its multiple color tools. Some interface programs offer color picker tools, so that appropriate colors can be selected from a palette. In contrast, handling colors from within X software requires that you know either the color name or its hex value. For those administrators who prefer to work directly with X, however, color management commands are relatively straightforward and easy to manage.

In dealing with color, X's primary function is to define default colors. These defaults apply to various screen elements like window borders, icons, typefaces, and so on. In addition, the various elements of a particular program might also have default color selections which take their values from the default X configuration. Change the values by changing the configuration for each element.

For personal configurations, the values of these defaults are contained in the file .Xresources, stored in your home directory. (If you have never changed an X default color, the file may not exist. You can copy the basic file from /etc/skel/.Xresources if necessary.) This file lists the various configurable elements and shows the current color name associated with each. Administrators who want to make system-wide changes to X default colors should place a file for each reconfigured program in the app-defaults subdirectory stored in the X tree, using the syntax of the .Xresources file.

Hex Values and Color Names

When editing a color configuration file, X will accept color identifications in three versions: RGB, color name, and hex value. All colors on a computer screen are made up of a mixture of red, green, and blue. The *RGB value* is a name which indicates the precise amount of each color, as in **rgb:FF/FF/FF**. FF is the highest possible amount of the color, and 00 is the complete absence of that color. The color rgb:FF/FF/FF has the color name white, and the hex name #FFFFFF. Although X uses RGB names as its native method of producing screen colors, it is easier to use hex names when editing various elements.

Hexadecimal notation is a way of describing an individual color through a six-digit number. Some RGB values translate directly to hex, like white or black (**rgb:00/00/00** and **#000000**), while other RGB values bear little resemblance to their hex equivalents. Anyone who works with Web design is already familiar with hex color values. The X color name is the least specific value, and is thus the least reliable. The best way to work with colors under X is to consult a comprehensive color chart that shows X color name, hex value, and RGB value for each possible X color. A number of such charts are available on the Web; consult the Internet Resources appendix for specific URLs.

X Windows and Security

In this age of viruses and malicious behavior, it is sometimes startling to realize that basic software, integral to the normal user experience, is not secure. The client and server software used to manage X Window System sessions is one of these programs. X's insecurity is due to several factors: it was developed in a more trusting era, it is intended primarily for local network use, and it still permits connections through nonsecure programs like telnet. Despite these issues, though, X is so critical that workarounds have been developed to address the legitimate security concerns of administrators and users.

Of all the remotely accessible services that run on a network or individual machine, X is certainly not the most attractive. Cracking X does not result in disguised Internet access for a cracker, nor does it unlock valuable files. Still, malicious attempts on X can result in local output being viewed by someone without appropriate clearance, including passwords, sensitive data, and the contents of open buffers. X settings can also be changed, sometimes with a virus-like program that causes system damage when the server is used remotely. Crackers can even interfere with active X sessions, closing down X windows while users are working within them. Where gaining illegal access to remote machines can sometimes be profitable, cracking X is more of a troublemaker's pastime.

If you are not a system administrator, there is little you can do about security just as there is little you can do directly with X on your machine. For those who administer X on their networks, there are a few protective steps which you can take to minimize the chances of an X crack and to lessen the chance of truly damaging invasion. Luckily, these are the same steps you would take to secure the network in general, so there is little extra work involved in tightening control over X functions.

Remote Access

In the current era of networking, there is no reason to run insecure remote access software on any network with valuable content, including Internet access. (A constant Internet connection is as valuable as any data file to the cracker community.) If your machines permit telnet or rlogin connections, stop accepting them. These programs are easily defeated and do nothing to protect passwords as they travel between local and remote computers.

Instead, change every remote access possibility on your network to require an SSH connection. Because SSH is a secure connection which employs encryption to scramble passwords, it provides much more control over people logging into your network remotely. SSH is easy to configure, and there are numerous SSH clients for every operating system that may connect to your network. SSH also forwards X connections without alteration, so users can run remote X sessions through SSH without noticing the difference.

Ports and Access

More specific security measures can be taken by restricting the ports which X connections may use, and by limiting those machines which can have access. X uses ports 6000 through 6063 to manage remote connections to the server. If you shut down access to those ports, except for users from a defined range of IP numbers, you will go a long way toward stopping unauthorized use of your X server. You can also configure the file /etc/x0.hosts. Machines listed in this file are the only ones allowed to access the X server; machines not listed in the file which attempt to connect will receive the error message

```
Xlib: connection to machinename0:0 refused by server
Xlib: Client is not authorized to connect to Server
Error: Can't Open display
```

There are other ways to enhance X security which involve cookies, small bits of data which live on an authorized machine's hard drive. Since X is a vast and complex subject, there are a number of security methods which have evolved for various parts of the standard. The important thing to remember is that the X Window System is inherently insecure. Any attempts to lock down ports, restrict access, or require security validation are excellent ways to tighten control over your network, but they do not change X into a secure system. As with any other administrative issue, the best solution is to control what you can and to keep a close eye on your system and your users.

X Windows and Adaptive User Environments

For the majority of Unix users, the graphical capabilities provided by the X Window System are a delight. Graphical displays make it possible to use sophisticated software, pointing devices, and other visual and spatial elements which bring new levels to the Unix user experience. For a small but significant minority of Unix users, however, graphical elements are actually a distraction; in some cases, they can even make Unix nearly impossible to use.

Users who need adaptive software, such as that designed for the visually impaired, often find that elements of graphical displays defeat the programs intended to make the computer easier to use. Many of the adaptive programs still available were written before X, so they require a shell interface to provide workable data. When confronted with a graphical user interface, some of these programs can't handle the new environment. Luckily, as concerns have been raised, new elements have been added to the X standard in order to meet the needs of the adaptive-software community.

There are three main categories of disability which require adaptive software: low vision, blindness, and limited mobility. Users with low vision need screen magnification and other adaptations which enhance the existing display with high contrast and no extraneous background decoration. Blind users must rely on screen readers, programs which translate the standard output into spoken output or into Braille type. Users with limited mobility require the largest range of adaptation; some need only minor configurations to make the keyboard and mouse easier to handle, while others must use a pointing device mounted on a headband or held in the mouth. Varying levels of fine and gross motor control can affect the level of adaptive assistance needed.

The X Window System offers elements which address each of these areas. Various X software has taken advantage of these hooks, including the graphical desktop environments. Keyboard configuration is particularly widespread, allowing users to determine whether a key will repeat when held down or whether it will print once. This is useful for those who move slowly. X also offers the StickyKeys option, which allows the keys in a keystroke combination to be pressed sequentially rather than simultaneously. X developers have done best with adaptations that involve time needed to complete a task or which address motor control issues.

Adaptations for visual impairment are not as easily integrated into mass-market software. Because visual interpreters were not initially developed to a standard, different kinds of software interpret output data in different ways. The X developers have addressed this issue by adding *hooks* to the standard; program developers can then incorporate these hooks into their programs so that a given hook can produce a consistent and repeatable effect.

Whether or not you have a physical impairment that affects your ability to use a Unix machine, your network may have users who do. The administrator must be aware of any adaptive needs among his user base, and should keep on top of new advances in adaptive technologies. Sometimes, the best solution is the easiest. Much adaptive software still works best with a plain shell interface, rather than an X-based graphical session. When possible, keep text-based software on your system even if it duplicates graphical programs. For example, keep the text-based Web browser Lynx available as well as graphical browsers like Netscape or Opera. Working with your users to keep the network accessible is a good idea, both ethically and legally.

Summary

Early Unix users worked only in the text-based shell environment. With the development of the X Window System, however, Unix has expanded into graphical user interfaces and graphics-intensive programs. The X Window System is a standard which defines how graphical elements should be displayed on a monitor. It is also the generic name for software which implements the X protocol. X uses client-server architecture, which provides exceptional stability for machines. This architecture means that X runs a server process, and individual X-based programs connect to the server as clients to receive the tools they need to draw individual graphical elements on the screen.

X is built for networks, so it is scalable and relatively frugal with system resources. Users can run a variety of software which takes advantage of X Windows, including the graphical interfaces called window managers or desktop environments. X programs can even be run across the Internet. Administrators can configure X to provide a wide range of character-based, pictographic, and ideographic fonts for users, as well as change the default system colors. Unfortunately, X has some known security risks, but the advantages of the service far outweigh them. Reasonable security precautions should avert most possible trouble. X is also a critical part of designing adaptive software for users with disabilities.

Review Questions

1. Define a graphical display and compare it to the shell interface.
2. What is the X Window System?
3. What does the X Window System standard define?
4. Explain the meaning of the saying "The X Window System is the middle of the GUI sandwich."
5. Why do personal computers need the XFree86 implementation of X?
6. Define a client-server architecture.
7. What are the advantages of client-server architecture as compared to an integrated graphics server like that in Windows or MacOS?
8. What elements of X are attributable to its networkability?
9. What is an X terminal? When would such a machine be a good investment?
10. How does a display manager work?
11. What is a window manager?
12. Define a graphical desktop environment.
13. What action restarts the X server if it should crash?
14. What generally causes problems with the X software?
15. What is the function of the DISPLAY variable?
16. How does Broadway provide X across the Internet?
17. Why are different fonts an integral part of a graphical user environment?
18. How are new fonts installed on Unix machines?
19. What is a font server?
20. How can you define colors for your personal user environment?
21. What is an RGB value?
22. What is hexadecimal notation?
23. What are the security risks of running X Windows?
24. List some of the ways to minimize X's security risks.
25. What X elements can be used to improve adaptive usability under Unix?

Exercises

1. Visit the Web site of the X Consortium at http://www.x.org. Read some of the introductory materials there to learn more about the X Window System. What advances have been made since the early releases of X? What elements remain the same?
2. Identify the window manager(s), display manager(s), and/or graphical desktop environment(s) running on your machine. What elements of the displays are user configurable? Are there additional elements which you can download? Which configurations appear to be X-related and which are specific to the display software? If you have the ability to install new software on your machine, download and install several window managers and desktops. Compare each and pick a favorite based on features and functions.
3. Look through the X directories on your network and identify the fonts that are installed. How many are there? Are they all Western European character-based fonts, or do you also have Asian and Cyrillic fonts available? What about mathematical, scientific, or artistic fonts? Figure out how to use those fonts in a word processor document or other graphical program, and explain the steps you took to use them.
4. Using a color chart which provides RGB and hex values along with X color names, as well as the X configuration files on the network, identify the various colors used as defaults. When you have determined how many default colors exist on your system, create several alternative palettes. Configure

your personal .Xresources file to display these palettes. WARNING: Do not create a tonal palette, where the colors are very close to each other in value or hue. You might not be able to see the characters on the screen in order to repair your selection.

5. Consult your school's computer department or disabilities office to learn what adaptive software is available to students. Is any of the software usable on a Unix platform? If so, run the software and evaluate the adaptations that it makes. If it is a text-based program, what elements could be transposed to a graphical display? If it is a graphical program, how does the display differ from the regular display you see on a standard monitor? Can you identify ways in which the program uses X hooks? If there is no adaptive software at your school, search the Web for information on similar products. Write a brief report explaining your findings.

CHAPTER 19

Running Servers

IN THIS CHAPTER

1. Services and servers
2. Selecting services
3. Web servers
4. Mail servers
5. FTP servers
6. News servers
7. Remote access services

Although a network can function with the normal commands and programs included in the basic operating system, many administrators want to offer content to the outside world as well as enable their users to bring content in from external networks. In order to provide material for users on other networks, such as the Internet, a network must run specialized software. These programs are called *servers*, and recognize the unique format of various requests sent to the network. Each request is then provided with appropriate files.

While running services is not necessary, many people choose to set up a network simply so they can provide services. For others, servers are their main job. Many businesses and other employers hire people specifically to manage individual servers, whether it be e-mail or Web. Once a server is in place, it can quickly assume a critical role in network management.

What Is a Service?

Services are usually involved with gathering or distributing information across a large network or mesh of networks. Most familiar services are Internet-related services like Web servers, mail servers, and the like. However, not all servers are Internet services. Some internal services which have already been described in this book include the X Window System and NFS, the Network File Server described briefly in Chapter 16, Basic System Administration: Part I.

All services, whether internal to the network or external, use client-server architecture as introduced in Chapter 18, The X Window System. In some cases, as with Web servers, the clients are usually external and connect across an open Internet connection. In other cases, as with X Windows, clients are usually from the internal network. Both client connections are managed by the server in the same way, barring any extra security precautions taken by the network for external connections through the Internet.

Selecting Services

It is common for administrators of new networks (and even some old ones) to run many services. In fact, quite a few networks run far more services than necessary. Some reasons for this include having the hardware or bandwidth to handle multiple services, wanting to serve your user base with locally managed services, or being curious about how the various servers work. All of these can be valid reasons, but there are drawbacks to running a variety of servers that don't get much use.

When a server process is running, it consumes system resources. If it is not being accessed frequently, that consumption is less than that of a busy server, but the program does still require resources to function. A running server process is also a security risk, especially if you do not know that it is running. There are some people who configure new servers just to see how they work, and then forget to turn them off or delete the programs. The service thus offers a convenient point of entry for someone who wants to break into the network.

Selecting an appropriate suite of services for a given network requires some research. The administrator must ask a series of questions that can help to narrow down the decision:

- What services does the user base need and use on a frequent basis?
- What is the purpose of the network?
- How does the network connect to the Internet?

- Does the Internet provider offer services which would otherwise need to be run locally?
- What file types would be served by the local network?

A network which is small and noncommercial may only need an e-mail server and possibly an FTP server. In fact, even e-mail may be provided by the upstream Internet connection. A large commercial network, however, may need to run multiple Web servers to manage their Web presence, as well as remote access and e-mail. A community network might offer a news server as well as e-mail and limited Web functions.

In selecting services, the network administrator must also consider any restrictions which are stipulated by upstream providers or other associated networks. A small home network connected to the Internet with a cable modem, for example, is probably barred from running a Web server across that modem unless the service agreement is for a business plan, not a personal plan; business plans are far more expensive. Before you make any choices about what services to run, check the terms of every user agreement affecting your network. The choice may have already been made for you if you are barred from running servers at all.

If you have permission to run services and you know the basic needs of your user base, you can begin to decide what servers to offer. Many networks need NFS to handle remote filesystem management, and you will need X if you plan to offer graphical interfaces anywhere on the network. Depending on your upstream service provider and your own time commitment or skill level, you may choose to run an e-mail server to handle mail locally. A Web server is useful for those with fast permanent Internet connections (where, of course, a Web server is permitted), while some administrators may want to offer an array of newsgroups.

Remember that your user base's service needs may change from time to time. Be sure to evaluate your service portfolio every few months, checking the logs to see how much an individual service is really being used. If your users claim to want a news server and yet never read news, it may be best to pull that service. Also, keep an eye on security. The more services, the more potential problems. If your operating system turns on services by default at installation, go through and turn off the services you neither want nor need.

World Wide Web Services

Web pages are provided by Web servers. When a user requests a page through a browser, the browser sends a specially formatted message to the appropriate Web server, asking for the desired page and any associated files that may be attached to it, such as images or sound files. To display properly in a Web browser, the files must be formatted according to the Hyper Text Markup Language (HTML) standard. File requests and transfers are handled according to the Hyper Test Transfer protocol, or HTTP. Any server chosen to handle Web traffic must be compliant with the HTTP standards.

The most popular Web server in the world is the Apache Web server. Apache runs on Unix, and is Free Software. It is released under the GNU Public License (see Chapter 1) and can be obtained free of charge. Although Microsoft's Internet Information Server, or IIS, is popular among those who administer Windows networks, IIS cannot be run on other platforms, where Apache has been ported to every known and stable operating system. Should you be interested in running a Web server, Apache is the best choice. It is robust, easy to manage, and unlikely to crash. Documentation and help are also freely available online.

Apache

Apart from being a powerful and easy-to-manage Web server, Apache has the added benefit of being modular. This means that, much like Unix itself, Apache functions are separated into individual units. An administrator can choose to run all Apache modules, a stripped-down set of modules that provides only the most basic functions, or a set somewhere between those extremes which meets the need of the site's community without adding extra system load. Modularity is one of the key Unix philosophies, and it is illustrated in the way Apache works.

Apache's modular nature is particularly useful when it comes to the machine resources it needs. The core server program is actually quite small. It can run on a machine with as little as eight MB of RAM and six MB of disk space. (Typical desktop systems currently on sale at your local big-box computer retailer will probably have at least 128MB of RAM and several gigabytes of hard disk space, costing well under $1,000.) Granted, the site being served by such a minimal installation must be text-only and low-bandwidth, but it is possible. One of those typical desktop systems would serve an average non-commercial site quite nicely for a few years. Apache can fit the resources available to it, though you may be limited in the modules you can use or the type of files you can serve if you are also limited in system resources.

> **Tech Tip**
>
> If you are interested in running Apache, there is a wealth of information available on the Web. See Appendix D, Internet Resources, for some sites. Apache skills are valuable additions to your Unix knowledge, and those who are considering a career in Unix will find that Apache experience often gives them an edge.

Installing Apache is unusually simple. Although working with the server is beyond the scope of this text, the Apache configuration file has been included in Appendix C, Common Configuration Files. It is a very well commented file, and is useful to read even if you have no interest in running the server, since it is an excellent example of program comments. The complexity of Apache comes from the interplay of modules and their work.

Other Web Servers

If, for some reason, you don't want to run Apache, there are other alternatives to it and IIS. Some administrators simply don't need a server that is as powerful as Apache. Others serve only particular file types or have security concerns that aren't addressed by various patches and workarounds. Still others just like running software that's different and unusual. Although Web servers are not as popular among the development community as other server types, mostly because Apache is the figurative 800-pound gorilla in this category, there are a few other servers which might be more attractive to certain network and Web administrators.

boa

A GNU program, boa is a Web server that handles multiple incoming requests in a different manner than Apache. Although it is still in limited use and under active development, boa can handle robust traffic and may be a good alternative for small sites.

Jigsaw

The Jigsaw server is a product of the World Wide Web Consortium (the people who manage the HTTP standard, among other functions). It is wholly HTTP compliant and is used by W3C programmers to test new HTTP functions. Jigsaw is unusual in that it's a Java program, making it wholly platform-independent.

WN

For those administrators who like Apache and its functions but don't have the space to spare for a full installation, the WN project offers a server with many of the same abilities but a smaller disk footprint. WN supports newer technologies like secure connections and new design tools like Server Side Includes (SSIs). It also offers great documentation, which is somewhat unusual in a small Open Source project.

Electronic Mail Servers

Most networks run mail servers. Once a user base gets to a certain size, it is more efficient to handle mail locally than it is to rely on software provided by upstream sites. E-mail has become a normal part of doing business and of personal communication, so most networks provide it to their users. However, getting a mail message from sender to recipient can be more complicated than it seems.

Mail travels from the sender's mail program, a client called the *user agent* or *mail user agent (MUA)*. The MUA transfers the finished message to a *mail transfer agent* located on the local network. This MTA is the program commonly referred to as an e-mail server. The MTA transfers the message out through the network's Internet connection, where it is delivered through a TCP connection. Once the message arrives at its intended destination, that network's *delivery agent* routes the message to the recipient.

User agents are usually a personal choice. On Unix systems, a user might select one of the programs described in Chapter 9: Internet Applications. On Windows or Mac systems, a user might use Eudora or another POP or IMAP compliant agent. POP and IMAP are two standards which define the way in which a mail client should connect to the mail spool and download waiting messages. In the same way, the delivery agent is a function of the operating system and is not really a matter of administrator choice. The decisions that administrators must make about e-mail servers are decisions about mail transfer agents.

Warning: Whenever possible, avoid Microsoft Outlook. Most viruses that spread through e-mail are written to exploit security holes in Outlook. You can greatly reduce your chance of getting an e-mail virus simply by switching to Eudora or another non-Outlook graphical mail client.

Mail Server Options

There are a number of mail servers available on the Unix platform. Some of them are quite old, while others are new and offer additional functions. No matter which server runs on your network, be aware that managing mail servers can be a complicated experience. Because so many different machines and processes are involved in getting a single message from Point A to Point B, many things can go wrong in mail delivery—and often do. Add to this complexity the fact that users are highly reliant on e-mail and become both frustrated and annoyed when mail does not arrive as expected, and you can see that mail server management is a specialized skill that requires both technical ability and solid people skills.

Choosing a mail server is something that any given administrator will do rarely, if at all. Because changing from one mail server to another is a significant undertaking, mail systems tend to run on the same server for years. The server will be upgraded as necessary, but **sendmail** systems tend to stay **sendmail** systems and Postfix systems tend to stay Postfix. It is doubtful that any readers of this book will be involved in selecting a mail server before developing skills far beyond the scope of this course. Therefore, this section of the chapter is limited to describing the four most popular mail servers and their functions.

sendmail

The **sendmail** program is the reliable warhorse of mail servers. sendmail has been around for years, has gone through multiple upgrades and new releases, and offers a level of flexibility and power for mail services that equals the strength of Apache for the Web. Those who work with old and robust networks will probably find a **sendmail** installation serving the e-mail needs of the network.

The downside of **sendmail** is that it is hard to use. Note that configuration alone—not using the program, troubleshooting it, or anything else—requires

FAQ documentation that is nearly 30 pages long. Documentation for other parts of the program is even longer. Networks running **sendmail** tend to have dedicated administrators who work with little else than the mail server. It is an amazing program that is still the most widely used mail server around the world, but it is not for the new administrator or the administrator of a small network.

Postfix

The Postfix mail server is a good alternative to sendmail, especially for smaller networks that don't handle vast floods of mail each day. One of the main benefits of Postfix is that it is very easy to configure, regardless of the network architecture or platform being used. In addition to helpful comments throughout the configuration files, there is excellent documentation available on the Postfix Web site. This server would be a good choice for a robust home network with multiple machines and users, or for small business or noncommercial use.

qmail

Although it is the youngest of the mail servers described here, the **qmail** server is rapidly being adopted by networks which handle large amounts of mail and which need a secure server that does not require excessive amounts of time to administer. In fact, **qmail** is so robust that it is the mail server of choice for Hotmail, Microsoft's free Web-based e-mail service. Microsoft has, in the past, tried to migrate Hotmail to its own Microsoft Exchange mail server, but Exchange hasn't been able to handle the load. While **qmail's** scale may be overkill for very small networks, it is reliable and easy to configure and works well even on those small networks.

Exim

The fourth mail server described here is Exim. This program, developed in England, has a small but growing following of people who want to run a Free Software mail server with some unique features like spam filtering and address verification. Exim is included in some Unix variant distributions as a replacement for **smail**, a GNU mail transfer agent. Because **smail** is simply not acceptable from a security standpoint, anyone working on a network which uses **smail** should replace that MTA immediately with **Exim**. Those who are interested in running a network which uses primarily or solely Free software should consider Exim, which is reliable on smaller networks but has also been tested at production levels against more powerful servers and has performed acceptably.

POP and IMAP

Those who administer electronic mail must also consider mail from the user's point of view. The vast majority of users neither know nor care what MTA is running on their system. To users, e-mail is managed by the mail client. For some users, that client is a Unix shell client like Pine or elm. These users are, from the administrative point of view, relatively low-impact. Such clients read directly from the mail spool, in text mode, and do not require additional configuration.

However, many more users prefer to work with their e-mail in a graphical environment. Those using a graphical desktop environment like KDE or Gnome can select the desktop's native graphical e-mail client. Other users, who pull their e-mail from a Unix mail server, will use Windows or Mac mail clients. To supply messages to these clients, the administrator must set up a POP or IMAP server to transfer messages from the mail spool to the individual client upon request.

Note: POP, or Post Office Protocol, and IMAP, Internet Message Access Protocol, are two methods of managing mail flow between graphical e-mail clients and the text mail spool hosted on the network.

POP and IMAP services offer an additional level of security for the administrator. Unlike Pine or elm users, POP and IMAP users never log directly into the network to get their mail. The users must have an account on the mail server machine, so that the POP or IMAP process can be authenticated and mail transferred, but there is no direct login as there must be with a direct-from-spool client. If you are running a mail server, it is probably a good idea to set up POP and IMAP servers so that your users can work with their messages remotely.

FTP Servers

One of the more traditional services that is routinely offered is FTP, the File Transfer Protocol. This service allows users to connect and upload or download files. In order to provide FTP service, you must install an FTP server. If your operating system's distribution does not come with an FTP server, there are several that are available on the Internet as Free Software. The two most popular FTP servers are WU-FTPD, and ProFTPD.

Note: If your file transfer needs are light, consider the **scp** utility that comes with the SSH suite of programs, as it is more secure than regular FTP.

Once installed and running, these servers will listen on port 21 for incoming connections. Those attempting to connect will be prompted for a username and password which will be checked just as if they would if they were logging in. The FTP server provides the ability to browse for a desired file and then download it.

Obviously, only users with accounts can access your system via FTP in this way. If you want to provide FTP service to the Internet at large, you must enable anonymous FTP service. In order to set up anonymous FTP service, you must first set up a file system for the use of anonymous users. The FTP server will restrict anonymous users to only this file system so that they cannot "fool around" on the rest of the system. You must then configure the server to accept anonymous connections.

Note: This procedure is different for each server, so read your server's documentation to learn how to do it.

News Servers

Of all the services described in this chapter, the average administrator is least likely to run a news server. Since the rise of the Web and various bulletin board programs written for HTTP transmission, USENET news has begun to fade as the primary method of time-independent online discussion. However, there are still many people who want access to newsgroups in order to participate in the myriad of discussions that happen on USENET daily.

Running a news server can be somewhat complicated due to the transmission method used by news posts. Unlike the Web, where a given page exists at a single location, an individual USENET post is mirrored on hundreds of sites around the world. The site at which you read news might have four or five upstream feeds, which provide redundant copies of some groups and unique copies of others. In turn, that site might feed a few downstream sites with some of the posts stored on the machine where you access news. The messages that exist on your local machine are all stored locally, and posts made locally are propagated out to every other news server on earth through this intermesh of feeds.

Small sites might have only one upstream feed and no downstream feeds. This practice is easiest to maintain, but it does run the risk of lost posts or incomplete propagation of local posts. In addition, the single upstream site might not carry every *hierarchy* of groups which you want to carry. For smaller hierarchies or those which cover non-local regions, you may need to obtain other feeds. Part of administering a news server involves managing feeds, checking for dropped messages, and interacting with news administrators at those other sites to be sure that traffic flows smoothly.

Note: As described in Chapter 9, Internet Applications, USENET groups are organized in hierarchies. Some sites only feed major hierarchies, while others feed smaller or more esoteric groups. Feeds are not restricted geographically; if you or your users want to read the Italian national hierarchy, you could get a feed from an Italian site if necessary. However, a feed closer to you geographically will feed faster and with less signal loss. When more than one upstream site can feed the same hierarchies, pick the one that is closest physically. It will usually provide the best service.

INN

The news server used by most heavy-traffic sites is INN, an acronym for Inter Net News. The INN server is capable of handling vast amounts of traffic through multiple streams of input. It is easily configured and is fairly straightforward to administer. The software is under active development. Because it is so widely used, there is little reason to choose any other program.

Once installed, INN can get up and running quickly. The administrator must define all incoming newsfeeds, specifying which hierarchies and groups are provided by each. The newsfeed configuration also determines what sites are served by your news server; even if you propagate only the posts made by your local users, you must set this properly or those posts will never appear on other servers.

Apart from newsfeed configuration, the other elements of INN configuration are more subjective. The administrator must define the various expirations for groups on the system. A group's expiration time defines how long messages in that group will age on the server before they are deleted. Some administrators set certain groups so that they never expire and all posts are always available. Other groups should be expired rapidly because they get so much traffic that they can overwhelm a news spool, such as the alt.binaries.* hierarchy.

Warning: Hierarchies like alt.binaries.*, with their massive traffic, are often havens for illegal activity. Much of the traffic in binaries groups consists of illegal copies of copyrighted software or images, like bootleg copies of Windows or photographs from pornographic magazines. Because the liability issues are unclear, more and more news administrators choose to carry only text groups, and not those groups which allow binary (encoded) posts.

Once the software is set up properly, most news administrators spend some time each day reviewing the news spool, checking INN's behavior, and fixing small problems. Good administrators also spend time on user behavior and education. Users who post commercial messages to inappropriate newsgroups, who persist in posting abusive or off-topic content, or who otherwise violate the USENET community standards must be disciplined; those who make errors inadvertently must be educated. As with other user issues, strong local policies go a long way toward making your site secure and respected for its user behavior.

One thing to remember is that, for a news administrator to be effective, the administrator should be an active USENET participant. USENET constantly discusses itself, its societal expectations of users and administrators, and its mechanics. An administrator who does not read USENET-related groups is one who may not know about the latest security risks, new releases of INN, or updated group lists. If you are not interested in news, it is better not to run a server than it is to run one badly or inattentively.

Remote Access Services

Apart from the major Internet-related services described in this chapter, there are other services which run on many Unix networks which help to manage the multiple incoming requests involved with those services. One of these services is **inet**. The **inet** process manages various services and controls the flow of information into your network in response to various client requests.

You can run servers without **inet**, allowing each server process to run constantly and respond whenever an incoming request is received. This is a fast way to respond to those client requests, but it is not particularly efficient. What if your Web site is not very popular? Should an Apache process run constantly to serve a few requests a day? The more services you run, the more CPU cycles are devoted to managing those processes even when idle.

A better solution might be to place all those servers under an umbrella program. That program would recognize the different formats of incoming requests, identify the program associated with each format, and start the necessary server to answer the client request. inet is such a program. Any server that receives requests from outside the network can be run under **inet**: Web, FTP, login programs, and other similar programs.

Note: Although Web servers can be run under **inet**, it is not a particularly good idea. People expect fairly rapid page loads. If the Web server must be started by **inet** to serve the page, the visitor may become frustrated and leave the site before the page loads. Web servers should be run independently. In the same vein, mail and news servers should not be run under **inet** because they pull new files on a regular basis.

Most administrators who use **inet** configure it to manage less frequently used programs which serve important purposes for the user base, but which can run only when needed. File transfer programs and remote logins are two of the most popular **inet** functions.

File Transfer Protocol

File transfer protocol programs, or FTP, allow users to move files between different accounts on the same network or between a local account and a remote one. Administrators can configure the FTP daemon, **ftpd**, to permit anonymous login or require a local account for remote access. Despite being one of the oldest Internet-related mechanisms, FTP is still quite popular and is one of the best ways to manage files across the Internet and on local networks. It runs well under **inet**, starting only when an external client requests access to the FTP filesystem.

Remote Login Access

Another function handled efficiently by **inet** is remote login. As discussed earlier in the text, a user can log into remote machines or execute commands on those machines with a number of programs: **telnet**, **rsh**, **rlogin**, and SSH. Although the first three of these four programs are security risks, some administrators still run them under **inet**. SSH can also be placed under the **inet** umbrella, opening secure channels only when prompted by an external request.

Configuring inetd

To set up the **inet** daemon **inetd**, you must configure two files: /etc/inetd.conf and /etc/services. (Note that these filenames may be slightly different depending on your Unix variant; as always, consult your documentation for the correct locations.) The /etc/inetd.conf file defines the various services which are controlled by the inet daemon, and /etc/services provides the path name for each of those servers and identifies the port on which each service listens for connections.

The inet configuration files are unusually well commented and reasonably easy to understand. The /etc/services file is quite long, and is included in Appendix C: Sample Configuration Files. The /etc/inetd.conf file is shown here, as an excellent example of a configuration file which you might encounter on your own system. A sample /etc/inetd.conf file, taken from a Debian or Red Hat Linux machine, might look like this:

```
# inetd.conf This file describes the services that will be
# available through the INETD TCP/IP super server.  To
# re-configure the running INETD process, edit this file,
# then send the INETD process a SIGHUP signal.
#
# Version: @(#)/etc/inetd.conf      3.10   05/27/93
#
# Authors: Original taken from BSD UNIX 4.3/TAHOE.
# Fred N. van Kempen, <waltje@uwalt.nl.mugnet.org>
#
# Modified for Debian Linux by Ian A. Murdock
# <imurdock@shell.portal.com>
#
# Modified for RHS Linux by Marc Ewing <marc@redhat.com>
#
# <service_name> <sock_type> <proto> <flags> <user>
# <server_path> <args>
#
# Echo, discard, daytime, and chargen are used primarily
# for testing.
#
```

```
# To re-read this file after changes, just do a 'killall
# -HUP inetd'
#
#echo    stream tcp    nowait root   internal
#echo    dgram  udp    wait   root   internal
#discard stream tcp    nowait root   internal
#discard dgram  udp    wait   root   internal
#daytime stream tcp    nowait root   internal
#daytime dgram  udp    wait   root   internal
#chargen stream tcp    nowait root   internal
#chargen dgram  udp    wait   root   internal
#time    stream tcp    nowait root   internal
#time    dgram  udp    wait   root   internal
#
# These are standard services.
#
#ftp stream tcp nowait root /usr/sbin/tcpd in.ftpd -l -a
#telnet stream tcp nowait root /usr/sbin/tcpd in.telnetd
#
# Shell, login, exec, comsat and talk are BSD protocols.
#
#shell stream tcp nowait root /usr/sbin/tcpd in.rshd
login stream tcp nowait root /usr/sbin/tcpd in.rlogind
#exec stream tcp nowait root /usr/sbin/tcpd in.rexecd
#comsat dgram udp wait root /usr/sbin/tcpd in.comsat
#talk dgram udp wait nobody.tty /usr/sbin/tcpd in.talkd
#ntalk dgram udp wait nobody.tty /usr/sbin/tcpd in.ntalkd
#dtalk stream tcp wait nobody.tty /usr/sbin/tcpd  \
#   in.dtalkd
#
# Pop and imap mail services et al
#
#pop-2 stream tcp nowait root /usr/sbin/tcpd ipop2d
pop-3 stream tcp nowait root /usr/sbin/tcpd ipop3d
#imap stream tcp nowait root /usr/sbin/tcpd imapd
#
# The Internet UUCP service.
#
#uucp stream tcp nowait uucp /usr/sbin/tcpd \
#   /usr/lib/uucp/uucico   l
#
# Tftp service is provided primarily for booting.  Most
# sites run this only on machines acting as "boot
# servers." Do not uncomment this unless you *need* it.
#
#tftp dgram udp wait root /usr/sbin/tcpd in.tftpd
```

```
#bootps dgram udp wait root /usr/sbin/tcpd bootpd
#
# Finger, systat and netstat give out user information
# which may be valuable to potential "system crackers."
# Many sites choose to disable some or all of these
# services to improve security.
#
#finger stream tcp nowait nobody /usr/sbin/tcpd  \
#    in.fingerd
#cfinger stream tcp nowait root /usr/sbin/tcpd  \
#    in.cfinger
#systat stream tcp nowait guest /usr/sbin/tcpd  \
#    /bin/ps -auwwx
#netstat stream tcp nowait guest /usr/sbin/tcpd  \
#    /bin/netstat -f inet
#
# Authentication
#
# identd is run standalone now
#
#auth stream tcp wait root /usr/sbin/in.identd  \
#    in.identd -e -o
## End of inetd.conf
```

Note that most of the file is commented out. There are actually very few active lines in the file, but the inactive lines are retained in case they need to be used at a later time. Entries in this file take the syntax

```
service socket protocol flags user path filename
```

The service entry defines the service; the socket and protocol entries define the data flow method used by the service; the flag entry defines how sockets manage incoming connections; the user entry defines the server process's owner; the path and filename entries locate the server in the filesystem.

If you choose to run **inet** on your system, you will need to review and update the configuration files regularly. **inet** may not be the most efficient way of managing certain processes on your machine, or you might find that it handles your incoming requests better than running individual servers constantly. Certainly, **inet** is a valuable tool for any network providing services across the Internet.

Note: Some systems are migrating from **inet** to the **xinetd** daemon. Xinetd is more secure and offers more variety in configuration for specific network needs. Although it is currently used mostly on Linux networks, there is no reason why **xinetd** cannot be used on other network platforms as a drop-in replacement for standard **inet**.

Summary

Functions which a network provides to external users are managed by services. These programs manage external client requests and return the desired file or files. Most networks run some services internally, like X Windows or NFS, but the most well-known services are Internet-related. Services use client-server architecture. Administrators should choose an array of services based on the needs of the local user base and the purpose of the network. Since unused services are a security risk, it is best to run only the services which are needed and actually used.

Web pages are transmitted according to the HTTP and HTML protocols. The most popular Web server is Apache, which offers modular construction. Apache can serve a number of different functions depending on the modules installed. For those uninterested in running Apache, several other Web servers are available for Unix. There are fewer choices for electronic mail servers; most choice in e-mail is limited to user clients. Mail servers pass messages to and from external networks, distributing them to the appropriate recipient. Some administrators may wish to run a USENET news server. News servers require a certain level of commitment since they should be monitored and reconfigured on a regular basis. Most news servers require multiple upstream feeds to provide the best range of newsgroups.

Many services do not need to run constantly. Rather, they can be started when an incoming request requires that service, and shut down when not needed. This saves CPU cycles and reduces overall system load. The inet program helps manage services in this way. Some programs commonly run under inet include file transfer and remote login access.

Review Questions

1. What is a server?
2. Name three different types of service, both Internet-related and non-Internet.
3. Describe client-server architecture and draw a schematic.
4. What are some good reasons to run multiple servers?
5. What are some drawbacks of running multiple servers?
6. How can you decide which services to run?
7. What is an upstream provider?
8. How can you ascertain your user base's service needs?
9. What is the HTTP protocol?
10. What is the HTML protocol?
11. Why is Apache's modular construction beneficial?
12. What is a module?
13. Why might an administrator choose to run a Web server other than Apache?
14. How does an electronic mail message travel from its sending machine to its destination?
15. Define MUA and MTA.
16. What are the POP and IMAP standards?
17. Why is Microsoft Outlook a security risk?
18. What are the advantages and disadvantages of **sendmail?**
19. What are the advantages of requiring users to use POP or IMAP mail clients?

20. How is a USENET post propagated?
21. What is an expiration time?
22. What is **inet**?
23. What are the reasons for and against running Web servers under **inet**?
24. Define FTP.
25. What is the function of /etc/inetd.conf?
26. What is the function of /etc/services?

Exercises

1. Determine what services are running on your network. Write a brief report describing each service and how it fits the needs of the network's user base.
2. Create three different scenarios in which you provide a list of services for three different network types. The first network is a small home network composed of fewer than five machines; the second, a small business network; the third, a large corporate or academic network. Describe the services (and servers) you recommend for each network, and why each is important.
3. Visit the Apache Web page and look at the list of available Apache modules. Describe the functions of the modules which are compiled in the default Apache installation. What additional modules do you think are important to a Web host?
4. On the Web, research electronic mail viruses. Are there any viruses which would affect a Unix user? How do viruses work, such as the Klez or Sircam viruses? Does this knowledge make you more interested in using Unix regularly?
5. Determine whether inet is running on your network by locating the /etc/inetd.conf file. Copy this file to a text file. Write a brief report explaining the various services configured under your network's inet daemon. Next, find the /etc/services file. What ports do each of these services use?

APPENDIX A

Common UNIX Commands

This appendix contains information about a selection of Unix shell commands. There are hundreds, if not thousands, more commands available to the Unix user, depending on the variant and shell which you have chosen. The commands included here are those which are generally available on any Unix installation, though your particular situation may offer different commands or may not have a particular command installed. Check your local documentation if commands do not appear to behave in the expected manner when you execute them.

About These Commands

The entries in this appendix use several typographical conventions to indicate the elements of each command:

- Any information within square brackets is optional, as in [*optional*]
- Any information within angle brackets must be replaced with an actual filename or program name without the angle brackets, as in <*filename*>
- Any string of elements separated by a pipe character are mutually exclusive, as in *a* | *b* | *c*
- If the string of elements appears within curly braces, one element must be selected, as in {*a* | *b* | *c*}
- If that string of elements appears within square brackets, however, the choice is optional. If you see [*a* | *b*], the choice may be *a*, *b*, or no selection.

Note: The entries here provide only the most common uses of the commands. Most of the commands have other options or an extended syntax which allows more sophisticated or targeted use. To see the complete list of elements for each command, consult its manual page to learn more. Manual pages can be found by issuing the command **man command** at the shell prompt; if your system does not have manual pages installed for some reason, use a Web search engine to find the appropriate page.

adduser

The adduser command is used to create a new user account. It takes the syntax

```
adduser [options] username
```

Options for adduser include

- -c adds a comment when creating the account
- -d specifies the user's home directory
- -e specifies an expiration date for this account
- -M creates a user account without a home directory
- -p specifies the initial password for the account (your system policies should require users to change their passwords immediately on first login)
- -s specifies the user's default shell environment if they do not want to use the default shell

apropos

The apropos command is used to search for a specified file in any directory on the computer, with a keyword. The command is often used to find a man page. apropos takes the syntax

```
apropos <keyword>
```

at

The at command schedules a command to be executed at a later specified time. It takes the syntax

```
at [options] <time>
```

By default, at takes its input from the standard input. If you issue the command

```
at <time>
```

the program will supply a prompt of

```
at>
```

where you can type the commands you wish to have executed at the specified time. at can also be used with a redirection operator, such as

```
at <time> < <command>
```

This command has a number of options, but one of the most useful is the –f flag, which causes at to take input from a specified file rather than from the keyboard. A series of commands can be stored in a file, which is invoked with the syntax

```
at -f <command file> <time>
```

bash

The bash command invokes the Bourne Again shell environment, taking the syntax

```
bash [<command>]
```

The command opens a bash shell session. If a shell command or the name of a script is given as an argument, that command or script will be run in a bash shell session regardless of what shell is currently being used.

cat

The cat command prints the contents of a named file to the standard output, usually the monitor. cat takes the syntax

```
cat [options] <file(s)>
```

cat has several options, including

- -n numbers the lines of output
- -s collapses consecutive blank lines into one single blank line

One of the more common uses of cat is to concatenate several files into one new file for easier reference to the data contained in the individual files, as in the command

```
cat <file 1><file2><file3> >> <newfile>
```

cd

The cd command is used to change directories in the file system. If the command is issued without a specified target directory, you will be taken to your home directory. cd takes the syntax

```
cd [directory]
```

cfdisk

Like the fdisk command, cfdisk is used to partition a hard disk. It takes the same basic syntax as that command but offers an interface which many users prefer.

chmod

The chmod command is used to define and change file permissions. This command can be used only on files that you own, or by the root account. chmod uses the syntax

```
chmod [u|g|a] {+|-} {r and/or w and/or x} <filename>
```

If you do not specify a level of permission, chmod assigns global permission to the file. That is, chmod uses the "a" option by default unless you specify "u" or "g" when issuing the command. There are several levels of permission used with chmod:

- u Permission only to the owner of the file
- g Permission to the user's groups
- a Global permissions, including those outside the local network
- \+ Declares that permissions on the named file are to be changed
- \- Declares that permissions on the named file are to be removed
- r *read* file permission, granting read-only access
- w *write* file permission, granting read and edit permissions
- x *execute* file permission, permitting the user to run the file if it is an executable binary: includes read and edit permissions

chmod also takes numerical arguments, which are explained on the chmod manual page. Some of the most commonly used chmod commands include

- chmod a+r <*filename*> — Gives read permission on the named file to all users
- chmod g+rw <*filename*> — Gives read and write permission on the named file to the user's group(s)
- chmod a-x <*filename*> — Removes execute permission from all users, including the file's owner; follow this command with another that grants execute permission to the owner and others who need to use the file

chown

The chown command is used to change the ownership of a named file, taking the syntax

```
chown <user> <filename>
```

This command must be issued by the root account or by the current owner of the target file.

cp

The cp command copies a named file to a new location, leaving the original file in its original location. cp takes the syntax

```
cp <file 1> <file 2>
```

where <*file 1*> is the original file and <*file 2*> is the new target file. Do not use the name of an existing file as <*file2*> unless you are prepared to have the contents of that file replaced by the contents of <*file1*>.

crontab

Use the crontab command to manage cron files, which are used for automated administrative tasks. This command edits the contents of the /etc/crontab file, and takes the syntax

```
crontab [-u <user>] {-l|-r|-e}
```

crontab has several options, including

- -u Defines the user who will issue the specified command. The default is the user issuing the crontab command
- -l Prints the contents of /etc/crontab to the standard output
- -r Removes the entire contents of the current /etc/crontab file
- -e Adds the specified entry to the data already in /etc/crontab

date

The date command prints the current time and date to the screen. If issued by the root account, the date command can also be used to set the system time and date. It takes the syntax

```
date [options]
```

When issued without argument, the current date and time will print. To set the date, log into the root account and issue the command with the –s option. Date takes two-digit numbers for the day, month, and year, using a 24-hour clock for time. For example, to set the clock to 30 seconds past 1:15 P.M., September 10, 1982, issue the command

```
date -s 1009821315.30
```

dd

The dd command is used to copy a specified file to another location. It is often used to copy files to removable media like floppy diskettes, because dd streams the data without formatting. dd takes the syntax

```
dd if=<input file> of=<output file>
```

<*output file*> is usually the device name of whatever drive holds the disk to which you are moving the file.

declare

The declare command is used to assign a particular type to a specified variable, and takes the syntax

```
declare [options] VAR[=<value>]
```

There are three options for declare:

- -i The variable is an integer
- -r The variable is read-only
- -a The variable is an array

This command can only be used to declare variable types in bash version 2.0 or later.

diff

The diff command is used to compare the contents of two named files. The differences between the two will be printed to the standard output. diff takes the syntax

```
diff <file 1> <file 2>
```

This command compares the files by checking each character in the first file against each character in the second file. If there are a number of differences, such as when the two files are completely different rather than being versions of the same file, diff's output is best piped to a file since it will be quite long.

du

The du command prints output showing the amount of disk space occupied by a specified file or directory. If issued without a specific target, du will show the disk space consumed by the user issuing the command. It takes the syntax

```
du [options] <file or directory name>
```

du's options include

- -b The size in bytes
- -c A listing of each directory and its size, including the total space used on the disk
- -h Uses common sizes, such as kilobytes or megabytes
- -k Uses kilobytes regardless of file or directory size
- -m Uses megabytes regardless of file or directory size
- -S Counts only the size of top-level directories
- -s Displays the size of the directory in which the command is issued

echo

The echo command prints a specified text string to the screen, and takes the syntax

```
echo [options] <string>
```

If issued without options or a string, echo will print a blank line. If issued with the syntax

```
echo -n <string>
```

echo will print the string without also printing a new line.

exit

The exit command ends the current shell process, and takes the syntax

```
exit [<value>]
```

The <*value*> component is used to indicate the exit status of the process, and is usually used only in shell programming.

export

The export command makes the specified variable available to the current shell process. export takes the syntax

```
export <variable>[=<value>]
```

As described in the text, you can change the value of a specified variable with this command. For example, to change the value of the EDITOR variable, you might issue the command

```
export EDITOR= "emacs"
```

exportfs

The exportfs command is used to export a filesystem across NFS. It takes the syntax

```
exportfs [options]
```

exportfs options include

- -s all filesystems listed in /etc/exports
- -r Re-exports all previously exported filesystems
- -u Removes, or "un-exports," one or more specified filesystems

expr

The expr command is used to specify numerical evaluation of a particular expression, and takes the syntax

```
expr <expression>
```

This command is used to define the variables as integers if you cannot or have not used the declare command to define the variable types. Use expr so that a string like "2+4" is evaluated as its arithmetical value of 6 rather than as the text string 2+4.

fdisk

The fdisk command is used to partition a specified device or disk. It takes the syntax

```
fdisk <device>
```

The fdisk program is interactive, and can be damaging to your computer if you use it without reading the documentation thoroughly before beginning to work with it.

fsck

The fsck command checks and reports on the integrity of a specified filesystem. It takes the syntax

```
fsck [options] <filesystem>
```

fsck offers several options, including

- -t Specifies filesystem type
- -A Checks all filesystems, using the /etc/fstab file as its guide
- -N Reports what would be checked, but does not actually check it
- -R Skips the root file system when using the –A option to check all filesystems
- -V Verbose mode
- -a Make all necessary repairs automatically while checking filesystems
- -r Converse of –a, requiring confirmation of each repair before it is made

Because filesystems must be mounted "read only" before they can be checked with fsck. With the –R option, the root filesystem can continue to be mounted "read-write" so that it will work properly, though all other filesystems checked on the machine will be read-only.

grep

The grep command is used to search a specified input for a particular text string. It takes the syntax

```
grep [options] <pattern> [filename]
```

grep takes a number of options, which are fully described in its manual page. Check the manual page because some options may not be enabled on your system.

grep can also be invoked using the output of another process as its input. To do this, invoke the command with the pipe, or |, character to connect the first command and the grep command, as in

```
w -x | grep -e root
```

This command would search the output of the w command for any occurrence of the string "root."

groups

The groups command reports all groups to which you belong. It can also be used to view the groups to which another user belongs. To see your own groups, issue the command simply as

```
groups
```

To see the groups to which another user belongs, issue the command as

```
groups <username>
```

gzip and gunzip

The gzip command compresses a specified file or group of files, while the gunzip command expands a file which was compressed with gzip. They take identical syntax:

```
gzip <filename>
gunzip <filename>
```

head and tail

The head command displays the first few lines of a specified file, and the tail command displays the last few lines of the specified file. They take the same syntax:

```
head <filename>
tail <filename>
```

ifconfig

A Linux command, ifconfig, is used to configure network devices. It takes the syntax

```
ifconfig [<device>] [options] [up|down]
```

If the command is issued without options, all active devices will be listed in the output. The <*device*> component is used to specify the path name of a device, such as eth0. ifconfig options include

- -a ifconfig will display all devices, regardless of status
- netmask <*address*> The specified IP number will be entered as a netmask
- <*address*> Specified address will be assigned as the device's IP number

init

The init command is used to start the init daemon, which is used to change the runlevel under Linux. The runlevel determines the set of commands and programs which will be automatically started upon boot or restart. init takes the syntax

```
init <runlevel>
```

where <*runlevel*> is one of the following: 0,1,2,3,4,5,6, or s.

- 0 shutdown
- 1 single user mode
- 2-5 locally defined
- 6 reboot
- s single user mode

insmod

The insmod command is used under Linux to add a kernel module into the modular kernel. It is a superuser-only command, and takes the syntax

```
insmod <module name>
```

kill

The kill command sends a specified signal to an active process, and takes the syntax

```
kill [-s <signal>] <process ID>
```

kill takes one of several signal numbers as an argument to the –s flag. If no signal number is specified, kill uses signal 15 (SIGTERM) as default. See a complete list of kill signals by issuing the command

```
kill -l
```

less

The less command is used to show a specified file in page-length sections. less takes the syntax

```
less <filename>
```

Press the spacebar to advance to the next page, and press the b key to view the previous page.

locate

The locate command identifies the path to a named program. It takes the syntax

```
locate [filename]
```

ls

The ls command is used to list the contents of a directory. If no directory is named, it will list the contents of the current directory. ls takes the syntax

```
ls [options] [directory]
```

Options for ls include

- -l Shows contents in long format, with additional information about file characteristics
- -a Shows all files in the directory, including hidden files that begin with a leading dot

- -i Shows the inode numbers of files
- -R Shows all subdirectories of the current directory and all files within those subdirectories
- -t Shows directory contents sorted by the time of the last modification

ln

The ln command is used to create a link to a named file. ln can create either symbolic links or hard links, and takes the syntax

```
ln [options] <linked-to file> <name of link>
```

ln options include

- -s Builds a symbolic link
- -b Creates a backup file of the linked file as well as creating the link
- -v Verbose output

logout

The logout command ends a user session. It takes the simple syntax

```
logout
```

lpc

The lpc command is used for line printer control. It uses the syntax

```
lpc [command [arguments]]
```

There are two important lpc commands:

- help Prints a short explanation of each command
- abort Stops an active spooling daemon

lpc takes several arguments, including

- all Terminate all printer spools
- printer Terminate a specified printer spool

- clean — Remove temporary files from spool directories
- disable — Terminate a spool
- down — Terminate a spool and print a message saying that it is off
- message — The message to be printed
- enable — Activates a spool
- exit — Stop lpc
- quit — Same as exit
- start — Begin a print queue and spooling daemon for the specified printer
- restart — Terminate the specified queue and restart it

lpq

The lpq command shows the queued jobs in a specified print spool. It uses the syntax

```
lpq [-l] [-P<printer>] [<job number>] [<user>]
```

lpq's main argument is the –l flag, which provides output in an extended format. The long format provides extra information about each job in the queue. If you add a user name to the command, lpq will print each of the queued print jobs owned by that user.

lpr

The lpr command sends a specified file to a print spool. It uses the syntax

```
lpr [options] [<file>]
```

Two common lpr options are

- -P<*printer*> — Specifies a printer name
- -#<*number*> — Print this number of copies

To send the file data.txt to the printer "room123," issue the command

```
lpr -Proom123 data.txt
```

To print eight copies of this file, issue the command as

```
lpr -Proom123 -#8 data.txt
```

lprm

The lprm command deletes a job from a print spool. It uses the syntax

```
lprm [-P<printer>] [-] [<job number>] [<user>]
```

Identify job numbers for specific print jobs by issuing the lpq command and reading the output.

make

The make command is one of the commands used in installing new software from source code. It is a user interface to the C compiler. make uses the syntax

```
make [options]
```

make takes different options, depending on the code being installed. Always check the Makefile (generated during the installation process) to see whether you should issue make with arguments. It is often useful to use the dep and install options: dep manages file dependencies, and install places the newly-configured software in appropriate locations of the file system.

man

The man command is used to display the manual page for a named program or command. It takes the syntax

```
man [options] <name of command or program>
```

man has several options, including

- -p Defines the pager which will display the manual page (default is less)
- -a Locates all manual pages that match the command-name text string
- -h Prints a help message
- -k Searches for the specified text string in the text of all manual pages, as well as in the title (may generate lengthy output)

mkdir

The mkdir command is used to make a new directory which takes the name supplied in the command. mkdir takes the syntax

```
mkdir <directory name>
```

mke2fs

The mke2fs command is used under Linux. It is used to build a filesystem (ext2 format) and also to format a named partition or file system. mke2fs uses the syntax

```
mke2fs [options] <device>
```

Some mke2fs options include

- -b Define block size: select 1024, 2048, and 4096 bytes per block
- -c Search for bad disk blocks while formatting
- -n Test run which does not create the filesystem, but reports what would have happened were it an active command
- -v Verbose mode

more

The more command is used to display a specified file in screen-size units. Press the spacebar to move forward one screen in the document or file. make takes the syntax

```
more <filename>
```

mount

The mount command makes a filesystem available for use. It takes the syntax

```
mount -t <fs type> <device> <mount point>
```

mount takes several arguments:

- *<fs type>* The file system type to be mounted
- *<device>* The path name to the file system being mounted, whether local or remote
- *<mount point>* An existing and empty local directory

mv

The mv command moves a designated file to a new location or gives it a new name. mv takes the syntax

```
mv <old> <new>
```

where <*old*> is the existing file, and <*new*> is the new location or new file name.

netstat

The netstat command is used to view the status of network functions. It takes the syntax

```
netstat [options]
```

Issuing netstat without options will show all open sockets. netstat options include

- -e Shows the userid of each socket user
- -r Reports the entire routing table

passwd

The passwd command changes the password for any user account. If you are logged in as root, you can use passwd to change the password on any user account; if you are logged in as a regular user, you can only change your own password. passwd takes the syntax

```
passwd [<user>]
```

ping

The ping command is used to test the connection between networks. ping works by sending data packets to a specified address, and reports the success or failure of that transmission. ping takes the syntax

```
ping [options] <remote machine>
```

ping has several options, including

- -c Defines the number of data packets to be used for the test. If ping is issued without this option, it will send packets until you instruct it to stop with the Ctrl+c keystroke combination.
- -i Specifies the number of seconds to wait between each packet; the default is ten seconds.

ps

The ps command is used to list all current processes. The output includes data showing how long each process has been running and the system resources used by each. ps takes the syntax

```
ps [options]
```

ps options include

- -a List all processes running on the computer, not just your own
- -x Include background processes
- -u Sort all processes by userid

pwd

The pwd command returns output that is the complete path name of the current directory. Use it to learn your current location in the file system by issuing the command

```
pwd
```

read

The read command is used in shell programming. It tells the computer to take input from the keyboard or other standard input device and assign the input as value to the variable $VAR. read takes the syntax

```
read $VAR
```

rm

The rm command deletes a named file. When used alone or with limited options, it is a safe command. However, certain option combinations can be quite destructive; rm should be used with caution when combining arguments. rm takes the syntax

```
rm [options] <filename>
```

rm options include

- -i Interactive mode: rm requires confirmation for each deletion. Many systems configure rm to use the –i flag automatically.

- -r Recursive mode: rm will delete the subdirectories stored in the current directory as well as the files contained in the subdirectories
- -f Force mode: rm will ignore all messages and warnings

Caution:

The –r and –f options are frequently combined as a shortcut, especially when removing filesystems or nested directories. Be extremely cautious when using this combination, however, since it can be devastating if issued unthinkingly. The command **rm –rf *.*** will completely erase the filesystem; if you are logged in as a user, it will remove your home directory, but if you are logged in as root, it will wipe the entire hard disk. Needless to say, do not use this command unless you know exactly what you are doing.

rmdir

The rmdir command is used to remove a named directory. If the specified directory has files in it, rmdir will give an error message and exit. rmdir takes the syntax

```
rmdir <directory name>
```

route

The route command provides information about the IP routing table. It can also be used to make changes to the table. route uses the syntax

```
route [options] <target>
```

route options include

- -v Verbose mode
- -n Display numerical IP addresses (host names are the route default)
- add Add a route
- del Delete a route
- -net Target is a network
- -host Target is a host
- netmask Netmask (if target is a network)
- default Defines the specified route as the default, to be used if no other route matches
- gw Defines a gateway through which packets must be routed

rsync

The rsync command synchronizes files and directories on a network. It takes the syntax

```
rsync [options] <source> <destination>
```

rsync has multiple options, including

- -e Define rsh or ssh as transport method (rsh is default)
- -a Archive mode: all file attributes preserved
- -r Recursive mode: copies all files in all subdirectories
- -u Update mode: copies only files with timestamps newer than those of the destination file copy
- -R Permits use of relative path names
- -v Verbose mode
- -b Backup mode: backs up files before replacing them
- -n Test run: reports what would have happened, but transfers no files
- -z Compresses data before transfer
- --delete If a file on the destination file system does not exist on the sending file system, it is deleted
- --exclude Used with the –R flag: excludes the named subdirectory from the transfer

set

The set command displays a list of environment variables with their current values. Issue the command

```
set
```

at a shell prompt to see the output.

setenv

The setenv command is used to change an environment variable under the C shell. It uses the syntax

```
setenv(VAR=<value>)
```

sh

The sh command starts a Bourne shell session. If a command is offered as an argument, the command will be run in a new Bourne shell session. sh takes the syntax

```
sh [<command>]
```

shutdown

The shutdown command is used to halt all current processes, then shut down the machine. This command has a complex syntax:

```
shutdown [options] <time> [<warning message>]
```

The time component defines the clock time until the machine shuts down. It has three options:

- now
- +<*m*> — the number of minutes to wait before shutting down
- <*hh*>:<*mm*> — the clock time in hours and minutes when the shutdown process will begin

Other shutdown options include

- <*warning message*> — A message printed to the standard output of all logged-in users, announcing the upcoming shutdown
- -h — Halt, or turn off, the machine
- -r — Reboot the machine

This command is most often issued as

```
shutdown -h now
```

sort

The sort command sorts the entries in a specified file. The sort is numerical or alphabetical depending on the first character of each entry. The sorted output is printed to the standard output. sort takes the syntax

```
sort <filename>
```

ssh

The ssh command is used to open a secure shell session using the SSH program. ssh takes the syntax

```
ssh [-l <login name>] [hostname] [command]
```

startx

The startx command starts an X Window System session. While it is possible to use arguments at the command line, it is more consistent and less likely to fail if you edit the .xinitrc configuration file instead. Thus, to open a new X session, issue the command

```
startx
```

su

The su command allows you to change between various user accounts, as long as you have the appropriate password. It is frequently used by system administrators to log into the root account, or to move between various user accounts used for administrative purposes. su uses the syntax

```
su [-] [<username>]
```

The – character determines whether or not your personal environment variables will be used when you move into another user account. If the – is used, the new account's environment variables will be used.

You can also use the su command to issue a single command as root, without logging into the superuser account. To do so, issue the command

```
su -c <command>
```

You will be prompted for the root password, and then the command will execute.

tar

The tar command is used to create an archive file, or *tarball.* tar can also be used to uncompress tarballs. tar takes one of two syntaxes:

```
tar [options] <file 1> <file 2>... <file N>
```

or

```
tar [options] <directory 1> <directory 2>... <directory N>
```

tar options are not given with the hyphen, unlike other flags. Options for tar include

- c Create an archive using the named files
- x Extract the files from the named archive
- f Compress the named file
- z Decompress the named file with gunzip
- v Verbose output

test

The test command is used in shell programming to evaluate a defined condition. test takes the syntax

```
test <condition>
```

or

```
[ <condition> ] (The square brackets are interpreted
  literally.)
```

or

```
test [options] <target>
```

test options include:

- -e File exists
- -f File exists and is a regular file
- -d Target exists and is a directory
- -s File exists and is not empty

test returns an exit value of 0, or "true," if the expression is valid. There are five possible forms for expressions used with this command:

1. **test ($VAR = "string")** where the variable $VAR is equal to the text string "string"
2. **test ($VAR –eq 5)** where the variable $VAR is equal to the integer 5
3. **[$VAR –eq 8]** where the variable $VAR is equal to integer 8
4. **test –e /var/run/*filename*** where the file /var/run/*filename* exists
5. **[–e /var/run/*filename*]** where the file /var/run/*filename* exists

top

The top command's output shows the table of processes. top takes the syntax

```
top [options]
```

top's options include

- d Define the interval between updates
- p Show only the process with this specified PID — can be used up to 20 times in a single command
- q Refresh constantly without delays
- i Ignore all zombie and idle processes

touch

The touch command is used to update the timestamp on a named file. It can also be issued with a file name that does not belong to an existing file, in which case touch creates a new empty file with the specified name. touch takes the syntax

```
touch <filename>
```

traceroute

The traceroute command lists the route which packets use to travel from your host to another specified remote network. It takes the syntax

```
traceroute [options] <remote machine>
```

traceroute options include

- -n Displays numerical IP numbers of machines (default is text host names)
- -w The time, in seconds, that traceroute waits for a response before timing out

ulimit

The ulimit command defines the resources available to shell processes, limiting the amount of system resources which can be used by any given process. It is particularly useful on heavily-used systems. ulimit takes the syntax

```
ulimit [options [limit]]
```

ulimit options include

- -S Set the soft resource limit (warns the process owner if the process exceeds the soft limit)
- -H Set the hard resource limit (does not permit a process to go over the hard limit)
- -a Print current limits to the standard output
- -c Define maximum size of core files
- -d Define the maximum size of a process's data segment
- -t Define the maximum amount of CPU time available to any given process, in seconds
- -f Define the maximum size of files created by the shell process
- -p Define the pipe buffer size
- -n Define the maximum number of open file descriptors
- -u Define the maximum number of user processes
- -v Define the size of the virtual memory

umask

The umask command sets default permissions for new files, using a previously defined mask. umask takes the syntax

```
umask [-S] [<mode>]
```

The –S option prints the current mask to the standard output. The mode is composed of either the letters or octal numbers used by chmod.

umount

The umount command unmounts a specified file system, so that it is no longer available for use. umount takes the syntax

```
umount [options] <filesystem>
```

The <*filesystem*> element is either a device or directory name. It is also possible to use umount to unmount every file system described in the /etc/mtab file with the –a option, as in

```
umount -a
```

useradd

The useradd command is used to create new user accounts. On some systems, useradd may be replaced by a nearly identical program called adduser. useradd takes the syntax

```
useradd [options] <username>
```

Options include:

- -c Include a comment
- -d Define home directory
- -e Define date account expires
- -p Define initial password
- -s Define default shell
- -u Define user ID

The file /etc/default/useradd contains the standard options for accounts created on your system.

userdel

The userdel command deletes a specified user account. On some systems, userdel is replaced by the nearly identical program deluser. userdel takes the syntax

```
userdel [-r] <username>
```

userdel is often issued with the –r flag. This flag deletes all files associated with the user's home directory as well as deleting the user account.

w

The w command displays a list of the users who are logged into the system. It uses the syntax

```
w [options]
```

Common w options include

- -h Print output without header information
- -s Show output in shortened format
- *<user>* Show all information about the specified user, ignoring all other logged-in users

wc

The wc command is used to count the number of words in a named file. A word is defined as a character string with a space on each end of the string (except for strings at the beginning and end of a line). wc takes the syntax

`wc [options] <filename>`

wc options include

- -c Count characters instead of words
- -l Count lines instead of words
- -L Print the length of the longest line

whereis

The whereis command is used to locate a specified program or file on the disk. whereis takes the syntax

`whereis [options] <filename>`

whereis options include

- -b Identify only binary files with the specified name
- -m Identify only manual pages with the specified name
- -s Identify only source code packages with the specified name

which

The which command is used to locate a given executable program on the disk. which takes the syntax

`which [options] <programname>`

Use the –a flag to see all matching executables from directories defined in the PATH environment variable. Using which without the –a flag will search all directories, not just those contained in PATH.

APPENDIX

B

Glossary

A

Acceptable Use Policy (AUP) An acceptable use policy is a set of guidelines and requirements which affects every user on a particular system. AUPs control user behavior, including disk space usage, activity on the Internet, remote connections, and other activities which might harm the system or external networks. Your school, if it offers computer access, as well as any commercial Internet Service Provider (ISP) you might use, will have AUPs to which you must agree before logging into the system.

Aliases In general terms, an alias is a particular string or name which actually refers to another location or machine on the network, just as a person may use a false name. There are three general types of alias:

1. A configuration parameter which allows one given command to be used as a synonym for another command. A common use of this type is to invoke the Bourne Again shell (bash) when a script calls for the regular Bourne shell (sh).
2. A machine which has several names, each defined in the /etc/hosts file, and each of which can be used to access services and files on that machine.
3. A service configuration which allows individual users to be defined as the person responsible for the service, rather than creating new accounts. In this case, an account like "webmaster" might be aliased to the user account "jennifer" rather than requiring Jennifer to log into a separate account to view webmaster mail.

Applet An applet is a small program which can be embedded into a number of file types, and which will run independently when it is activated or the file is opened. Applets are most commonly found in Web files, but are also part of the graphical desktop environments like KDE and Ximian.

Application Programming Interface An Application Programming Interface, or API, defines the particular programming conventions that must be used when writing software for a particular operating system or application. For example, if you were to write a new graphical widget or application for the Gnome integrated desktop, you would need to read the Gnome API and adhere to its guidelines when writing your own program. Ignoring the API means that your program may not work, or that it might even damage the parent program when run.

Archive Files Archive files are composite files which are created by compressing multiple files together into one file. The programs **tar** and **gzip** are the most common Unix compression utilities. In order to use an archive file, it must be uncompressed and the files restored to their regular state.
See **Tarball**.

Argument An argument is issued as part of a shell command. Arguments may define the file or location which is the target of the command, or they may be used to identify a user whose account will be affected by the command.
See **Option**.

Array Variable Array variables take a value which is a series of items, whether numbers or words.
See **String Variable**.

B

Bits A discrete unit of binary data. Bits are the smallest possible data unit, and take either the value of 1 or 0.

Boot Block The boot block is the first designated block on the disk, and is read first when the computer is powered on. It contains information about how the file system is organized and prepares the disk to have the operating system booted.

Buffer A buffer is a section of system memory which contains currently-used data. Buffers speed program response because the data need not be retrieved from the hard disk each time it is required. The buffer concept is also used in text editors, especially GNU Emacs.

C

Case Sensitive Case sensitive programs consider capital letters to be different elements than lower case letters. For example, a case sensitive system does not parse A and a in the same way. Many programs can be toggled between case sensitivity and insensitivity, as with the Web server Apache, which can be configured to ignore case in browser URL requests. However, Unix systems are generally case sensitive by default.

Client-Server Architecture Client-server architecture is a way of constructing services and networks. In this method, a particular service is run on a central machine, or server. Individual client programs then connect to the server and receive their requested data. The Web is probably the best-known client-server service, but many other services also use this architecture whether they are Internet services or not.

Command Interpreter A command interpreter is any program which takes instructions from the user or from a program and translates them into language which the computer's processor can understand. Shell environments are command interpreters.

Command Line Interface The command line interface is unique to text-based operating systems. In such systems, instructions are given to the operating system through typed commands.

Command Prompt A short text string which indicates the place where commands may be typed. The prompt can be configured to show a variety of data about the user or system.

Command Shell The shell interprets user input for the kernel and processor. There are a number of command shells available for Unix variants, including the Bourne Again shell on which this text concentrates. Shells are text-based and use the command prompt; even within a graphical user environment, shells can be used within terminal windows.

Command Substitution The act of using the output of one command as the argument to another.

Command Syntax Each shell command has a particular syntax, which is the way in which the command must be phrased so that it can be interpreted and return the appropriate result.

Command Word The text string which is entered at the command prompt to invoke the desired program. Most programs use their names as the command word, though some use an abbreviated version or acronym.

Comments Sections of a program which are intended for human eyes, and which contain explanations or helpful advice about running the program. Each line of a comment is begun with the #, or hashmark, character, which indicates to the compiler or command interpreter that those lines should be ignored and not executed.

Commodity Software Software which can be purchased independently from a computer. Most software today is commodity software, including all the programs which can be purchased at an electronics store or downloaded over the Internet.

Compilers A program which translates code from programming language to a language understood by the specific Unix variant on which the program will be used. Compilers allow programmers to write a single version of a program, rather than writing a version for each possible Unix variant upon which the program will be run. Programs are compiled as part of the software installation process.

Configuration Files Configuration files are used by a wide variety of Unix programs. These files contain variables which define the way in which the program appears to the user, or the way in which the program runs. Most configuration files can be edited in a text editor.

D

Directories A file type which serves as a container for other files. Directories are the core of the Unix file system, and directions to an individual file are given as the list of directories in which that file is nested.

Display Manager Part of a graphical user interface. The display manager controls login and logout, and manages the various processes which are displayed on the screen.

Distributions A distribution is a particular version of Linux. There are more than a hundred different Linux distributions, each of which has the same kernel but offers a different array of programs, shells, and other elements which distinguish that variant from another.

Dot Files The term used to describe system files which have names beginning with the dot, or period, character. These files are not usually shown in a directory listing unless a particular flag is used. Configuration files and other system information files are often stored as dot files.

E

Environment Variables These variables define the appearance and activity of various programs running on the system. Some environment variables are program-specific, but most are used as part of the shell environment interface. Environment variables are almost always user-configurable.

Escape Sequence A text string or keystroke combination which indicates that a normally running process must be modified in some way. These sequences can be used in programming to manage the way in which programs handle metacharacters, or can be used to pause or halt a running process.

Ethernet A method of network construction, Ethernet involves the use of cables which are strung between machines on the network. These cables are dedicated to data transfer.

Exit Status Each process returns an exit value that indicates whether the process succeeded or failed. These values can be incorporated into a shell program which would perform different actions depending on the exit value. Values are usually expressed as 0 for success, with any other number indicating failure; particular numbers might indicate various reasons for the failure.

F

File The basic data storage concept under Unix. Files may be directories, text files, executable binaries, storage devices, or disk partitions.

File Permissions Settings which determine who has access to a particular file. File permissions may be granted to the file's owner, the owner's group(s), or all users. Levels of permission are read, write, and execute. Regardless of the permissions set on a particular file, the superuser always has access to every file on the system.

Flag
See **Option**.

Flow Control Programming constructs which determine how a program will execute. There are two types of flow control: conditional and iterative. Under conditional flow control, a particular segment of the program will execute only if a specified condition is met. Under iterative flow control, a particular segment will repeat until or unless a specified condition is met.

Free Software Software which meets the license conditions set by the Free Software Foundation. Free Software is generally considered to be that which

1. Permits anyone to use the program for any reason;
2. Permits anyone to modify the program;
3. Permits anyone to redistribute the program;
4. Requires that any derivative work carry the same license conditions.

Function Calls A programming construct used to pull an external function into a shell program. Functions allow small code elements to be used in a number of different programs so that the programmer does not need to rewrite that function with each new program.

G

GPL (GNU Public License)
The license developed by the Free Software Foundation which incorporates all elements of the Free Software definition. Much Linux software is released under the GPL, as are programs found on other Unix variants.

Graphical Text Editor A text editor which can be used with a mouse or other input device, and which is used within a graphical user interface. Graphical text editors usually use menu systems to show available commands. Though they appear much like a word processor, they do not share the same level of functionality.

Graphical User Interface A program which displays operating system elements on the screen with visual widgets like windows and desktop wallpaper. Graphical user interfaces usually permit the use of pointing devices like light pens or mouses, and organize the file system in a visual manner. Although GUIs are more technically sophisticated than text environments, a user can run a text session within a terminal window on the GUI desktop.

H

Heterogeneous A network type. A heterogeneous network is a network which has machines of more than one operating system. That is, a network with a Windows machine, a Linux machine, and a Macintosh is heterogeneous. These networks are managed with software which translates the different operating systems so that they understand each other.

Homogeneous A network type. On a homogeneous network, all machines are running the same operating system.

I

Inode The description of which disk blocks are occupied by a particular file. The inode information is stored in an inode table, which is used to allocate disk space to new files. See **Superblock**.

Integer Any whole number: positive, negative, or zero. Integers cannot contain fractions or decimals.

Integrated Desktop Environment Graphical user interfaces which supply a suite of software designed to work directly with the GUI. Popular desktops include KDE, Ximian, and Gnome.

Interface The method by which the user interacts with the operating system. Unix interfaces can be text-based or graphical.

Internet A type of network which connects several networks together. For example, the Internet is an internet. In general, an internet is any network which connects multiple LANs or WANs.

J

Job Number A unique identifying number assigned to each job started by a particular user. See **Process Identification Number**.

K

Kernel The lowest level component of the operating system. The kernel manages input and output for hardware devices, controls task scheduling, and manages memory.

Key Bindings Functions which are evoked by a keystroke combination or a particular key with an assigned function. These bindings are usually found in text editors, particularly GNU Emacs, but can also be found in other elements of the operating system.

L

Libraries A collection of programming functions. With libraries, a programmer can place a function call into a program rather than rewriting the needed function each time he wants to use it.

Line Editor A type of text editor which handles only one line at a time. Line editors have been supplanted by visual editors like vi, and by graphical editors.

Links An alias for a file. There are two types of links: symbolic and hard. Symbolic links are pointers which refer to another actual file. Hard links involve a separate inode with a different file name; this inode refers to the same disk blocks as the original file's inode.

M

Macro There are two definitions for macro:

1. A series of commands or operations performed on a selected section of data, invoked with a keystroke combination or single command. This definition is often used in the context of an application or program.
2. The substitution of a short command for a lengthy function. This definition is used in programming, where macros can save a number of keystrokes.

Manual Page A text file which describes the function of a specified Unix program or shell command. Manual pages are accessed with the **man** command.

Message Of The Day (MOTD) A message displayed at login. The text of this message is usually stored in the file /etc/motd and can be changed only by the root account.

Metacharacter A keyboard key which is usually pressed in combination with a regular letter to invoke a macro or function. Common metacharacters include Ctrl and Alt.

Modularity A construct in which multiple small elements combine to make a complex system like an operating system. Unix is modular, and each simple module can be combined into larger chains to create sophisticated outcomes. However, each module can be controlled, modified, repaired, or configured individually.

Multitasking An operating system which can perform several tasks at the same time. Multitasking may be accomplished through one of two methods: task switching and time slicing. See **Task Switching** and **Time Slicing**.

N

Name Server A computer which translates text domain names into numerical IP addresses. Most network connections are configured so that two domain name servers are specified for redundancy.

O

Open Source A term defined by the Open Source Initiative. Like Free Software, Open Source software must be freely redistributable and the source code must always be made available to users. However, Open Source software licenses may restrict modifications to the original source code as long as users can distribute patches, or small changes which can be applied to the original code.

Operating System The software which lies between the user and the machine hardware. Operating systems, as the name implies, allow the user to operate the machine by running programs, manipulating the hardware, and configuring various software. This book covers the Unix operating system and its variants; other operating systems include Windows and MacOS.

Operator An item used in programming which can perform a number of actions including mathematics, comparisons, and other operations which involve evaluation of two or more values.

Option An optional element of a command. Options affect the way in which the program operates, or the manner in which its output is reported. Options are often preceded by the hyphen. See **Argument**.

P

Packages An archive file which contains the various files needed to install a given program. Packages might include software libraries, source code, formatted programs designed to be installed with a package management program, documentation, and other files important for smooth and successful installation.

Packet Sniffer A program usually used for illicit purposes. Packet sniffers watch the incoming data stream and attempt to grab user names and passwords sent in clear text. These programs can be defeated by the use of encrypted secure transmissions.

Path The exact location of a given file within the total file system. Path names are made up of a series of directory and subdirectory names.

Password The text string which a user supplies to gain access to her home directory and the system as a whole. Passwords should be strong passwords when possible, incorporating both upper- and lower-case letters as well as numbers. Dictionary words are extreme security risks. Never share passwords.

Peripheral Devices Any device which can be attached to the main computer or removed from it. Peripherals include scanners, printers, and pointing devices.

Permissions
See **File Permissions**.

Pipes A method of identifying and transferring the data output from one program to be used as input for another.

Port Rewriting software for a different platform or operating system.

Process Identification Number A unique identifying number assigned to each process running on a particular machine. See **Job Number**.

Protocol A standard which defines the way in which particular transactions must occur. Protocols are used to define the way in which mail is transferred between machines, as well as many other interactions and data transfers.

R

Recursive Acronym An acronym which uses itself as one of the components. GNU, for example, is an acronym for "GNU's Not Unix." Recursive acronyms are so named in reference to recursive programming functions, which call themselves. Recursive functions take the form

```
function {
   function()
   }
```

Redirection Operators Elements used to change the default destination of a program's input or output. Redirection operators include the characters < and >, as well as the pipe.

Regular Expression An expression which is used to match one or more text strings within a specified target file or segment of data. Regular expressions usually use metacharacters to define potential matches. They can be used at the command line or within a shell program.

Rescue Kit A diskette or CD-ROM which contains a bare-bones version of the operating system and a few critical administrative tools like a text editor. When a Unix machine is damaged to the point where it will not boot, a rescue kit can be used to boot the machine and search for the problem so that it can be repaired. Rescue kits usually provide only the vi text editor, which is why vi skills are important no matter what your preferred text editor might actually be.

Root The user ID of the superuser account.

Router A computer with specialized software designed to manage data transfer around a network. Some routers are configured to stand at the intersection between a local network and an external network, in which case they may be called gateways.

Run Control Files Configuration files which determine the way in which a given program will boot up and how it will appear to the user.
See **Dot Files**.

S

Scripts Short programs, often written for a single purpose, which are often written in a native shell scripting language like that of bash, or in an interpreted language like Perl.

Shell
See **Command Shell**.

Shell Account A user account which opens a shell session for interaction with the operating system.

Shell Command A command which the shell's interpreter passes as direction to the operating system.
See **Command Word**.

Shell Environment The "look and feel" of a given user's shell sessions. This look and feel can be altered by editing configuration files and environment variables. Most systems have a default set of variables which define the shell environment, which can then be altered by individual users.

Shell Prompt
See **Command Prompt**.

Source Code A program as it is written by a programmer. This code must be compiled or interpreted before it can be run by users or used within a shell program. Software can often be downloaded either as source code or as precompiled packages.
See **Packages**.

Spool A specified file which contains incoming data, such as electronic mail messages or unread news posts.

Standard Input The default source for input data. Usually the keyboard is the standard input, but some programs may take input from other devices. Standard input can also be altered with redirection operators or pipes.

Standard Output The default location for output data. Usually, the monitor is the standard output, but under some circumstances it may be a printer or another program that has been defined through redirection operators.

Strings A set of alphanumeric characters. Text processing, regular expressions, and many other elements of the operating system and various programs rely on strings as their basic data unit.

String Variable A variable which takes a text string as its value.
See **Array Variable**.

Subshell A shell process started by an existing shell session. Subshells often open long enough to run a particular command and then close themselves when finished.

Superblock The disk block which boots directly after the boot block. The superblock contains information about the file system itself, including the various blocks occupied or vacant and basic inode information.

Superuser The supreme user. The superuser can run any program or view any file on the machine regardless of its permissions. The superuser can start or stop the machine, add or delete users, manage software, and any other function possible. Every Unix machine has a superuser, an account created when the operating system was installed.

System Administrator The person who runs the system and has access to the superuser account. A machine may have more than one administrator who shares access to root. System administrators do routine machine management and maintenance.

System Call A programming construct that makes use of native kernel functions rather than those provided by software libraries.

T

Tarball An archive file created with the tar compression program.
See **Archive File**.

Task Switching A type of multitasking in which the operating system lets a given process complete its work before switching system resources to the next process.
See **Multitasking** and **Time Slicing**.

Terminal Window A window opened within a graphical user interface which provides access to a system prompt and a shell session.

Text-Mode Editor A text editor which uses keystroke combinations to perform various editing functions. Text editors include both line and visual editors.

Time Slicing A type of multitasking where the operating system provides a defined period of access to system resources to each active process in turn.
See **Multitasking** and **Task Switching**.

Timestamp A file notation which carries the last time the file was modified, taken from the system clock.

Topology The mapped layout of a network's architecture.

U

Unices The plural form of Unix.

User Interface
See **Interface**.

V

Variable A term which has an associated value and can be used in programming without knowing the exact value.

Verbose Mode A mode which generates output while a program is running. Verbose mode provides information about what is happening at each step of the program's execution. Some programs offer several levels of verbosity, while others do not offer verbose mode at all.

W

Widgets Graphical elements which can be reused in multiple programs written for the same graphical user interface. Like programming functions, widgets are often supplied as libraries known as "widget sets."

Wildcard Used in regular expressions, a wildcard is a metacharacter which represents a range of characters.

Window Manager Part of a graphical user interface, the window manager controls the "look and feel" of the screen including window appearance and placement.

X

X Window System A standard which defines how graphical elements must be programmed and executed. Any graphical interface which meets the standard can be called an X Window System.

x86 Processor An Intel processor chip or a chip which meets the Intel specifications. x86 chips include the 386, 486, and Pentium chip families. All personal Unix variants, like Linux and FreeBSD, have been written for, or ported to, the x86 architecture.

APPENDIX C

Sample Configuration Scripts

- gdm.conf
- pine.conf
- rc.sysinit
- XF86Config

gdm.conf

This file is the configuration file for the Gnome display manager. It controls the login screen appearance, as well as the behavior and appearance of various desktop programs and elements. It can be edited to change these system parameters, either with a text editor or with Gnome's graphical administrative tools.

```
[daemon]
AutomaticLoginEnable=false
AutomaticLogin=
# If you are having trouble with using a single server for a long time and
# want gdm to kill/restart the server, turn this on
AlwaysRestartServer=false
Configurator=/usr/sbin/gdmconfig --disable-sound --disable-crash-dialog
GnomeDefaultSession=/usr/share/gnome/default.session
Chooser=/usr/bin/gdmchooser --disable-sound --disable-crash-dialog
DefaultPath=/bin:/usr/bin:/usr/bin/X11:/usr/local/bin:/usr/games :\
  /opt/gnome/bin
DisplayInitDir=/etc/X11/gdm/Init
Greeter=/usr/bin/gdmlogin --disable-sound --disable-crash-dialog
Group=gdm
HaltCommand=/sbin/shutdown -h now
KillInitClients=true
LogDir=/var/lib/gdm
PidFile=/var/run/gdm.pid
```

```
PostSessionScriptDir=/etc/X11/gdm/PostSession/
PreSessionScriptDir=/etc/X11/gdm/PreSession/
# Distributions:  If you have some script that runs an X server in say
# VGA mode, allowing a login, could you please send it to me?
FailsafeXServer=
XKeepsCrashing=/etc/gdm/XKeepsCrashing
RebootCommand=/sbin/shutdown -r now
RootPath=/sbin:/usr/sbin:/bin:/usr/bin:/usr/bin/X11:/usr/local/bin:/usr/bin
ServAuthDir=/var/lib/gdm
SessionDir=/etc/X11/gdm/Sessions/
SuspendCommand=
User=gdm
UserAuthDir=
UserAuthFBDir=/tmp
UserAuthFile=.Xauthority
TimedLoginEnable=false
TimedLogin=
TimedLoginDelay=30
StandardXServer=/usr/bin/X11/X
FlexibleXServers=5
Xnest=/usr/bin/X11/Xnest -name Xnest

[security]
# If any distributions ship with this one off, they should be shot
# this is only local, so it's only for say kiosk use, when you
# want to minimize possibility of breakin
AllowRoot=true
# If you want to be paranoid, turn this one off
AllowRemoteRoot=true
AllowRemoteAutoLogin=false
RelaxPermissions=0
RetryDelay=3
UserMaxFile=65536
SessionMaxFile=524388

[xdmcp]
# Distributions: Ship with this off.  It is never a safe thing to leave
# out on the net.  Alternatively you can set up /etc/hosts.allow and
# /etc/hosts.deny to only allow say local access.
Enable=false
HonorIndirect=true
MaxPending=4
MaxPendingIndirect=4
MaxSessions=16
MaxWait=15
MaxWaitIndirect=15
DisplaysPerHost=1
```

```
Port=177
# Willing script, none is shipped and by default we'll send
# hostname system id
Willing=/etc/gdm/Xwilling

[gui]
GtkRC=/usr/share/themes/Default/gtk/gtkrc
MaxIconWidth=128
MaxIconHeight=128

[greeter]
TitleBar=false
ConfigAvailable=true
Browser=false
DefaultFace=/usr/share/pixmaps/nobody.png
DefaultLocale=en_US
# These are things excluded from the face browser, not from logging in
Exclude=bin,daemon,adm,lp,sync,shutdown,halt,mail,news,uucp,operator, \
  nobody,gdm,postgres,pvm,rpm
Font=-*-helvetica-bold-r-normal-*-*-180-*-*-*-*-*-*,*
GlobalFaceDir=/usr/share/faces/
Icon=/usr/share/pixmaps/gdm.xpm
LocaleFile=/etc/X11/gdm/locale.alias
Logo=/usr/share/pixmaps/ximian/ximian-gdm-screen.png
Quiver=true
SystemMenu=true
Welcome=Welcome to %n
Welcome[es]=Bienvenido a %n
Welcome[de]=Willkommen auf %n
Welcome[fr]=Bienvenue sur %n
Welcome[cs]=Vítejte na %n
Welcome[no]=Velkommen til %n
Welcome[nn]=Velkomen til %n
Welcome[ru]=äÏÂÒÏ _ÏÖÁÌÏ_ÁÔØ ÎÁ %n
LockPosition=false
SetPosition=false
PositionX=0
PositionY=0
XineramaScreen=0
#Type can be 0=None, 1=Image, 2=Color
BackgroundType=2
BackgroundImage=
BackgroundScaleToFit=true
BackgroundColor=#363047
BackgroundRemoteOnlyColor=true
BackgroundProgram=
ShowGnomeChooserSession=true
```

```
ShowGnomeFailsafeSession=true
ShowXtermFailsafeSession=true
Use24Clock=false

[chooser]
DefaultHostImg=/usr/share/pixmaps/nohost.png
HostImageDir=/usr/share/hosts/
ScanTime=3
Hosts=
Broadcast=true

[debug]
# This will enable debugging into the syslog, usually not necessary
# and it creates a LOT of spew of random stuff to the syslog
Enable=false

[servers]
0=Standard
#1=Standard
#Note: If you want to make sure X runs on a specific virtual console on
#   linux, you can use the following (for console 7).  However this can cause
#   problems for some users.  Be careful about this, getting this wrong
#   can lead to an unusable console.  Best solution is to make sure gdm
#   starts as the last thing, and that will make it not necessary to
#   do hacks like this.
#0=Standard vt7

[server-Standard]
name=Standard server
command=/usr/bin/X11/X
flexible=true
```

pine.conf

This file is the configuration file for the PINE electronic mail and news reader. It affects the appearance and behavior of PINE, and can be edited by the user or can take system defaults set by the local administrator.

```
# Pine system-wide defaults file -- customize as needed.
#
# This file sets the system-wide configuration defaults used by Pine.
# If you have questions about specific settings see the section on
# configuration options in the Pine notes. Run pine -conf to see how
# system defaults have been set.  For variables that accept multiple
```

```
# values, list elements are separated by commas.  A line beginning with
# a space or tab is considered to be a continuation of the previous line.
# For a variable to be unset its value must be blank.
# To set a variable to the empty string its value should be "".
# Switch variables are set to either "yes" or "no", and default to
# "no".  Lines beginning with "#" are comments, and ignored by Pine.

# Over-rides your full name from Unix password file.
personal-name=

# Sets domain part of From: and local addresses in outgoing mail.
user-domain=

# List of SMTP servers for sending mail. If blank: Unix Pine uses sendmail.
smtp-server=

# NNTP server for posting news. Also sets news-collections for news reading.
nntp-server=

# Path of (local or remote) INBOX, e.g. ={mail.somewhere.edu}inbox
# Normal Unix default is the local INBOX (usually usr/spool/mail/$USER).
inbox-path=

# List of incoming msg folders besides INBOX, e.g. ={host2}inbox, {host3}inbox
# Syntax: optnl-label {optnl-imap-host-name}folder-path
incoming-folders=

# List of directories where saved-message folders may be. First one is
# the default for Saves. Example: Main {host1}mail/[], Desktop mail\[]
# Syntax: optnl-label {optnl-imap-hostname}optnl-directory-path[]
folder-collections=

# List, only needed if nntp-server not set, or news is on a different host
# than used for NNTP posting. Examples: News *[] or News {host3/nntp}[]
# Syntax: optnl-label *{news-host/protocol}[]
news-collections=

# List of folder pairs; the first indicates a folder to archive, and the
# second indicates the folder read messages in the first should
# be moved to.
incoming-archive-folders=

# List of context and folder pairs, delimited by a space, to be offered for
# pruning each month.  For example: {host1}mail/[] mumble
pruned-folders=

# Over-rides default path for sent-mail folder, e.g. =old-mail (using first
```

```
# folder collection dir) or ={host2}sent-mail or ="" (to suppress saving).
# Default: sent-mail (Unix) or SENTMAIL.MTX (PC) in default folder collection.
default-fcc=

# Over-rides default path for saved-msg folder, e.g. =saved-messages (using
# first folder collection dir) or ={host2}saved-mail or ="" (to suppress
  saving).
# Default: saved-messages (Unix) or SAVEMAIL.MTX (PC) in default folder
  collection.
default-saved-msg-folder=

# Over-rides default path for postponed messages folder, e.g. =pm (which uses
# first folder collection dir) or ={host4}pm (using home dir on host4).
# Default: postponed-msgs (Unix) or POSTPOND.MTX (PC) in default fldr coltn.
postponed-folder=

# If set, specifies where already-read messages will be moved upon quitting.
read-message-folder=

# If set, specifies where form letters should be stored.
form-letter-folder=

# Over-rides default path for signature file. Default is ~/.signature
signature-file=

# List of file or path names for global/shared addressbook(s).
# Default: none
# Syntax: optnl-label path-name
global-address-book=
# List of file or path names for personal addressbook(s).
# Default: ~/.addressbook (Unix) or \PINE\ADDRBOOK (PC)
# Syntax: optnl-label path-name
address-book=

# List of features; see Pine's Setup/options menu for the current set.
# e.g. feature-list= select-without-confirm, signature-at-bottom
# Default condition for all of the features is no-.
feature-list=allow-changing-from,
   enable-unix-pipe-cmd,
   enable-tab-completion,
   enable-full-header-cmd,
   enable-flag-screen-implicitly,
   enable-flag-cmd,
   enable-8bit-esmtp-negotiation,
   enable-8bit-nntp-posting,
   enable-bounce-cmd,
   enable-aggregate-command-set,
   enable-search-and-replace,
```

```
    enable-sigdashes,
    enable-reply-indent-string-editing,
    signature-at-bottom,
    enable-dot-folders,
    enable-msg-view-urls,
    enable-msg-view-web-hostnames,
    enable-dot-files,
    enable-newmail-in-xterm-icon,
    enable-suspend,
    show-plain-text-internally

# Pine executes these keys upon startup (e.g. to view msg 13: i,j,1,3,CR,v)
initial-keystroke-list=
# Only show these headers (by default) when composing messages
default-composer-hdrs=

# Add these customized headers (and possible default values) when composing
customized-hdrs=

# When viewing messages, include this list of headers
viewer-hdrs=

# Determines default folder name for Saves...
# Choices: default-folder, by-sender, by-from, by-recipient, last-folder-used.
# Default: "default-folder", i.e. "saved-messages" (Unix) or "SAVEMAIL" (PC).
saved-msg-name-rule=

# Determines default name for Fcc...
# Choices: default-fcc, by-recipient, last-fcc-used.
# Default: "default-fcc" (see also "default-fcc=" variable.)
fcc-name-rule=

# Sets presentation order of messages in Index. Choices:
# subject, from, arrival, date, size. Default: "arrival".
sort-key=

# Sets presentation order of address book entries. Choices: dont-sort,
# fullname-with-lists-last, fullname, nickname-with-lists-last, nickname
# Default: "fullname-with lists-last".
addrbook-sort-rule=

# Sets presentation order of folder list entries. Choices: .
#
# Default: "alpha-with-directories-last".
folder-sort-rule=

# Sets the default folder and collectionoffered at the Goto Command's prompt.
goto-default-rule=
```

```
# Sets message which cursor begins on. Choices: first-unseen, first-recent,
# first, last. Default: "first-unseen".
incoming-startup-rule=

# Reflects capabilities of the display you have. Default: US-ASCII.
# Typical alternatives include ISO-8859-x, (x is a number between 1 and 9).
character-set=ISO-8859-1

# Specifies the program invoked by ^_ in the Composer,
# or the "enable-alternate-editor-implicitly" feature.
editor=

# Specifies the program invoked by ^T in the Composer.
speller=/usr/bin/pine-spellcheck

# Specifies the column of the screen where the composer should wrap.
composer-wrap-column=

# Specifies the string to insert when replying to a message.
reply-indent-string=

# Specifies the introduction to insert when replying to a message.
reply-leadin=

# Specifies the string to use when sending a message with no to or cc.
empty-header-message=

# If "user-domain" not set, strips hostname in FROM address. (Unix only)
use-only-domain-name=

# Your default printer selection
printer=

# List of special print commands
personal-print-command=

# Which category default print command is in
personal-print-category=

# This names the path to an alternative program, and any necessary arguments,
# to be used in posting mail messages.  Example:
#               /usr/lib/sendmail -oem -t -oi
# or,
#               /usr/local/bin/sendit.sh
# The latter a script found in Pine distribution's contrib/util directory.
# NOTE: The program MUST read the message to be posted on standard input,
#   AND operate in the style of sendmail's "-t" option.
```

```
sendmail-path=

# This names the root of the tree to which the user is restricted when reading
# and writing folders and files.  For example, on Unix ~/work confines the
# user to the subtree beginning with their work subdirectory.
# (Note: this alone is not sufficient for preventing access.  You will also
# need to restrict shell access and so on, see Pine Technical Notes.)
# Default: not set (so no restriction)
operating-dir=

# This variable takes a list of programs that message text is piped into
# after MIME decoding, prior to display.
display-filters=

# PGP disabled by default due to some users security concerns.
# Feb 14, 2001 Mike A. Harris <mharris@redhat.com>
#display-filters=_LEADING("-----BEGIN PGP MESSAGE-----")_ /usr/bin/gpg-check,
#   _LEADING("-----BEGIN PGP SIGNED    MESSAGE-----")_ /usr/bin/gpg-check

# This defines a program that message text is piped into before MIME
# encoding, prior to sending
sending-filters=

# PGP disabled by default due to some users security concerns.
# Feb 14, 2001 Mike A. Harris <mharris@redhat.com>
#sending-filters=/usr/bin/gpg-sign,
#   /usr/bin/gpg-encrypt _RECIPIENTS_,
#   /usr/bin/gpg-sign+encrypt _RECIPIENTS_

# A list of alternate addresses the user is known by
alt-addresses=

# This is a list of formats for address books.  Each entry in the list is made
# up of space-delimited tokens telling which fields are displayed and in
# which order.  See help text
addressbook-formats=

# This gives a format for displaying the index.  It is made
# up of space-delimited tokens telling which fields are displayed and in
# which order.  See help text
index-format=

# The number of lines of overlap when scrolling through message text
viewer-overlap=

# Number of lines from top and bottom of screen where single
# line scrolling occurs.
scroll-margin=
```

```
# The number of seconds to sleep after writing a status message
status-message-delay=

# The approximate number of seconds between checks for new mail
mail-check-interval=

# Full path and name of NEWSRC file
newsrc-path=

# Path and filename of news configation's active file.
# The default is typically "/usr/lib/news/active".
news-active-file-path=

# Directory containing system's news data.
# The default is typically "/usr/spool/news"
news-spool-directory=

# Path and filename of the program used to upload text from your terminal
# emulator's into Pine's composer.
upload-command=

# Text sent to terminal emulator prior to invoking the program defined by
# the upload-command variable.
# Note: _FILE_ will be replaced with the temporary file used in the upload.
upload-command-prefix=

# Path and filename of the program used to download text via your terminal
# emulator from Pine's export and save commands.
download-command=

# Text sent to terminal emulator prior to invoking the program defined by
# the download-command variable.
# Note: _FILE_ will be replaced with the temporary file used in the download.
download-command-prefix=

# Sets the search path for the mailcap cofiguration file.
# NOTE: colon delimited under UNIX, semi-colon delimited under
# DOS/Windows/OS2.
mailcap-search-path=

# Sets the search path for the mimetypes cofiguration file.
# NOTE: colon delimited under UNIX, semi-colon delimited under
# DOS/Windows/OS2.
mimetype-search-path=

# If no user input for this many hours, Pine will exit if in an idle loop
```

```
# waiting for a new command.  If set to zero (the default), then there will
# be no timeout.
user-input-timeout=

# Sets the time in seconds that Pine will attempt to open a network
# connection.  The default is 30, the minimum is 5, and the maximum is
# system defined (typically 75).
tcp-open-timeout=

# Sets the time in seconds that Pine will attempt to open a UNIX remote
# shell connection.  The default is 15, min is 5, and max is unlimited.
# Zero disables rsh altogether.
rsh-open-timeout=0

# Sets the name of the command used to open a UNIX remote shell connection.
# The default is tyically /usr/ucb/rsh.
rsh-path=

# Sets the format of the command used to open a UNIX remote
# shell connection.  The default is "%s %s -l %s exec /etc/r%sd"
# NOTE: the 4 (four) "%s" entries MUST exist in the provided command
# where the first is for the command's path, the second is for the
# host to connnect to, the third is for the user to connect as, and the
# fourth is for the connection method (typically "imap")
rsh-command=

# Sets the version number Pine will use as a threshold for offering
# its new version message on startup.
new-version-threshold=

# List of programs to open Internet URLs (e.g. http or ftp references).
url-viewers=_TEST("test -e /usr/bin/htmlview")_ /usr/bin/htmlview,
    _TEST("test -e /usr/bin/mozilla")_ /usr/bin/mozilla,
    _TEST("test -e /usr/bin/konqueror")_ /usr/bin/konqueror,
    _TEST("test -e /usr/bin/netscape -a -n '${DISPLAY}'")_ /usr/bin/netscape,
    _TEST("test -e /usr/bin/links")_ /usr/bin/links,
    _TEST("test -e /usr/bin/lynx")_ /usr/bin/lynx,
    _TEST("test -e /usr/bin/w3m")_ /usr/bin/w3m

# List of mail drivers to disable. See technical notes.
disable-these-drivers=

# Set by Pine; contains data for caching remote address books.
remote-abook-metafile=

# How many extra copies of remote address book should be kept. Default: 3
remote-abook-history=
```

```
# Patterns and their actions are stored here.
patterns=

# Controls display of color
color-style=use-termdef

# Sets the time in seconds that Pine will attempt to open a UNIX secure
# shell connection.  The default is 15, min is 5, and max is unlimited.
# Zero disables ssh altogether.
ssh-open-timeout=

# Sets the name of the command used to open a UNIX secure shell connection.
# Tyically this is /usr/local/bin/ssh.
ssh-path=

# Sets the format of the command used to open a UNIX secure
# shell connection.  The default is "%s %s -l %s exec /etc/r%sd"
# NOTE: the 4 (four) "%s" entries MUST exist in the provided command
# where the first is for the command's path, the second is for the
# host to connnect to, the third is for the user to connect as, and the
# fourth is for the connection method (typically "imap")
ssh-command=

# Minimum number of minutes between checks for remote address book changes.
# 0 means never check except when opening a remote address book.
# -1 means never check. Default: 5
remote-abook-validity=

# Choose: black,blue,green,cyan,red,magenta,yellow,or white.
normal-foreground-color=white
normal-background-color=black
reverse-foreground-color=
reverse-background-color=
title-foreground-color=
title-background-color=
status-foreground-color=
status-background-color=
keylabel-foreground-color=
keylabel-background-color=
keyname-foreground-color=
keyname-background-color=
selectable-item-foreground-color=
selectable-item-background-color=
quote1-foreground-color=cyan
quote1-background-color=black
quote2-foreground-color=green
quote2-background-color=black
```

```
quote3-foreground-color=blue
quote3-background-color=black
prompt-foreground-color=
prompt-background-color=
index-to-me-foreground-color=
index-to-me-background-color=
index-important-foreground-color=
index-important-background-color=
index-deleted-foreground-color=
index-deleted-background-color=
index-answered-foreground-color=
index-answered-background-color=
index-new-foreground-color=
index-new-background-color=
index-recent-foreground-color=
index-recent-background-color=
index-unseen-foreground-color=
index-unseen-background-color=

# When viewing messages, these are the header colors
viewer-hdr-colors=
```

rc.sysinit

This file is the master configuration file for SysV-style Linux. It is the first file run at boot after the kernel is loaded. It starts all other processes that run automatically at boot, and calls all the other boot scripts, including those which affect the user environment.

```
#!/bin/bash
#
# /etc/rc.sysinit - run once at boot time
#
# Taken in part from Miquel van Smoorenburg's bcheckrc.
#

# Rerun ourselves through initlog
if [ -z "$IN_INITLOG" ]; then
[ -f /sbin/initlog ] && exec /sbin/initlog $INITLOG_ARGS -r
etc/rc.sysinit
fi

# If we're using devfs, start devfsd now - we need the old device names
[ -e /dev/.devfsd -a -x /sbin/devfsd ] && /sbin/devfsd /dev

# Set the path
```

```
PATH=/bin:/sbin:/usr/bin:/usr/sbin
export PATH

HOSTNAME=`/bin/hostname`

# Read in config data.
if [ -f /etc/sysconfig/network ]; then
    . /etc/sysconfig/network
else
    NETWORKING=no
fi

if [ -z "$HOSTNAME" -o "$HOSTNAME" = "(none)" ]; then
    HOSTNAME=localhost
fi

# Source functions
. /etc/init.d/functions

# Print a banner. ;)
echo -en $"\t\t\tWelcome to "
[ "$BOOTUP" != "serial" ] && echo -en $"\\033[1;31m"
echo -en $"Red Hat"
[ "$BOOTUP" != "serial" ] && echo -en $"\\033[0;39m"
echo $" Linux"
if [ "$PROMPT" != "no" ]; then
   echo -en $"\t\tPress 'I' to enter interactive startup."
   echo
   sleep 1
fi

# Fix console loglevel
/bin/dmesg -n $LOGLEVEL

# Mount /proc (done here so volume labels can work with fsck)

action $"Mounting proc filesystem: " mount -n -t proc /proc /proc

# Configure kernel parameters

action $"Configuring kernel parameters: " sysctl -e -p /etc/sysctl.conf

# Set the system clock.
ARC=0
SRM=0
UTC=0
```

```
if [ -f /etc/sysconfig/clock ]; then
   . /etc/sysconfig/clock

   # convert old style clock config to new values
   if [ "${CLOCKMODE}" = "GMT" ]; then
      UTC=true
   elif [ "${CLOCKMODE}" = "ARC" ]; then
      ARC=true
   fi
fi

CLOCKDEF=""
CLOCKFLAGS="--hctosys"

case "$UTC" in
   yes|true)
      CLOCKFLAGS="$CLOCKFLAGS -u";
      CLOCKDEF="$CLOCKDEF (utc)";

   ;;
   no|false)
      CLOCKFLAGS="$CLOCKFLAGS --localtime";
      CLOCKDEF="$CLOCKDEF (localtime)";
   ;;
esac

case "$ARC" in
   yes|true)
      CLOCKFLAGS="$CLOCKFLAGS -A";
      CLOCKDEF="$CLOCKDEF (arc)";
   ;;
esac

case "$SRM" in
   yes|true)
      CLOCKFLAGS="$CLOCKFLAGS -S";
      CLOCKDEF="$CLOCKDEF (srm)";
   ;;
esac

/sbin/hwclock $CLOCKFLAGS

action $"Setting clock $CLOCKDEF: `date`" date


if [ "`/sbin/consoletype`" == "vt" ]; then
   # Load keymap
   if [ -x /bin/loadkeys ]; then
```

```
    KEYTABLE=
    KEYMAP=
    if [ -f /etc/sysconfig/console/default.kmap ]; then
     KEYMAP=/etc/sysconfig/console/default.kmap
    else
     if [ -f /etc/sysconfig/keyboard ]; then
       . /etc/sysconfig/keyboard
     fi
     if [ -n "$KEYTABLE" -a -d "/usr/lib/kbd/keymaps" -o -d \
        /lib/kbd/keymaps" ]; then
       KEYMAP=$KEYTABLE
     fi
fi
if [ -n "$KEYMAP" ]; then
    # Since this takes in/output from stdin/out, we can't use initlog
    if [ -n "$KEYTABLE" ]; then
       echo -n $"Loading default keymap ($KEYTABLE): "
    else
       echo -n $"Loading default keymap: "
    fi
    loadkeys $KEYMAP < /dev/tty0 > /dev/tty0 2>/dev/null && \
    success $"Loading default keymap" || failure $"Loading default keymap"
   echo
  fi
  fi

  # Load system font
  if [ -x /sbin/setsysfont ]; then
     [ -f /etc/sysconfig/i18n ] && . /etc/sysconfig/i18n
     if [ -f /etc/sysconfig/console/$SYSFONT.psf.gz -o \
          -f /usr/lib/kbd/consolefonts/$SYSFONT.psf.gz -o \
          -f /etc/sysconfig/console/$SYSFONT.gz -o \
          -f /usr/lib/kbd/consolefonts/$SYSFONT.gz -o \
          -f /lib/kbd/consolefonts/$SYSFONT.gz -o \
          -f /lib/kbd/consolefonts/$SYSFONT.psf.gz ]; then
        action $"Setting default font ($SYSFONT): " /sbin/setsysfont
     fi
  fi
fi

# Start up swapping.
action $"Activating swap partitions: " swapon -a -e

# Set the hostname.
```

```
action $"Setting hostname ${HOSTNAME}: " hostname ${HOSTNAME}

# Initialize USB controller and HID devices
usb=0
if ! grep -iq "nousb" /proc/cmdline 2>/dev/null && ! grep -q "usb" \
   proc/devices 2>/dev/null ; then
   aliases=`/sbin/modprobe -c | egrep -s "^alias [[:space:]]+usb- \
      controller" | awk '{ print $3 }'`
   if [ -n "$aliases" -a "$aliases" != "off" ] ; then
      modprobe usbcore
      action $"Mounting USB filesystem: "  mount -t usbdevfs usbdevfs \
         /proc/bus/usb
      for alias in $aliases ; do
        action $"Initializing USB controller ($alias): " modprobe $alias
      done
      [ $? -eq 0 -a -n "$aliases" ] && usb=1
   fi
fi

if ! grep -iq "nousb" /proc/cmdline 2>/dev/null && grep -q "usb" \
     /proc/devices 2>/dev/null ; then
   usb=1
fi

needusbstorage=
if [ $usb = "1" ]; then
   sleep 5
   mouseoutput=`cat /proc/bus/usb/devices 2>/dev/null|grep -E \
      "^I.*Cls=03.*Prot=02"`
   kbdoutput=`cat /proc/bus/usb/devices 2>/dev/null|grep -E \
      "^I.*Cls=03.*Prot=01"`
   needusbstorage=`cat /proc/bus/usb/devices 2>/dev/null|grep -e \
      "^I.*Cls=08"`
   if [ -n "$kbdoutput" ] || [ -n "$mouseoutput" ]; then
      action $"Initializing USB HID interface: " modprobe hid 2> /dev/null
   fi
   if [ -n "$kbdoutput" ]; then
      action $"Initializing USB keyboard: " modprobe keybdev
   fi
   if [ -n "$mouseoutput" ]; then
      action $"Initializing USB mouse: " modprobe mousedev
   fi
fi

if [ -f /fastboot ] || grep -iq "fastboot" /proc/cmdline 2>/dev/null ; then
      fastboot=yes
   else
```

```
        fastboot=
fi

if [ -f /fsckoptions ]; then
        fsckoptions=`cat /fsckoptions`
    else
        fsckoptions=
fi

if [ -f /forcefsck ]; then
        fsckoptions="-f $fsckoptions"
fi

if [ "$BOOTUP" != "serial" ]; then
        fsckoptions="-C $fsckoptions"
else
         fsckoptions="-V $fsckoptions"
fi


_RUN_QUOTACHECK=0
ROOTFSTYPE=`grep " / " /proc/mounts | awk '{ print $3 }'`
if [ -z "$fastboot" -a "$ROOTFSTYPE" != "nfs" ]; then

    STRING=$"Checking root filesystem"
    echo $STRING
    initlog -c "fsck -T -a $fsckoptions /"
    rc=$?

    if [ "$rc" = "0" ]; then
            success "$STRING"
            echo
    elif [ "$rc" = "1" ]; then
        passed $"$STRING"
            echo
    fi

    # A return of 2 or higher means there were serious problems.
    if [ $rc -gt 1 ]; then
            failure "$STRING"
            echo
            echo
            echo $"*** An error occurred during the file system check."
            echo $"*** Dropping you to a shell; the system will reboot"
            echo $"*** when you leave the shell."

            PS1=$"(Repair filesystem) \# # "; export PS1
```

```
            sulogin

            echo $"Unmounting file systems"
            umount -a
            mount -n -o remount,ro /
            echo $"Automatic reboot in progress."
            reboot -f
    elif [ "$rc" = "1" ]; then
            _RUN_QUOTACHECK=1
    fi
fi

# check for arguments

if grep -iq nopnp /proc/cmdline >/dev/null 2>&1 ; then
    PNP=
else
     PNP=yes
fi

# set up pnp
if [ -x /sbin/isapnp -a -f /etc/isapnp.conf -a ! -f /proc/isapnp ]; then
    if [ -n "$PNP" ]; then
       action $"Setting up ISA PNP devices: " /sbin/isapnp /etc/isapnp.conf
    else
       action $"Skipping ISA PNP configuration at users request: " /bin/true
    fi
fi

# Remount the root filesystem read-write.
state=`awk '/(^\/dev\/root| \/ )/ { print $4 }' /proc/mounts`
[ "$state" != "rw" ] && \
    action $"Remounting root filesystem in read-write mode: " mount -n -o \
       remount,rw /

# LVM initialization
if [ -e /proc/lvm -a -x /sbin/vgchange -a -f /etc/lvmtab ]; then
       action $"Setting up LVM:" /sbin/vgscan && /sbin/vgchange -a y
fi

# Clear mtab
>/etc/mtab

# Remove stale backups
rm -f /etc/mtab~ /etc/mtab~~

# Enter root, /proc and (potentially) /proc/bus/usb and devfs into mtab.
```

```
mount -f /
mount -f /proc
[ -f /proc/bus/usb/devices ] && mount -f -t usbdevfs usbdevfs /proc/bus/usb
[ -e /dev/.devfsd ] && mount -f -t devfs devfs /dev

# Turn on harddisk optimization
# There is only one file /etc/sysconfig/harddisks for all disks
# after installing the hdparm-RPM. If you need different hdparm parameters
# for each of your disks, copy /etc/sysconfig/harddisks to
# /etc/sysconfig/harddiskhda (hdb, hdc...) and modify it.
# each disk which has no special parameters will use the defaults.

disk[0]=s; disk[1]=hda; disk[2]=hdb; disk[3]=hdc;
disk[4]=hdd; disk[5]=hde; disk[6]=hdf; disk[7]=hdg; disk[8]=hdh;


if [ -x /sbin/hdparm ]; then
   for device in 0 1 2 3 4 5 6 7 8; do
   unset MULTIPLE_IO USE_DMA EIDE_32BIT LOOKAHEAD EXTRA_PARAMS
      if [ -f /etc/sysconfig/harddisk${disk[$device]} ]; then
            . /etc/sysconfig/harddisk${disk[$device]}
            HDFLAGS[$device]=
            if [ -n "$MULTIPLE_IO" ] && [ "$MULTIPLE_IO" != "0" ]; then
               HDFLAGS[$device]="-q -m$MULTIPLE_IO"
            fi
            if [ -n "$USE_DMA" ] && [ "$USE_DMA" != "0" ]; then
                HDFLAGS[$device]="${HDFLAGS[$device]} -q -d$USE_DMA"
            fi
            if [ -n "$EIDE_32BIT" ]; then
                HDFLAGS[$device]="${HDFLAGS[$device]} -q -c$EIDE_32BIT"
            fi
            if [ -n "$LOOKAHEAD" ]; then
                HDFLAGS[$device]="${HDFLAGS[$device]} -q -A$LOOKAHEAD"
            fi
            if [ -n "$EXTRA_PARAMS" ]; then
                HDFLAGS[$device]="${HDFLAGS[$device]} $EXTRA_PARAMS"
            fi
         else
            HDFLAGS[$device]="${HDFLAGS[0]}"
         fi
         if [ -e "/proc/ide/${disk[$device]}/media" ] ; then
            hdmedia=`cat /proc/ide/${disk[$device]}/media`
            if [ "$hdmedia" = "disk" ]; then
                 if [ -n "${HDFLAGS[$device]}" ]; then
                    action $"Setting hard drive parameters for \
                       ${disk[$device]}: "  /sbin/hdparm
```

```
{HDFLAGS[$device]} /dev/${disk[$device]}
                fi
            fi
        fi
    done
fi

# Update quotas if fsck was run on /.
if [ X"$_RUN_QUOTACHECK" = X1 -a -x /sbin/quotacheck ]; then
    if [ -x /sbin/convertquota ]; then
        if [ -f /quota.user ]; then
            /sbin/convertquota -u / && rm -f /quota.user
        fi
        if [ -f /quota.group ]; then
            /sbin/convertquota -g / && rm -f /quota.group
        fi
    fi
    action $"Checking root filesystem quotas: "  /sbin/quotacheck -v /
fi

# The root filesystem is now read-write, so we can now log via syslog()
# directly..
if [ -n "$IN_INITLOG" ]; then
    IN_INITLOG=
fi

if ! grep -iq nomodules /proc/cmdline >/dev/null 2>&1 && [ -f /proc/ksyms ];
   then
    USEMODULES=y
else
    USEMODULES=
fi

# Our modutils don't support it anymore, so we might as well remove
# the preferred link.
rm -f /lib/modules/preferred
rm -f /lib/modules/default
if [ -x /sbin/depmod -a -n "$USEMODULES" ]; then
    # If they aren't using a recent sane kernel, make a link for them
    if [ ! -n "`uname -r | grep -- "-"`" ]; then
        ktag="`cat /proc/version`"
        mtag=`grep -l "$ktag" /lib/modules/*/.rhkmvtag 2> /dev/null`
        if [ -n "$mtag" ]; then
            mver=`echo $mtag | sed -e 's,/lib/modules/,,' -e 's,/.rhkmvtag,,' \
                -e 's,[        ].*$,,'`
        fi
```

```
        if [ -n "$mver" ]; then
           ln -sf /lib/modules/$mver /lib/modules/default
        fi
     fi
     if [ -L /lib/modules/default ]; then
        INITLOG_ARGS= action $"Finding module dependencies: " depmod -A default
     else
        INITLOG_ARGS= action $"Finding module dependencies: " depmod -A
     fi
  fi

  # tweak isapnp settings if needed.
  if [ -n "$PNP" -a  -f /proc/isapnp -a -x /sbin/sndconfig ]; then
     /sbin/sndconfig --mungepnp >/dev/null 2>&1
  fi


  # Load sound modules iff they need persistent DMA buffers
  if grep -q "options sound dmabuf=1" /etc/modules.conf 2>/dev/null ; then
     RETURN=0
     alias=`/sbin/modprobe -c | egrep -s "^alias[[:space:]]+sound[[:space:]] \
        +" | awk '{ print $3 }'`
     if [ -n "$alias" -a "$alias" != "off" ] ; then
        action $"Loading sound module ($alias): " modprobe $alias
        RETURN=$?
     fi
     alias=`/sbin/modprobe -c | egrep -s "^alias[[:space:]]+sound-slot-0 \
        [[:space:]]+" | awk '{ print $3 }'`
     if [ -n "$alias" -a "$alias" != "off" ] ; then
        action $"Loading sound module ($alias): " modprobe $alias
        RETURN=$?
     fi
     # Load mixer settings
     if grep -q "\(sparcaudio\|sound\)" /proc/devices 2>/dev/null ; then
        if [ $RETURN -eq 0 -a -f /etc/.aumixrc -a -x /bin/aumix-minimal ]; then
           action $"Loading mixer settings: " /bin/aumix-minimal -f
           /etc/.aumixrc -L
        fi
     fi
  fi

  if [ -f /proc/sys/kernel/modprobe ]; then
     if [ -n "$USEMODULES" ]; then
        sysctl -w kernel.modprobe="/sbin/modprobe" >/dev/null 2>&1
        sysctl -w kernel.hotplug="/sbin/hotplug" >/dev/null 2>&1
```

```
    else
      # We used to set this to NULL, but that causes 'failed to exec'
        messages"

      sysctl -w kernel.modprobe="/bin/true" >/dev/null 2>&1
      sysctl -w kernel.hotplug="/bin/true" >/dev/null 2>&1
    fi
fi

# Load modules (for backward compatibility with VARs)
if [ -f /etc/rc.modules ]; then
      /etc/rc.modules
fi

# Add raid devices
if [ ! -f /proc/mdstat ]; then
      modprobe md >/dev/null 2>&1
fi

if [ -f /proc/mdstat -a -f /etc/raidtab ]; then
      echo -n $"Starting up RAID devices: "

      rc=0

      for i in `grep "^raiddev" /etc/raidtab | awk '{print $2}'`
      do
            RAIDDEV=`basename $i`
         RAIDSTAT=`grep "^$RAIDDEV : active" /proc/mdstat`
            if [ -z "$RAIDSTAT" ]; then
               # Try raidstart first...if that fails then
               # fall back to raidadd, raidrun.  If that
               # also fails, then we drop to a shell
               RESULT=1
               if [ -x /sbin/raidstart ]; then
                      /sbin/raidstart $I
                      RESULT=$?
               fi
               if [ $RESULT -gt 0 -a -x /sbin/raid0run ]; then
                   /sbin/raid0run $I
                   RESULT=$?

               fi
               if [ $RESULT -gt 0 -a -x /sbin/raidadd -a -x /sbin/raidrun ];
                  then
                   /sbin/raidadd $I
```

```
                    /sbin/raidrun $I
                    RESULT=$?
                fi
                if [ $RESULT -gt 0 ]; then
                    rc=1
                fi
                 echo -n "$RAIDDEV "
            else
                 echo -n "$RAIDDEV "
            fi
      done
   echo

   # A non-zero return means there were problems.
   if [ $rc -gt 0 ]; then
      echo
      echo
      echo $"*** An error occurred during the RAID startup"
      echo $"*** Dropping you to a shell; the system will reboot"
      echo $"*** when you leave the shell."

      PS1=$"(RAID Repair) \# # "; export PS1
      sulogin

      echo $"Unmounting file systems"
      umount -a
      mount -n -o remount,ro /
      echo $"Automatic reboot in progress."
      reboot -f
   fi
fi

_RUN_QUOTACHECK=0

# Check filesystems
if [ -z "$fastboot" ]; then
   STRING=$"Checking filesystems"
   echo $STRING
   initlog -c "fsck -T -R -A -a $fsckoptions"
   rc=$?
   if [ "$rc" = "0" ]; then
         success "$STRING"
         echo
   elif [ "$rc" = "1" ]; then
      passed "$STRING"
         echo
```

```
    fi

    # A return of 2 or higher means there were serious problems.
    if [ $rc -gt 1 ]; then
       failure "$STRING"
          echo
          echo
          echo $"*** An error occurred during the file system check."
          echo $"*** Dropping you to a shell; the system will reboot"
          echo $"*** when you leave the shell."

          PS1=$"(Repair filesystem) \# # "; export PS1

          sulogin

          echo $"Unmounting file systems"
          umount -a
          mount -n -o remount,ro /
          echo $"Automatic reboot in progress."
          reboot -f
    elif [ "$rc" = "1" -a -x /sbin/quotacheck ]; then
          _RUN_QUOTACHECK=1
    fi
fi

# Mount all other filesystems (except for NFS and /proc, which is already
# mounted). Contrary to standard usage,
# filesystems are NOT unmounted in single user mode.
action $"Mounting local filesystems: " mount -a -t nonfs,smbfs,ncpfs

if [ X"$_RUN_QUOTACHECK" = X1 -a -x /sbin/quotacheck ]; then
    if [ -x /sbin/convertquota ]; then
       # try to convert old quotas
       for mountpt in `cat /etc/mtab | awk '$4 ~ /quota/{print $2}'`; do
          if [ -f "$mountpt/quota.user" ]; then
             /sbin/convertquota -u $mountpt && \
                rm -f $mountpt/quota.user
          fi
          if [ -f "$mountpt/quota.group" ]; then
             /sbin/convertquota -g $mountpt && \
                rm -f $mountpt/quota.group
          fi
       done
    fi
    action $"Checking filesystem quotas: "  /sbin/quotacheck -v -R -a
fi
```

```
# Turn on process accounting
if [ -x /sbin/accton ] ; then
   action $"Turning on process accounting" /sbin/accton /var/log/pacct
fi

# Configure machine if necessary.
if [ -f /.unconfigured ]; then
   if [ -x /usr/bin/passwd ]; then
      /usr/bin/passwd root
   fi
   if [ -x /usr/sbin/netconfig ]; then
      /usr/sbin/netconfig
   fi
   if [ -x /usr/sbin/timeconfig ]; then
      /usr/sbin/timeconfig
   fi
   if [ -x /usr/sbin/authconfig ]; then
      /usr/sbin/authconfig -nostart
   fi
   if [ -x /usr/sbin/ntsysv ]; then
      /usr/sbin/ntsysv --level 35
   fi

   # Reread in network configuration data.
   if [ -f /etc/sysconfig/network ]; then
      . /etc/sysconfig/network

      # Reset the hostname.
      action $"Resetting hostname ${HOSTNAME}: " hostname ${HOSTNAME}
   fi

   rm -f /.unconfigured
fi

if [ -x /sbin/quotaon ]; then
   action $"Turning on user and group quotas for local filesystems: "
      /sbin/quotaon -a
fi

# Clean out /etc.
rm -f /fastboot /fsckoptions /forcefsck /halt /poweroff

# Do we need (w|u)tmpx files? We don't set them up, but the sysadmin
# might...
_NEED_XFILES=
```

```
[ -f /var/run/utmpx -o -f /var/log/wtmpx ] && _NEED_XFILES=1

# Clean up /var
# I'd use find, but /usr may not be mounted.
for afile in /var/lock/* /var/run/*; do
   if [ -d "$afile" ]; then
      [ "`basename $afile`" != "news" -a "`basename $afile`" != "sudo" -a \
        "`basename $afile`" != "mon" ]
& rm -f $afile/*
   else
      rm -f $afile
   fi
done

# Reset pam_console permissions
[ -x /sbin/pam_console_apply ] && /sbin/pam_console_apply -r

{
# Clean up utmp/wtmp
>/var/run/utmp
touch /var/log/wtmp
chgrp utmp /var/run/utmp /var/log/wtmp
chmod 0664 /var/run/utmp /var/log/wtmp
if [ -n "$_NEED_XFILES" ]; then
   >/var/run/utmpx
   touch /var/log/wtmpx
   chgrp utmp /var/run/utmpx /var/log/wtmpx
   chmod 0664 /var/run/utmpx /var/log/wtmpx
fi

# Delete X locks
rm -f /tmp/.X*-lock

# Delete Postgres sockets
rm  f /tmp/.s.PGSQL.*

# Now turn on swap in case we swap to files.
swapon -a
action $"Enabling swap space: " /bin/true

# Initialize the serial ports.
if [ -f /etc/rc.serial ]; then
  . /etc/rc.serial
fi
```

```
# If a SCSI tape has been detected, load the st module unconditionally
# since many SCSI tapes don't deal well with st being loaded and unloaded
if [ -f /proc/scsi/scsi ] && grep -q 'Type: Sequential-Access' /proc/scsi/
  scsi 2>/dev/null ; then
   if grep -qv ' 9 st' /proc/devices ; then
      if [ -n "$USEMODULES" ] ; then
         # Try to load the module.  If it fails, ignore it...
         insmod -p st >/dev/null 2>&1 && modprobe st >/dev/null 2>&1
      fi
   fi
fi

# Load usb storage here, to match most other things
if [ -n "$needusbstorage" ]; then
   modprobe usb-storage >/dev/null 2>&1
fi

# If they asked for ide-scsi, load it
if grep -q "ide-scsi" /proc/cmdline ; then
   modprobe ide-cd >/dev/null 2>&1
   modprobe ide-scsi >/dev/null 2>&1
fi

# Generate a header that defines the boot kernel.
/sbin/mkkerneldoth

# Adjust symlinks as necessary in /boot to keep system services from
# spewing messages about mismatched System maps and so on.
if [ -L /boot/System.map -a -r /boot/System.map-`uname -r` ] ; then
   ln -s -f System.map-`uname -r` /boot/System.map
fi
if [ ! -e /boot/System.map -a -r /boot/System.map-`uname -r` ] ; then
   ln -s -f System.map-`uname -r` /boot/System.map
fi

# Now that we have all of our basic modules loaded and the kernel going,
# let's dump the syslog ring somewhere so we can find it later
dmesg > /var/log/dmesg
sleep 1
kill -TERM `/sbin/pidof getkey` >/dev/null 2>&1
} &
if [ "$PROMPT" != "no" ]; then
   /sbin/getkey i && touch /var/run/confirm
fi
wait
```

XF86Config

This is the configuration file for XFree86, an X Window System designed to work on x86 chip architecture, such as that found in personal computers. Thus, XFree86 is most commonly used with Linux and FreeBSD, since they are designed for personal computer use. This file defines display variables for use with the specific hardware installed on the current machine, such as video cards or monitors.

```
# File generated by XConfigurator.

# **********************************************************************
# Refer to the XF86Config(4/5) man page for details about the format of
# this file.
# **********************************************************************

# **********************************************************************
# Files section.  This allows default font and rgb paths to be set
# **********************************************************************

Section "Files"

# The location of the RGB database.  Note, this is the name of the
# file minus the extension (like ".txt" or ".db").  There is normally
# no need to change the default.

    RgbPath   "/usr/X11R6/lib/X11/rgb"

# Multiple FontPath entries are allowed (they are concatenated together)
# By default, Red Hat 6.0 and later now use a font server independent of
# the X server to render fonts.

    FontPath   "unix/:7100"

EndSection

# **********************************************************************
# Server flags section.
# **********************************************************************

Section "ServerFlags"

    # Uncomment this to cause a core dump at the spot where a signal is
    # received.  This may leave the console in an unusable state, but may
    # provide a better stack trace in the core dump to aid in debugging
```

```
    #NoTrapSignals

    # Uncomment this to disable the <Crtl><Alt><BS> server abort sequence
    # This allows clients to receive this key event.
    #DontZap

    # Uncomment this to disable the <Crtl><Alt><KP_+>/<KP_-> mode switching
    # sequences.  This allows clients to receive these key events.
    #DontZoom

EndSection

# **********************************************************************
# Input devices
# **********************************************************************

# **********************************************************************
# Keyboard section
# **********************************************************************

Section "Keyboard"

    Protocol    "Standard"

    # when using XQUEUE, comment out the above line, and uncomment the
    # following line
    #Protocol   "Xqueue"

    AutoRepeat  500 5

    # Let the server do the NumLock processing.  This should only be
    # required when using pre-R6 clients
    #ServerNumLock

    # Specify which keyboard LEDs can be user-controlled (eg, with xset(1))
    #Xleds      1 2 3

    #To set the LeftAlt to Meta, RightAlt key to ModeShift,
    #RightCtl key to Compose, and ScrollLock key to ModeLock:

    LeftAlt       Meta
    RightAlt      Meta
    ScrollLock    Compose
    RightCtl      Control

# To disable the XKEYBOARD extension, uncomment XkbDisable.
```

```
#   XkbDisable

# To customise the XKB settings to suit your keyboard, modify the
# lines below (which are the defaults).  For example, for a non-U.S.
# keyboard, you will probably want to use:
#    XkbModel    "pc102"
# If you have a US Microsoft Natural keyboard, you can use:
#    XkbModel    "microsoft"
#
# Then to change the language, change the Layout setting.
# For example, a german layout can be obtained with:
#    XkbLayout   "de"
# or:
#    XkbLayout   "de"
#    XkbVariant  "nodeadkeys"
#
# If you'd like to switch the positions of your capslock and
# control keys, use:
#    XkbOptions  "ctrl:swapcaps"

# These are the default XKB settings for XFree86
#    XkbRules    "xfree86"
#    XkbModel    "pc101"
#    XkbLayout   "us"
#    XkbVariant  ""
#    XkbOptions  ""

   XkbKeycodes     "xfree86"
   XkbTypes        "default"
   XkbCompat       "default"
   XkbSymbols      "us(pc101)"
   XkbGeometry     "pc"
   XkbRules        "xfree86"
   XkbModel        "pc101"
   XkbLayout       "us"
EndSection

# **********************************************************************
# Pointer section
# **********************************************************************

Section "Pointer"
   Protocol    "PS/2"
   Device      "/dev/mouse"
   ZAxisMapping 4 5
```

```
# When using XQUEUE, comment out the above two lines, and uncomment
# the following line.

#    Protocol   "Xqueue"

# Baudrate and SampleRate are only for some Logitech mice

#    BaudRate   9600
#    SampleRate 150

# Emulate3Buttons is an option for 2-button Microsoft mice
# Emulate3Timeout is the timeout in milliseconds (default is 50ms)

#    Emulate3Buttons
#    Emulate3Timeout    50

# ChordMiddle is an option for some 3-button Logitech mice

#    ChordMiddle

EndSection


# **********************************************************************
# Monitor section
# **********************************************************************

# Any number of monitor sections may be present

Section "Monitor"

   Identifier   "SAM1CB3"
   VendorName   "Unknown"
   ModelName    "Unknown"

# HorizSync is in kHz unless units are specified.
# HorizSync may be a comma separated list of discrete
  values, or a
# comma separated list of ranges of values.
# NOTE: THE VALUES HERE ARE EXAMPLES ONLY.  REFER TO YOUR MONITOR'S
# USER MANUAL FOR THE CORRECT NUMBERS.

   HorizSync    30 - 69

# VertRefresh is in Hz unless units are specified.
# VertRefresh may be a comma separated list of discrete values, or a
```

```
# comma separated list of ranges of values.
# NOTE: THE VALUES HERE ARE EXAMPLES ONLY.  REFER TO YOUR MONITOR'S
# USER MANUAL FOR THE CORRECT NUMBERS.

    VertRefresh 50 - 160

# Modes can be specified in two formats.  A compact one-line format, or
# a multi-line format.

# These two are equivalent

#    ModeLine "1024x768i" 45 1024 1048 1208 1264 768 776 784 817 Interlace

#    Mode "1024x768i"
#        DotClock   45
#        HTimings   1024 1048 1208 1264
#        VTimings   768 776 784 817
#        Flags      "Interlace"
#    EndMode

# This is a set of standard mode timings. Modes that are out of monitor spec
# are automatically deleted by the server (provided the HorizSync and
# VertRefresh lines are correct), so there's no immediate need to
# delete mode timings (unless particular mode timings don't work on your
# monitor). With these modes, the best standard mode that your monitor
# and video card can support for a given resolution is automatically
# used.

# 512x384  @ 78 Hz, 31.50 kHz hsync
Modeline "512x384"    20.160 512  528  592  640   384  385  388  404 \
  -HSync -VSync
# 512x384  @ 85 Hz, 34.38 kHz hsync
Modeline "512x384"    22     512  528  592  640   384  385  388  404 \
  -HSync -VSync

# 640x400  @ 70 Hz, 31.5 kHz hsync
Modeline "640x400"     25.175 640  664  760  800   400  409  411  450
# 640x400  @ 85 Hz, 37.86 kHz hsync
Modeline "640x400"     31.5   640  672 736   832   400  401  404  445 \
  -HSync +VSync

# 640x480  @ 100 Hz, 53.01 kHz hsync
Modeline "640x480"     45.8   640  672  768  864   480  488  494  530 \
  -HSync -VSync
# 640x480  @ 60 Hz, 31.5 kHz hsync
Modeline "640x480"     25.175 640  664  760  800   480  491  493  525
```

```
# 640x480  @ 72 Hz, 36.5 kHz hsync
Modeline "640x480"     31.5   640  680  720  864   480  488  491  521
# 640x480  @ 75 Hz, 37.50 kHz hsync
ModeLine  "640x480"    31.5   640  656  720  840   480  481  484  500 \
   -HSync -VSync
# 640x480  @ 85 Hz, 43.27 kHz hsync

Modeline "640x480"     36     640  696  752  832   480  481  484  509 \
   -HSync -VSync
# 800x600  @ 100 Hz, 64.02 kHz hsync
Modeline  "800x600"    69.65  800  864  928 1088   600  604  610  640 \
   -HSync -VSync
# 800x600  @ 56 Hz, 35.15 kHz hsync
ModeLine "800x600"     36     800  824  896 1024   600  601  603  625
# 800x600  @ 60 Hz, 37.8 kHz hsync
Modeline "800x600"     40     800  840  968 1056   600  601  605  628 \
   +hsync +vsync
# 800x600  @ 72 Hz, 48.0 kHz hsync
Modeline "800x600"     50     800  856  976 1040   600  637  643  666 \
   +hsync +vsync
# 800x600  @ 85 Hz, 55.84 kHz hsync
Modeline  "800x600"    60.75  800  864  928 1088   600  616  621  657 \
   -HSync -VSync


# 1024x480 for certain Vaios
Modeline "1024x480"   65 1024 1032 1176 1344 480 491 493 525 -HSync \
   -VSync

# 1024x768  @ 100Hz, 80.21 kHz hsync
Modeline "1024x768"   115.5  1024 1056 1248 1440  768  771  781  802 \
   -HSync -VSync
# 1024x768  @ 60 Hz, 48.4 kHz hsync
Modeline "1024x768"    65     1024 1032 1176 1344   768  771  777  806 \
   -hsync -vsync
# 1024x768  @ 70 Hz, 56.5 kHz hsync
Modeline "1024x768"    75     1024 1048 1184 1328   768  771  777  806 \
   -hsync -vsync
# 1024x768  @ 76 Hz, 62.5 kHz hsync
Modeline "1024x768"    85     1024 1032 1152 1360   768  784  787  823
# 1024x768  @ 85 Hz, 70.24 kHz hsync
Modeline "1024x768"   98.9  1024 1056 1216 1408   768 782 788 822 \
   -HSync -VSync

# 1152x864  @ 100 Hz, 89.62 kHz hsync
Modeline "1152x864"   137.65 1152 1184 1312 1536   864  866  885  902 \
   -HSync -VSync
```

```
# 1152x864  @ 60 Hz, 53.5 kHz hsync
Modeline  "1152x864"   89.9  1152 1216 1472 1680   864  868  876  892 \
  -HSync -VSync
# 1152x864  @ 70 Hz, 62.4 kHz hsync
Modeline  "1152x864"   92    1152 1208 1368 1474   864  865  875  895
# 1152x864  @ 78 Hz, 70.8 kHz hsync
Modeline "1152x864"   110   1152 1240 1324 1552   864  864  876  908
# 1152x864  @ 84 Hz, 76.0 kHz hsync
Modeline "1152x864"   135    1152 1464 1592 1776   864  864  876  908

# 1280x960  @ 60 HzModeline "1280x960"  108 1280 1376 1488 1800 960 961 964
  1000 +HSync + VSync
# 1280x960  @ 85 HzModeline "1280x960"   148.5 1280 1344 1504 1728 960 961
  964 1011  +HSync +VSync

# 1280x1024  @ 100 Hz, 107.16 kHz hsync
Modeline "1280x1024"  181.75 1280 1312 1440 1696  1024 1031 1046 1072 \
  -HSync -VSync
# 1280x1024  @ 61 Hz, 64.2 kHz hsync
Modeline "1280x1024"  110    1280 1328 1512 1712  1024 1025 1028 1054
# 1280x1024  @ 70 Hz, 74.59 kHz hsync
Modeline "1280x1024"  126.5 1280 1312 1472 1696  1024 1032 1040 1068 \
  -HSync -VSync
# 1280x1024  @ 74 Hz, 78.85 kHz hsync
Modeline "1280x1024"  135    1280 1312 1456 1712  1024 1027 1030 1064
# 1280x1024  @ 76 Hz, 81.13 kHz hsync
Modeline "1280x1024"  135    1280 1312 1416 1664  1024 1027 1030 1064
# 1280x1024  @ 85 Hz, 91.15 kHz hsync
Modeline "1280x1024"  157.5  1280 1344 1504 1728  1024 1025 1028 1072 \
  +HSync +VSync

# 1400x1050  @ 60Hz, 65.8 kHz hsync
Modeline "1400x1050"  129   1400 1464 1656 1960 1050 1051 1054 1100 \
  +HSync +VSync
# 1400x1050  @ 70Hz, 76.8 kHz hsync
Modeline "1400x1050"  151   1400 1464 1656 1960 1050 1051 1054 1100 \
  +HSync +VSync
# 1400x1050  @ 75Hz, 82.3 kHz hsync
Modeline "1400x1050"  162   1400 1464 1656 1960 1050 1051 1054 1100
  +HSync +VSync
# 1400x1050  @ 85Hz, 93.2 kHz hsync
Modeline "1400x1050"  184   1400 1464 1656 1960 1050 1051 1054 1100 \
  +HSync +VSync

# 1600x1200  @ 60Hz, 75.00 kHz hsync
```

```
Modeline "1600x1200"  162   1600 1664 1856 2160  1200 1201 1204 1250 \
   +HSync +VSync
# 1600x1200  @ 70 Hz, 87.50 kHz hsync
Modeline "1600x1200"  189    1600 1664 1856 2160  1200 1201 1204 1250 \
   -HSync -VSync
# 1600x1200  @ 75 Hz, 93.75 kHz hsync
Modeline "1600x1200"  202.5  1600 1664 1856 2160  1200 1201 1204 1250 \
   +HSync +VSync
# 1600x1200  @ 85 Hz, 105.77 kHz hsync
Modeline "1600x1200"  220    1600 1616 1808 2080  1200 1204 1207 1244 \
   +HSync +VSync

# 1800x1440  @ 64Hz, 96.15 kHz hsync
ModeLine "1800X1440"  230    1800 1896 2088 2392 1440 1441 1444 1490 \
   +HSync +VSync
# 1800x1440  @ 70Hz, 104.52 kHz hsync
ModeLine "1800X1440"  250    1800 1896 2088 2392 1440 1441 1444 1490 \
   +HSync +VSync

# Low-res Doublescan modes
# If your chipset does not support doublescan, you get a 'squashed'
# resolution like 320x400.

# 320x200  @ 70 Hz, 31.5 kHz hsync, 8:5 aspect ratio
Modeline "320x200"     12.588 320  336  384  400   200  204  205  225 \
   Doublescan
# 320x240  @ 60 Hz, 31.5 kHz hsync, 4:3 aspect ratio
Modeline "320x240"     12.588 320  336  384  400   240  245  246  262 \
   Doublescan
# 320x240  @ 72 Hz, 36.5 kHz hsync
Modeline "320x240"     15.750 320  336  384  400   240  244  246  262 \
   Doublescan
# 400x300  @ 56 Hz, 35.2 kHz hsync, 4:3 aspect ratio
ModeLine "400x300"     18     400  416  448  512   300  301  302  312 \
   Doublescan
# 400x300  @ 60 Hz, 37.8 kHz hsync
Modeline "400x300"     20     400  416  480  528   300  301  303  314 \
   Doublescan
# 400x300  @ 72 Hz, 48.0 kHz hsync
Modeline "400x300"     25     400  424  488  520   300  319  322  333 \
   Doublescan
# 480x300  @ 56 Hz, 35.2 kHz hsync, 8:5 aspect ratio
ModeLine "480x300"     21.656 480  496  536  616   300  301  302  312 \
   Doublescan
# 480x300  @ 60 Hz, 37.8 kHz hsync
Modeline "480x300"     23.890 480  496  576  632   300  301  303  314 \
```

```
   Doublescan
# 480x300  @ 63 Hz, 39.6 kHz hsync
Modeline "480x300"     25     480  496  576  632   300  301  303  314 \
   Doublescan
# 480x300  @ 72 Hz, 48.0 kHz hsync
Modeline "480x300"     29.952 480  504  584  624   300  319  322  333 \
   Doublescan

EndSection


# **********************************************************************
# Graphics device section
# **********************************************************************

# Any number of graphics device sections may be present

Section "Device"
    Identifier        "Generic VGA"
    VendorName        "Unknown"
    BoardName "Unknown"
    Chipset   "generic"

#    VideoRam 256

#    Clocks   25.2 28.3

EndSection

# Device configured by Xconfigurator:

Section "Device"
     Identifier  "Matrox Mystique"
     VendorName  "Unknown"
     BoardName   "Unknown"
     #VideoRam    2048
     # Insert Clocks lines here if appropriate
EndSection


# **********************************************************************
# Screen sections
# **********************************************************************

# The Colour SVGA server
```

```
Section "Screen"
   Driver      "svga"
   # Use Device "Generic VGA" for Standard VGA 320x200x256
   #Device      "Generic VGA"
   Device      "Matrox Mystique"
   Monitor     "SAM1CB3"
   DefaultColorDepth   32
   Subsection "Display"
      Depth       24
      Modes       "800x600" "640x480"
      ViewPort    0 0
   EndSubsection
   Subsection "Display"
      Depth       32
      Modes       "800x600" "640x480"
      ViewPort    0 0
   EndSubsection
EndSection

# The 16-color VGA server

Section "Screen"
   Driver      "vga16"
   Device      "Generic VGA"
   Monitor     "SAM1CB3"
   Subsection "Display"
      Modes       "640x480" "800x600"
      ViewPort    0 0
   EndSubsection
EndSection

# The Mono server

Section "Screen"
   Driver      "vga2"
   Device      "Generic VGA"
   Monitor     "SAM1CB3"
   Subsection "Display"
      Modes       "640x480" "800x600"
      ViewPort    0 0
   EndSubsection
EndSection

# The accelerated servers (S3, Mach32, Mach8, 8514, P9000, AGX, W32, Mach64
# I128, and S3V)
Section "Screen"
```

```
    Driver      "accel"
    Device      "Matrox Mystique"
    Monitor     "SAM1CB3"
    DefaultColorDepth   32
    Subsection "Display"
       Depth       24
       Modes       "800x600" "640x480"
       ViewPort    0 0
    EndSubsection
    Subsection "Display"
       Depth       32
       Modes       "800x600" "640x480"
       ViewPort    0 0
    EndSubsection
EndSection
```

APPENDIX D

Internet Resources

Because information about technology can change rapidly, the Internet is often one of the most reliable sources of up-to-date knowledge and news about computers and software. In this appendix, you will find the URLs of some good sites which can help you answer questions which may not be addressed in this book or which you need answered before you can see your instructor. Should you need information beyond the sites shown here, a good search engine like Google (http://www.google.com) can help you find the answer.

Note: Internet sites are usually not reviewed for accuracy. While you can usually trust the information found on corporate sites, such as Sun's or Red Hat's, it is not always the case that you can trust personal sites. Be cautious about downloading software or configuration files from random sites unless you have a good idea of what you are looking for.

What Is Unix?

The sites in this section cover Unix history, as well as the cultural aspects of the Unix community.

http://www.levenez.com/unix/

A chart of Unix history, which spans 14 pages. The author included only Unix variants which were significant—the chart could have been much larger!

http://www.bell-labs.com/history/unix/

The "official" history of Unix, as told through the eyes of AT&T. The site also includes biographies of Ken Thompson and Dennis Ritchie.

http://www.uwsg.iu.edu/usail/library/history.html

Copies of some of the seminal documents in Unix's history. This site collects most of the critical documents in one location, though you can find each of them in various other places on the Web.

http://www.gnu.org/

The home of the GNU project. Here, you can download all the GNU software to install on your own system, as well as get documentation for all GNU applications and programs. While there is some philosophical material here, it is primarily devoted to programming and software released under the GNU Public License.

http://www.fsf.org/

A more political site than the GNU page, the Free Software Foundation page provides information about supporting the foundation and the philosophical positions behind Free Software.

http://www.opensource.org/

The main site of the Open Source iniative, this site offers links to other program sites. However, its main strength is information about Open Source, especially that which is targeted at the media so that it will cover Open Source software and describe it correctly.

http://www.tuxedo.org/~esr/writings/

The home page of Eric Raymond, the major figure behind Open Source. This site contains his seminal paper "The Cathedral and the Bazaar," as well as the two other papers in the Open Source trilogy: "Homesteading the Noosphere" and "The Magic Cauldron."

http://www.linux.org

Linux Online provides links to documentation, the wide range of Linux variants, and software downloads. It also offers news and its own editorial content. A good place to start your search for Linux information.

http://www.freebsd.org

The FreeBSD project's home site offers documentation, links to other sites reflecting the FreeBSD community, downloads, and a good depository of information about bugs in the software. You'll also find links for user groups and other community elements.

Basic Unix Concepts

The sites in this section offer help on the basic elements of the Unix operating system, including command structure, file system organization and navigation, and simplified documentation.

http://www.linuxnewbie.org

Not just for Linux users. This site offers simplified manual pages and help files on a variety of Unix-related topics which might be more useful to someone who finds standard manual pages to be a bit confusing.

http://www.nmt.edu/tcc/help/unix/unix_cmd.html

A brief introduction to some of the most common Unix commands, intended for those new to working with the operating system.

http://wks.uts.ohio-state.edu/unix_course/intro-137.html

A good reference card for commonly used commands. Print this one out if you have trouble remembering the name or syntax of the commands needed for your work.

http://www.isu.edu/departments/comcom/unix/workshop/fstour.html

An overview of the Unix file system. The documents pay particular attention to file type and how the disk is organized, with a good explanation of inodes.

http://www.no.embnet.org/unixhelp/shell_jobz.php3

A good description of how jobs and processes are organized under Unix, and how to manage processes by moving them between foreground and background.

http://www.ncl.ac.uk/ucs/unix/job_process.html

Another approach to jobs and processes. This site pays particular attention to the batching of non-interactive processes to run at more convenient times.

The Shell Environment

These sites introduce various shells, and offer guidance for those who are interested in exploring the capabilities of their shell environments.

http://www.nscp.umd.edu/shells.html

An excellent overview of several different shells. This site provides links to each shell's home page and to other documentation. There is a great table which compares a wide range of features across the various shells. A good place to start if you are interested in changing your shell.

http://www.mmm.ucar.edu/computing/doc/guide/ch_2.html

A more detailed comparison of the Bourne shell, the C shell, and the T C shell. If sh, csh, and tcsh are the main shells available to you, this site will help you figure out the differences.

http://www.gnu.org/manual/bash-2.02/html_chapter/bashref_toc.html

The complete bash manual. It can be a bit dry, but it will answer almost any question you can ask about the bash shell. Use this in conjunction with the FAQ described in the next entry.

http://www.faqs.org/faqs/unix-faq/shell/bash/

The bash FAQ. Use this along with the bash manual from the link above. The FAQ addresses the most common questions and problems with the shell.

Text Editors

Sites in this section discuss various aspects of Unix text editors, offer helpful hints on making editors simpler to use, and introduce some editors which are less widely used.

http://www.thomer.com/vi/vi.html

This site, the "vi Lovers' Home Page," is an excellent collection of vi-related links and tutorials. You'll also find extensive information about macros and other vi functions.

http://www.math.fu-berlin.de/~guckes/vi/

The other major vi site, vi-editor pulls together a number of vi resouces. This site is especially strong in discussion of vi clone programs, like the vim editor, which may be installed on some systems by administrator preference.

http://www.eng.hawaii.edu/Tutor/vi.html

A thorough vi tutorial that will teach you the basic skills you need to use the editor efficiently. The tutorial includes hints for programming with the editor and for configuring vi's environment to your liking.

http://www.gnu.org/software/emacs/emacs.html

This is the basic home site for GNU Emacs information and downloads. New releases, bugfixes, documentation, and other important information will be placed here before it is released to any other sites or software archives.

http://www.gnu.org/software/emacs/emacs-faq.text

The FAQ for Emacs, written by its developers. Most basic questions can be answered by this document. Read it before you start working with GNU Emacs.

http://www.geek-girl.com/emacs/refcard.html

A quick reference card for commonly used GNU Emacs functions. Print this out and slip it under your keyboard.

http://www.oceanwave.com/technical-resources/unix-admin/editors.html

A wonderful overview of text editors. Though the site focuses on GNU Emacs and vi, it offers links and information about other editors as well. Easy to navigate and well designed.

Internet Applications

The sites in this section introduce various applications and clients used for Internet services, such as e-mail, Web, and news.

http://www.washington.edu/pine/

The home of the PINE mail/news reader. Download packages here, or read documentation and FAQs. An easily navigated site with lots of great information.

http://www.eng.hawaii.edu/Tutor/elm.html

A good tutorial introducing the elm electronic mail reader. The tutorial walks you through composing, sending, retrieving, and saving mail messages.

http://www.netscape.com

The same browser you use on Windows or Macintosh computers. Download Netscape 6.2 packages for Linux, or Netscape Navigator for a vast range of Unix variants.

http://www.mozilla.org

Linux users can check out the Open Source browser right now; other Unix variant users will probably have to wait until the program is more thoroughly developed before it is ported to other platforms. Builds are available for other platforms, but require more skill to install and use.

http://www.opera.com

Download the HTML-compliant Opera browser, read documentation, or find the latest news. This site offers Opera downloads for Linux and Solaris Unix variants.

http://www.ocf.berkeley.edu/help/usenet/trnint-3.3.html

An excellent overview of USENET in general, and the threaded news reader trn in particular. This document will get you up and running in short order.

http://www.landfield.com/usenet/usenet.html

Before you jump into the world of USENET, read some of the user documents housed on this site. You'll learn about USENET etiquette, how posts are propagated, and how to find the right newsgroup for your post.

Unix Networking

These sites provide information about Unix networking on both heterogeneous and homogeneous networks.

http://www.tldp.org/HOWTO/Networking-Overview-HOWTO.html

The nuts and bolts of networking under Linux, as well as an introduction to networking in general. This HOWTO document is part of the Linux Documentation Project.

http://www.yale.edu/pclt/COMM/TCPIP.HTM

A brief overview of TCP/IP, its history, and how it works. There are some graphics. While not as in-depth as other sites in this section, this is a quick way to learn the basics.

http://www.private.org.il/tcpip_rl.html

A comprehensive collection of links about TCP/IP and networking topics. The site lists FAQs, tutorials, newsgroups, printed books, and other resources which will help the network professional or someone new to the concept.

http://www.sangoma.com/fguide.htm

A tutorial which walks you through setting up a network. This is a commercial site which emphasizes its own network cards, but the information is usable whether you have one of Sangoma's cards or not. Not Unix-specific.

http://www.itprc.com/tcpipfaq/default.htm

The TCP/IP FAQ, which answers the most common questions about TCP/IP, how it works, and how to troubleshoot network installations. It also provides an exhaustive explanation of the various protocols involved in network transmissions.

http://www.cisco.com/warp/public/535/4.html

A complete introduction to TCP/IP, with good graphics and solid information. Cisco routers are the industry standard, so this is trustworthy information.

http://www.samba.org

For those interested in running heterogeneous networks which have both Unix and Windows machines, consider Samba. This wonderful program handles networking connections in ways that both operating systems understand, and is critical for Windows-involved networks.

http://www.umich.edu/~rsug/netatalk/

As Samba is used with Windows/Unix heterogeneous networks, netatalk is used for Macintosh/Unix networks. This site provides downloads and information about netatalk, which offers file and print sharing using Appletalk.

Shell Programming

Sites in this section offer help with shell programming, including excellent information on the various elements and constructs of good shell scripts.

http://www.tldp.org/LDP/abs/html/

An excellent tutorial for shell programming. This is targeted at Linux users, but can be read and used by people working under a number of operating systems. It begins with simple topics and progresses to far more complicated and advanced mechanisms. Well worth the time.

http://www.tldp.org/HOWTO/Bash-Prog-Intro-HOWTO.html

A tutorial more specifically devoted to bash shell programming than the previous document. This file includes information about various program constructs, including tables, and has a section on debugging.

http://www.docs.uu.se/~matkin/documents/shell/

A Swedish site which goes into more detail than many other shell scripting pages. Although the author notes that the site is undergoing revision, it is quite complete and offers a great range of ideas for your own shell programs.

http://dmoz.org/Computers/Software/Operating_Systems/Unix/Shell/Scripting/

The dmoz.org directory offers a lengthy list of links for those interested in shell scripting. You'll find resources for scripting under bash, sh, and a range of other shells. Not a search engine, so some links may be outdated since the directory is a managed resource.

http://pegasus.rutgers.edu/~elflord/unix/bash-tute.html

A brief overview of bash scripting, and a simple tutorial. While this is not the most in-depth resource, it can provide just enough help to get you going in your own scripting.

http://steve-parker.org/sh/sh.shtml

Should you not have the Bourne (Again) shell available on your system, this site provides a tutorial for programming under the Bourne shell. It provides the manual pages for a number of important shell functions, as well as assistance in writing elegant sh scripts.

System Administration

The sites shown here are a good starting point for those interested in the administrative elements of Unix, including user management, software installation, security, and other tasks.

http://www.washington.edu/R870/

The home for a course taught at the University of Washington by Dave Dittrich. Dittrich's site contains notes and a syllabus from his regular class, as well as a series of sample problems that describe real-life system administration situations. An excellent hands-on introduction to the tasks in such a job.

http://www.ee.siue.edu/~bnoble/classes/

A great series of links about network administration, including security, scripting, and LAN administration. The information linked here should answer almost any network administration question.

http://www.freshmeat.org

One of the larger software archives devoted solely to Unix programs. You'll find mostly FreeBSD and Linux packages here, but it's a good place to search for other programs that you might want to use. Part of the Slashdot-related universe: Slashdot (http://www.slashdot.org) is the wildly popular tech-related news site.

http://www.rpm.org

For those using the RPM package manager to install software, the program's home page can be a helpful site. It has documentation, downloads, and help in making your installations run more smoothly.

http://www.alw.nih.gov/Security/Docs/network-security.html

This site, provided by the National Institutes of Health, gives a good introduction to Unix networks and their security risks. The focus is on firewalls and gateways.

www.cert.org/

The first place to read about new security risks, viruses, worms, security holes in newly released software, and the like. CERT advisories are thoroughly fact-checked and are reliable, unlike virus warnings that people pass through e-mail without checking first. If you get a scary e-mail, check it out at CERT before passing it on.

X Window System

These sites introduce the X Window System and offer help in configuring this often frustrating, yet critical, element of Unix.

http://www.x.org

The main site for the X Consortium, the group which administers the X Window System standard. This site is not particularly targeted toward users, but does offer a great introduction to how X works and where graphics on Unix platforms is heading.

http://www.xfree86.org/

The site for people running X on personal computers using x86 architecture chips. The site offers downloads and documentation, as well as assistance in configuring X for particular chips and video hardware.

http://www.plig.org/xwinman/

An excellent compendium of information and links about the various window managers and desktop environments that work with X. Each section shows a number of screenshots to illustrate how the manager or desktop will look when installed on your system.

http://www.gnome.org

The home of the Gnome integrated desktop. This program is a graphical user interface with a wide variety of embedded and native software. At the site, you can download software and documentation, as well as read Gnome-related news.

http://www.kde.org

The KDE site also offers an integrated desktop environment which is highly configurable and provides a very comfortable interface to Unix. The KDE site is especially useful to those whose first language is not English, as it is mirrored in multiple languages. Software downloads, news, documentation, and bugfixes are all here.

http://www.ximian.com

A more commercial site than Gnome or KDE, Ximian is the current project of the person who first developed Gnome. Ximian is a smooth and appealing integrated desktop. Learn more about it, or download packages, here.

Running Services

The sites in this section offer assistance in installing, configuring, and administering the servers which provide data to various clients across local networks or the Internet.

http://www.apache.org

The site of the Apache Software Foundation, providers of the best and most popular Web server available. Links, documentation, downloads, and Apache news. You'll find more specific help at some of the sites linked from here, but this is the central clearinghouse for Apache news and packages.

http://www.irt.org/articles/js180.index.htm

If you run Apache, you may want to configure it to fit more specific needs at some point. This site offers some suggestions about working with Apache configuration files, and emphasizes Apache's modular nature as the key to a fully customized Apache installation.

http://www.sendmail.org

The home page for the "big kahuna" of mail servers. Learn more about sendmail here, including troubleshooting help for installations gone wrong. The big strength of this site is its attention to security and ensuring that your sendmail installation is as tight as possible.

http://cr.yp.to/qmail.html

The site for the Qmail mail server. You can download the server here, as well as read various documents about running a safe and efficient Qmail server.

http://www.postfix.cs.uu.nl/start.html

The home site for the Postfix mail server. Although it offers the same documentation and downloads that most project sites have, Postfix's site also provides links to manuals that cover general problems associated with e-mail administration.

http://www.isc.org/products/INN/

The home site for the INN USENET news server. INN is under reasonably active development, so the current version is quite stable but a new version will be released in the next year or so. Downloads, documentation, and everything else you'll need to run INN.

http://www.uwsg.iu.edu/security/inetd.html

This site explains how to configure inetd in the most secure manner. The site focuses on TCP wrappers as the best method to thwart crack attempts that come through processes managed by inetd.

Index

Symbols and Numbers

A

B

C

D

G

H

P